slow
wine

A YEAR
IN THE LIFE
OF THE
VINEYARDS
AND WINES
OF THE USA

slow wine

A YEAR IN THE LIFE OF THE VINEYARDS AND WINES OF THE USA

2022

ORO Editions
Publishers of Architecture, Art, and Design
Gordon Goff: Publisher

www.oroeditions.com – info@oroeditions.com

Published by ORO Editions

Authors:
Giancarlo Gariglio, Editor-in-chief
Deborah Parker Wong, Coordinating Editor

California
Pam Strayer, Senior Editor
Contributing editors:
Gwendoyln Alley, Peg Champion, Catherine Fallis, MS, Charles Kelly, Laurie Love, Sally Ohlin, Karla Ravandi, Leslie Rosa, Amber Turpin

Oregon
Contributing editors:
L.M. Archer, Sophia McDonald Bennett, Catherine Fallis, MS, Ellen Landis, Neal D. Hulkower, Ph.D.

Washington
Contributing editor:
Nancy Crosier

New York
Contributing editors:
Robin Shreeves, Kathleen Wilcox

Editorial Assistants: Jonathan Gebser, Maddalena Schiavone, Stella Ricciardelli
Book Design: Francesco Perona
Cover Design: Alice Iuri and Mauro de Toffol / theWorldofDot
Project Coordinator: Alejandro Guzman-Avila
Managing Editor: Jake Anderson

10 9 8 7 6 5 4 3 2 1 First Edition

ISBN: 978-1-954081-76-5

Color Separations and Printing: ORO Group Ltd. – Printed in China.

ORO Editions makes a continuous effort to minimize the overall carbon footprint of its publications. As part of this goal, ORO Editions, in association with Global ReLeaf, arranges to plant trees to replace those used in the manufacturing of the paper produced for its books. Global ReLeaf is an international campaign run by American Forests, one of the world's oldest nonprofit conservation organizations. Global ReLeaf is American Forests' education and action program that helps individuals, organizations, agencies, and corporations improve the local and global environment by planting and caring for trees.

INDEX

MAP

PREFACE

Last year's edition of the Slow Wine Guide USA marked an important step for our annual publication, with its promotion from simple appendix of the translated Italian edition to an independent publication in its own right. Now, just one year later, we can mark off yet another important milestone, namely US publisher, Goff Books, embracing our project and deciding to publish it under their name. This is a great acknowledgement for a venture born as an experiment and grown over the years thanks to the support of our readers, the dedication and hard work of so many contributors and the enthusiasm of the wine producers who have opened their doors to us.

Slow Wine is in fact not your ordinary wine guide, especially considering its presence in the US market that has basically invented scores when judging wine. We have decided to go down a different road, privileging description, narrative and a visit to the winery. Of course, we also evaluate the wines from a pure sensory perspective, otherwise we wouldn't be wine critics. Without that in-depth knowledge of the wines and wineries, our reviews and accolades would have far less value to consumers.

After the 2021 emergency edition, realized for obvious reasons through virtual interviews with the producers, this year we've gone back to making winery visits – a great way to celebrate the return of something at least a little closer to normality. This return to a face-to-face approach means one important thing: the Snail, our most significant accolade awarded to a winery, is back. In response to the positive feedback of last year's interviews made available online for everyone to view, this time around we made a series of brief videos taken directly at the winery, thus offering a unique insight of the people behind the wines, their philosophy and approach in the vineyards and the cellar.

And speaking about news and outstanding times, there's more. These last two years have allowed us to conceive, plan and prepare what is going to be the biggest and most ambitious project by Slow Food in the world of wine thus far: the Slow Wine Coalition, a new international thematic network uniting wine lovers and professionals under one umbrella. By sharing of a series of core values as described in the Slow Wine Manifesto for Good, Clean and Fair Wine, we've dedicated much of our lives, through our activity as critics, to educate people and steer them towards wines that are respectful of the environment, the landscape and the people who produce. them.

Action has never been so urgent and now is the time to radically rethink viticulture and winemaking practices. Wine is in fact the most glamourous among agricultural products; as the subject of books and documentaries, movies and novels, it's a trailblazer with the opportunity and responsibility to set new standards and ignite a transition away from the conventional productivist paradigm that has caused so much harm to our planet.

Looking back at the eleven previous editions of the Slow Wine Guide, this voyage is a recurring topic. Now, with the Slow Wine Coalition we're embarking on a new adventure that will require us to take on a pirate-like mentality. Because only the anarchic, rebellious and determined nature of the opportunist will help us reshape a world of wine in desperate need of new standards. We hope and we're confident that many of you will get onboard and join us in this new and exciting journey.

Giancarlo Gariglio
Editor-in-chief

INTRODUCTION

Over the past year as National Editor of the Slow Wine Guide USA, I've seen the daily conversations we're having about wine expand far beyond the immediate concern for the health of our planet to address a broader view of the practices outlined in the Slow Wine Manifesto. Both I and Senior Editor Pam Strayer have lent our voices to the subjects of diversity within the industry, domestic and global migrant labor, and the profitability of organic farming among many others.

In 2021 we joined forces with Slow Food USA both as the verifying body for their coveted Snail Award for wineries and as their "voice" of wine for the national and international press which has enabled us to address industry issues that rarely see the light of day.

As advocates for the wineries that grace the pages of this guide and for the consumers who rely on its contents when making purchase decisions, we strive to be inclusive while upholding the baseline criterion - the choice not to farm with synthetic herbicides - that qualifies wineries to be listed. The understanding of and adaptation by winegrowers of low-intervention practices in the vineyard is enabling more and more wineries to forgo chemical weeding.

Being back in the field again making in-person winery visits has invigorated our national team of coordinators which includes for the first time L.M. Archer and Ellen Landis both of whom contribute for Oregon; Nancy Crosier who has grown our presence in Washington; Robin Shreeves who teamed up with Kathleen Wilcox in New York State, and the astoundingly prolific Gwendolyn Alley along with Karla Ravandi who are both covering wineries in California for the first time. I'm immensely proud of our returning field coordinators whose efforts have propelled the guide forward during the most challenging of times.

Senior editor Pamela Strayer shines in her instrumental role as subject matter expert in viticulture and her rigorous field work continues to evolve the guide forward. As national editor, it is an honor and a privilege to collaborate with each and every writer who makes the Slow Wine Guide possible.

The Slow Wine Guide USA is produced in collaboration with the Italian Slow Wine Guide editorial team led by Jonathan Gebser who, in addition to his role in the Italian guide, expertly shepherds the production of our manuscript which will be published this year by Goff Books. We've got a tough act to follow as the 2021 guide which I refer to as our "pandemic miracle" continues to achieve milestones by making the *Self-Publishing News'* top ten list of best-sellers in 2021.

Join me in celebrating the wineries whose slow wines are farmed conscientiously and bring immense enjoyment to our lives.

Deborah Parker Wong
National Editor, US

HOW TO READ THE GUIDE

THE WINERY

BOTTLE — Symbol awarded to wineries whose bottles represented excellent average quality at our tastings.

$ COIN — Symbol awarded to wineries whose bottles are good value for money.

SNAIL — Symbol awarded to a winery that we recognize for the way it interprets Slow Food values (sensory perceptions, territory, environment, identity) and also offers good value for money.

The QR code at the bottom of some of the reviews is linked to the video-interviews documenting our virtual visits of the wineries.

Prices — The prices indicated represent the suggested retail price as listed by the wineries.

THE WINES

TOP WINE
(TOP)

The finest bottles from a sensory point of view.

SLOW WINE
`SLOW WINE`

Top Wines that, beyond their outstanding sensory quality, demonstrate terroir-related values such as history and identity, as well as offering good value for money. The attribution of this accolade implies the absence of any chemical herbicides in the vineyard. The Slow Wine accolade also considers value for money, taking into account the time and place of production.

EVERYDAY WINE
`EVERYDAY WINE`

Top Wines retailing up to 30 $.

Wine type — ○ White wine ● Red wine ● Rosé wine ⁂ Sparkling wine ● Dessert wine ◎ Orange wine

Type of ageing — ⊍ Stainless steel ⊓ Concrete ⊞ Small barrels ⊚ Large casks ⧖ Amphora

Aabbreviations — **ac** Acres of land, owned or leased, managed and cultivated directly by the winery
cs Number of 12-bottle cases produced

The data regarding viticultural and enological practices were provided by the producers.

SLOW WINE COALITION

A COLLABORATIVE WINE NETWORK

Slow Food®
Slow Wine Coalition

the Slow Food Manifesto for good, clean and fair wine

The Manifesto for good, clean and fair wine is born from Slow Food's experience over the years, a long-standing relationship in which wine has played a crucial role, thanks to the passionate involvement of wine experts, winemakers and technicians.

Through the production and consumption of wine made according to the Manifesto, we aim to positively influence the future of viticulture, by breaking the ties from the use of chemicals and monocultures, and re-establishing our connection to biodiversity across terroirs and regions.

For some years now, vanguard vignerons from across the globe have understood and communicated that we must change course. This change, however, cannot happen by acting alone. For this reason, we are calling on wine lovers and professionals alike to come together and play a fundamental role in the promotion and consumption of wines with strong environmental, ethical and social values. This is important now, more than ever, as we navigate a period of economic and ecological reconstruction.

Through this interaction with other actors in the network, winemakers themselves will have the opportunity to be exposed to other fundamental subjects such as education to conscious consumption, the centrality of a narration focused on what is really important to tell (and to know) about each wine and the territory from which it comes from, as well as recognizing the right value of one's product.

SLOW FOOD MANIFESTO
FOR GOOD,CLEAN AND FAIR WINE

Wineries must grow a **minimum 70% of the grapes used in the production of their wine** themselves. Exceptions are given for regions in which widespread sourcing is common, e.g. Madeira, Napa Valley, the south of Spain, etc.

Wineries **may not use chemically synthesized fertilizers**, herbicides, or anti-botrytis fungicides.

A conscious and sustainable **approach to the use of environmental resources** in winemaking must be applied. Dependence on irrigation systems must be limited and should only aim to avoid critical water-stress conditions.

Winery buildings, should they need to be constructed, must respect their environmental surroundings. Management, upkeep and eventual restauration of extant buildings should take **sustainability into account.**

Wineries should not utilize techniques like reverse osmosis or other physical methods of must concentration. Furthermore, the addition of RCGM (rectified concentrated grape must) or sugar (according to the country of production) is not permitted, with the exception of sparkling wines or wines where these practices fall under traditional techniques. Oak chips used to aromatize wines are also prohibited.

Permitted levels of sulfites should not exceed the limits listed under the European Union's regulations for organic wine.

 The wines must **show terroir and reflect their place of origin.** It is for this reason that we encourage the use of indigenous yeasts, as well as scientific research to isolate native yeasts which can then be replicated and used by the winery or other winemakers of the same area and geographical denomination.

 The wines **must be free of any winemaking defects,** as they tend to homogenize the wines and stamp out any regional identity.

 Wineries should actively engage and **collaborate with the entire surrounding farming community** in order to strengthen and enhance the agricultural system of the area. In this vein, the winery must maintain a principled relationship with its associates, as well as its employees, fostering personal and professional growth. It is moreover important that the winery cooperates and shares knowledge with other producers, avoiding unfair competition.

 Sustainable winemakers **encourage biodiversity** through practices such as: alternating vineyards with hedges and wooded areas; soil management practices that include grass and green manure and exclude, in any case, bare soil, with potential exceptions for short, seasonal periods; the protection of pollinating insects and useful fauna through the use of insecticides which are allowed in organic farming, where such interventions are necessary, and in any case avoiding their use during the flowering of the vine and of other herbaceous species present in the vineyard; the breeding of animals with respect for their welfare and the production of manure on the farm, as well as the production of compost from pruning residues and other organic materials.

TOP WINES

California

108 Adelaida District Paso Robles
Esprit de Tablas 2019 ●   SLOW WINE
Tablas Creek Vineyard

81 Alexander Valley Bell Mountain
Estate Sauvignon Blanc 2020 ○
Medlock Ames

26 Alisos Canyon Thompson
Vineyard Grenache Blanc 2020 ○
A Tribute to Grace

26 Amador County Shake Ridge Ranch
Vineyard Grenache 2019 ●
A Tribute to Grace

102 Anderson Valley China Block
Pinot Noir 2018 ●   EVERYDAY WINE
Sean Walker McBride

48 Anderson Valley Dach Vineyard
Pinot Noir 2018 ●   SLOW WINE
Domaine Anderson

74 Anderson Valley Grand Cuvée 2012 ⊛
Lichen Estate

62 Anderson Valley Handley Estate Vineyard Pinot
Noir 2017 ●   SLOW WINE
Handley Cellars

49 Anderson Valley Lily's Pet Nat Sparkling
Chardonnay 2020 ⊛   SLOW WINE
Donkey & Goat

90 Arroyo Grande Valley Rim Rock Vineyard
Syrah 2019 ●
Piedrasassi

67 Arroyo Seco Zabala Vineyard P'tit Paysan
Sauvignon Blanc 2020 ○   EVERYDAY WINE
I Brand & Family

33 Ballard Canyon 1ngredient 2019 ◎   SLOW WINE
Beckmen Vineyards

60 Calaveras County Faux Picpoul
Blanc 2020 ○   EVERYDAY WINE
Guthrie Family Wines

117 California Chardonnay 2020 ○   SLOW WINE
ZD Wines

53 California Citrine Chardonnay 2019 ○
Enfield Wine Co.

76 California Maglite Blanc 2020 ○
Los Angeles River Wine Co.

79 California Post Flirtation
White Blend 2020 ○   EVERYDAY WINE
Martha Stoumen Wines

101 California The Prince In His Caves 2018 ◎   SLOW WINE
Scholium Project

96 Carneros Estate Pinot Blanc 2020 ○
Ram's Gate Winery

66 Carneros Hyde Vineyard Chardonnay 2018 ○
Hyde de Villaine - HdV

49 Carneros White Barn Single Block Reserve
Pinot Noir 2020 ●
The Donum Estate

47 Cienega Valley Cardillo Vineyard
Cabernet Franc 2019 ●   EVERYDAY WINE
DeRose Vineyards

47 Cienega Valley Cedolini Vineyard
Zinfandel 2019 ●   SLOW WINE
DeRose Vineyards

79 Clarksburg Wilson Vineyard
Chenin Blanc 2020 ○   SLOW WINE
Margins Wine

34 Contra Costa Areio e Vento e Amor Red
Blend 2018 ●   SLOW WINE
Bedrock Wine Co.

93 Contra Costa County Rosehaze
Pinot Gris 2021 ◓   EVERYDAY WINE
Purity Wine

---

54 Coombsville Napa Valley
Cabernet Sauvignon 2018 ●
Favia

94 Dry Creek Valley Anderson Ranch
Zinfandel 2017 ●
Quivira Vineyards

92 Dry Creek Valley Carignane 2018 ●
Preston Farm & Winery

47 Dry Creek Valley Estate
Sagrantino Riserva 2013 ●   SLOW WINE
DaVero Farms & Winery

94 Dry Creek Valley Fig Tree Vineyard
Sauvignon Blanc 2019 ○   EVERYDAY WINE
Quivira Vineyards

78 Dry Creek Valley Kierkegaard Vineyard
Chenin Blanc 2018 ○   EVERYDAY WINE
Mâitre de Chai

112 Edna Valley Sawyer Lindquist
Vineyard Albariño 2019 ○   SLOW WINE
Verdad Wine Cellars

50 El Dorado County Edio
Albariño 2020 ○   SLOW WINE
Edio Vineyards at Delfino Farms

83 El Dorado Dunamis Block Head-Trained
Grenache 2017 ●
Narrow Gate Vineyards

83 El Dorado Roussanne 2020 ○   EVERYDAY WINE
Narrow Gate Vineyards

109 Fiddletown Terre Rouge Syrah 2014 ●   SLOW WINE
Terre Rouge/Easton Wines

65 Fort-Ross Seaview San Andreas Fault
Estate Pinot Noir 2019 ●
Hirsch Vineyards

83 Howell Mountain
Cabernet Sauvignon 2017 ●
Neal Family Vineyards

27 Howell Mountain QUINTVS
Cabernet Sauvignon 2016 ●   SLOW WINE
ADAMVS

110 Knights Valley Lisa's Vineyard
Cabernet Sauvignon 2017 ●
Thumbprint Cellars

60 Lodi Cresci Vineyard Chenin Blanc 2020 ○
Haarmeyer Wine Cellars

26 Lodi Grenache Blanc 2020 ○   EVERYDAY WINE
Acquiesce Winery

36 Lodi Terra Alta Vineyard
Albariño 2019 ○   EVERYDAY WINE
Bokisch Vineyards

26 Lodi Viognier 2020 ○
Acquiesce Winery

69 Los Alamos Clairette Blanche 2020 ○
Jolie-Laide Wines

105 Los Chuchaquis Champelli Sparkling
Albariño 2020 ⬚   EVERYDAY WINE
Stirm Wine Co.

25 Los Olivos Marsanne 2020 ○   EVERYDAY WINE
âmevive

96 Madera Jonquille Viognier 2020 ○   EVERYDAY WINE
Raft Wines

31 Mendocino Carignane 2017 ●   EVERYDAY WINE
Azolla

97 Mendocino County Buddha's Dharma
Vineyard Carignan 2019 ●   EVERYDAY WINE
Ramble Wines

56 Mendocino County
Shangra-Li Mendo Savvy-B
Sauvignon Blanc 2020 ○   EVERYDAY WINE
Florez Wines

99 Mendocino Fox Hill Vineyard
Feints 2020 ●   EVERYDAY WINE
Ruth Lewandowski Wine

53 Mendocino Ridge Mariah Vineyard ENA
Pinot Noir 2020 ●   SLOW WINE
ENA Wines

99 Mendocino Testa Vineyard Boaz 2019 ● SLOW WINE
Ruth Lewandowski Wine

92 Mokelumne River Kirschenmann
Vineyard Zinfandel 2019 ●   SLOW WINE
Precedent Wine

116 Monterey Swan/828 Pinot Noir 2018 ●
Wrath Wines

28 Moon Mountain District
Cabernet Sauvignon 2016 ●   SLOW WINE
Amapola Creek Vineyards & Winery

39 Mount Harlan Jensen Vineyard
Pinot Noir 2018 ●
Calera

91 Mount Veeder Space & Time
Cabernet Franc Blend 2019 ●
Pott Wines

78 Napa Gala Vineyard
Cabernet Sauvignon 2019 ●
Mâitre de Chai

80 Napa Valley Annia 2020 ○ EVERYDAY WINE
Massican

38 Napa Valley Burgess
Cabernet Sauvignon 2021 ●
Burgess Cellars

52 Napa Valley Chockablock
Red Blend 2018 ● EVERYDAY WINE
Elizabeth Rose

37 Napa Valley Cooper's Reeds
Cabernet Sauvignon 2018 ● SLOW WINE
Brendel

51 Napa Valley Eisele Vineyard
Cabernet Sauvignon 2018 ● SLOW WINE
Eisele Vineyard

70 Napa Valley Estate
Cabernet Sauvignon 2018 ●
Kelly Fleming Wines

80 Napa Valley Hyde Vineyard
Chardonnay 2020 ○
Massican

113 Napa Valley Las Flores
Cabernet Sauvignon 2013 ●
Volker Eisele Family Estate

107 Napa Valley Mayacamas Range
Zinfandel 2018 ● SLOW WINE
Storybook Mountain Vineyards

59 Napa Valley Paris Tasting Commemorative
Chardonnay 2017 ○ SLOW WINE
Grgich Hills Estate

80 Napa Valley Phoenix Vineyard
Cabernet Sauvignon 2018 ●
Matthiasson

72 Napa Valley Solari 2018 ●
Larkmead Vineyards

84 Napa Valley The Puzzle
Bordeaux Blend 2018 ● SLOW WINE
Newton Vineyard

45 North Coast Lignaggio 2019 ●
Coturri Winery

85 Oakville Oakville Ranch
Bordeaux Blend 2016 ●
Oakville Ranch

85 Oakville Zinfandel 2018 ● SLOW WINE
Oakville Winery

78 Paso Robles Before Anyone Else 2019 ○ SLOW WINE
MAHA | Villa Creek

41 Paso Robles Charbono 2018 ● EVERYDAY WINE
Castoro Cellars

29 Paso Robles Decorus 2020 ◉ SLOW WINE
AmByth Estate

41 Paso Robles Falanghina 2019 ○ EVERYDAY WINE
Castoro Cellars

111 Paso Robles Pesenti Vineyard
Zinfandel 2019 ●
Turley Wine Cellars

66 Petaluma Gap Saltonstall Vineyard
Pinot Noir 2017 ●
House Family Vineyards

63 Red Hills Lake County Petite Sirah 2017 ● SLOW WINE
Hawk and Horse Vineyards

32 Redwood Valley Girasole Vineyards
Pinot Blanc 2020 ○ EVERYDAY WINE
BARRA of Mendocino

65 Redwood Valley Lolonis Family
Vineyard Folk Machine Film & Camera
Valdiguié 2019 ● EVERYDAY WINE
Hobo Wine Company

111 Redwood Valley Lolonis Vineyard Sémillon 2020 ○
Trinafour

81 Redwood Valley Petite Sirah 2016 ● EVERYDAY WINE
Mia Bea Wines

68 Russian River Valley Endless Crush
Rosé of Pinot Noir 2020 ◍
Inman Family Wines

90 Russian River Valley George's Hill Vineyard
Old Vine Chardonnay 2018 ○ SLOW WINE
Porter Creek Vineyards

57 Russian River Valley
Grenache Blanc 2019 ○ SLOW WINE
Front Porch Farm

68 Russian River Valley Inman Family OGV Estate
Pinot Noir 2018 ● SLOW WINE
Inman Family Wines

110 Rutherford Napa Valley Zinfandel **2019** ●
   Tres Sabores

31 Rutherford Vineyard 1
   Cabernet Sauvignon **2016** ●
   Ashes and Diamonds

105 San Benito County Siletto
   Cabernet Pfeffer **2020** ●　　　SLOW WINE
   Stirm Wine Co.

76 San Diego County Grenache **2020** ●EVERYDAY WINE
   Los Pilares

76 San Diego County La Dona Sparkling
   Muscat **2019** ✹　　　EVERYDAY WINE
   Los Pilares

42 San Diego County Valentina Vineyard
   Darkstar **2019** ✹　　　EVERYDAY WINE
   Charlie & Echo

42 San Diego County Valentina Vineyard
   Whoa Jake **2019** ✹　　　EVERYDAY WINE
   Charlie & Echo

103 San Luis Obispo Bassi Vineyard
   Whole Cluster Pinot Noir **2018** ●　　SLOW WINE
   Sinor-LaVallee

39 Santa Barbara County Christy
   and Wise Vineyard Grenache **2020** ●
   Camins 2 Dreams

75 Santa Barbara County Clos Mullet
   Cabernet Franc **2020** ●　　　SLOW WINE
   Lo-Fi Wines

86 Santa Barbara County
   Duvarita Vineyard Syrah **2017** ●　　SLOW WINE
   The Ojai Vineyard

75 Santa Barbara County
   Gamay Noir **2020** ●　　　EVERYDAY WINE
   Lo-Fi Wines

71 Santa Barbara County Grenache
   Nouveau **2020** ●　　　EVERYDAY WINE
   Land of Saints Wine Company

108 Santa Barbara County Kick-On Ranch
   Clone 239 Riesling **2019** ○
   Tatomer

71 Santa Barbara County
   Sauvignon Blanc **2019** ○　　　EVERYDAY WINE
   Land of Saints Wine Company

86 Santa Barbara County
   Puerta del Sol Chardonnay **2018** ○
   The Ojai Vineyard

91 Santa Clara Valley Estate
   Pinot Noir **2015** ●　　　SLOW WINE
   Portola Vineyards

91 Santa Clara Valley
   Rosé of Pinot Noir **2020** ◉　　EVERYDAY WINE
   Portola Vineyards

79 Santa Clara Valley Sattler's Family
   Vineyard Mourvedre **2020** ●　　EVERYDAY WINE
   Margins Wine

28 Santa Cruz Mountains Alfaro Family
   Vineyard Estate Pinot Noir **2019** ●
   Alfaro Family Vineyard & Winery

33 Santa Cruz Mountains Coast Grade
   Vineyard Pinot Noir **2018** ●
   Beauregard Vineyards

73 Santa Cruz Mountains Domingo
   Pinot Noir **2018** ●
   Lester Estate Wines

82 Santa Cruz Mountains Estate
   Cabernet Sauvignon **2017** ●
   Mount Eden Vineyards

103 Santa Cruz Mountains Estate
   Chardonnay ○　　　SLOW WINE
   Silver Mountain Vineyards

115 Santa Cruz Mountains Estate Cuvée
   Pinot Noir **2019** ●
   Windy Oaks

55 Santa Cruz Mountains Estate
   Pinot Noir **2018** ●　　　SLOW WINE
   Ferrari Ranch Wines

55 Santa Cruz Mountains Estate
   Rosé of Pinot Noir **2020** ◉　　EVERYDAY WINE
   Ferrari Ranch Wines

107 Santa Cruz Mountains Hidden Springs
   Chardonnay **2017** ○　　　SLOW WINE
   Storrs Winery & Vineyards

100 Santa Cruz Mountains Lester Family Vineyard
   Chardonnay **2019** ○
   Sante Arcangeli Family Wines

97 Santa Cruz Mountains Monte Bello Estate
   Cabernet Sauvignon **2018** ●　　SLOW WINE
   Ridge Vineyards

35 Santa Cruz Mountains Old Corral
Pinot Noir **2018** ●   SLOW WINE
Big Basin Vineyards

35 Santa Cruz Mountains Peter Martin Ray
Vineyard Cabernet Sauvignon **2018** ●   SLOW WINE
Birichino

109 Santa Cruz Mountains Rapley Trail Vineyard
Pinot Noir **2017** ●
Thomas Fogarty

32 Santa Cruz Mountains Regan Vineyard Reserve
Pinot Noir **2019** ●
Bargetto Winery

100 Santa Cruz Mountains
Split Rail Vineyard
Pinot Noir **2019** ●   SLOW WINE
Sante Arcangeli Family Wines

77 Santa Cruz Mountains Toyon Vineyard
Chardonnay **2019** ○
Madson Wines

74 Santa Maria Valley Bien Nacido
Vineyard Z Block Syrah **2019** ●
Lindquist Family Wines

71 Sierra Foothills
Cabernet Franc **2020** ●   EVERYDAY WINE
La Clarine Farm

71 Sierra Foothills Chardonnay **2019** ○ EVERYDAY WINE
La Clarine Farm

109 Sierra Foothills Saureel
Vineyard Easton
Vermentino **2020** ○   EVERYDAY WINE
Terre Rouge/Easton Wines

89 Sonoma Coast Armaugh Vineyard
Syrah **2018** ●
Pax Wines

30 Sonoma Coast Peter's Vineyard
Syrah **2018** ●
Anthill Farms Winery

89 Sonoma Coast Pomarium Estate
Pinot Noir **2019** ●
Peay Vineyards

75 Sonoma Coast The Pivot Vineyard
Pinot Noir **2018** ●
Littorai Wines

98 Sonoma Coast UV Chardonnay **2019** ○ SLOW WINE
Rocca Family Vineyards

56 Sonoma Coast Yu-ki Estate
Pinot Noir **2018** ●
Freeman Vineyard & Winery

27 Sonoma County Centennial
Mountain Rosso **2018** ●
Aeris Wines

113 Sonoma County Split Rock
Cabernet Sauvignon **2016** ●
Viluko Vineyards

73 Sonoma Mountain Lot 48
Cabernet Sauvignon **2016** ●
Laurel Glen Vineyard

115 Sonoma Mountain Mountains
of Sonoma-Dos Limones Syrah **2018** ● SLOW WINE
Winery Sixteen 600

87 Sonoma Valley Bedrock Vineyard
Zinfandel **2019** ●   SLOW WINE
Once & Future Wine

101 Sonoma Valley Estate Pinot Noir **2018** ●
Scribe

63 Sonoma Valley Hanzell Vineyards
Chardonnay **2018** ○   SLOW WINE
Hanzell Vineyards

87 Sonoma Valley Old Hill Ranch
Zinfandel **2019** ●
Once & Future Wine

38 Spring Mountain District Cain Five **2017** ●
Cain Vineyard And Winery

105 St. Helena Napa Valley Spottswoode Estate
Cabernet Sauvignon **2018** ●   SLOW WINE
Spottswoode Estate Vineyard & Winery

114 Sta. Rita Hill Estate Pinot Noir **2016** ●
Wenzlau Vineyard

99 Sta. Rita Hills Bentrock Vineyard
Chardonnay **2018** ○
Sandhi Wines

69 Sta. Rita Hills Holus Bolus Syrah **2019** ● SLOW WINE
The Joy Fantastic | Holus Bolus

29 Sta. Rita Hills Lambda
Pinot Noir **2018** ●   SLOW WINE
Ampelos Cellars

48 Sta. Rita Hills Sous Le Chêne **2020** ●
Domaine de la Côte

70 Sta. Rita Hills Spear Vineyard
Grenache **2018** ●
Kings Carey Wines

39 Sta. Rita Hills Spear Vineyard
Syrah 2018 ● SLOW WINE
Camins 2 Dreams

40 Suisun Valley Gomes Vineyard
Sparkling Albariño 2020 ⊛ EVERYDAY WINE
CARBONISTE

44 Syrah White ○
Côte des Cailloux

30 The Meadow Rosé 2020 ⊛ EVERYDAY WINE
Angeleno Wine Co.

82 Valporone 2015 ●
Mora Estate

112 Yolo County Windmill Vineyard Natty
Pets Picpoul 2020 ○ EVERYDAY WINE
Two Shepherds

Oregon

145 Applegate Valley Mae's Vineyard
Cabernet Franc 2019 ●
Quady North

150 Applegate Valley Pét tanNat 2020 ⊛ SLOW WINE
Troon Vineyard

127 Applegate Valley Sentience Syrah 2016 ●
Cowhorn Vineyard & Garden

127 Applegate Valley Spiral 36 2020 ○ SLOW WINE
Cowhorn Vineyard & Garden

146 Chehalem Mountains Laurelwood
District Flora's Reserve Pinot Noir 2015 ●
Ruby Vineyard & Winery

121 Columbia Gorge Mosier Hills Estate
Blanco 2019 ○ SLOW WINE
Analemma Wines

123 Dundee Hills Bergström Vineyard
Chardonnay 2018 ○
Bergström Wines

130 Dundee Hills Cuvée Laurène
Pinot Noir 2018 ●
Domaine Drouhin Oregon

139 Dundee Hills Maresh Vineyard
Pinot Noir 2019 ●
Kelley Fox Wines

147 Dundee Hills Old Vineyard
Block 50th Anniversary
Pinot Noir 2018 ● SLOW WINE
Sokol Blosser Winery

130 Dundee Hills Pinot Noir 2019 ● SLOW WINE
Domaine Drouhin Oregon

125 Eola-Amity Hills Brooks Estate
Riesling 2018 ○ SLOW WINE
Brooks Wine

122 Eola-Amity Hills Eola Springs Vineyard
Pinot Noir 2017 ●
Authentique Wine Cellars

125 Eola-Amity Hills Rastaban Pinot Noir 2018 ●
Brooks Wine

142 Eola-Amity Hills Temperance
Hill Vineyard Aligoté 2019 ○ EVERYDAY WINE
Lumos Wine Co.

143 McMinnville Arsheen
Pinot Gris 2020 ○ EVERYDAY WINE
Maysara Winery

143 McMinnville Asha Pinot Noir 2015 ● SLOW WINE
Maysara Winery

153 McMinnville Bailey Family Pinot Noir 2017 ●
Youngberg Hill

147 McMinnville Momtazi Vineyard
Pinot Noir 2017 ● SLOW WINE
St. Innocent Winery

124 Ribbon Ridge House Red
Pinot Noir ● EVERYDAY WINE
Brick House Wines

124 Ribbon Ridge
Pinot Noir Les Dijonnais 2019 ●
Brick House Wines

151 Rogue Valley Avra Vineyard
Grenache 2018 SLOW WINE ●
Weisinger Family Winery

128 Rogue Valley Ecarté Pinot Noir 2018 ●
DANCIN

151 Rogue Valley Grenache 2019 ● SLOW WINE
Upper Five Vineyard

151 Rogue Valley Sauvignon Blanc 2020 ○ EVERYDAY WINE
Upper Five Vineyard

129 Tualatin Hills Black Jack Estate Block 21
Pinot Noir 2019 ●
David Hill Vineyards and Winery

143 Tualatin Hills Pinot Gris **2019** ○   EVERYDAY WINE
Montinore Estate

136 Umpqua Valley Petit Blanc **2017** ○   EVERYDAY WINE
HillCrest Vineyard

141 Van Duzer Corridor Cali's Cuvée
Pinot Noir **2018** ●   EVERYDAY WINE
Left Coast Estate

141 Van Duzer Corridor Estate White
Pinot Noir **2020** ○
Left Coast Estate

136 Willamette Valley 1899
Pinot Noir **2019** ●   SLOW WINE
Illahe Vineyards

129 Willamette Valley Chardonnay **2019** ○
Domaine Divio

127 Willamette Valley Cooper Mountain
Pinot Noir **2018** ●   EVERYDAY WINE
Cooper Mountain Vineyards

132 Willamette Valley Estate
Pinot Gris **2020** ○   EVERYDAY WINE
Elk Cove Vineyards

144 Willamette Valley Estate Pinot Noir **2018** ●
Open Claim Vineyards

147 Willamette Valley Freedom Hill Vineyard
Cuvée la Liberté Chardonnay **2018** ○
St. Innocent Winery

127 Willamette Valley Life Pinot Noir **2019** ●   SLOW WINE
Cooper Mountain Vineyards

135 Willamette Valley
Melon de Bourgogne **2020** ○   EVERYDAY WINE
Grochau Cellars

147 Willamette Valley
Rosé of Pinot Noir **2020** ◐   EVERYDAY WINE
Sokol Blosser

126 Willamette Valley
Sparkling Rosé **2020** ❋   EVERYDAY WINE
Bryn Mawr Vineyards

134 Willamette Valley The Eyrie Pinot Noir **2017** ●
The Eyrie Vineyards

141 Willamette Valley Thea's Selection
Pinot Noir **2018** ●   SLOW WINE
Lemelson Vineyards

141 Willamette Valley Tikka's Run
Pinot Gris **2019** ○   EVERYDAY WINE
Lemelson Vineyards

142 Willamette Valley Wren Vineyard
Chardonnay **2018** ○   SLOW WINE
Lumos Wine Co.

123 Yamhill-Carlton Belle Pente Vineyard
Chardonnay **2017** ○   EVERYDAY WINE
Belle Pente Vineyard & Winery

130 Yamhill-Carlton Bishop Creek
Chardonnay **2018** ○
Domaine Nicolas-Jay

152 Yamhill-Carlton Clairière
Pinot Noir **2019** ●
WillaKenzie Estate

120 Yamhill-Carlton Due North
Pinot Noir **2019** ●
Abbott Claim Vineyard

152 Yamhill-Carlton Estate Cuvée
Chardonnay **2019** ○   SLOW WINE
WillaKenzie Estate

140 Yamhill-Carlton Estate
Müller-Thurgau **2019** ○   EVERYDAY WINE
Kramer Vineyards

140 Yamhill-Carlton Estate Pinot Gris **2018** ○
Kramer Vineyards

132 Yamhill-Carlton Mount Richmond
Pinot Noir **2019** ●
Elk Cove Vineyards

146 Yamhill-Carlton Roots Estate Vineyard
Pinot Noir **2019** ●   SLOW WINE
Roots Wine Co.

New York

156 Finger Lakes #239 Dry Riesling **2019** ○
Boundary Breaks

156 Finger Lakes Barrel Fermented
Chardonnay **2019** ○   EVERYDAY WINE
Damiani Wine Cellars

157 Finger Lakes Cabernet Franc **2019** ●
Fox Run Vineyards

158 Finger Lakes Estate Riesling **2020** ○   SLOW WINE
Silver Thread Vineyard

158 Finger Lakes Tango Oaks
Vineyard Riesling **2016** ○
Red Newt Cellars

160 Long Island Perle Chardonnay 2019 ○
Wölffer Estate Vineyard

161 Seneca Lake Timeline Dry Riesling 2019 ○
Standing Stone Vineyards

Washington

166 Columbia Gorge Estate Grown
Gamay Noir 2019 ● SLOW WINE
Syncline

163 Columbia Valley Estate Barbera 2019 ●
Cascade Cliffs Vineyard and Winery

164 Columbia Valley GSM 2020 ●
Foundry Vineyards

167 Columbia Valley Organic
Chenin Blanc 2020 ○ EVERYDAY WINE
Tagaris Winery

164 Lake Chelan Whole Picture Au Naturel
Pét Nat 2019 ⬡ SLOW WINE
Hard Row to Hoe Vineyards

167 Naches Heights Wilridge
Vineyard Estate Organic & Biodynamic
Sagrantino 2016 ● SLOW WINE
Wilridge Vineyard, Winery & Distillery

162 Puget Sound Madeleine
Angevine 2018 ○ SLOW WINE
Bainbridge Vineyards

165 Red Mountain Hedges Family Estate
Biodynamic Syrah 2018 ●
Hedges Family Estate

163 Walla Walla Valley Cayuse
Vineyards Cailloux Syrah 2018 ● SLOW WINE
Bionic Wines

163 Walla Walla Valley No Girls
La Paciencia Vineyard Grenache 2018 ● SLOW WINE
Bionic Wines

CALIFORNIA

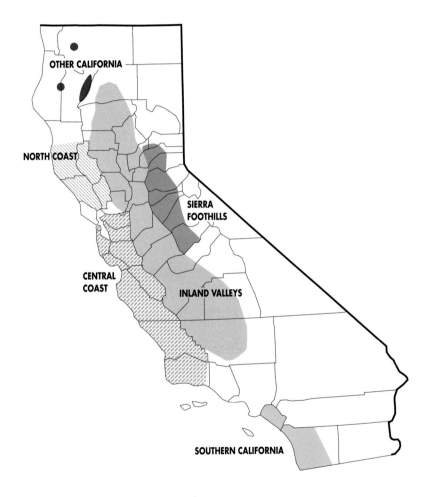

OTHER CALIFORNIA

NORTH COAST

SIERRA
FOOTHILLS

CENTRAL
COAST

INLAND VALLEYS

SOUTHERN CALIFORNIA

Snail 🌀

25 Á Deux Têtes
27 ADAMVS
27 Aeris Wines
29 AmByth Estate
29 Ampelos Cellars
33 Beckmen Vineyards
37 Brendel
43 Chateau Davell
47 DaVero Farms & Winery
51 Eisele Vineyard
52 Elizabeth Rose
52 Elkfield Wines
57 Frog's Leap
57 Front Porch Farm
58 Ghost Block
59 Grgich Hills Estate
62 Handley Cellars
63 Hanzell Vineyards
63 Hawk and Horse Vineyards
68 Inman Family Wines
72 Larkmead Vineyards
72 Lasseter Family Winery
80 Matthiasson
81 Medlock Ames
83 Neal Family Vineyards
84 Nicholson Ranch
85 Oakville Ranch
85 Oakville Winery
88 Ovis
90 Porter Creek Vineyards
91 Portola Vineyards
91 Pott Wines
92 Preston Farm & Winery
94 Quintessa
94 Quivira Vineyards
95 Radio-Coteau
95 RAEN
97 Ramble Wines
97 Ridge Vineyards
98 Robert Sinskey Vineyards
98 Rocca Family Vineyards
104 Snowden Vineyards
105 Spottswoode Estate
    Vineyard & Winery
106 Stony Hill Vineyard
107 Storybook
    Mountain Vineyards
113 Volker Eisele Family Estate
115 Winery Sixteen 600

Bottle 🍾

26 A Tribute to Grace
28 Amapola Creek
    Vineyards & Winery
25 âmevive
30 Anthill Farms Winery
31 Ashes and Diamonds
33 Beauregard Vineyards
34 Bedrock Wine Co.
35 Big Basin Vineyards
35 Birichino
37 Bonterra Organic Vineyards
38 Burgess Cellars
39 Calera
46 Crosby Roamann
48 Domaine de la Côte
49 Donum Estate
50 Edio Vineyards
    at Delfino Farms
60 Haarmeyer Wine Cellars
66 Hyde de Villaine - HdV
67 Idlewild
69 Jolie-Laide Wines
69 The Joy Fantastic | Holus Bolus
73 Lester Estate Wines
74 Lindquist Family Wines
75 Littorai Wines
76 Los Angeles River Wine Co.
77 Madson Wines
78 MAHA | Villa Creek
78 Maître de Chai
79 Martha Stoumen Wines
80 Massican
82 Mora Estate
82 Mount Eden Vineyards
83 Narrow Gate Vineyards
84 Newton Vineyard
86 The Ojai Vineyard
87 Once & Future Wine
87 Opus One
89 Pax Wines
90 Piedrasassi
99 Sandhi Wines
101 Scholium Project
101 Scribe
103 Silver Mountain Vineyards
107 Storrs Winery & Vineyards
108 Tablas Creek Vineyard
108 Tatomer
110 Tres Sabores
111 Trinafour
111 Turley Wine Cellars
112 Verdad Wine Cellars
114 Wenzlau Vineyard
115 Windy Oaks
116 Wrath Wines
117 ZD Wines

Coin $

26 Acquiesce Winery
28 Alfaro Family
    Vineyard & Winery
31 Azolla
32 Bargetto Winery
32 BARRA of Mendocino
39 Camins 2 Dreams
40 Carol Shelton Wines
41 CARY Q WINES
41 Castoro Cellars
60 Guthrie Family Wines
62 Hammerling Wine
71 Land of Saints
    Wine Company
75 Lo-Fi Wines
76 Los Pilares
77 Madroña
79 Margins Wine
81 Mia Bea Wines
92 Precedent Wine
93 Prima Materia
    Vineyard and Winery
93 Purity Wine
96 Raft Wines
99 Ruth Lewandowski Wine
100 Sante Arcangeli
    Family Wines
102 Sean Walker McBride
112 Two Shepherds
114 Wild Hog Vineyard
117 Yamakiri Wines

SANTA MARIA

ÂMEVIVE

2705 Aviation Way – tel. (209) 872-2420
www.amevivewine.com – alice@amevivewine.com

PEOPLE - Alice Anderson graduated from Cal Poly San Luis Obispo and soon found herself in New Zealand absorbing biodynamics at Rippon Winery. Through a friend in New Zealand, she landed a two-year stint in the Rhône at Domaine Pierre Gaillard. She then made her way back to the States at Tyler in Sta Rita Hills. Meanwhile, the lease for the historic Ibarra-Young Vineyard in Los Olivos had been relinquished. She assumed the lease in 2020.

VINEYARDS - Anderson sources 40% of her output, all gamay, from Presqu'il Vineyard and Shokrian Vineyards in the Santa Maria Valley which features sandy loam soils. The other 60% of her grapes come from the Ibarra-Young Vineyard, Anderson's estate. It is farmed regeneratively with biodynamic protocols and animals roaming the vineyards at intervals. Currently marsanne, graciano and a field blend are estate produced.

WINES - The name amevive means "lively souls," and the wines are unfined and unfiltered.

(TOP) Los Olivos Marsanne 2020 EVERYDAY WINE ○ 78 cs; $ 30 - 🍷⊞ - Shows aromas of acacia, yellow apple and baked goods with a racy peach and green apple palate.
Santa Barbara County Gamay Noir 2020 ● 80 cs; $ 30 - ⊞ - Has light nutmeg woven into strawberry and raspberry aromas and a palate that adds red apple and an earthy seasoning.
Los Olivos Ibarra Young Vineyard Syrah 2020 ● 75 cs; $ 34 - ⊞ - Spiced cherry and meaty aromas emanate from this wine, while fresh, ripe dark cherry and cranberry fruit are on the palate shot with a mineral streak.

---

acres 10 - **cases** 800
Fertilizers compost, organic-mineral
Plant protection organic, sulfur, synthetic pesticides
Weed control mechanical
Yeasts spontaneous fermentation
Grapes purchase 60%
Certification none

SONOMA

Á DEUX TÊTES

589 1st Street – tel. (707) 721-1805
www.winerysixteen600.com – info@winerysixteen600.com

 For cultivating a climate friendly varietal, Grenache, and taking its vinification to new heights–the team's forward looking approach and its impeccable wines.

PEOPLE - In 2018, Sonoma's organic viticulture rockstar Phil Coturri launched Á Deux Têtes, a collaboration with Rhône superstar winemaker Philippe Cambie. Coturri is known as a vineyard manager growing grapes for 100 point wines. Robert Parker named Cambie Oenologist of the Year in 2010 and more than 15 of his wines have been rated 100 points.

VINEYARDS - Coturri could be said to be the Johnny Appleseed of Grenache. The Miller site, the source for the brand's rosé, was planted for rosé based on Cambie's direct guidance. At Oakville Ranch, in Napa's Vaca Mountains, the soils are red and volcanic. At Rossi Ranch in Sonoma Valley, an historic site, the soils are light volcanic ash and obsidian shards. The two latter sites provide a comparison for starpower Grenache wines grown in different terroirs.

WINES - Southern Rhone native Isabel Gassier is the hands on winemaker working with Cambie's protocols.

Napa Valley Miller Vineyard Rosé 2019 ● 100 cs; $ 49 - 🍷 - Aromatic, textured and intensely flavorful, with peach and citrus notes. A delicate, distinctive licorice note–essential for Grenache rosé, Cambie says–persists from the nose through to the finish. Shows rosé's potential to achieve great heights.
Oakville Oakville Ranch Grenache 2018 ● n/a; $ 88 - ⊞ - A blend with 7 percent Mourvèdre, it offers deep cherry notes coupled with red fruits, exhibiting impressive concentration and depth.
Sonoma Valley Rossi Ranch Grenache 2018 ● n/a; $ 88 - ⊞ - More feminine, compared to the Oakville, this impresses with its floral nose before developing into cherry and blackberry notes and a long finish.

---

acres 0 - **cases** 1,000
Fertilizers compost, cover crops
Plant protection organic, sulfur
Weed control mechanical
Yeasts spontaneous fermentation
Grapes purchase 100%
Certification some of the vineyards are certified organic

A TRIBUTE TO GRACE

ACQUIESCE WINERY $

490 Bell Street, #5 – tel. (805) 633-0598
www.gracewinecompany.com
angela@gracewinecompany.com

PEOPLE - 'Granache is my normal mode, I just take a few sidesteps now and then', so says Angela Osborne who has made many single vineyard grenaches since 2007 and is a master of the grape in California. Grace was Angela's treasured grandmother and there is a through line from the name and the virtue that is Angela's watchword in winemaking and life writ large. She has a home base and tasting room in Los Alamos in the Santa Maria Valley. Jason is her husband and partner. There is a brood of three.

VINEYARDS - Osborne typically sources from all over the state and this year has gone to lengths to make sure that 6 grenaches from three sites were all picked on the same day, October 24th 2020, recommended by the biodynamic calendar. High elevation Shake Ridge Ranch is farmed by the legendary Ann Kramer. Thompson vineyard is certified organic, nearby in the Santa Maria Valley and Spear, also certified, is also close, in the eastern Sta Rita Hills.

WINES - Substantial acidity is expressed in all her wines as is ripeness. Differences in perfume, structure and earthiness distinguish them.

Amador County Shake Ridge Ranch Vineyard Grenache 2019 ● 61 cs; $ 75 - - Marries whole cluster fermentation with 1/3 new oak for a broad-shouldered version, with incense aromas, a fine tannic structure and dry strawberry and sous bois flavors.

Alisos Canyon Thompson Vineyard Grenache Blanc 2020 ○ 200 cs; $ 33 - - Has earthy aromas including white flower and pollen. Pear fruit appears on the palate with almond and bright green apple.
Sta. Rita Hills Spear Vineyard Grenache 2019 ● 87 cs; $ 60 - - Osborne makes tactile winemaking choices such as chewing on many of the stems of her Spear Vineyard to Grenache to decide on whole cluster inclusion. Results this time: none. Still, the aromatics are extravagant of fresh rose and strawberry while the concentrated palate of currant and strawberry is anchored in earth spices.

acres 0 - cases 3,000
Fertilizers compost, cover crops
Plant protection copper, organic, sulfur
Weed control mechanical
Yeasts spontaneous fermentation
Grapes purchase 100%
Certification some of the vineyards are certified organic

22353 N Tretheway Road – tel. (209) 333-6102
www.whitewinery.com – sue@av-wine.com

PEOPLE - To acquiesce is to agree, go along; corporate executive Rodney Tipton was listening to k.d.lang's song "Acquiesce" when he knew he and wife Sue would own a winery with that name. After raising three sons and living abroad, they moved to Portland, OR where Sue owned a successful mail-order business, and she developed an appreciation for wine pairing. They found their vineyard in Lodi; when they decided to make wine, Sue became a winemaker, and "surrender to the grapes."

VINEYARDS - In a region known for red wine, Lodi's Acquiesce grows obscure white Rhone varietals. After tasting a white wine blend from Chateau Beaucastel, they decided to plant Grenache Blanc in 2008. Pleased with results, they added Roussanne, Viognier and Picpoul Blanc with cuttings from Tablas Creek Winery in Paso Robles which partners with Beaucastel where these varietals originated.

WINES - Grapes are hand picked, whole cluster pressed, and fermented with yeast indigenous to the Rhone. Sue started Slow Food Lodi; making balanced wine that pairs well with food matters to her. Lovely tastings by reservation include pairings with small bites featuring homemade crackers.

Lodi Grenache Blanc 2020 EVERYDAY WINE ○ 659 cs; $ 28 - - They grow 3 acres of their signature 100% Grenache Blanc which beguiles with intense floral aromatics and follows with vivid lemon and nectarine with a lingering mineral finish.

Lodi Viognier 2020 ○ 208 cs; $ 30 - - Crisp and dry, this 100% Viognier offers an enticing floral nose violets and a voluminous mouthfeel.
Lodi Ingénue 2019 ○ Grenache Blanc, Clairette Blanche, Bourboulenc, Picpoul; 340 cs; $ 34 - - Named after a k.d. Lang album, Ingénue's blend speaks to the new varietals at Acquiesce offering abundant aromas of white flowers and farmer's market basket of summer fruit on the palate.

acres 10.5 - cases 3,000
Fertilizers compost, cover crops, manure, mineral fertilizer
Plant protection copper, organic, sulfur
Weed control mechanical
Yeasts commercial cultured yeasts, selected indigenous yeasts
Grapes 100% estate-grown
Certification none

ANGWIN

ADAMVS

501 White Cottage Road N – tel. (707) 965-0555
www.adamvs.com – info@adamvs.com

 As of 2018 ADAMVS' wines have been 100% estate and exemplify their farming practices.

PEOPLE - According to Denise Adams, co-owner of ADAMVS, George Yount once owned the Howell Mountain estate she and husband Stephen purchased in 2008. Adams' discovered her passion for biodynamic agriculture when they lived in Montecito, CA and has since transformed the 80-acre property. Viticulturist and winemaker Alberto Bianchi joined the team in early 2021 and will oversee all aspects of the estate with long-time consultant Philippe Melka.

VINEYARDS - Recent additions to the estate include a large insectary planted adjacent to the winery with a plant mix specifically created to support bee hives. A herd of cattle have joined mule "McGee" and donkey "Buttercup" furthering biodiversity. Adams' has replanted one third of the 27 acres under vine which comprise five soils series and have some of the highest elevation plantings on Howell mountain.

WINES - The winery's estate Cabernet Sauvignons bear the names ADAMVS meaning "born from our red earth," TÉRES, meaning "round, smooth, polished," and QUINTVS, meaning "five." A yeast strain native to the ADAMVS Estate is used for the estate wines.

TOP **Howell Mountain QUINTVS Cabernet Sauvignon 2016** SLOW WINE ● 632 cs; $ 174 - ▦ - Powerful yet elegant mountain fruit with markers of resinous dried herbs and patchouli. Deeply-colored with mullberry and black plum layered over fine, dense tannins.
Howell Mountain ADAMVS Cabernet Sauvignon 2016 ● 200 cs; $ 350 - ▦ - Lush with blackberry, boysenberry, plum and blood orange zest, a marker often found in this wine, umami, star anise and sous bois add savory depth to this fresh vintage.
Howell Mountain TÉRES Cabernet Sauvignon 2016 ● 1,200 cs; $ 128 - ⬭ - Radiating blackberry, boysenberry, mullberry with licorice and dried herbs over ample resolved tannins and a dark, fresh saline finish.

acres 27 - cases 2,000
Fertilizers biodynamic compost
Plant protection biodynamic preparations, organic
Weed control animal grazing, mechanical
Yeasts selected indigenous yeasts
Grapes purchase 30%
Certification some of the vineyards are certified organic, some of the vineyards are certified biodynamic

UKIAH

AERIS WINES

1265 Masonite Road – tel. (650) 419-2060
www.aeriswines.com

 Aeris promotes preservation of ancient varieties and homage to Mount Etna terroir, along with impeccable winemaking.

PEOPLE - The label is a collaboration with the Rhys Vineyard team in northern California and Sicilian Salvo Foti, champion for preserving rare, indigenous varieties from Mount Etna. In 2011, only 25 acres of true Carricante, a white grape variety, were left on Mount Etna. Rhys imported vines to plant in Sonoma, a task that took five years (for legal permissions). Aeris' team is owner Kevin Harvey, vineyard manager Javier Meza, and winemaker Jeff Brinkman.

VINEYARDS - Aeris has two sites on Mount Etna and one in northern Sonoma on a remote coastal ridge west of Lake Sonoma called Centennial Mountain (at 2,000 feet of elevation). The Mount Etna vines include 7.5 acres of true Carricante. Another vineyard is planted with about an acre of old-vine Nerello Mascalese, as well as some new plantings.

WINES - Winemaker Jeff Brinkman says, "You can't make these wines like Pinot Noir (the Rhys specialty), so we really had to start from scratch in our winemaking program."

TOP **Sonoma County Centennial Mountain Rosso 2018** ● 333 cs; $ 59 - ⬭ - A very unusual red blend with 50% Nebbiolo. This interesting juxtaposition of varieties produces a floral, red fruit nose with dark toned, herby and savory finish.
Etna Rosso Centenari 2016 ● 130 cs; $ 79 - ⬭ - From an abandoned vineyard that Foti decided was a sweet spot for Nerello Mascalese on the north part of Mount Etna. This wine takes the Italian word for 100-year-olds, or centenarians, to give homage to the old-vines that lend prominent dusty rose and red fruit characteristics.
Etna Bianco Superiore 2017 ○ 291 cs; $ 59 - ⬭ ⬭ - This wine does take time to evolve, and bottle aging for a couple of years to really show, but then unfolds with a waxy, rainwater precision. Rich and round yet ending with great acidity.

acres 32 - cases 833
Fertilizers n/a
Plant protection organic, sulfur
Weed control
Yeasts spontaneous fermentation
Grapes 100% estate-grown
Certification none

ALFARO FAMILY VINEYARD & WINERY $

420 Hames Road – tel. (831) 728-5172
www.alfarowine.com – mail@alfarowine.com

PEOPLE - Alfaro is very familiar to most long-time Santa Cruz residents as a pioneering local bread business. But in 1997, Mary Kay and Richard Alfaro transitioned to the wine industry when they bought a 75 acre property in Corralitos and have since grown an equally recognizable wine label, primarily showcasing distinct Chardonnay and Pinot Noir. In 2019, their son Ryan Alfaro took over the winemaking role, while Richard continues to oversee the farming.

VINEYARDS - The winery has six different vineyards, all dry farmed and planted to Chardonnay, Pinot Noir, Syrah and Merlot. Alfaro also planted two acres of Gruner Veltliner, an Austrian variety. The family recently bought the historic 42 year old, dry farmed Trout Gulch Vineyard in Aptos, which Richard had been farming for 10 years, and plan to continue to dry farm it as well as put in some new rootstock and graft some vines.

WINES - Though it started making wine during the days of Robert Parker, with full bodied wines, the house style has now lightened up to please consumer's desires for lighter bodied wines.

🔴 **Santa Cruz Mountains Alfaro Family Vineyard Estate Pinot Noir 2019** ● 425 cs; $ 45 - One of the more robust of the Alfaro estate Pinots, retaining a savory component with a full, velvety mouthfeel. It is compelling, with earthy, almost minty aromatics and tons of acid.
Santa Cruz Mountains Trout Gulch Chardonnay 2019 ○ 250 cs; $ 30 - From Ryan's favorite vineyard, four miles from the ocean, produces wines with ripping acidity. Crisp and citrusy it's made in stainless tanks.
Santa Cruz Mountains Trout Gulch Pinot Noir 2018 ● 225 cs; $ 45 - Blended from two clones, fermented separately. There's a bit of stem influence from the whole cluster is along with a super bright, dark berry flavor profile with excellent tannin balance.

acres 60 - **cases** 8,000
Fertilizers compost
Plant protection organic, sulfur, synthetic pesticides
Weed control mechanical
Yeasts selected indigenous yeasts
Grapes 100% estate-grown
Certification none

AMAPOLA CREEK VINEYARDS & WINERY

392 London Way – tel. (707) 938-3783
www.amapolacreek.com – info@amapolacreek.com

PEOPLE - Arrowwood's history is the stuff of legend, showing wine critics—back in the 1980's—that Sonoma Cabs were on equal footing with those from Napa. He teamed up with Sonoma's leading organic vineyardist Phil Coturri, a left leaning hippie who wears tie dye shirts, and began championing organic grapes, which Arrowood says make better tasting wine. When Richard retired, he sold to neighbor Brion Wise, but will continue making the wines through 2021.

VINEYARDS - The estate vineyard (certified organic) grows Cabernet and red Rhone varietals on red and white volcanic soils in the Moon Mountain District AVA, a landscape of hardened lava flows. Chardonnay comes from Joseph Belli Vineyard (certified organic) in the Russian River Valley AVA. In 2018, for one vintage only, a single vineyard bottling of Zinfandel came from Coturri-farmed Nuns Canyon (certified biodynamic) where the vines are 60 to 80 years old.

WINES - Arrowood's elegant and complex wines are widely recognized as consistently among the best in Sonoma. The 2021 harvest marks his 56th year as a winemaker.

🔴 **Moon Mountain District Cabernet Sauvignon 2016** SLOW WINE ● 1,700 cs; $ 100 - Grown on early ripening clones (chosen for that reason), an ageworthy wine that sports plum, blackberry, and blueberries notes. **Nuns Canyon Zinfandel 2016** ● 130 cs; $ 50 - A singular wine made only in this vintage (the vineyard was later damaged by fire), expressing the Pinot like flights an old vine Zin can take in the hands of a master who adores the variety. Raspberry and blueberry aromas deepen into brambleberry and bright, tart cherry notes. **Russian River Valley Jos. Belli Vineyards Chardonnay 2018** ○ 780 cs; $ 50 - Bottle fermented and aged in barrel, delicate and rounded, it offers elegant lemon, citrus and stone fruit notes and a long finish.

acres 14 - **cases** 5,000
Fertilizers compost, cover crops
Plant protection sulfur, synthetic pesticides
Weed control chemical, mechanical
Yeasts commercial cultured yeasts
Grapes purchase 25%
Certification some of the vineyards are certified organic

AMBYTH ESTATE

AMPELOS CELLARS

510 Sequoia Lane – tel. (805) 319-6967
www.ambythestate.com – info@ambythestate.com

312 N 9th Street – tel. (805) 736-9957
www.ampeloscellars.net – rebecca@ampeloscellars.com

 AmByth stewards the land and its wines with deep sincerity.

 Attention to farming practices makes this winery stand out.

PEOPLE - Ambyth founder Phillip Hart grew up in the green hills of North Wales. In the rolling golden hills of Paso Robles, he realized his dream of owning a winery which he named AmByth, from the Welsh word meaning 'forever.' Biodynamic farmers from the start in 2003, second gen Gelert now manages the vineyards, fruit, farm, and olive orchards, and makes the wine.

PEOPLE - Life can change in a flash. A missed appointment on Sept. 11, 2001 at the World Trade Center led busy executives Rebecca and Peter Work to reassess their lives, and decide to change to a slow paced lifestyle closer to the land by moving from Los Angeles to Lompoc to grow grapes and make wine. In 2006, they committed to biodynamics. Ampelos means "wine" in Greek; they also own a hotel in Greece by the same name.

VINEYARDS - Of 42 acres, AmByth has 17 planted with Demeter certified Mourvèdre, Grenache, Syrah, Counoise, Tempranillo, Sangiovese, Roussanne, Marsanne, Viognier, & Grenache Blanc with 2/3 of the vines on their own roots. Dry farmed, vines are headtrained and widely spaced with roots exploiting cracks in the limestone to survive. Low yields and high demand means Gelert has expanded to embrace vineyards farmed with a similar philosophy.

VINEYARDS - Saving soil is of primary importance to Peter Work. First in the US to be certified organic, sustainable, and biodynamic, Ampelos vines grow in the Sta. Rita Hills AVA close to the Pacific which brings cooling afternoon breezes, deep marine fog at night, and sunshine during the day. Justly famous for pinot noir, they also grow grenache, syrah, viognier, and riesling.

WINES - The winery specializes in natural wines that are foot stomped and have zero additives. Whites typically have extended skin contact. Wines age in amphorae or neutral oak barrels.

WINES - Work makes still, sparkling, and dessert wines in a minimalist style using native yeasts.

🔴 **Paso Robles Decorus 2020** SLOW WINE ◎ Viognier, Marsanne, Grenache Blanc, roussanne; 84 cs; $ 38 - 🍷 - A cloudy deep orange sunset, with complex aromas of honeysuckle, garden flowers, sandalwood, orange oil, and fresh mint, the palate offers bee pollen, apricot, orange pith, and oxalis with a dry chalky texture, and a resonating, mouthwatering finish.

🔴 **Sta. Rita Hills Lambda Pinot Noir 2018** SLOW WINE ● 620 cs; $ 39 - 🍴 - Hand picked, hand sorted, with some stem inclusion, three days of pumpover with native fermentation and 8-10 days on skin, this pinot noir blend develops into translucent raspberry with tart fruit, herbs, and earth.

Santa Barbara County Sauvignon Blanc O.W. 2020 ◎ 230 cs; $ 28 - 🍷 - From Coquelicot Vineyard: a golden cloud presenting a complex melange of white stone fruit when first opened, moving toward herbal notes of bell pepper, oxalis, jalapeno jelly, with the same changes on the palate, and a consistent, amazing textural experience.

Sta. Rita Hills Delta Grenache 2017 ● 216 cs; $ 38 - 🍴 - Lean and clean, this pale translucent raspberry hued gem tickles the palate with bright acidity, fresh raspberry fruit, and a hint of cinnamon.

Paso Robles Zinfandel 2018 ● 78 cs; $ 38 - 🍷 - A balanced, textural zin laden with earth, mint spice, fruitcake, rhubarb, bramble fruit.

Sta. Rita Hills Gamma Syrah 2017 ● 263 cs; $ 35 - 🍴 - An explosion of baked cherry brownie, Christmas fruitcake, cardamom, spearmint hit the nose while cherry, lean acidity, and chalky minerals delight the palate.

acres 17 - **cases** 1,500
Fertilizers biodynamic compost, cover crops, organic-mineral
Plant protection biodynamic preparations, organic, sulfur
Weed control animal grazing, mechanical
Yeasts spontaneous fermentation
Grapes purchase 30%
Certification some of the vineyards are certified biodynamic, some of the vineyards are certified organic

acres 25 - **cases** 3,500
Fertilizers biodynamic compost, manure, organic-mineral
Plant protection biodynamic preparations
Weed control mechanical
Yeasts spontaneous fermentation
Grapes purchase 5%
Certification some of the vineyards ore certified organic, some of the vineyards ore certified biodynamic

LOS ANGELES

ANGELENO WINE CO.

1646 North Spring Street, Unit C
www.angelenowine.com – jasper@angelenowine.com

PEOPLE - The winery is leading a renaissance in the Los Angeles wine industry, exploring adventurous varietals. In order to deal with the challenges of the pandemic, Jasper Dickson and Amy Luftig Viste expanded their space this year, and devised a delivery program for large swaths of Los Angeles, becoming expert at logging orders on spreadsheets and dispatching deliveries.

VINEYARDS - The Alonso vineyard in the Sierra Paloma Valley AVA was planted by owner Juan Alonso in the '80s to ungrafted Spanish varietals such as Garnacha, Tempranillo, Albarino and Treixadura. It is in a slightly cooler valley than the Swayze vineyard, which is hot, high desert. Swayze is the source for Alicante Bouschet and Sauvignon Blanc. Sulfur is the sole input at these vineyards. Some wine is also made at Bokisch in Lodi from organic grapes.

WINES - The wines are vibrant, aromatic and refreshing.

🔝 **The Meadow Rosé 2020** EVERYDAY WINE 🍷 300 cs; $ 25 - 🗄 - 100% graciano, is an alluring hot-weather wine with watermelon and peach on the nose and a surprisingly grown-up tangy palate of peach and red berry enhanced by aging in neutral barrel.
Alonso Vineyard Grenache 2019 ● 99 cs; $ 35 - 🗄 - Offers loamy strawberry and spice aromas and earthy dried strawberry and currant flavors aided by 20% syrah.
Swayze Vineyard Alicante Bouschet 2019 ● 160 cs; $ 35 - 🗄 - Is noteworthy for its harmony of dark cherry and cranberry fruit, slightly chewy tannins and moderate alcohol. On the nose, a whiff of fruit compote, earth and smoke.

acres 0 - cases 1,800
Fertilizers compost
Plant protection organic, sulfur
Weed control none
Yeasts spontaneous fermentation
Grapes purchase 100%
Certification none

HEALDSBURG

ANTHILL FARMS WINERY

4791 Dry Creek Road – tel. (707) 385-939
www.anthillfarms.com – hello@anthillfarms.com

PEOPLE - Anthill Farms was started in 2004 by Anthony Filberti, David Low and Webster Marquez as a winery dedicated to pinot noir from single sites in Sonoma and Mendocino. They tackled the hands-on work from the outset and pursue organic and biodynamic principles in farming their grapes. Their goal is to successfully express a vineyard which isn't possible if chemical farming is obscuring the site and the vine.

VINEYARDS - The winery leases and farms one half of their production from three vineyards: Abbey Harris and Comptche Ridge in Mendocino and Campbell Ranch in Sonoma. They prefer cool climate sites with elevation and/or ocean influence. They also participate in farming most of their other sources. In this drought season, extra care is being taken to establish cover crops and vine balance. Broadcasting compost before presumptive fall rains is considered crucial.

WINES - All three partners made wine at Williams-Selyem and in that vein, the wines express vintage character.

🔝 **Sonoma Coast Peter's Vineyard Syrah 2018** ● 310 cs; $ 38 - 🗄 - Thyme, wintergreen, olive and blackberry leap from the glass. Black currant and iodine add to the palate with converging then pleasantly subsiding fine tannins.
Mendocino County Comptche Ridge Pinot Noir 2019 ● 295 cs; $ 49 - 🗄 - Has nose of bay and cedar forest lurking below shimmering red cherry/ berry fruit. Cherry Jolly Rancher greets the palate. Mushroom and earth flavors should transform to truffle with time.
Russian River Valley Peugh Vineyard Mixed Blacks 2019 ● 310 cs; $ 38 - 🗄 - Has aromas of Mediterranean herbs, pencil lead and dark cherry which translate to the palate along with a touch of oak.

acres 30 - cases 6,800
Fertilizers compost, organic-mineral
Plant protection organic, sulfur, synthetic pesticides
Weed control mechanical
Yeasts spontaneous fermentation
Grapes purchase 50%
Certification none

ASHES AND DIAMONDS

AZOLLA $

4130 Howard Lane – tel. (707) 666-4777
www.ashesdiamonds.com – info@ashesdiamonds.com

P.O. Box 93 – tel. (510) 495-7224
www.yamakiriwines.com – info@yamakiriwines.com

PEOPLE - Music producer Kashy Khaledi made a big statement when he opened his winery in 2017, announcing this was the new Napa–millennials welcome. First act: an attention getting, sleek, Instagrammable building designed by a prominent L.A. designer. But Khaledi was also about wine style–old school–getting back to the classic Napa Cabs of the 1960's. He's cultivated relationships with top winemakers–Matthiasson and Snowden-Seysses–who make the wines.

PEOPLE - Mendocino winemaker Alex Crangle made his mark in Anderson Valley at the former Balo Vineyards. Today he makes affordable, natural wines under his own micro label, Azolla, named for the tiny fern that sequesters carbon in a big way. His knowledge of azolla comes from Christ Tebbutts of Filigreen Farm, a biodynamic farm and vineyard in Boonville where it's grown in irrigation ponds and used as fertilizer–vegan fertilizer, in fact–for the entire farm.

VINEYARDS - The winery sources from vineyards from Napa to the Santa Cruz Mountains, but its heart is in its Oak Knoll District vines with 25 acres of Merlot and Cab Franc (certified organic). Sémillon comes from the Yount Mill vineyard (certified organic) nearby while Sauvignon Blanc is sourced from an Oak Knoll District site Matthiasson farms organically. Cab Franc for rosé is from a site Matthiasson farms (organically farmed).

VINEYARDS - Crangle sources fruit from a wide variety of vineyards that range from the renowned Angel Camp in Anderson Valley for Pinot to an historic, organic (not certified) dry farmed, backyard vineyard in inland Ukiah for Carignane. Angel Camp sits on alluvial soils, where 7 different clones of Pinot are planted. The Carignane comes from gnarly old vines sitting on clay clod soils mixed with volcanic rock.

WINES - In Rutherford, a block of the famed George III Cab was farmed to A&D's organic specifications. This site was the source for many renowned, mid century Napa Cabs made by the legendary Andre Tchelistcheff when he was at Beaulieu.

WINES - All of the wines are made without added sulfites or additives and are 50 percent whole cluster. They're aged in neutral oak puncheons.

🔝 **Rutherford Vineyard 1 Cabernet Sauvignon 2016** ● 1,646 cs; $ 125 - ▦ - The piece de resistance–from the renowned George III site. Elegant and beautifully balanced with layers of complex dark berry notes, a fitting homage to the classic wines of yesteryear. 2016 is A&D's vintage for this wine.

🔝 **Mendocino Carignane 2017** EVERYDAY WINE ● 50 cs; $ 41 - Ⓜ - Offers dark cherries and an earthy quality that reflects the rocky soils it comes from.

Anderson Valley Angel Camp Pinot Noir 2017 ● 65 cs; $ 26 - Ⓜ - A step up in quality–richer and heartier–than the entry level Pinot. Though it is young now, savvy buyers are laying it down with the expectation it will grow in depth and complexity with a few years of aging in the cellar. (The vineyard and the winemaker have impressive track records).

Carneros Rosé of Cabernet Franc 2020 ◍ 5,400 magnum; $ 39 - 🗋 - A stylistic success, weaving savory salinity with tender creaminess that comes from spending 8 months on the lees.

Anderson Valley Pinot Noir 2017 ● 50 cs; $ 21 - Ⓜ - An entry level, handmade wine–rustic and affordable–for easy drinking.

Napa Valley Blanc 2018 ○ 1,100 cs; $ 45 - ▦ - A 50-50 blend of Sémillon and Sauvignon Blanc (a takeoff on a white Bordeaux), and barrel fermented, impresses for complex, citrusy notes and tart, grapefruit finish. Aged 12 months in barrel and 24 more months in bottle.

acres 25 - **cases** 8,000
Fertilizers compost, cover crops, organic
Plant protection organic, sulfur
Weed control mechanical
Yeasts spontaneous fermentation
Grapes purchase 83%
Certification some of the vineyards are certified organic

acres 0 - **cases** 170
Fertilizers cover crops, organic
Plant protection organic, synthetic pesticides
Weed control mechanical
Yeasts spontaneous fermentation
Grapes purchase 100%
Certification none

SOQUEL

BARGETTO WINERY $

3535 N Main Street – tel. (831) 475-2258
www.bargetto.com – jbargetto@bargetto.com

PEOPLE - Founded in 1933 right after the repeal of Prohibition by two brothers who immigrated to Santa Cruz from Piedmont, Italy, Bargetto Winery is run by three Bargettos representing the third generation. Bobby Graviano is the winemaker since 2016.

VINEYARDS - The Regan Vineyard, 40 acres planted in 1992, lies 7 miles inland from the Monterey Bay in the Corralitos area of the Santa Cruz Mountains AVA. Twelve grape varieties and clones, including several Italian varietals, are planted on loamy-clay soil. John Bargetto, director of winemaking, manages the vineyard. Since 2018, Regan Vineyard and Bargetto Winery are certified sustainable by the CSWA.

WINES - Winemaking is terroir-driven with minimal intervention to allow expression of the Regan Vineyard: rich with good acidity and deep color.

🔝 **Santa Cruz Mountains Regan Vineyard Reserve Pinot Noir 2019** ● 427 cs; $ 44 - ⊞ - Composed of 4 Pinot Noir clones, the wine offers aromas of dark cherry, cherry cola, fresh strawberry, and dried rose petals, with good acidity and crunchy red fruits on the palate rounded out with vanilla and spice.
Santa Cruz Mountains Regan Vineyard Dolcetto 2018 ● 267 cs; $ 35 - ⊞ - Dark fruits, black pepper, and oak, the wine has a well-balanced structure with good acid, full body, and rich tannins.
Santa Cruz Mountains Regan Vineyard Pinot Grigio 2018 ○ 428 cs; $ 28 - 🍷 - Lemon, peach, lemongrass, and orange blossom in a ripe Pinot Gris style.

acres 40 - **cases** 30,000
Fertilizers compost, organic-mineral
Plant protection organic
Weed control mechanical
Yeasts commercial cultured yeasts, spontaneous fermentation
Grapes purchase 10%
Certification converting to organics

REDWOOD VALLEY

BARRA OF MENDOCINO $

7051 N. State Street – tel. (707) 485-0322
www.barraofmendocino.com – info@barraofmendocino.com

PEOPLE - Born in Mendocino in 1926 to first generation Italian immigrants, Charlie Barra grew up working in a vineyard and began growing professionally in 1945 while still in high school. He organized growers to fight for better contracts, started North Coast AVA and was the first to use water on vines for frost protection in the US in 2011. After Charlie's passing at 92 his wife, Martha, took over the mulit-faceted family business with two brands, and a custom crush facility.

VINEYARDS - Barra bought the 175 acre Redwood Valley vineyard in 1955 and eventually added 90 more acres. Two other vineyards, "Bella Collina" and "Tasting Room" are nearby (certified organic). Varieties include Chardonnay, Pinot Blanc, Muscat Canelli, Pinot Noir, Sangiovese, Merlot, Petite Sirah, Zinfandel and Cabernet Sauvignon with 60% of grapes being sold. Current focus is to reduce fuel loads on the lands after nearly losing everything to the Mendocino Complex Fire in 2018.

WINES - Winning many national and local wine competitions, these wines are crafted to represent their locale and are within a price range that make them easily accessible.

🔝 **Redwood Valley Girasole Vineyards Pinot Blanc 2020** EVERYDAY WINE ○ 2,000 cs; $ 15 - 🍷 - Light and refreshing with fig and green apple on the front palate followed by lemon zest. Crisp acids are well balanced carrying a signature "Mendocino minerality".
Redwood Valley Girasole Vineyards Charlie's Blend 2019 ● 2,500 cs; $ 16 - ⊞ - erlot and Cabernet Sauvignon blend presents raspberry, boysenberry, caramel, vanilla with earthy aromas and flavors with full-bodied mouthfeel and edgy tannins. Drink now or age.
Redwood Valley Barra of Mendocino Petite Sirah 2018 ● 232 cs; $ 26 - ⊞ - Blueberry jam, wild blackberry, mint, chocolate on nose and palate with a light peppery finish. Tannins structured, balanced, firm, full-bodied

acres 250 - **cases** 20,000
Fertilizers compost
Plant protection copper, organic, sulfur
Weed control mechanical
Yeasts commercial cultured yeasts
Grapes 100% estate-grown
Certification organic

BONNY DOON

BEAUREGARD VINEYARDS

10 Pine Flat Road – tel. (831) 425-7777
www.beauregardvineyards.com
tastingroom@beauregardvineyards.com

PEOPLE - Beauregard's history goes back four generations. Amos Beauregard purchased the Beauregard Ranch in 1945. Amo's son, Bud farmed the vineyard for a lifetime until his son Jim assumed management. In 1982, Jim established the Ben Lomond Mountain AVA. Jim currently manages the estate vineyards plus hundreds of acres of vineyards throughout the Santa Cruz Mountains. Jim's son, Ryan, is the winemaker and since 2020 owns the estate Bald Mountain vineyard.

VINEYARDS - Beauregard's three estate vineyards are in the Santa Cruz Mountains AVA. The 12-acre Beauregard Ranch Vineyard sits above the fogline at 1800 feet elevation on sandy loam and is in the heart of the Ben Lomond Mountain AVA. The 16-acre Coast Grade Vineyard, 1300 feet on limestone, is planted to four clones of Pinot Noir. Bald Mountain vineyard, 40 acres below the fogline with heavy coastal influence, is comprised of rare sandy Zayante soil and is being converted to organic certification.

WINES - Since 2000, Ryan has been the winemaker, with an eye toward old-world, terroir-driven winemaking practices.

TOP Santa Cruz Mountains Coast Grade Vineyard Pinot Noir 2018 ● 480 cs; $ 60 - 🍷 - Lovely, lively, and complex, this Pinot showcases the terroir and vintage beautifully with sous bois berries, redwood duff, mushroom, salinity, baking spice and vanilla (20% new French oak), deserving of quiet attention.
Ben Lomond Mountain Bald Mountain Vineyard Sand Hill Chardonnay 2018 ○ 550 cs; $ 50 - 🍷 - Outstanding example of a mineral-driven, terroir-focused Chardonnay from an excellent vintage, the wine shows lemon curd, yuzu, ripe pear, sandalwood, sea spray, minerality, and vanilla notes.
Ben Lomond Mountain Beauregard Ranch Cabernet Sauvignon 2017 ● 250 cs; $ 75 - 🍷 - A cool-climate, aromatic classic presenting black fruit, cedar, menthol, forest floor, firm well-integrated tannin balanced by good acidity.

acres 69 - **cases** 7,000
Fertilizers organic-mineral
Plant protection sulfur
Weed control mechanical
Yeasts spontaneous fermentation
Grapes purchase 10%
Certification none

LOS OLIVOS

BECKMEN VINEYARDS

2670 Ontiveros Road – tel. (805) 688-8664
www.beckmenvineyards.com – info@beckmenvineyards.com

A Ballard Canyon benchmark, Beckmen's biodynamic farming and acclaimed wines make it a winner.

PEOPLE - Electronic music technology pioneer Tom Beckmen founded Beckmen Vineyards in Los Olivos in 1994. Today his son Steve is the winegrower and winemaker. The winery was one of the first in the region to be organic and biodynamic. Older son Jeff left Wall Street in 2016 and now works as the national sales director for the wines.

VINEYARDS - Their two vineyards are located in two different appellations. In Los Olivos, their 25 acre estate vineyards sits on gravely, well-drained soil and is planted primarily to Cabernet Sauvignon with small amounts of Rhone grapes. Their Ballard Canyon site, known for Rhone wines, has 125 acres planted on clay and clay loam with an all important limestone subsoil. There they grow Chardonnay, Sauvignon Blanc, and red and white Rhone varieties.

WINES - The Beckmens are best known for their Syrahs and for their leadership in being Ballard Canyon pioneer. A new side project of very small lot wines - 1ngredient - features wines made without sulfites.

TOP Ballard Canyon Purisima Vineyard 1ngredient 2019 SLOW WINE ◎ 53 cs; $ 65 - 🍷 - A golden rich beer color, this "off the grid" wine went through ML to offer an unusual vibrant nose of intense florals, stone fruit, and spice, with a well structured, textural palate of ginger, apricot, and mango with a long mineral finish.
Ballard Canyon Purisima Mountain Vineyard Grenache 2019 ● 425 cs; $ 56 - 🍷 - Twenty year old vines allowed to bush out provide one third whole cluster to add texture to the mid-palate for this juicy, spicy, pretty grenache with a lovely carnation and herbal nose.
Ballard Canyon Purisima Mountain Vineyard Clone #1 Syrah 2019 ● 525 cs; $ 72 - 🍷 - From the first harvest in 2001, this limestone grown syrah is a stunner in deep plum with a big rich bacon gaminess yet balance and elegance on the palate.

acres 150 - **cases** 18,000
Fertilizers compost, cover crops, humus, manure
Plant protection biodynamic preparations, organic
Weed control mechanical
Yeasts spontaneous fermentation
Grapes 100% estate-grown
Certification some of the vineyards are certified biodynamic, some of the vineyards are certified organic

SONOMA

BEDROCK WINE CO.

414 1st Street E – tel. (707) 364-8763
www.bedrockwineco.com – chris@bedrockwineco.com

PEOPLE - Born into a Zin loving family, Morgan Twain-Peterson is a vintner and an MW with a passion for wine history and old vines. He started making wine in a chicken coop and grew a devoted fanbase for his excellent, well priced wines. Business partner Chris Cottrell co-pilots. Bedrock's received 100 point scores from Robert Parker and honors from Wine Spectator and the New York Times, yet remains a down home brand that honors growers and their grapes.

VINEYARDS - Bedrock sources from 25 different vineyards, including the belle of the ball–its 120 acre estate (organically farmed but not certified), first planted in the 1890's with 28 different varieties. Geographically, its growers range from Mendocino in the north, east to Amador and south to Santa Maria Valley. Peterson recently bought Katushas in Lodi with own rooted Zin and the legendary Evangelho vineyard in Antioch planted by Portuguese in the 1890s.

WINES - Traditional practices are used–from foot treading and carbonic maceration to partial whole cluster inclusion–to create fresh, vibrant wines.

🔝 **Contra Costa Areio e Vento e Amor Red Blend 2018** SLOW WINE ● n/a; $ n/a - 🍷 - Translated rom the Portuguese as "Sand and Wind and Love," this elegant, aromatic, Mourvèdre dominant field blend comes from the late grower Frank Evangelho's favorite block, marrying the subtle power of Mourvèdre with red fruited deliciousness from Carignan and Zinfandel. Accordingly it's named as an homage to the grower who preserved these old vines.
Lodi Zinfandel-Schmiedt Road 2015 ● 250 cs; $ 40 - 🍶 - An ode to the heights Lodi field blends can achieve in the hands of a fine winemaker–delicate and nuanced–with raspberry and cherry notes.
Cole Ranch Ester Riesling 2018 ○ 200 cs; $ 28 - 🍶 - An outstanding dry white wine that's a delicious whorl of bright, floral aromas and flavors–a perfect match for Asian food.

acres 152 - **cases** 5,700
Fertilizers compost, cover crops, mineral fertilizer
Plant protection organic, sulfur, synthetic pesticides
Weed control chemical, mechanical
Yeasts spontaneous fermentation
Grapes purchase 80%
Certification some of the vineyards are certified organic

GLEN ELLEN

BENZIGER FAMILY WINERY

1883 London Ranch Road – tel. (707) 935-3000
www.benziger.com – buywine@benziger.com

PEOPLE - Benziger celebrated its 40th anniversary in 2021 and continues its long run as a model of sustainability in Sonoma County. Winemaker Lisa Amaroli began her career at Benziger in 1999 and was promoted to winemaker after founding winemaker Mike Benziger retired and the winery was first certified as biodynamic in 2015. Amaroli grew up immersed in Italian wine culture and found her calling when living in Europe and Italy.

VINEYARDS - In response to a lower water table, Amaroli and her vineyard team are pursuing dry farming and only selectively irrigating. She credits the long-standing vineyard team for their ability to spot symptomatic vines and take preemptive measures to maintain balance. The estate has insectaries that act as "insect super highways" radiating throughout the vineyard to keep pests under control and they rotate their resident flock of sheep until bud break to manage weeds.

WINES - Amaroli believes that a gentle hand is required when natural fermentation is used and relies on early picking decisions for freshness.

Sonoma Valley Tribute 2016 ● 2,366 cs; $ 85 - 🍶 - Cabernet Sauvignon dominates this blend like a thoroughbred race horse with muscular mountain fruit sourced from all of the sweet spots on the slopes. Intended to age.
Sonoma Valley Joaquin's Inferno 2018 ● 470 cs; $ 56 - 🍶 - A blend of 46% Zinfandel, 41% Grenache, and 13% Petite Sirah with spicy, unctuous flavors of raspberry, plum, licorice and a fresh, bold black pepper finish.
Sonoma Mountain Paradiso de Maria Sauvignon Blanc 2021 ○ 406 cs; $ 36 - 🍶 - Meyer lemon, lime zest and a hint of white nectarine are balanced with crisp, delicate green apple and a saline, mineral core.

acres 85 - **cases** 12,000
Fertilizers biodynamic compost, compost, cover crops
Plant protection biodynamic preparations, sulfur, synthetic pesticides
Weed control animal grazing, mechanical
Yeasts spontaneous fermentation
Grapes purchase 10%
Certification biodynamic, organic

BOULDER CREEK

BIG BASIN VINEYARDS

830 Memory Lane – tel. (831) 621-8028
www.bigbasinvineyards.com – bradley@bigbasinvineyards.com

PEOPLE - Bradley Brown purchased an overgrown Santa Cruz Mountains property in 1998 with the vision of restoring it to its former, historic glory. An early consultant, Rhône Ranger, John Alban, led Brown down his intuitive winemaking path. Brown recently handed off winemaking duties to his assistant winemaker, Blake Yarger in early 2021, yet they continue to blend and make most of the stylistic decisions together.

VINEYARDS - The organic certified estate sits on land that was originally homesteaded in the 1880s. Grapes were grown there until Prohibition. In 2020, the CZU Lightning Complex Fire in the Santa Cruz Mountains, burned part of the vines and Brown's home. Damaged vines are now growing back. The steep property has high rainfall and fog from three directions. Fruit is also sourced from Coastview Vineyard in the Gabilan Mountains.

WINES - Both the Pinots and the Syrahs are all whole cluster fermentation. Additionally, all the corks they are using are made out of sugar cane.

🔴 **Santa Cruz Mountains Old Corral Pinot Noir 2018** SLOW WINE ● 155 cs; $ 65 - ▦ - Using a basket press for the reds has improved this which now shows greater clarity, precision and purity of fruit. The site produces wines with remarkable aromatics, floral and wild brambly earthiness.
Santa Cruz Mountains Rattlesnake Rock Syrah 2017 ●
200 cs; $ 55 - ▦ - From the oldest vines (18 years old) 2% Viognier. The floral nose is full of lavender and violets. Its significant tannins will soften with time. A spicy, brooding aspect.
Santa Cruz Mountains Sixty-Two Terraces Syrah 2017 ● 155 cs; $ 65 - ▦ - Named for the number of west facing terraces of younger vines and two different field selections. A classic, savory, peppery syrah and the first vintage done with 100% whole cluster fermentation.

acres 10 - **cases** 4,166
Fertilizers compost, organic
Plant protection organic, sulfur, synthetic pesticides
Weed control mechanical
Yeasts spontaneous fermentation
Grapes purchase 60%
Certification some of the vineyards are certified organic

SANTA CRUZ

BIRICHINO

204 Church Street – tel. (831) 425-4811
www.birichino.com – info@birichino.com

PEOPLE - John Locke and Alex Krause met working at Bonny Doon Vineyard in the 1990's. In 2007, they both decided to pursue a joint venture, a Malvasia Bianca made specifically for an international client. Since then, the Birichino label has grown steadily, bootstrapping the whole operation from harvest to winemaking to marketing. They create distinct, thoughtful wines and have many loyal patrons.

VINEYARDS - Birichino showcases historic, old vine California vineyard sites, specifically those planted in the late 19th century. They work with small family farms, and find sites that are farmed beautifully, often organically, paying attention to the uniqueness of each site. They have recently started working with a couple of new vineyard sites, both planted in the 1960s. One is in Yountville (Napa) and the other is the Wirz Vineyard in the Cienega Valley.

WINES - Combatting wildfire smoke and drought in 2020, the winery made six roses that year.

🔴 **Santa Cruz Mountains Peter Martin Ray Vineyard Cabernet Sauvignon 2018** SLOW WINE ● 150 cs; $ 40 - ▦ - From an historic vineyard: deep red with a lovely, savory nose. Chocolate, black cherry or plum with mountain fruit grippiness and signs of a cooler vintage than the 2017. Delicious now, it could easily age for 10 years.
Napa Valley Yount Mill Vineyard Sémillon 2020 ○ 100 cs; $ 28 - ▯ - Unfined and unfiltered, it evolves from spice to citrus to floral. History suggests that this wine will age very well in the bottle, becoming more oily yet stay bright. Certified organic grapes.
Santa Cruz Mountains Lilo Vineyard Pinot Noir 2018 ● 175 cs; $ 40 - ▦ - From a site that is 3 1/2 miles from the ocean on a south facing slope surrounded by redwood and douglas fir trees with cooling fog. This is a classic, cool climate Santa Cruz Mountains Pinot Noir.

acres 0 - **cases** 10,000
Fertilizers compost, cover crops, mineral fertilizer, organic, organic-mineral
Plant protection copper, organic, sulfur, synthetic pesticides
Weed control chemical, mechanical
Yeasts spontaneous fermentation
Grapes purchase 100%
Certification some of the vineyards are certified organic

LODI

BOKISCH VINEYARDS

18921 Atkins Road – tel. (209) 642-8880 - (209) 642-8880
www.bokischvineyards.com – info@bokischvineyards.com

PEOPLE - With roots in Catalan, Markus Bokisch studied enology at UC Davis where he met wife Liz. After graduating, they traveled and worked in Spain where Markus made Cava and Liz taught English. In 1995 they purchased land in Clement Hills; in 1998, they imported Spanish budwood. Two years later, their dream came true: to make wine made from Spanish grapes for Americans. A steward for the land, in 2005, he began farming organically. In 2016, Elyse Perry became winemaker.

VINEYARDS - At one time, Bokisch had 3000 acres, but they went to 880 with 303 acres of the Las Cerezas, Vista Luna, and the Terra Alta Vineyard certified organic. The remaining acres follow Lodi Rules, farmed organically and sustainably but not certified. The Bokisch Vineyards label offers nine Spanish varieties including Garnacha Blanca, Verdejo, Garnacha, Monastrell. The Tizona label includes Malbec, Petit Verdot, Old Vine Zin, and blends.

WINES - From sparkling Albariño to rosado to Tempranillo to late harvest Graciano, Bokisch speaks to a passion for food friendly wines made from Spanish grapes grown sustainably and produced with respect for people and planet. Eleven of 25 bottlings are certified organic.

TOP · **Lodi Terra Alta Vineyard Albariño 2019**
EVERYDAY WINE O 1,100 cs; $ 22 - 🍷 🗃 - With citrus, stone fruit, and vibrant acidity, this organic wine's roundness on the palate comes from 30% neutral oak.
Lodi Vista Luna Garnacha Blanca 2020 O 312 cs; $ 24 - 🍷 🗃 - Fragrant with gardenia and cherry, this organic wine offers tangy acidity, lingering tangerine, and nutmeg on the finish.
Lodi Terra Alta Vineyard Graciano 2018 ● 300 cs; $ 27 - 🗃 - Tart berries and a finish of mouthwatering salinity and acidity follow a perfumed nose of mulberry, roses, and forest floor.

---

acres 880 - **cases** 6,000
Fertilizers compost, humus, mineral fertilizer
Plant protection organic, sulfur
Weed control n/a
Yeasts spontaneous fermentation
Grapes 100% estate-grown
Certification converting to organics and biodynamics, some of the vineyards are certified organic

---

DAVENPORT

BONNY DOON VINEYARD

450 Highway 1 – tel. (831) 425-3625
www.bonnydoonvineyard.com
tastingroom@bonnydoonvineyard.com

PEOPLE - Randall Grahm, one of the original Rhone Rangers, is well known and loved in the California wine industry and beyond. His soulful, esoteric and honest approach to growing Rhone and other grapes and packaging them with quirky labels is like nothing else. He recently sold the winery to War Room Ventures and continues as Director or Winemaking with long-time winemaker Nicole Walsh continuing to craft naturally soulful and original wines.

VINEYARDS - Fruit is purchased from vineyards selected and known for farming following biodynamic principles. Many are with long-standing arrangements. After many years of research, in 2010 Grahm finally settled on a 400-acre estate in San Juan Batista, Popelouchum, or "paradise" in the language of the Mutsun, where he continues to push the viticultural bar for the state and beyond.

WINES - While production includes whites, reds, and roses, that is where the connection to the rest of California wines ends. Each product is utterly unique if not downright weird and quirky.

Central Coast Le Cigare Volant Red Wine of the Earth 2020 ● Grenache, cinsault, Syrah, Petite Sirah, Counoise; 11,000 cs; $ 15 - 🍷 - Light, tart and dry with notes of cherry cola, charred meat, mushroom and cedar.
Central Coast Le Cigare Blanc White Wine of the Earth 2020 O Grenache Blanc, Vermentino, Clairette Blanche; 2,600 cs; $ 15 - 🍷 - Light, silky and dry with notes of lemon curd, apricot, cantaloupe, sage, almond and pine nut.
Central Coast Vin Gris De Cigare Pink Wine of the Earth 2020 ◉ Grenache, Cinsault, Grenache Blanc, Vermentino, Clairette Blanche, Mourvèdre; 26,000 cs; $ 15 - 🍷 - Crisp and refreshing with notes of strawberry, watermelon, cucumber and celery.

---

acres 0 - **cases** 41,800
Fertilizers compost
Plant protection organic, sulfur, synthetic pesticides
Weed control chemical, mechanical
Yeasts commercial cultured yeasts
Grapes purchase 100%
Certification none

BONTERRA ORGANIC VINEYARDS

2231 McNab Ranch Road – tel. (707) 744-1250
www.bonterra.com – rachel.newman@bonterra.com

PEOPLE - As Mendocino's pioneering organic and biodynamic producer, Bonterra continues to pursue climate initiatives for the 1,000 acres it has under vine. In 2021 the winery became the world's first organically-farmed winery to achieve Climate Neutral certification for its entire business, and to make its climate footprint public. Director of Winemaking Jeff Cichocki works with winemaker Sebastian Donoso and vineyard director Joseph Brinkley..

VINEYARDS - While its own 900+ acre estate in Mendocino and grapes from local growers started the brand off way back when, the winery now buys 80 percent of its grapes—mostly from growers in coastal and central California. It owns 290 acres of biodynamic vines on three Mendo sites (which go into its 500+ cases of high end biodynamic wines). An addition 605 acres in Mendocino are organic..

WINES - The first vintage for The McNab was 2000 and The Butler followed in 2007. Vintage variation can be seen in the wines but Donoso hasn't shifted the winemaking style.
Mendocino County The McNab 2019 ● 350 cs; $ 68 - ⊞ - Petite Sirah lends additional depth and nuance to aromas of blackcurrant, fig, and dark chocolate, and energetic flavors of cassis, toast, tobacco and star anise are framed by firm, finely textured tannins.
Mendocino County The Butler 2019 ● 1,000 cs; $ 85 - ⊞ - This Rhone-style blend of 77% Syrah, 15% Petite Sirah, 7% Mourvèdre and 1% Viognier is dark and brooding with black currant, plums, black pepper, and mushrooms layered over herbaceous notes of oregano and bay leaf.
Mendocino County Dry Muscat 2019 ○ 220 cs; $ 27 - 🍷 - A lean and lively wine that delivers fragrant notes of honeysuckle and lychee with juicy mango, stone fruit, tangerine and a crisp, dry finish.

acres 1,000 - **cases** 500,000
Fertilizers biodynamic compost, compost
Plant protection organic
Weed control mechanical
Yeasts spontaneous fermentation, commercial cultured yeasts
Grapes purchase 80%
Certification organic, some of the vineyards are certified biodynamic

BRENDEL

1227 1st Street – tel. (707) 963-8774
www.brendelwines.com – hello@brendelwines.com

 A new label that offers artisanal, affordably priced (for Napa), organically grown wines made by top winemakers and focusing on diverse varietals.

PEOPLE - Named for an early Italian grower in St. Helena, Leon Brendel, this new label debuted in 2021, under the rapidly expanding Demeine Estates owned by the Lawrence family, whose wealth comes from Tennessee banking and U.S. ag. Brendel the man famously grew Grignolino, a grape from Italy's Piemonte region. The Heitz family bought his vines and kept the Grignolino tradition alive. Cassandra Felix heads the winery. Brittany Sherwood leads winemaking.

VINEYARDS - The winery sources from Demeine Estates' 450 acres of organically certified vineyards in Napa, which were acquired by the Heitz family. Grignolino comes from vines the Heitz family planted in St. Helena at their historic winery site. Chardonnay comes from their Oak Knoll vines while the Cabernet is sourced mainly from Rutherford.

WINES - Brendel offers its winemakers a chance to showcase lesser known grapes—like port wine varieties—in adventurous blends, in addition to the traditional Chardonnay, Sauvignon Blanc, and Cabernet.
Napa Valley Cooper's Reeds Cabernet Sauvignon 2018 SLOW WINE ● 15,073 cs; $ 40 - ⓦ - Adventurously aged in a supersized, 60 year old, 20,000 liter upright oak barrel (to minimize the oak impact) and sealed with reeds, it's fresh and on the light side—not your average Napa cab—with black cherries and soft tannins. You could drink it tonight.
Napa Valley Noble One Chardonnay 2019 ○ 1,867 cs; $ 30 - 🍷 - Young and filled with citrus and lemon, it's a drink now wine with a bright finish.
Napa Valley Sparkling Young Leon Grignolino 2019 ⦂ 900 cs; $ 30 - 🍷 - A reinvention of a Heitz Cellars tradition, a dry, lightly carbonated (frizzante) rosé, its gracefully shows off citrus and pomegranate flavors. Like Processo, it's carbonated via the Charmat method.

acres 450 - **cases** n/a
Fertilizers compost, cover crops, organic
Plant protection organic, sulfur
Weed control mechanical
Yeasts commercial cultured yeasts
Grapes 100% estate-grown
Certification organic

NAPA

BURGESS CELLARS

3800...

2921 Silverado Trail – tel. (707) 963-4766
www.burgesscellars.com – meghan@burgesscellars.com

PEOPLE - In 2020 Burgess Cellars, founded in 1972 by Tom Burgess, was sold to Lawrence Wine Estates, overseen by Memphis based Gaylon Lawrence Jr., a principal investor in one of the country's largest agricultural businesses, the Arkansas-based The Lawrence Group and Carlton McCoy – Master Sommelier and current CEO of Heitz Cellar. Burgess Cellars was founded in 1972 making it one of the older privately-owned, continuously-operating wineries in Napa Valley.

VINEYARDS - Shortly after the sale, the Glass Fire destroyed the winery's buildings but left the Sorenson Vineyard, planted in 1979, intact. Under the direction of winemaker Meghan Zobeck, the estate some of which is organic is coverting to biodynamics and will pursue Rodale's Regenerative certification. The Xerez Society has planted a Monarch Educator Garden and by baling her cover crop, Zobeck will establish a closed-system for the estate's flock of sheep.

WINES - The 2021 vintage will be reflective of Zobeck's winemaking which includes native fermentations and the addition of a sparkling wine.

🔝 **Napa Valley Burgess Cabernet Sauvignon 2021 ●** 250 cs; $ 175 - Ⓜ - Sourced from the estate's pollinator block, the fruit is foot trod and spends 24 to 36 months in a neutral puncheon for a wine that defies the Valley floor stereotype.
Napa Valley Burgess Estate Cabernet Franc 2021 ● 650 cs; $ 110 - Ⓜ Ⓖ - Classic blue floral notes with raspberry, cherry, blackberry bramble moving to bluer fruit, cocoa and savory herbs on the palate.
St. Helena Sorenson Vineyard Cabernet Sauvignon 2021 ● 1,000 cs; $ 250 - Ⓜ - Classic markers for Sorenson include crisp blue and red fruit, savory herbal aromatics of rosemary and thyme and a subtle oak signature of earthy graphite.

SAINT HELENA

CAIN VINEYARD AND WINERY

3800 Langtry Road – tel. (707) 963-1616
www.cainwines.com – winery@cainfive.com

PEOPLE - Jerry and Joyce Cain planted about 1/5th of this Mayacamas mountaintop estate to vines in 1980, adding a stone winery in 1982. Today the Meadlocks, friends of the Cain's, own the property. General Manager and Winegrower Chris Howell joined the winey in 1991. 2020 was Chris's 31st harvest, when the Glass fire caused extensive damage, destroying the winery and most of the vineyards. They are planning to rebuild, with vineyard rehabilitation first.

VINEYARDS - In house vineyard manager Ashley Anderson Bennett and her full-time crew of ten organically farm the steep, terraced hillsides here at 2100' elevation atop the Mayacamas mountains, which form the western border of Napa Valley. Recovery of the vines is still being assessed in the short and long term. Cain purchases additional fruit from Napa growers for two of its three wines.

WINES - With his extensive training in winegrowing and winemaking in France, Chris takes a classical, terroir-driven approach. Cain Five is in an elite group of Bordeaux Blends from Napa Valley that are known the world over.

🔝 **Spring Mountain District Cain Five 2017 ●** Cabernet Sauvignon, Merlot, Cabernet Franc, Malbec, Petit Verdot; 4,100 cs; $ 120 - 🛢 - Very young and gripping with notes of cassis, graphite, tobacco and black olive.
Napa Valley NV17 Cain Cuvée ● Cabernet Sauvignon, Cabernet Franc, Merlot; 5,300 cs; $ 36 - 🛢 - Elegant and approachable Left-bank style Bordeaux blend with notes of cassis, dark chocolate, tobacco and vanilla. Unfiltered so decant off of sediment first.

---

acres 46 - cases 6,000
Fertilizers compost, green manure, organic-mineral
Plant protection biodynamic preparations, organic, sulfur
Weed control mechanical
Yeasts selected indigenous yeasts, spontaneous fermentation
Grapes 100% estate-grown
Certification converting to biodynamics, some of the vineyards are certified organic and/or biodynamic

acres 90 - cases 12,000
Fertilizers manure, organic-mineral
Plant protection organic, synthetic pesticides
Weed control mechanical, chemical
Yeasts spontaneous fermentation
Grapes purchase 75%
Certification some of the vineyards are certified organic

HOLLISTER

CALERA 🍾

11300 Cienega Road – tel. (831) 637-9170
www.calerawine.com – info@calerawine.com

PEOPLE - Pioneer Josh Jensen saw great Pinot potential in the early 1970's in the Central Coast's remote Gavilan Mountains with its high elevation limestone soils. He quickly succeeded in making impeccable wines in this undiscovered terroir. In 2017, at 73, Jensen sold Calera to Duckhorn which sources from estate and non-estate fruit. Calera veteran winemaker Mike Waller provides stylistic continuity. The brand also produces lower priced non-estate wines.

VINEYARDS - In 1975, Jensen got his estate sites (certified organic) their own AVA–Mount Harlan–planted to six Pinot Noir vineyards, one Chardonnay, one Aligote and one Viognier. In 2020, the estate evaluated the impact of wildfire smoke and ash but found that their grapes were fine. The resulting research and data gathering they did benefited the entire state's winemaking industry. Additional wines for its Central Coast appellated wines come from growers.

WINES - 2018 was a short vintage with low yields and an early harvest. Many fans are expected to cellar the vintage for 10 years.

🔝 **Mount Harlan Jensen Vineyard Pinot Noir 2018** ●
500 cs; $ 100 - ⊞ - This wine is a legend, very highly regarded and even cult-worthy in Japan. The old-vines present a layer of complexity in the finish, with allspice and brambly fruit that just keeps going.
Mount Harlan de Villiers Vineyard Pinot Noir 2018
● 500 cs; $ 75 - ⊞ - The current vintages are more fruit driven than many of their other wines, and are probably the most approachable Calera Pinot Noirs, with lovely red fruit characteristics.
Mount Harlan Ryan Vineyard Pinot Noir 2018 ●
710 cs; $ 75 - ⊞ - Deep red, with a lush mouthfeel and dark fruit characteristics in a vintage that produced, on this site, what the winemaker calls the softest wine made from Mt Harlan.

acres 83 - **cases** 20,000
Fertilizers compost, green manure
Plant protection organic, sulfur
Weed control animal grazing, mechanical
Yeasts spontaneous fermentation
Grapes purchase 75%
Certification some of the vineyards are certified organic

LOMPOC

CAMINS 2 DREAMS $

313 N F Street – tel. (805) 741-7041
www.camins2dreams.com

PEOPLE - With a degree in Enology, Tara Gomez, who is Chumash, was working as a winemaker in central California when she met intern Mireia Taribó, who is Spanish. They visited each other's countries, traveled to taste wine, and helped with each other's projects. In 2014, they married, and Mireia joined Tara in Lompoc on the road (camino) to their dreams. Both keep busy with consulting, and Tara is winemaker at Kita where Mireia also works.

VINEYARDS - With a focus on the Sta. Rita Hills AVA near their home in Lompoc, they purchase grapes that are certified or use organic and biodynamic practices. They eschew the typical grapes of the AVA, preferring lesser known "underdog" varietals like gruner veltliner, grenache, graciano, and syrah. Their first vintage was only 25 cases in 2017, but their Lompoc facility and tasting room offers plenty of room to grow. In addition to still white, rose, and red wines, in 2020 they made a Grüner Veltliner Pétillant Naturel.

WINES - Working closely with the vineyards, they make wines from purchased organic grapes with natural yeast, and minimal intervention to allow the pristine fruit to shine.

🔝 **Sta. Rita Hills Spear Vineyard Syrah 2018**
SLOW WINE ● 120 cs; $ 42 - ⊞ - With Northern Rhone syrah as a model, the certified organic Spear Vineyard fruit offers a lighter style with high acidity, black pepper, spice, and big black fruit flavors.
🔝 **Santa Barbara County Christy and Wise Vineyard Grenache 2020** ● 48 cs; $ 48 - ⊞ - Located just outside the Sta Rita Hills AVA, the Demeter certified Christy and Wise Vineyard is cool and breezy which brings out zippy yet ripe raspberry with black pepper on the finish.
Sta. Rita Hills Spear Vineyard Grüner Veltliner 2018 ○
60 cs; $ 30 - 🍷 - Grapes from the certified organic Spear vineyard are foot stomped and fermented with natural yeasts to produce a tart, bright, acidic, and food friendly wine with grapefruit, licorice, and minerality.

acres 0 - **cases** 1,000
Fertilizers biodynamic compost
Plant protection biodynamic preparations
Weed control n/a
Yeasts spontaneous fermentation
Grapes purchase 100%
Certification some of the vineyards are certified biodynamic, some of the vineyards are certified organic

NAPA

CARBONISTE

3 Executive Way – tel. (707) 536-8451
www.carboniste.com – jacqueline@carboniste.com

PEOPLE - Carboniste is an innovative California sparkling wine brand founded by winemakers Jacqueline and Dan Person. The couple met at UC Davis, and then worked around the world before settling into careers in Napa. Dan worked at Schramberg for three years. The two wanted to reimagine sparkling wine not as an imitation of Champagne but wine with a sunnier, more Californian disposition. That is to say—juicier and fresher.

VINEYARDS - The couple use grapes from many appellations throughout the state, often working with new growers every year. Yet their flagship wine, using Albarino from Andres Island in the Sacramento Delta, is a core offering. Pinot Noir grapes come from Corralitos in the Santa Cruz Mountains, Dan says is like the wild west for wines.

WINES - Most of the Carboniste wines simply say "California" on the label, representing the state and the sunshine expression of the fruit.

TOP Suisun Valley Gomes Vineyard Sparkling Albariño 2020 EVERYDAY WINE ⟡ 1,950 cs; $ 28 - 🍶 - A signature wine for Carboniste, and what Dan likes to call "a breakfast wine." It is electric, zippy and full of citrus–an expressive Albarino with shining through, made with no added sulfites.
Santa Cruz Mountains Corralitos Brut 2017 ⟡ 72 cs; $ 44 - 🔲 - The first release of an older vintage from two very small vineyards in the Pleasant Valley area of Corralitos. Expressive, with superb acid yet a full richness at the same time.
California Brut V.19 ⟡ 150 cs; $ 36 - 🔲 - A nonvintage blend that's half 2018 and 2019, it's a perennial reserve. Has a beautiful, ethereal hue, almost pink yet golden at the same time, like a sunset or an ombre rose blossom.

acres 0 - **cases** 3,000
Fertilizers compost, mineral fertilizer
Plant protection organic, sulfur, synthetic pesticides
Weed control chemical, mechanical
Yeasts commercial cultured yeasts, spontaneous fermentation
Grapes purchase 100%
Certification none

SANTA ROSA

CAROL SHELTON WINES $

3354-B Coffey Lane – tel. (707) 575-3441
www.carolshelton.com – wines@carolshelton.com

PEOPLE - One of the first women to get her degree in Enology from U.C.Davis in the late 1970's, legendary Carol Shelton had a 23-year career in the wine industry before starting her own label in 2000. Her focus is on her true love - single vineyard Zinfandels which she will soon be making in her own winery in Windsor now in the planning stages. In 2021 Carol was awarded Best Woman Winemaker in the International Women's Wine Competition, adding to her 9 other "Winemaker of the Year" awards.

VINEYARDS - Shelton works with exceptional vineyards in crafting exemplary wines. Mendocino County's Cox Vineyard (certified organic) with 65-year-old vines sources Wild Thing Zin and Rendezvous Rosé. In southern California's Cucamonga Valley lies an historic and nearly forgotten wine region. Planted in 1918 the Jose Lopez Vineyard (certified organic) dry-farmed Zinfandel grows as 2-foot-high "pygmy" bush vines on 30-50 ft roots in sand and rocks with 6-8" of yearly rainfall.

WINES - Shelton's portfolio also includes Chardonnay, Viognier, Petite Sirah, Carignane, Cabernet Sauvignon and both white and red Rhone-style blends.

Cucamonga Valley Lopez Vineyard Monga Zin Old Vine Zinfandel 2019 ● 914 cs; $ 26 - 🔲 - Yielding $1/8$ ton an acre, these old vines offer flavors of black cherry, chocolate, warm spices, vanilla and caramel. Creamy and lively with solid tannins and a long, delicious finish. Drink now or age.
Mendocino County Cox Vineyard Wild Thing Old Vine Zinfandel 2018 ● 9,085 cs; $ 19 - 🔲 - Terroir-driven from 65 year old vines, Shelton relies on a healthy wild yeast population. Luscious black raspberry and black cherry with baking spice. Smooth mouthfeel with a long jammy finish.
Mendocino County Cox Vineyard Wild Thing Rendezvous Rosé 2020 ● 476 cs; $ 18 - 🍶 - From Carignane and Zinfandel it presents crisply dry, juicy strawberry, watermelon, with a bright cranberry color.

acres 0 - **cases** 16,000
Fertilizers n/a
Plant protection n/a
Weed control n/a
Yeasts commercial cultured yeasts, spontaneous fermentation
Grapes purchase 100%
Certification some of the vineyards are certified organic

SANTA ROSA

CARY Q WINES $

1160 Hopper Ave. #B – tel. (305) 586-6666
www.caryqwines.com – cary@caryqwines.com

PEOPLE - Cary Quintana, of Cary Q Wines, is a self-taught winemaker and a minimalist at heart. She produces low intervention, organically-farmed wines with a winemaking philosophy that encourages the purest expression of site, variety and vintage. She cut her teeth working in Berkeley's Gilman District and her first vintage was 2014 . She began with Grenache but experiments with each passing vintage. She has a light touch in the cellar and her wines have a freshness and vibrancy that's undeniable.

VINEYARDS - Cary's 2019 and 2020 vintages were sourced from the Shake Ridge Ranch vineyard, a high-elevation site at 1750 ft. in Amador County with a mix of volcanic soils including quartz, basalt, shale and soapstone. Iberian varieties like Garnacha and Tempranillo are her calling card and she's included Mourvèdre in the mix as well. She likes extended macerations to help build layers of dimension in the wines.

WINES - Varying percentages of whole cluster are a thread that connects the wines while aging vessels vary by variety. Her objective is to make wines that are clean and tasty. Low to minimal sulfur, no additives, no fining, and no filtering are part of her winemaking philosophy.
Amador County Shake Ridge Ranch hey PRETTY! 2019 ● 85 cs; $ 45 - ◉ - Co-fermented with floral and red fruit aromas from the Grenache, a touch of dried herb and tobacco from the Tempranillo, and savory dark fruit from the Mourvèdre.
Amador County Shake Ridge Ranch Hollis 2019 ● 40 cs; $ 45 - ◔ - A light-bodied, monovarietal Mourvèdre that's unfined and unfiltered with bright, peppery red fruit, dusty leather notes and silky tannins. Absolutely charming.
Amador County Shake Ridge Pink Lola 2020 ◍ 50 cs; $ 27 - ◔ ⊞ - A rosado of Graciano that's high-toned and vibrant with floral aromas, strawberry and cherry and a vinous, whole cluster quality.

acres 0 - **cases** 150
Fertilizers compost, cover crops
Plant protection sulfur, organic
Weed control mechanical
Yeasts spontaneous fermentation
Grapes purchase 100%
Certification organic

TEMPLETON

CASTORO CELLARS $

1315 North Bethel Road – tel. (805) 238-0725
www.castorocellars.com – events@www.castorocellars.com

PEOPLE - With a name like Castoro, it would seem this Paso Robles winery has deep roots in Italian soil. After all, many Italian immigrants settled in the region and planted vineyards. Not so with Castoro. Founder Niels Udsen grew up in Ventura CA and visited his father's home country of Denmark where he met his future wife Bimmer when they were children. While Castoro is inspired by Italian grapes, the word translates to Beaver which is Niels' nickname.

VINEYARDS - With an agricultural background, Niels and Bimmer began Castoro in 1983, and they've been at the forefront of sustainability for 30 years, Over 1,400 acres of estate vineyards are certified organic by CCOF and all vineyards are SIP Certified. Vineyards benefit from the Templeton Gap; Whale Rock, with its limestone, clay and river rock, is their best known vineyard and lends its name to their annual music festival.

WINES - Winemaker Tom Myers guides Castoro toward their accessible, affordable, playful style designed to go with daily dining and to be "Dam Fine Wine" that's also organic with limited sulfites.
🔝 **Paso Robles Charbono 2018** EVERYDAY WINE ● n/a; $ 30 - ⊞ - It's a special day when Charbono comes across the palate: only 76 acres in CA exist from this almost extinct grape with 6 at Castoro offering flavors of smokey grape with a black pepper finish that reveals more complexity as it opens.
🔝 **Paso Robles Falanghina 2019** EVERYDAY WINE ○ 425 cs; $ 30 - ◔ - From the Whale Rock and Double Black vineyards comes a chamomile colored and scented blend with refreshing acidity, bartlett pear, eureka lemon, valencia orange pith, and a full, smooth, luscious mouthfeel.
Paso Robles Primitivo 2019 ● n/a; $ 30 - ⊞ - Lushly dense with complex aromas of baking spices, fruits, and both fresh and dried florals, the Primitivo palate delivers big bold bramble fruit with cherry pipe tobacco, and very nice tannins.

acres 1,422 - **cases** 35,000
Fertilizers compost
Plant protection organic
Weed control mechanical
Yeasts commercial cultured yeasts
Grapes 100% estate-grown
Certification organic

LOS ANGELES

CENTRALAS

3953 Somerset Drive – tel. (310) 663-3542
www.centralaswine.com – info@centralaswine.com

PEOPLE - "I love wine, but I love the world more" says Adam Huss, winemaker and owner, with wife Wendy, of Centralas Wines. A chef by trade, his property bursts with grapes, herbs and fruit trees. In his mission toward all aspects of sustainability, he has mounted "The Organic Wine Podcast" that he hosts with a range of guests whose subject matter goes beyond agricultural to issues of access and social justice in the wine world.

VINEYARDS - For 2019 and 2020, Centralas sourced pinot noir from the organic Spear vineyards in the Sta Rita Hills and syrah and grenache from the biodynamic Martian Ranch vineyard in the new Alisos Canyon AVA. More recently, the search for more local grape sources has led to Lopez vineyard, a centenary desert vineyard in Fontana, one hour east of Los Angeles and a meticulously tended practicing organic vineyard in Hemet, yet another hour east. So, there will be new wines in 2022.

WINES - While his grape wines display ample focus, in the name of localism, Huss is experimenting with fermenting cactus fruit.
Santa Barbara County Syren Pinot Noir 2019 ● 100 cs; $ 50 - ▦ - Shows powerful red florals, menthol and red and dark cherry/berry aromas leading to a red and dark cherry palate imbued with earth and cedar.
Santa Barbara County Hussy Rosé 2019 ● 100 cs; $ 35 - 🍷 - Grenache and syrah and emulates certain French rosés that incorporate oak aging. With ample floral notes, the palate shows elegant cherry/berry fruit with subtle vanilla and nuttiness.
Santa Barbara County Noctilucence Rosé Noir 2020 ● 175 cs; $ 28 - ▦ - As advertised is a very dark rosé of syrah that shows extravagant rose and gamey dark cherry aromatics that belie a light-bodied palate of cherry and blackberry fruit.

---

acres 0 - **cases** 6,000
Fertilizers biodynamic compost, green manure, organic-mineral
Plant protection organic, sulfur
Weed control mechanical
Yeasts spontaneous fermentation
Grapes purchase 100%
Certification some of the vineyards are certified organic, some of the vineyards are certified biodynamic

SAN DIEGO

CHARLIE & ECHO

8680 Miralani Drive #113 – tel. (877) 592-9095
charlieandecho.com

PEOPLE - Charlie & Echo came about from the inquiry of Eric Van Drunen, a former physicist, of how to make more food-friendly wine than what he found around him. The story of the winery is how, largely insulated from the "wine world", he invented his wine with few peers or mentors. An exception was the San Diegan Los Pilares crew who were after the same lighter styles and purity of fruit vinified with no inputs. Wife Clara (retired Air Force) is the 'Charlie' in Charlie & Echo and came up with the name.

VINEYARDS - C & E lays claim to expressing San Diego County terroir, both in its understanding of 'natural wine' and marketing strategy. Keeping it simple, Van Drunen makes a red, a white and a rosé in still and sparkling versions with varieties and blends subject to change. He remarks that in the past, finding clean grapes was challenging. Currently, he has settled on Valentina Vineyard in Dulzura.

WINES - Now, with a suitable a grape source, his current releases are remarkably concentrated and interesting.
TOP **San Diego County Valentina Vineyard Whoa Jake 2019** EVERYDAY WINE ☼ 90 cs; $ 25 - 🍷 - A sparkling blanc de noir of sangiovese and grenache. Biscuit, fennel and ripe yellow apple are on the nose with apple and grapefruit pith flavors.
TOP **San Diego County Valentina Vineyard Darkstar 2019** EVERYDAY WINE ☼ 217 cs; $ 25 - 🍷 - A blend of nebbiolo, petite sirah, syrah and zinfandel. Rose, pepper and dark cherries rise out of the glass which features flavors of loamy strawberries and cherries.
San Diego County Uncharted 2020 ○ 28 cs; $ 23 - 🍷 - A riesling with a green herb and peach syrup aroma presiding over a rich white peach and lemon palate.

---

acres 0 - **cases** 502
Fertilizers organic-mineral
Plant protection organic, sulfur
Weed control mechanical
Yeasts spontaneous fermentation
Grapes purchase 100%
Certification none

CAMINO

CHATEAU DAVELL

3020 Vista Tierra Drive – tel. (530) 644-2016
www.chateaudavell.com – chateaudavell@att.net

 Vintages speak with minimal interference using organic and biodynamic farming so the Sierra Foothills fruit shines.

PEOPLE - Chateau Davell is named after Davell Hays, the mother of winemaker Eric Hays. Along with Eric's wife Emily, the three manage the winery operations. Following a 15 year career in the restaurant business where Eric discovered his passion for wine, Eric worked as an Assistant Winemaker at nearby Lava Cap; he also paints the art for the labels. Emily keeps the business green and operates the tasting room, while Davell is the master gardener.

VINEYARDS - Located at 1100' elevation, Chateau Davell's Estate Vineyard's organic and biodynamic practices support the vitality of the surrounding ecosystem with cover crops and other natural farming techniques. Most of the 12.5 acre estate is set aside for wildlife habitat, forest, riparian, orchards, and 30 varieties of heirloom tomatoes.

WINES - Grapes are purchased from small organic family farms in Amador and El Dorado Countie. With a philosophy that wine is made in the vineyard, winemaker Eric Hays lets each vintage speak for itself with minimal interference and leaves wines unfiltered and unfined. Yeasts are native to where the grapes originated.

El Dorado Chloe Reserve Chardonnay 2018 ○ 22 cs; $ 34 - ▦ ⓦ - This all organic estate wine had extended skin contact to create the intense color and flavor profile with roasted apple, sweet tartness, pear texture, and acidity.
El Dorado Estate Zinfandel 2017 ● n/a; $ 34 - ▦ - Great body yet light and easy to drink, this zinfandel is fruit forward without being too jammy.
El Dorado Gaia 2015 ● n/a; $ 71 - ▦ - This is one of those wines that slows down time: earthy complexity, a mix of dark fruits, with a meaty smoky bacon savoriness on the nose, and black pepper on the finish.

acres 2 - **cases** 2,000
Fertilizers biodynamic compost, compost, cover crops, humus
Plant protection biodynamic preparations, organic, sulfur
Weed control animal grazing, mechanical
Yeasts commercial cultured yeasts
Grapes purchase 70%
Certification none

ST. HELENA

CLIF FAMILY WINERY

709 Main Street – tel. (707) 968-0625
www.cliffamily.com – winery@cliffamily.com

PEOPLE - Avid bicyclists and organic philanthropists, co-owners Gary Erickson and Kit Crawford co-founded their CLIF Bar company in 1992. In 2004, they bought a weekend getaway on Howell Mountain and started their own winery and a farm. Manager Linzi Gray oversees the winery, farm and their food products. Laura Barrett makes the wines. In 2020, the owners generously donated $500,000 to found the California Organic Institute with the University of California.

VINEYARDS - While Clif Family currently sources from various sites (about half of which are organic), in 2020, it took a major step towards becoming an all organic, all estate producer, with the purchase of an 80 acre vineyard on the valley floor in the Oak Knoll District AVA. It also owns 11 acres of certified organic vineyards on Howell Mountain. It buys organic grapes from growers in Yountville and Sonoma Valley. Erik Dodd manages the estate vines.

WINES - In keeping with their love of bicycles, Clif Family's wine labels feature bike chain graphics, name their wines after bike routes, and rent bikes at the tasting room.

Yountville Rte. Blanc Sauvignon Blanc 2020 ○ 1,000 cs; $ 48 - 🍴 - Bursting with fruit flavors, this is a white wine for people who like their Sauvignon Blanc big and bold.
Sonoma Valley Grenache 2019 ● 500 cs; $ 72 - ▦ - Tangy notes of strawberry, cherry and plums and tannins.
Howell Mountain Kit's Killer Cab 2018 ● 750 cs; $ 137 - ▦ - Sourced from its two Howell Mountain vineyards, a vibrant, drink now wine, with integrated cassis, cherry, and plum notes.

acres 11 - **cases** 12,000
Fertilizers compost, cover crops, mineral fertilizer, organic
Plant protection organic, sulfur, synthetic pesticides
Weed control chemical, mechanical
Yeasts commercial cultured yeasts
Grapes purchase 30%
Certification converting to organics, some of the vineyards are certified organic

CLIFF LEDE VINEYARDS

CÔTE DES CAILLOUX

1473 Yountville Cross Road – tel. (707) 944-8642
www.cliffledevineyards.com – info@cliffledevineyards.com

565 Mountain Avenue – tel. (707) 320-3564
Ma2@cotedescailloux.com

PEOPLE - Comprising sixty acres in the northern end of the Stags Leap District with views of the Stags Leap palisades, Cliff Lede Vineyards has continued to evolve its sustainability practices under the direction of vineyard manager Allison Wilson. Conversion to no-till, mechanical weed control, IPM and solar panels that produce 90% of the wineries energy needs are among their initiatives. The Lede Family Wines' brand family includes sister winery FEL Wines which are grown in the Anderson Valley.

VINEYARDS - The winery produces Sauvignon Blanc and Cabernet Sauvignon from the Twin Peaks and Poetry vineyards after some of his favorite rock songs and albums. Block names such as "My Generation" and "Dark Side of the Moon" created what is known today as the Cliff Lede Vineyards' "Rock Blocks." Winemaker Chris Tynan crafts Cliff Lede and the flagship, Poetry Cabernet Sauvignon and Ryan Hodgins is winemaker for FEL.

PEOPLE - Second-generation winemaker Cody Mathieu works with his father, Cailloux's founding winemaker, Jacques growing eleven varieties on their vineyard in Sonoma. In addition to their estate fruit, they purchase Carignan and white varieties for the "Mathieu" label, a white Rhone blend sourced from Mendocino's Potter Valley. To keep winemaking close to to vineyard sourcing, they'll vinify those wines at Potter Valley Wine Works.

VINEYARDS - The estate vineyard of mixed Rhône varietals is planted on volcanic bedrock with very shallow topsoil. The different varieties are planted to various aspects on the hillside site which helps them ripen about the same time. 2020 was the last vintage the wines were made at Coturri vineyard in Glen Ellen. The 2021 wines are being made at Magnolia Wine Service in Healdsburg.

WINES - Tynan has shifted the blend for High Fidelity and Hodgins continues to dial-in the profiles of the Anderson Valley sites.

Napa Valley High Fidelity 2018 ● 1,142 cs; $ 162 - ⊞ - With 50% Cabernet Franc this blend feels fresher and more complex with cocoa and black pepper embellishing dark fruits and firm tannins.

WINES - The Matheiu family specializes in sulfite-free wine and prefers neutral oak casks.

⬤ **Syrah White** ○ 50 cs; $ 36 - ⊚ - A white blend rom Syrah with a melange of white Rhône varieties showing fresh floral aromas, alluding to darker fruit like plums and blackberries with savory herbs and peppery notes.
Grenache Enox ● 40 cs; $ 36 - ⬚ - Estate grown Grenache raised in a stainless steel (Inoxidable) tank creates a sharp mix of dark red fruits and pepper flavors. The stainless tank process is a distinct experience from the rest of the oak-aged wines the family produces.
Sonoma Côte des Cailloux Estate GSM 2020 ● 250 cs; $ 38 - ⊚ - Grenache, Syrah and Mourvèdre are joined by Cinsault, Counoise and and Chasselas in this unique blend that savory plums and raspberries seasoned with umami and black pepper.

---

acres 11 - **cases** 12,000
Fertilizers compost, cover crops, mineral and organic fertilizer
Plant protection organic, sulfur, synthetic pesticides
Weed control chemical, mechanical
Yeasts comercial cultured yeasts
Grapes purchase 30%
Certification converting to organics, some of the vineyards are certified organic

acres 2.5 - **cases** 450
Fertilizers green manure
Plant protection sulfur
Weed control mechanical
Yeasts spontaneous fermentation
Grapes purchase 20%
Certification none

GLEN ELLEN

COTURRI WINERY

6725 Enterprise Road – tel. (707) 525-9126
www.coturriwinery.com – tony@coturriwinery.com

PEOPLE - Above Sonoma Valley sits the Coturri Estate which was founded by Harry "Red" Coturri and his sons Tony and Phil in 1975. Originally from Lucca, Italy, winemaking was handed down in the family from Enrico Coturri who immigrated to San Francisco in 1901. Tony Coturri has been making wine since 1964 and oversees the estate. He makes wine the way his forefathers did– using organically grown grapes, adding nothing, allowing the wild yeast and grapes to create without interruption.

VINEYARDS - The estate vineyard is planted with Zinfandel, organically dry farmed in soils of decomposed volcanic ash and lava adding complexity to the grapes. Cover crops feed the soil and vines while supplying yeast and bacteria specific to the place which is crucial in the winemaking here. The micro-climate is unique at 750 feet, tucked into the southeastern facing mountain receiving coastal fog in the summer avoiding the extreme heat nearby.

WINES - Coturri uses organically grown grapes, wild native yeasts, open fermentation tanks and neutral barrels allowing the wine to make itself: truly natural.

North Coast Lignaggio 2019 ● 50 cs; $ 45 - 🛢 - Cranberry, cooking spice, plum, balsamic on the nose- juicy cherry, boysenberry, blueberry, umami, cured meat. Acid balanced with tannins leaving a long silky finish. Drink now or age to 10 years.
Sonoma Valley Grenache 2019 ● 50 cs; $ 45 - 🛢 - Rich black raspberry, cherry, star anise on the nose and palate with licorice, earthy and herbaceous flavors. Well balanced with smooth lengthy finish. Drink now or age to 10 years.
Sonoma Valley Estate Zinfandel 2019 ● 50 cs; $ 50 - 🛢 - Blackberry, strawberry, sweet tobacco, taste of candied cherry, licorice with pronounced tannins.

acres 5 - **cases** 750
Fertilizers green manure
Plant protection none
Weed control mechanical
Yeasts spontaneous fermentation
Grapes purchase 90%
Certification none

SEBASTOPOL

COUNTY LINE VINEYARDS

2040 Barlow Lane – tel. (707) 823-2578
www.countylinevineyards.com
info@countylinevineyards.com

PEOPLE - In 2003 Eric Sussman and the skilled folks at Radio-Coteau winery set out to make high-quality, affordable Rosé from California's North Coast. In 2008, they added Pinot Noir, Syrah, Chardonnay, and Zinfandel, completing an affordable line of handcrafted, food-friendly wines to drink in the present. The pandemic inspired collaborating with local artist Molly Kars, resulting in new whimsical labels showing reverence for the wild and domestic animals that cohabitate with the vines.

VINEYARDS - The County Line name was born while driving between counties and checking on the vineyards in Anderson Valley (Mendocino) and Russian River and the Sonoma Coast (Sonoma) where the grapes are farmed. The vineyards are organically farmed with some being certified. The long-time relationships between the winemaker and the vineyard owners are solid, creating stability and consistency in the wine quality.

WINES - Using traditional winemaking techniques, and a shorter élevage in neutral French Oak barrels or stainless steel, each wine is made to provide a cool-climate snapshot of the appellation it comes from.

Sonoma Coast Syrah 2020 ● 60 cs; $ 32 - 🛢 - Inviting blueberry, warm spice and licorice on the nose followed by charismatic blueberry pie, ripe plum, warm spices on the palate. Tannins and acidity are nicely balanced, this delicious Syrah does not disappoint.
Sonoma Coast Chardonnay 2020 ○ 400 cs; $ 32 - 🍸 🛢 - Golden delicious apple, marshmallow, spice and white flowers on the nose and palate with an unfolding of white peach and light citrus. The lush viscosity gives a full mouthfeel mid-palate.
Sonoma Coast Pinot Noir 2020 ● 1,300 cs; $ 32 - 🛢 - Bright red fruits of cherry, cranberry, strawberry followed by earthy, green leaf, and licorice. The tannins are light, balanced with a lingering cocoa finish. This wine has many layers to discover.

acres 7 - **cases** 4,000
Fertilizers compost, organic-mineral
Plant protection organic
Weed control mechanical
Yeasts spontaneous fermentation
Grapes purchase 70%
Certification some of the vineyards are certified organic, some of the vineyards are certified biodynamic

CROSBY ROAMANN

45 Enterprise Court, #6 – tel. (707) 258-8599
www.crosbyroamann.com – sean@crosbyroamann.com

PEOPLE - A lawyer by training, Sean Walker Mc-
Bride founded his small lot, artisanal brand in 2006.
He works with winery businesses in an industrial
office complex south of the town of Napa called
the Crusher District, where he also makes Sean
Walker McBride wines. His tiny lots of Cabernets
have won impressive attention, getting scores from
Wine & Spirits magazines, included in its issue focusing on the Best Cabernets of the Year.

VINEYARDS - The white wine comes from Crosby
Roamann's new, four acre Carneros vineyard (purchased in 2020) which is in the process of being
converted to organic farming. Cabernet comes
from Harmony School Vineyard, which sits on
Haire loam soils in Coombsville where the cooling
influences from San Pablo Bay are felt.

WINES - The winery is moving to an estate wine
model, after purchasing a four acre site in the Carneros in 2020.

Carneros Sauvignon Blanc 2020 O 100 cs; $ 60 - 🗋 🍷
🍾 - A singular Sauvignon Blanc that expresses both a
unique texture and focused concentration. Fermented in
concrete, it's aged in both stainless steel and French oak.
Napa Valley Reserve Cabernet Sauvignon 2017 ●
123 cs; $ 90 - 🍾 - A blend with 18 percent Merlot and
2 percent Cabernet Franc, there's a minty note on the
nose before it shifts gears into an elegant, savory Cab.

DASHE CELLARS

1951 Monarch Street, Hangar 25 – tel. (510) 452-1800
www.dashecellars.com – info@dashecellars.com

PEOPLE - U.C. Davis-educated winemaker Mike
Dashe worked at Ridge Vineyards from 1989 to
1998, learning pre-industrial winemaking at the
foot of the renowned Paul Draper. Meanwhile,
French born Anne Dashe was one of the first wom-
en to graduate in enology at the University of Bordeaux before she came to work in Napa. Two years
after meeting Anne and Michael made their first
Zinfandel together — and married. Today their urban winery in Alameda is renowned for Old World-
style Zinfandel.

VINEYARDS - With a preference toward cool-climate vineyards, the couple source old vine Zinfandel, Carignane, and Riesling from a wide swath of
northern California, including Louvau Vineyard
and West Vineyard in Sonoma County, McFadden
Farm (certified organic) and Heart Arrow Ranch
in Mendocino County and Heringer Vineyard in
Clark County.

WINES - Mike and Anne are intent on creating
wines that reflect the unique terroir of each of the
vineyards they source fruit from.

Dry Creek Valley Zinfandel Reserve 2017 ● 1,526 cs;
$ 35 - 🍾 - This big but well-structured wine presents
lush fruit flavors of blueberry and cherry, with touches of
cinnamon, licorice and violets.
**Eagle Peak Heart Arrow Ranch Les Enfants Terri-
bles 2018** ● 373 cs; $ 350 - 🍷 - This medium-bodied
red offers nuanced layers of dark berries, chocolate,
spice and minerals.
Potter Valley McFadden Farm Dry Riesling 2019 O
328 cs; $ 26 - 🗋 - A is a textured and crisp blend of ripe
pineapple, lemon, pear and chalky mineral.

---

acres 4 - **cases** 1,000
Fertilizers compost, cover crops
Plant protection sulfur
Weed control mechanical
Yeasts spontaneous fermentation
Grapes 100% estate-grown
Certification none

acres - **cases** 8,300
Fertilizers compost, organic-mineral
Plant protection sulfur
Weed control mechanical
Yeasts spontaneous fermentation
Grapes purchase 100%
Certification some of the vineyards are certified
organic, some of the vineyards are certified biodynamic

HEALDSBURG

DAVERO FARMS & WINERY

766 Westside Road – tel. (707) 431-8000
www.davero.com

 "Nature drives" at DaVero Farms & Winery.

PEOPLE - In 1982, Ridgley Evers laid his eyes on what is now DaVero Farms & Winery and knew he had found his home. The estate was transformed into the agricultural wonder it is with the help of his wife Colleen McGlynn, whereas the idea for making wine came after Evers tasted a bottle of Paolo Bea's Sagrantino di Montefalco. Winemaker Evan LaNouette and the rest of the DaVero team have become a tightly woven family making wines from mainly Italian grape varieties, appropriate for the Northern California climate.

VINEYARDS - DaVero's estate vineyards in Dry Creek Valley, in the midst of olive groves, gardens, chickens, pigs, and even an Italian willow-constructed Pantheon (complete with oculus), are a sight to be seen. The winery also sources fruit from vineyards in Russian RIver, Mendocino and Lodi. All are long-term contracts, paid by acre than by ton, and are farmed biodynamically.

WINES - DaVero wines are a reflection of the terroir and vintage. As Evers state, "Our wines are time capsules."

TOP **Dry Creek Valley Estate Sagrantino Riserva 2013** SLOW WINE ● 300 cs; $ 95 - ⊞ - A powerhouse of a wine with a firm varietally-correct tannic core and a multi-layered palate of opulent dark berries and savory undertones.
Dry Creek Valley Altobasso Red Blend 2017 ● Sangiovese, barbera; 235 cs; $ 75 - ⊞ - Has a vibrant acidity and an alluring mix of rich currants, cranberry, and underbrush.
Mendocino Trovato Red Blend 2018 ● 650 cs; $ 34 - ⊞ - A medium-bodied, food-friendly wine showing crunchy pomegranate and a touch of black pepper.

HOLLISTER

DEROSE VINEYARDS

9970 Cienega Road – tel. (831) 636-9143
www.derosewine.com – info@derosewine.com

PEOPLE - Derose is a second-generation business with Al Derose in charge of winemaking. The winery and 50 acre vineyard go back to 1851 making it among the oldest in the state. As a mostly direct-to-consumer business with many visitors, Al compensated for the covid year drop-off with generous delivery policies which included complementary foods provided by a caterer friend. As restrictions lifted, he added a patio and wine by carafe with a popular self-service glass caddy.

VINEYARDS - The vineyards are at 1100' and benefit from cool Pacific winds. Soils are granitic to the east of the San Andreas Fault, which bisects the property, and include limestone to the west. 25 acres are head-trained, dry-farmed old vines, mostly zinfandel, but also rare negrette (166 years-old!). The continuing drought is leading to vine die-off which is prompting consideration of shrinking outer vineyard blocks. Grafting to hearty Derose cabernet franc rootstalk may help.

WINES - Gravity-only racking and transfers of wine encourage clean fermentations.

TOP **Cienega Valley Cedolini Vineyard Zinfandel 2019** SLOW WINE ● 450 cs; $ 35 - ⊞ - Has a nose of cedar and dark cherry while the palate offers distinct smokey, flinty minerality to go with rich dark fruit.
TOP **Cienega Valley Cardillo Vineyard Cabernet Franc 2019** EVERYDAY WINE ● 350 cs; $ 28 - ⊞ - Shows smoked paprika and orange peel on the nose with rich black currant and dark cherry framed by smooth tannins on the palate.
Cienega Valley Chardonnay 2019 ○ 1,000 cs; $ 20 - ▯ - Displays concentrated, racy peach and yellow apple on the palate with honeysuckle and pastry on the nose.

---

acres 17 - **cases** 4,500
Fertilizers compost
Plant protection sulfur
Weed control mechanical
Yeasts spontaneous fermentation
Grapes purchase 60%
Certification some of the vineyards are certified organic, some of the vineyards are certified biodynamic

acres 50 - **cases** 60,000
Fertilizers compost, organic
Plant protection organic, sulfur
Weed control mechanical
Yeasts spontaneous fermentation
Grapes purchase 5%
Certification none

PHILO

DOMAINE ANDERSON

9201 CA-128 – tel. (707) 895-3626
www.domaineanderson.com – info@domaineanderson.com

PEOPLE - With five years under his belt as wine-maker at Domaine Anderson, Darrin Low has rehabilitated the estate's vineyards and continues to fine-tune its biodiversity. Low incorporated additional bee hive boxes and relocated the chicken coop to a more prominent part of the vineyard to discourage pests. Their flock of sheep arrived for grazing a few weeks late as spring drought conditions severely restricted cover crop growth in 2021.

VINEYARDS - The timeline for organic conversion of the estate under the direction of Vineyard Director Bob Gibson will be complete by 2022. Currently 34 acres are certified organic, and the remaining 3 acre vineyard will be so by summer 2022. Of the projected total of 37 acres certified organic, 17 acres are also certified biodynamic. An additional 14 acres are farmed using biodynamic practices and preparations but the winery is not seeking certification at this time.

WINES - In response to lower yields in 2020, Low turned to smaller fermentation vessels and adjusted his winemaking regime with more hand work and foot treading. With drought years increasing concentration, Low has focused on less extraction to adhere to his less is-more wine style.

Anderson Valley Dach Vineyard Pinot Noir 2018 SLOW WINE ● 86 cs; $ 65 - ▦ - This warmer site reveals rich dark cherries and plums with the Anderson Valley garrigue marker of pennyroyal framed by silky, amplified tannins.
Anderson Vally Estate Pinot Noir 2018 ● 1,950 cs; $ 48 - ▦ - Sourced from Dach and cooler sites, characteristic red fruits with sweet brown spice, lifted citrus and black tea are the hallmarks of the blend.
Anderson Valley Estate Chardonnay 2019 O 890 cs; $ 35 - ▦ - Barrel fermented, full ML and barrel aging served to amplify not hide the intensity and mineral expression of the fruit showing lemon zest, golden apple and pear.

acres 53 - **cases** 3,250
Fertilizers compost, green manure, humus
Plant protection biodynamic preparations, organic, sulfur
Weed control animal grazing, mechanical
Yeasts spontaneous fermentation
Grapes 100% estate-grown
Certification some of the vineyards are certified organic, some of the vineyards are certified biodynamic

LOMPOC

DOMAINE DE LA CÔTE

1712 Industrial Way, Suite B – tel. (805) 695-4119
www.domainedelacote.com – wine@domainedelacote.com

PEOPLE - Planted in 2007 on a former Evening Land property, Domaine de la Côte is the result of the convergence of resources and ambition. Sashi Moorman, then a consultant to the previous ownership, was tasked with replanting the estate to pinot noir and decided that he would take a chance in opting for an unheard-of planting density that he felt was the way to produce truly superior pinot. By 2013, Moorman had a partner in Rajat Parr and also the opportunity to buy the property.

VINEYARDS - The Domaine is a series of vineyard blocks plunging down a south-facing grade of diatomaceous earth. The site is windy and cool. The grapes are exceptionally thin-skinned and with few seeds because of low temperatures, high-density planting and fruit shading. Grape yield on average is a mere 1 lb per vine.

WINES - Carbonic maceration is practiced in addition to vigorous extraction, which is possible because of the minimal grape tannins. Stem inclusion provides aromatic lift and control of bringing tannins into the wine. Cherry fruit predominates in these wines.

Sta. Rita Hills Sous Le Chêne 2020 ● 170 cs; $ 120 - ▦ - Is refined in its florality and lightish body, but its impact is expressed in complex levels of flavor including delicate blood orange, currant and sous bois.
Sta. Rita Hills Bloom's Field Pinot Noir 2020 ● 660 cs; $ 90 - ▦ - Shows aromatic beauty with rose and purple flowers. Concentrated fruit joins with loam and dark miso notes into a supple linearity.
Sta. Rita Hills Memorious Pinot Noir 2020 ● 400 cs; $ 80 - ▦ - Thrillingly savory, veering off into floral, roasted and herbal aromas and flavors which are initially confusing and appropriately memory stirring. There is surprising integration in this young wine.

acres 25 - **cases** 2,300
Fertilizers compost, organic-mineral
Plant protection organic, sulfur
Weed control mechanical
Yeasts spontaneous fermentation
Grapes 100% estate-grown
Certification none

BERKELEY

DONKEY & GOAT

1340 5th Street – tel. (510) 868-9174
www.donkeyandgoat.com – dgorders@donkeyandgoat.com

PEOPLE - After a career in tech, Jared and Tracey Brandt took a break in 2002, heading to France for a wine sabbatical. There they interned with renowned Rhone natural winemaker Eric Texier. After returning to Berkeley, in 2004 they opened their own urban winery in Berkeley. As natural wine pioneers, they rely on time, vessels, blending and other natural factors to achieve their honest wines.

VINEYARDS - The winery sources fruit from El Dorado, Mendocino and Napa. In El Dorado, they work closely with the Barsotti family who has planted vines specifically for their wines. While Rhone grape varieties predominate, the winery also buys Bordeaux and Burgundian varieties. One source, Filigreen Farm, is certified biodynamic. Several other vineyards are certified organic. All vineyards will be certified organic within 3 years. Grapes are vinified at the Berkeley winery.

WINES - The Brandt's winemaking ethos requires "nothing added." All wines are unfined and unfiltered.

🔴 **Anderson Valley Lily's Pet Nat Sparkling Chardonnay 2020** SLOW WINE ⁘ 502 cs; $ 35 - 🍶 - Probably the oldest continuously made pet nat in the US; this zesty sparkler is a celebration of citrus fruit, small white flowers and brioche.
Napa Valley Linda Vista Vineyard Chardonnay 2019 ⃝ 200 cs; $ 36 - ⊞ - The richly textured Napa Valley Chardonnay has a opulent nose of lemon, butterscotch, pineapple and flint, and a nice acidity on the palate.
El Dorado Gigi Syrah 2019 ● 125 cs; $ 36 - Ⓠ - Delivers light aromatics of berries, violets and rose petals, and a touch of spice alongside a refreshing acidity.

SONMA

THE DONUM ESTATE 🍾

24500 Ramal Road – tel. (707) 732-2200
www.thedonumestate.com – dfishman@thedonumestate.com

PEOPLE - Donum, Latin for "gift of the land," offers visitors a redesigned hospitality center by David Thulstrup, and a new state-of-the-art winery run by VP of Winemaking and Vineyards Daniel Fishman. Biodynamic and organic farming practices were implemented in 2019 and the estate is on track for CCOF certification in 2022. Fishman and Associate Winemaker Tony Chapman have introduced a portable chicken coop, beehives, and resident sheep to the bucolic Carneros estate.

VINEYARDS - In addition to the 91-acre Carneros vineyard, the estate includes three additional vineyards: Ferguson Vineyards, the Winside Vineyard and the Bodega Vineyards. Ferguson Vineyards will produce a first Pinot Noir in the vintage 2021. The Russian River Winside Vineyard produces intense Pinot Noir along with Wente clone Chardonnay. The Bodega Vineyard was planted in 2020 and won't see its first harvest for the next few years.

WINES - Fishman never forces extraction and crafts expressive, well balanced wines that are reflective of vintage.

🔴 **Carneros White Barn Single Block Reserve Pinot Noir 2020** ● 150 cs; $ 85 - ⊞ - Well-structured with notes of bramble giving way to watermelon, cranberry and black cherry with a lingering sassafras and white pepper finish.
Carneros West Slope Pinot Noir 2020 ● 250 cs; $ 85 - ⊞ - Tasted from the barrel, the wine showed intense red plum, stone fruit and blood orange notes with well integrated brown spice.
Carneros Rosé of Pinot Noir 2020 ◍ 330 cs; $ 50 - ⊞ - Celebrating Donum's 20th anniversary, a small amount of Pinot Noir was devoted to rose with cherry, apple, lemon, peach and a fresh saline finish.

---

acres 0 - **cases** 6,500
Fertilizers biodynamic compost, compost, organic-mineral
Plant protection organic, sulfur
Weed control mechanical
Yeasts spontaneous fermentation
Grapes purchase 100%
Certification converting to organics, some of the vineyards are certified organic and/or biodynamic

acres 158 - **cases** 9,000
Fertilizers biodynamic compost, compost, green manure, organic-mineral
Plant protection organic
Weed control mechanical
Yeasts spontaneous fermentation
Grapes 100% estate-grown
Certification converting to organics

ECO TERRENO WINES

1055 Broadway Suite D – tel. (707) 938-3833
www.ecoterreno.com – info@ecoterreno.com

PEOPLE - Mark Lyon has been making wine for over 40 years at Sebastiani and under his own brand, Eco Terreno, since 2017. He purchased the 122-acre Lyon Vineyard in 1980 first planted in the early 70's by Rodney Strong, and the nearby 27-acre Cisne Ranch in 2008 - both sites certified biodynamic and organic. Set to open in 2022 in Jackson Square, San Francisco, a fantastic three-story wine and food hub will bring wine tasting, food pairings, history, education and entertainment all under one roof.

VINEYARDS - Bordeaux varietals thrive here as do some of the oldest Sauvignon Blanc and Cabernet in the county. Divided between two vineyards, the Cisne has two ideal soils: volcanic loam for Cabernet Franc and clay loam for Sauvignon Blanc. Nearby Lyon has Cortina and Yolo Loam where the deeper reds flourish. The vineyards cohabitate with wild animals and riparian woodlands as well as domestic animals, olive trees and a vegetable and bee garden.

WINES - Mark's winemaking techniques are a mix of Old and New World styles highlighting the enlivening effects of biodynamic farming.

Alexander Valley Old Vine Cabernet Sauvignon 2017 ● 400 cs; $ 100 - 🍴 - Multi-layered and complex, it slowly unfolds with dark and jammy purple fruits, spice, cedar and vanilla with smooth,and refined tannins. Drink now or age.
Alexander Valley Lyon Vineyard Petit Verdot 2018 ● 101 cs; $ 80 - 🍴 - Bold and full-bodied with violet, lilac, ripe plum lifting out of the glass, black cherry, plum, chocolate on the palate. Drink now or age.
Alexander Valley Old Vine Sauvignon Blanc 2020 ○ 140 cs; $ 40 - 🍷 🍴 - Aroma lifts with tropical fruits, fresh tarragon followed by white peach, hay with a crisp, dry finish.

---

acres 90 - cases 5,000
Fertilizers biodynamic compost, green manure, manure
Plant protection biodynamic preparations, organic
Weed control animal grazing, mechanical
Yeasts commercial cultured yeasts, spontaneous fermentation
Grapes 100% estate-grown
Certification biodynamic, organic

EDIO VINEYARDS AT DELFINO FARMS

3205 N. Canyon Road, Bldg. 1 – tel. (530) 622-0184
www.delfinofarms.com – hello@delfinofarms.com

PEOPLE - Third-generation winegrowers and siblings Christine, Peter, Ben and Derek Delfino established Edio Vineyards on the agricultural foundation laid by their grandfather Edio Delfino and father Chris in El Dorado County. Graduates of Cal Poly San Louis Obispo with wine-related majors, Peter Delfino leads winemaking while Derek manages viticulture and Christine Delfino Noonan handles hospitality and operations. They began the winery in 2015, debuted their first vintage in 2018 and opened the doors to their tasting room in April 2020.

VINEYARDS - At elevations of 2,800 feet, alpine viticulture here is defined by plenty of UV light, extreme slopes and well drained, granitic and volcanic soils which means vines are concentrated on ripening fruit. The Delfinos grow Mourvedre, Grenache, Chardonnay, Cabernet Sauvignon, Primativo and Albarino which is planted to a bowl-shaped vineyard that provides a glorious view from the deck of their new tasting room.

WINES - Picking early at physiological ripeness for delicate flavors and higher acidity is the rule of thumb at Edio where the focus is on freshness and structure.
TOP **El Dorado County Edio Albariño 2020** SLOW WINE ○ 244 cs; $ 28 - 🍷 - Granite-loving Albarino shines here with pronounced floral perfume, crisp lime and creamy white peach flavors and nervy acidity.
El Dorado Frank's Rhone Blend 2019 ● 84 cs; $ 60 - 🍴 - Perfumed Mourvèdre showing purity of fruit makes a bold statement in this Mourvèdre, Grenache, Syrah blend with piney Sierra spice, dark cherries and bittersweet cocoa.
El Dorado County Edio Grenache 2019 ● 244 cs; $ 40 - 🍴 - "Sierra spice" describes the garrigue-like notes that are a marker for this site with juicy strawberry, tobacco and savory tannins.

---

acres 15 - cases 2,500
Fertilizers cover crops
Plant protection sulfur
Weed control mechanical
Yeasts commercial cultured yeasts
Grapes 100% estate-grown
Certification none

ST. HELENA

EHLERS ESTATE

3222 Ehlers Lane – tel. (707) 963-5972
www.ehlersestate.com – info@ehlersestate.com

PEOPLE - Originally known as the Bale Mill Winery, the historic property was purchased by Jean and Sylviane Leducq in 1996, the estate releasing its first vintage in 2000. Now held in trust by the Leducq Foundation, proceeds fund international research combating cardiovascular disease and strokes. Winemaker Laura Diaz Muñoz, a native of Spain, took over winemaking in 2018 and collaborates with Michael Wolf who manages the estate's vines.

VINEYARDS - Napa Valley's narrowest point, between the Mayacamas and the Vacas Mountains, the vineyards benefit from a unique microclimate with fog in the morning and full sun at midday ensuring the grapes get a slow ripening. Cabernet Sauvignon, Merlot, Cabernet Franc, Petit Verdot and Sauvignon Blanc flourish in rocky and gravelly soils. Muñoz will implement a regenerative wastewater system taking winery wastewater and, using the digestive power of worms and microbes, clean it for reuse in agriculture.

WINES - Diaz Muñoz and her team focus on achieving vineyard expression in the wines, relying on a light hand in the cellar using 50-70 percent new French oak.

St. Helena Estate Merlot 2018 ● 734 cs; $ 65 - 🔲 - Picked first in harvest to capture the freshness, the aromas of raspberry and cassis lead to juicy red fruits forward on the palate followed by white pepper, mocha and sweet spice. Full mouthfeel, bright acidity and strong tannins. Age or drink now.
St. Helena J. Leducq Cabernet Sauvignon 2018 ● 500 cs; $ 90 - 🔲 - Traditionally, each year one block stands out and is chosen to make into "Leducq", a tribute to the founder. Presents flavors of ripe red fruit, bay leaves, and warm spice. Drink now or age to 15 years.
St. Helena Estate Cabernet Franc 2018 ● 653 cs; $ 72 - 🔲 - Aromatic with red fruits, purple flowers, blueberries and comforting earthiness. Lively on the palate with red raspberry, blueberry, dry herbs. Drink now or hold.

acres 42 - cases 8,500
Fertilizers compost
Plant protection sulfur
Weed control mechanical
Yeasts commercial cultured yeasts, spontaneous fermentation
Grapes 100% estate-grown
Certification organic

CALISTOGA

EISELE VINEYARD

2155 Pickett Road – tel. (707) 942-6061
www.eiselevineyard.com – wine@eiselevineyard.com

 This historic Napa Valley vineyard is dual-certified and committed to adaptive viticultural practices.

PEOPLE - After the dramatic impact of forest fires on the surrounding terroir, increasing biodiversity at Eisele has been winemaker Helene Mingot's primary goal. "We've planted insectaries with drought-resistant grasses and plants for biodynamic preparations." An increased population of bluebirds has helped keep pressure from pests at bay and owls do the same for gophers. Constant finetuning of the estate in response to both weather and climate is essential.

VINEYARDS - After experimenting with shade cloth to mitigate increasing temperatures, Mingot believes "the best shade cloth is the canopy" and is trialing an espalier trellising style from the Rhone. Mingot has now adopted a wing-shaped plow that flutters the soil surface of the vineyard without disturbing the deeper microbiome and the Clemens weed knife for under vine mechanical weeding and less erosion.

WINES - Mingot has moved to using large-format, high-toast oak foudres for the 2018 Alta Gracia in a vintage that required little or no sorting in the cellar.

🔝 **Napa Valley Eisele Vineyard Cabernet Sauvignon 2018** SLOW WINE ● 1,790 cs; $ 435 - 🔲 - Compelling aromas of rose and tobacco with red and black currants, black plums, blackberries and richly textured tannins scented with umami, cinnamon and cocoa.
Napa Valley Eisele Vineyard Altagracia Cabernet Sauvignon 2018 ● 2,680 cs; $ 120 - Ⓒ - Cabernet Franc brings floral lift to black and blue fruits scented with nutmeg, cardamom and cool, well-knit flavors with a fine mineral expression.
Napa Valley Eisele Vineyard Sauvignon Blanc 2019 ○ 1,180 cs; $ 154 - 🔲 - Lengthy lees aging lends a bright richness to floral and tropical aromas of passionfruit, guava and grapefruit with white peaches, pears and tangerine on the palate.

acres 38 - cases 5,420
Fertilizers biodynamic compost, green manure, humus, manure
Plant protection organic, sulfur
Weed control mechanical
Yeasts commercial cultured yeasts, spontaneous fermentation
Grapes purchase 10%
Certification some of the vineyards are certified organic and biodynamic

OAKVILLE

ELIZABETH ROSE

7830-40 St. Helena Highway – tel. (800) 848-9630
www.ghostblockwine.com – drinkcab@ghostblockwine.com

 Made by Napa's largest organic growers (for three decades), by a family with more than 100 harvests in Napa Valley, this value brand's wines overdeliver year after year.

PEOPLE - A rare, value brand in Napa, Elizabeth Rose offers affordable, organically grown wines from an historic Italian farming family. Napa's largest organic growers, the descendants of Pelissa family reserve 15 percent for their own three labels. Pelissa descendant and managing partner Andy Hoxsey was one of the first in Napa to be organic starting in 1992. In 2019 he was honored by the California Association of Wine as California Grower of the Year.

VINEYARDS - The family's Yount Mill Vineyard s grow 13 different wine grape varieties in Yountville and Oakville. Napa settler George Yount first planted grapes on their Block House property in 1838. Hoxsey's vast composting facility, which provides compost for their 557 acres of vines, takes up an entire acre.

WINES - Jeff Onysko makes the wines, which are all bottled with screwtops. It also offers ecofriendly refillable growlers for sale at the wine.

Napa Valley Chockablock Red Blend 2018
EVERYDAY WINE ● 1,850 cs; $ 28 - ▦ - Pleasingly herbaceous, this Bordeaux blend of Cabernet Sauvignon (55%), Merlot (27%) and Malbec (18%) brims with red fruits and cherries, overdelivering for a wine in this price range. It's aged 30 percent in new French oak.
Yountville Pinot Noir 2018 ● 3,125 cs; $ 26 - ▦ - Aged nine months in 30% new French Oak, discover its strawberry and cherry notes.
Yountville Flora 2018 ○ 95 cs; $ 20 - ▢ - The family is also the only grower of Flora, a rare cross between Gewürztraminer and Sémillon. The perfect aperitif or complement to Asian or spicy food, this refreshing and novel variety offers with a light touch of sweetness, showing its Gewürztraminer roots, fleshed out by the richness of Sémillon.

acres 557 - cases 4,000
Fertilizers compost, cover crops
Plant protection organic
Weed control mechanical
Yeasts commercial cultured yeasts
Grapes 100% estate-grown
Certification organic

UKIAH

ELKFIELD WINES

7801 State Highway 20 – tel. (707) 895-3626
www.elkfieldwines.com – jane@elkfieldwines.com

 A back to the land farm and winery making natural and certified Biodynamic Wine, free from additives.

PEOPLE - Greek Orthodox immigrants from Palestine, founders Gaby and Amal Khoury came to San Francisco in 1967 to join other family members in the grocery business, before realizing their dream of owning a vineyard and a winery. Gaby grew up making sacrificial wine with monks at a monastery in Jerusalem. Winemaker Jane Khoury, a part time ICU nurse in Ukiah, trained at U.C. Davis. Brother Nicholas is the assistant winemaker, and sister Sema handles marketing.

VINEYARDS - In 1994, the Khoury's bought 260 acres of wooded land east of Ukiah, naming it Elkfield for the elk that roamed the property. Located on the south side of Highway 20, Elkfield has a wide variety of different microclimates and 10 soil types. In keeping with biodynamic practices, the Khoury's have animals on the property—25 sheep—along with chickens, who are pastured year round.

WINES - Winemaker Jane Khoury, who once worked at Domaine Anderson, credits Gloria Decater, a biodynamic farming pioneer who studied with Alan Chadwick and runs Live Power farm in Covelo, as a mentor.

Mendocino Merlot 2019 ● n/a; $ 24 - ▦ - Offers restrained cherry and black fruit notes and a long lingering finish.
Mendocino Pinot Noir 2016 ● n/a; $ 35 - ▦ - Taste black cherries with a black pepper note framed by gentle tannins.

acres 60 - cases 3,000
Fertilizers biodynamic compost, cover crops
Plant protection biodynamic preparations, sulfur
Weed control animal grazing, mechanical
Yeasts spontaneous fermentation
Grapes 100% estate-grown
Certification biodynamic, organic

ENA WINES

5029 Gregory Court – tel. (707) 338-1551
www.enawinemakers.com – enawinemakers@gmail.com

PEOPLE - Leading the charge by sourcing from the world's first Ecological Outcome Verification (EO-VTM) regenerative vineyard, Eglantine Chauffour, a native of Cote d'Azur-Provence, France, and husband Alberto Bianchi who hails from Milan are the winemaking team behind ENA Wines. The brand name includes their initials and also represents a winemaking philosophy that combines American terroirs with their European personalities. 2019 was their debut vintage focused on Pinot Noir and Sauvignon Blanc and they've already expanded their portfolio to include a cool-climate Primitivo based in 2021.

VINEYARDS - ENA sources fruit solely from Mariah Vineyard at 2,400 ft. in the coastal mountains of the Mendocino Ridge AVA. The vineyard is owned and operated by Dan and Vicki Dooling who have partnered with Land to Market and the Savory Institute to pilot the Ecological Outcome Verification (EOVTM) which is the world's first verified sourcing solution for regenerative agriculture.

WINES - Eglantine and Alberto have a light hand in the cellar which results in wines with precise balance and striking freshness. Native yeast fermentation and careful barrel selection are used to highlight the vineyard expression rather than pursue a specific wine style.

🔝 **Mendocino Ridge Mariah Vineyard ENA Pinot Noir 2020** SLOW WINE ● 195 cs; $ 43 - ▦ - The addition of 18% clone 777 added structure and length to the pronounced floral aromas, tart red cherry, cranberries and crisp, savory finish.
Mendocino Ridge Mariah Vineyard ENA Sauvignon Blanc 2020 ○ 110 cs; $ 38 - ▦ - Neutral oak, less than 20% ML and six months of lees stirring frame the bright citrus, freshly-cut grass and saline mineral expression from this high-altitude site.
Mendocino Ridge Mariah Vineyard ENA Pinot Noir 2019 ● 194 cs; $ 43 - ▦ - Medium-bodied with bright cranberries, raspberries and red plums up front moving to darker, savory fruit, silky tannins and a more expansive finish.

acres 30 - **cases** n/a
Fertilizers compost
Plant protection copper, sulfur
Weed control mechanical
Yeasts spontaneous fermentation
Grapes 100% estate-grown
Certification converting to organics

ENFIELD WINE CO.

1160b Hopper Avenue – tel. (707) 287-4519
www.enfieldwine.com – info@enfieldwine.com

PEOPLE - John Lockwood started Enfield Wine Co with partner Amy Seese Lockwood in 2010 while working as Vineyard Manager at Failla, even making his first three vintages there. When his daughter was born and he was a stay-at-home dad, he made his first commercial vintage of Enfield wines, the 2014's, which caught the attention of Jon Bonne and Eric Asimov, who called him a "winemaker to watch." Production has grown from 900 to 2500 cases.

VINEYARDS - John works with "sites that are naturally powerful" including Brousseau (certified organic), Haynes, the 10 acre Heron Lake in Napa Valley's Wild Horse AVA which he has been managing and farming exclusively since 2018 and the 2-acre Waterhorse Ridge in Fort Ross-Seaview AVA adjacent to Hirsch and Marcassin on the Sonoma Coast, owned by Jesus and Patricia Vasquez.

WINES - John concentrates on unique cool climate vineyards, where he can coax site expression rather than winemaking imprint.

🔝 **California Citrine Chardonnay 2019** ○ 1,000 cs; $ 28 - ◉ - Soft and inviting, delicate, fresh and dry with notes of almond croissant, mushroom and nutmeg.
Wild Horse Valley Heron Lake Vineyard Pinot Noir 2019 ● 150 cs; $ 42 - ◉ - Energetic, silky, tart and dry with notes of strawberry, raspberry, cherry tomato and leaf.
Fort Ross-Seaview Waterhorse Ridge Cabernet Sauvignon 2018 ● 200 cs; $ 60 - ▦ - Very light, tart and youthfully austere with notes of cassis, fennel seed, cumin and cedar.

acres 11 - **cases** 2,500
Fertilizers compost
Plant protection copper, organic, sulfur
Weed control mechanical
Yeasts spontaneous fermentation
Grapes purchase 60%
Certification none

ETTORE

FAVIA

14160 Mountain House Road – tel. (707) 744-1114
www.ettore.wine – contact@ettore.wine

2031 Coombsville Road – tel. (707) 256-0875
www.faviawine.com – info@faviawine.com

PEOPLE - Ettore launched in 2021, making some of its wine using Purovino®, a new approach developed at the University of Tuscia in Viterbo, Italy. Italian born winemaker Ettore Biraghi, recognized by Gault Millau as a rising star in Switzerland, makes the wines with Sofia Riviera. Swiss co-proprietor Paolo Buonvicini also owns Olivino, an olive oil production facility, which houses Ettore's new winery as well as the Terra Savia wine brand.

PEOPLE - In 2003 renowned viticulturist Annie Favia and Napa Valley cult winemaker Andy Erickson started Favia in the century old stone building that became their home and winery. The 6.5 acre property along Coombsville Road is just east of downtown Napa in the foothills of the Vaca Mountains at the center of a west-facing horseshoe that comprises the appellation. Ella Brooks is Director of Operations

VINEYARDS - The 35 acre, certified organic vineyard sits on gravelly benchland, loamy soils in hot, sunny Hopland in Mendocino's inland Sanel Valley. It grows Chardonnay along with Cabernet Sauvignon and Merlot. The four different blocks of Chardonnay contain a variety of vine ages, including some that are 25-30 years old.

VINEYARDS - Favia works with 11 vineyards, many for over a decade, most certified organic. All are sustainable including the 40-year old block of Cabernet Franc on the Rancho Chimiles high in the Vaca Mountains, Coombsville in the southeast corner of Napa Valley with gravelly soils and cooling from nearby San Pablo Bay, and in the red, iron-rich soils of Oakville Ranch across the valley in the eastern hills of Oakville.

WINES - The Zero wines are made without added sulfites using the unique Purovino® process (in which the grapes are cooled with ozone and cold tanks) to produce a fresher style of wine.
Mendocino Zero Chardonnay 2018 ○ 93 cs; $ 50 - 🛢 - Full bodied, bold and creamy (the result of multiple pumpovers) with fruity tropical notes along with apricot, peach and a bit of fennel.
Mendocino Zero Merlot 2018 ● 197 cs; $ 65 - 🛢 - Fresh and lively, offers up tightly wound black and red berries and a hint of licorice.
Mendocino Red Wine 2018 ● 448 cs; $ 65 - 🛢⊞ - A new take on a Bordeaux blend, with pleasing cherry and currant flavors from a blend of Merlot, Cabernet Sauvignon, and Petit Verdot.

WINES - Andy crafts some of the richest, most powerful Cabernet Sauvignons in the world for his famous, wealthy clients. This however is a personal family project and there is a bit more restraint while still showcasing the power and beauty of the Napa Valley.
TOP **Coombsville Napa Valley Cabernet Sauvignon 2018** ● 450 cs; $ 250 - ⊞ - Very rich, intense, gripping and dry with notes of blueberry, fig, spice bread and clove.
Napa Valley Cerro Sur Red Wine 2018 ● Cabernet Franc, Cabernet Sauvignon; 350 cs; $ 250 - ⊞ - Very full, gripping, chewy and dry with notes of mulberry, cassis, nougat and white chocolate.
Coombsville Napa Valley Carbone Chardonnay 2020 ○ 1,000 cs; $ 48 - ⊞ - Unctuous, fresh, dry and long with notes of lemon curd, peach, nutmeg, vanilla and toasted almond.

acres 21 - cases 4,000
Fertilizers compost, cover crops
Plant protection organic
Weed control mechanical
Yeasts spontaneous fermentation
Grapes 100% estate-grown
Certification organic

acres 0 - cases 2,500
Fertilizers compost, green manure, organic-mineral
Plant protection copper, organic, sulfur
Weed control mechanical
Yeasts commercial cultured yeasts, spontaneous fermentation
Grapes purchase 100%
Certification none

CORRALITOS

FERRARI RANCH WINES

65 Magnifico Vita Lane – tel. (408) 667-4506
www.ferrariranchwines.com – info@ ferrariranchwines.com

PEOPLE - One of the newest wineries in Corralitos making wine from some of the oldest vines in the region. Dave and Liz Ferrari purchased their Santa Cruz Mountains ranch on a hillside in 2016, where 40-year-old Pinot Noir vines were planted. The Ferraris brought in Santa Cruz Mountains viticulture consultant, Prudy Foxx, who uses sustainable and holistic farming practices to farm this unique old-vine site in the Corralitos area. Ross Reedy deftly leads the winemaking.

VINEYARDS – Ferrari Ranch's 40-year-old Pinot Noir vines dig 40 foot deep in a terraced, dry-farmed, west-facing vineyard sitting at 700 feet. The steep slopes vary from 20-50% gradient. The soils are deep colluvial, sand, and gravel with ancient dune deposits. Redwoods stand sentry around the vineyard.

WINES - Ferrari Ranch wines are handcrafted in very small lots, elegant and terroir-focused, honoring the heritage of the vineyard and keeping the natural expression of the vineyard front and center.

🔝 Santa Cruz Mountains Estate Pinot Noir 2018
SLOW WINE ● 60 cs; $ 58 - ⊞ - This outstanding Santa Cruz Pinot Noir from an outstanding vintage is rich and smooth loaded with red fruit, rose and violet, black tea, mushroom, Asian 5-spice, leather, and caramel notes, while 25% carbonic maceration lends cinnamon and vanilla.
🔝 Santa Cruz Mountains Estate Rosé of Pinot Noir 2020 EVERYDAY WINE ◍ 50 cs; $ 28 - 🍶 - This fresh and lively direct-press rosé is like summer in a glass: fresh strawberries, raspberries, watermelon, and rose petals. Minerality adds a clean finish.
Santa Cruz Mountains Estate Chardonnay 2018 O 60 cs; $ 42 - ⊞ - Lemon curd, graham cracker, tangerine, apple, pear, vanilla with a touch of butterscotch on the finish, this Chardonnay is round and fresh with good acidity.

acres 12 - cases 240
Fertilizers organico-mineral
Plant protection organic
Weed control mechanical
Yeasts spntaneous fermentation
Grapes 100% estate-grown
Certification none

PLACERVILLE

FIELD NUMBER FIFTEEN

4771 Greenhills Road – tel. (530) 536-0621
www.fieldnumberfifteen.com – info@fieldnumberfifteen.com

PEOPLE - Forty years ago, Kenyon Elliot's uncle by marriage planted 11.5 acres of wine grapes plus fruit trees on his 20 acres. Years later, the opportunity arose for Kenyon to purchase and revitalize the abandoned vineyard, fulfilling a lifelong dream. He and his wife Lizzy think outside of the box as they focus on making wine from organic, sustainable, loved, grapes with an emphasis on rosé because he likes it.

VINEYARDS - At 2500' in elevation near Placerville in the Sierra Foothills surrounded by forests, the sloped 11.5 acres of vineyards at Field Number Fifteen include Chardonnay, Zinfandel, Cabernet Sauvignon, Merlot, and Barbera. Because the vineyards had been neglected, Kenyon could easily attain CCOF organic certification prior to releasing the first wines in 2020. As the tended vines begin to produce more, Kenyon won't need to purchase organic fruit.

WINES - With 2020 the first commercial release, only a few estate wines are available: big, bold, flavorful wines designed to be enjoyed cold during the heat of a summer's day yet they still offer that special "Sierra spice." For whites and rosé he uses stainless, and for reds, oak.

El Dorado Chardonnay 2020 O 220 cs; $ 24 - 🍶 - Harvested a bit late and with about 10% raisins, the grapes were pressed off quickly to offer a clean crisp yet unique chardonnay profile.
El Dorado Cabernet Sauvignon Rosé 2020 ◍ 66 cs; $ 24 - 🍶 - Great acidity, light cherry fruit on the palate, and Sierra spice make this an easy to enjoy rosé.
El Dorado Barbera Rosé 2020 ◍ 77 cs; $ 24 - 🍶 - Fresh fruit bursts onto the palate up front, but the finish is bone dry and very balanced in this intentionally made rosé.

acres 11.5 - cases 600
Fertilizers cover crops
Plant protection organic, sulfur
Weed control n/a
Yeasts commercial cultured yeasts, selected indigenous yeasts
Grapes purchase 12%
Certification some of the vineyards are certified organic

WATSONVILLE

FLOREZ WINES

2487 Freedom Boulevard – tel. (530) 760-5140
www.florezwines.com – james@florezwines.com

PEOPLE - As many college graduates do, James Jelks wanted to travel abroad post-graduation. He ended up looking at the UC Davis summer abroad program, and for some reason the Intro to Winemaking course in Burgundy jumped out. "I had always been a hobbyist, always had eccentric and focused interests," he says, "and then at some point, wine just clicked." The trip to Burgundy eventually led to the launch of his own label, Florez Wines, in 2017.

VINEYARDS - Initially, Jelks planned to only make wines from Santa Cruz grapes but could not find enough organic fruit there. He now personally farms two sites in Santa Cruz, one of which was originally planted in the 1970s, first with Riesling and then Chardonnay. He just planted some Gamay there and is about to plant the more obscure varietal, Savignen. At another, gently sloped, south-facing site is an acre of Chardonnay and a little bit of Syrah.

WINES - Jelks likes to consider his winemaking as experimental, and while his wines are whimsical and playful, he also has the experience to pull them off with precision.

Mendocino County Shangra-Li Mendo Savvy-B Sauvignon Blanc 2020 `EVERYDAY WINE` ○ 250 cs; $ 26 - 🍷 - A signature wine for Jelks. The 2020 is from Upton Vineyard in Redwood Valley, planted 1968 and certified organic. Reminiscent of an Italian orange wine, wonderfully salty, with lush salinity.
Dunnigan Hills The Pope's Smoke Grenache 2020 2020 ● 192 cs; $ 28 - 🛢 - A pretty, light bodied, low alcohol wine, which some could even classify as a rose. Yet it is structured, with good tannins and juicy strawberry notes.
Santa Cruz Mountains Moonmilk Chardonnay 2020 ○ 200 cs; $ 40 - 🛢 - The grapes come from the Glenwood Vineyard in Scotts Valley that he farms, resulting in a very delicate, classic Chardonnay, which he has been making since the start of his label in 2017.

acres 3 - **cases** 1,333
Fertilizers compost, green manure, mineral fertilizer, organic
Plant protection organic, sulfur, synthetic pesticides
Weed control mechanical
Yeasts spontaneous fermentation
Grapes purchase 100%
Certification some of the vineyards are certified organic

SEBASTOPOL

FREEMAN VINEYARD & WINERY

1300 Montgomery Road – tel. (707) 823-6937
www.freemanwinery.com – info@freemanwinery.com

PEOPLE - Ken and Akiko Freeman returned to California after living in Asia and fell head over heels in love with Russian River Valley Pinot Noir. They visited more than 300 properties before establishing their winery in 2001 on the cool, western edge of the Green Valley of Russian River Valley. Akiko took over as winemaker in 2010 and leads an all-female winemaking team.

VINEYARDS - Gloria Vineyard next to the winery, planted in 2006, is at 400' elevation, 10 miles from the ocean, and has the classic goldridge sandy loamy soil. Art Robledo Jr farms the estate vineyards. Greg Adams helped plant the vineyards and began moving to fully organic. In 2007 they acquired a 14-acre sheep ranch in West Sonoma in the cool Sonoma Coast AVA and planted it with seven clones of Pinot Noir. Yu-Ki is at 1,000' elevation, 4 miles from the ocean and enjoys the shelter of Redwoods.

WINES - Ken and Akiko Freeman stood fast to their beliefs while the world went for candied, super-ripe and lavishly oaked California Pinot Noirs. Today they are considered a founder of the movement towards elegant, understated, site and vintage expressive wines.

Sonoma Coast Yu-ki Estate Pinot Noir 2018 ● 400 cs; $ 68 - 🛢 - Light, tart, elegant and dry with notes of pomegranate, raspberry, white rose, cedar and nutmeg.
Russian River Valley Gloria Estate Pinot Noir 2019 ● 450 cs; $ 68 - 🛢 - Gentle and delicate, silky and dry with notes of cranberry, red currant, sage leaf and red rose.

acres 24 - **cases** 5,000
Fertilizers compost, green manure, organic-mineral
Plant protection copper, organic, sulfur
Weed control none
Yeasts spontaneous fermentation
Grapes purchase 25%
Certification none

RUTHERFORD

FROG'S LEAP

8815 Conn Creek Road – tel. (707) 963-4704
www.frogsleap.com – ribbit@frogsleap.com

 One of the first to be organic in Napa (in 1997), its farm to table approach (chickens, veggie gardens and fruit orchards), solar energy, labor policies and pioneering ecostewardship make it a leader.

PEOPLE - The poster child for organic farming in Napa, Frog's Leap, founded by John Williams in 1981, is popular for its ecofriendliness, witty sense of humor, and finely balanced wines. It went solar in 2005 and built a Silver LEED certified farmhouse tasting room in 2006–the first winery to achieve this milestone. On the worker front, it employs its staff year round. Employees receive healthcare and other benefits, a claim few wineries can make.

VINEYARDS - The winery farms 200 acres of organic vines in Rutherford, St. Helena and the Carneros. Additional fruit comes from Mendocino and Napa. Committed to preserving heritage varieties, it grows Valdiguie and field blends. The Red Barn site (built in 1884) houses the winery and 30 acres of Cabernet.

WINES - The winery acquired the historic 52 acre Rossi Ranch (with old vines and an iconic water tower) in 2007, preserving more Napa history. With Pablo Polanco and Xochilt Polanco, winemaker Rory Williams, John's son, continues the house style of pure and balanced wines. Many wines are unfined and unfiltered.

Napa Valley Shale and Stone Chardonnay 2019 ○ 8,348 cs; $ 60 - 🍷▦ - Harvested in 8 separate picks, whole cluster pressed and aged sur lie (without stirring)–the delicate attention is reflected in this crisp, vibrant, fresh wine, outstanding for balance and elegance.
Napa Valley Zinfandel 2019 ● 11,200 cs; $ 60 - 🍷▦ - Rose-scented aromas on the nose, delicate cherry notes on the palate–it's almost Pinot-esque in its lightness and grace.
Rutherford Estate Cabernet Sauvignon 2018 ● 13,982 cs; $ 111 - ▦ - Light on its feet–and unfined and unfiltered–it offers up cherry and black fruit notes on the palate. Cab is 88 percent of the blend.

acres 200 - **cases** 60,000
Fertilizers compost, cover crops, organic
Plant protection copper, organic, sulfur
Weed control mechanical
Yeasts commercial cultured yeasts, spontaneous fermentation
Grapes purchase 25%
Certification organic

HEALDSBURG

FRONT PORCH FARM

2550 Rio Lindo Avenue – tel. (707) 433-8683
www.fpfarm.com – info@fpfarm.com

 "The health of the soil is at the forefront of our thinking." – Sebastien Pochan, winemaker.

PEOPLE - Owners Mimi and Peter Buckley started Front Porch Farm with a vision — to grow healthy food and to gather people together. Their estate wines are very much part of that vision. Sébastien Pochan oversees all of the viticulture as well as the winemaking. He believes that when you farm well, everything else falls into place, and that the balance and diversity of the terroir should be reflected in the wines.

VINEYARDS - Front Porch Farm's idyllic, organically-certified estate vineyards, planted on well-drained, steep hillsides, frame their picturesque 110-acre farm in a small and sunny valley that looks up at Fitch Mountain and runs beside the Russian River. They are planted to Rhône grape varieties including Syrah, Grenache, Viognier, Grenache Blanc, and Mourvèdre. Everything is farmed by hand.

WINES - Front Porch Farm's aim is to produce organic and balanced wine that are meant to be enjoyed with food and in good company.

TOP **Russian River Valley Grenache Blanc 2019**
SLOW WINE ○ 148 cs; $ 32 - 🍷 - Vibrant and fleshy, redolent of roasted pineapple, lemon, melon, white flowers, almond and flint.
Russian River Valley Grenache 2018 ● 199 cs; $ 28 - ▦ - Well-balanced, complex and intense with an alluring mix of blackberry, raspberry, chocolate, baking spices and rose petals.
Russian River Valley Rosé 2020 ◕ Grenache, Mourvedre, Syrah; 390 cs; $ 26 - 🍷 - Fresh and with a pleasing velvety texture this rosé offers gentle flavors of strawberry, peach, and orange blossom.

acres 12 - **cases** 1,250
Fertilizers compost
Plant protection organic, sulfur
Weed control mechanical
Yeasts spontaneous fermentation
Grapes 100% estate-grown
Certification organic

GALLICA

GHOST BLOCK

2300 Vallejo Street – tel. (707) 963-1096
www.gallicawines.com – info@gallicawines.com

7830-40 St. Helena Highway – tel. (800) 848-9630
www.ghostblockwine.com – drinkcab@ghostblockwine.com

PEOPLE - Rosemary Cakebread, known for wines of elegance and balance, started her own winery in 2007 after serving as winemaker at Spottswoode (one of Napa's most classic producers) for 15 years. Previously she worked in sparkling wine production, an experience leading her to develop a more subtle palate and gain insight into the nuanced craft of blending. For her label, Gallica, she handcrafts single vineyard wines with a commitment to organic farming.

VINEYARDS - Gallica sources from their estate's valley floor in St. Helena (certified organic) for Rosé and Cabernet Sauvignon as well as three distinguished growers (two are certified organic). Cabernet Franc is from eastern Oakville HIlls (certified organic). Cakebread uses compost tea to strengthen the vines, better water management, electric vehicles, solar panels and battery back-up, continually looking for responsible approaches in every avenue of farming.

WINES - Cakebread creates graceful and elegant wines allowing the unique signature of the single vineyards and vintage to be experienced through a gentle hand in the cellar.

St. Helena Estate Cabernet Sauvignon 2018 ● 91 cs; $ 185 - 🍷 - Elegance meets you on the nose with plum, spice, cinnamon, raspberry and vanilla with a light and ethereal entry of fresh berries, plum and baking spices wrapped in refined tannins. Drink now or age.
Oakville Ranch Vineyard Cabernet Franc 2018 ●131cs; $ 185 - 🍷 - Subtle yet complex with earthy rose, raspberry and faint bell pepper the tannins are softened and balance the acidity nicely.
St. Helena Estate Rosé 2020 ● 65 cs; $ 27 - 🍷🍷 - White peach, lime, blood orange and floral notes on nose and palate; dry and crisp. Drink now

 It's one of the largest organic growers in Napa and one of the biggest in California and the U.S.

PEOPLE - A brand created by one of the oldest farming families in Napa, the descendants of the Pelissa family, Ghost Block is known for top quality. In 1993, the family purchased the Napa Wine Co. (originally constructed in 1877), turning it into a custom crush winery where clients' cult wines were made. Fourth generation Pelissa descendant Andy Hoxsey manages the vines and wines with daughters Morgaen and Kendall. Kristi Koford makes the wines.

VINEYARDS - The family's farming history in Napa dates back to 1903. In 1938, after Prohibition ended, the family bought 1,000 acres in Oakville and Yountville locally known as the Pelissa Hills. Their compost facility covers an entire acre. The soils are gravelly loam. Their Oakville vineyards border renowned sites–Opus One and the fabled To Kalon vineyard.

WINES - Its 2018 wines won widespread acclaim in the mainstream wine press, selling out rapidly after getting a 95 pt. score.
Yountville MorgaenLee Sauvignon Blanc 2019 ○ 1,300 cs; $ 44 - 🍷🍷 - Picked at three different sugar levels, partially whole cluster, partly fermented in barrel, and aged sur lie, it's blended with Sémillon (four percent) to enhance texture and flavor. It's complex, creamy, lively, and filled with delicious tropical fruit and citrus notes.
Oakville Pelissa Vineyard Zinfandel 2018 ●15,000 cs; $ 68 - 🍷 - The family preserves precious, 25 to 30 year old Zin vines (where others would have planted Cab) for this wine, offering up briary red fruit and lovely berry and cherry notes on the palate.
Oakville Oakville Estate Cabernet Sauvignon 2018 ● 4,700 cs; $ 128 - 🍷 - A steal by Napa prices, the flagship Cab (rated 95 points by Wine Spectator) is aged two years in 70 percent new French oak. Elegant and restrained, offers dark cherries and dark red fruits, cassis and more.

acres 2 - cases 1,500
Fertilizers compost, green manure
Plant protection organic
Weed control mechanical
Yeasts spontaneous fermentation
Grapes purchase 60%
Certification some of the vineyards are certified organic

acres 557 - cases 4,000
Fertilizers compost, cover crops
Plant protection sulfur
Weed control mechanical
Yeasts commercial cultured yeasts
Grapes 100% estate-grown
Certification organic

GRGICH HILLS ESTATE

1829 St. Helena Highway – tel. (707) 963-2784
www.grgich.com – info@grgich.com

 A model of regenerative organic farming for more than 15 years, Grgich Hills wines are perennial favorites.

PEOPLE - Possibly the most famous winemaker in America for the role he played in putting California wines on the world stage, 98 year old Mike (or Miljenko) Grgich was a Croatian immigrant who arrived in Napa with just a few bucks in his pocket in 1958. In 1973, at 50, Grgich made the Chardonnay that won the 1976 Paris Tasting, besting the French. His daughter Violet is president.

VINEYARDS - Grgich Hills has five estate vineyards (certified organic) that span the entire length of Napa Valley. The winery's prized old vines go into its top tier "Legacy" wines. In the Carneros, its oldest blocks of Chardonnay, sought after Old Wente clones, were planted in 1989. In Yountville, its heritage Cabernet vineyard preserves precious clones and old vines dating back to 1959. Some of its Calistoga Zin vines data back to the 1880s.

WINES - Grgich's nephew Ivo Jeramaz manages winemaking and production. The wines are certified to be free from synthetic additives (except for the limited use of sulfites).

TOP Napa Valley Paris Tasting Commemorative Chardonnay 2017 SLOW WINE ○ 942 cs; $ 100 - 🍷 Ⓤ - Gorgeously complex, barrel fermented, and slightly creamy with a rounded texture, it's light on the entry, then bursts into bright lemon, peach, and citrus.
Napa Valley Miljenko's Old Vine Zinfandel 2017 ● 396 cs; $ 125 - 🍷 Ⓤ - With grapes from 100 year old Zinfandel vines blended with a healthy dollop of Petite Sirah (17 percent)–it offers elegant black fruits, leading into plums and cherry notes on the mid palate.
Yountville Old Vine Cabernet Sauvignon 2016 ● 617 cs; $ 150 - 🍷 - Sourced entirely from 62 year old vines, shows cassis and plums on the nose, followed by red berries on the palate–a worthy homage to the historic Inglenook clone it comes from.

acres 366 - cases 65,000
Fertilizers biodynamic compost, cover crops
Plant protection biodynamic preparations, organic, sulfur
Weed control mechanical
Yeasts spontaneous fermentation
Grapes 100% estate-grown
Certification organic

GUST WINES

24737 Arnold Drive – tel. (707) 815-2869
gustwines.com – megan@gustwines.com

PEOPLE - The newest 2018 California AVA, Petaluma Gap, ranging from the Pacific coast to San Pablo Bay just south of Sonoma, is unique for its early morning fog leading to brisk cool shore breezes coming in from Bodega Bay. Fred and Nancy Cline recognized this mixture of warm and unusually cool temperatures as the perfect formula for making prized cool-climate Pinot, Chardonnay and Syrah wines. Inspired by this region, second-generation vintners Megan Cline and Hilary Cline launched GUST in 2017.

VINEYARDS - Gust Wines is overseen since 2016 by Director of Winemaking and Viticulture Tom Gendall who believes "if you look after the vines, the vines will look after you and produce great fruit." This native New Zealander continues the "Green String" farming system originally developed by Fred Cline, embracing the most rigorous beyond organic/regenerative farming practices in order to produce exceptional wines.

WINES - Sourced from the Catapult and Diamond Pile estate vineyards, the combination of these two creates well balanced, complex wines offering distinct flavors based on terroir and climate of each location.

Petaluma Gap Gust Chardonnay 2019 ○ 500 cs; $ 38 - 🍷 - Planted in 2001 in heavy clay, 52% Diamond Pile Vineyard and 48% Catapult Vineyard, this Chardonnay delights the pallet with of bursts of citrus, lemon-curd and delicate notes of honeysuckle.
Petaluma Gap Gust Pinot Noir 2017 ● 400 cs; $ 48 - 🍷 - Planted in 1997, this Pinot Noir is a complex blend of 55% Catapult and 45% Diamond Pile vineyard making a strikingly well-structured wine with an array of red fruits, earthy undertones, with a spicy finish.
Petaluma Gap Gust Syrah 2018 ● 400 cs; $ 48 - 🍷 - This Rhone-inspired Syrah is a small, hand-picked blend of both Catapult and Diamond Pile vineyards. Enjoy flavors of black pepper with layers of blue and black fruit intertwined with lots of secondary expressions.

acres 15 - cases 16,000
Fertilizers compost, humus, organic, organic-mineral
Plant protection sulfur
Weed control animal grazing, mechanical
Yeasts spontaneous fermentation
Grapes 100% estate-grown
Certification none

GUTHRIE FAMILY WINES $

HAARMEYER WINE CELLARS

tel. (707) 307-3614
www.guthriefamilywines.com – blair@guthriefamilywines.com

610 Harbor Boulevard
www.haarmeyerwinecellars.com – visit@haarmeyercellars.com

PEOPLE - In 2013, Guthrie Family Wines was launched by a young winemaking couple who wanted to showcase a minimalist approach to winemaking. With a day job making high end Cabernet Sauvignon in Napa, Blair Guthrie desired to create something very different on his own time, with complete freedom to make New California style wines that were low intervention at accessible prices. they always tend to pick early to make a racier style

PEOPLE - Craig Haarmeyer's interest in wine originated from his mother's career running restaurants. He was a home winemaker and helped with some harvests around Sacramento. Haarmeyer ditched his career in IT when he was offered a job as winemaker at a friend's troubled winery. Eventually his own project exceeded the scope of the day job and he quit. With the encouragement of son, Alex, he moved his project into the recently shuttered, historic Harbor Wine facility. Alex works beside Haarmeyer and they often complete each other's sentences.

VINEYARDS - Guthrie works only with vineyards that farm organically or biodynamically. The last vintage was an early harvest year, due to continued drought conditions that result in very low water in the vines and soil. However, the wildfire season of 2020 was especially hard, with widespread smoke damage cutting their typical production down to only three wines being produced that year.

VINEYARDS - Sourced vineyards must have no chemical inputs. Palmero Family Vineyard in Lodi produces chenin in its no-till site. Wirz in Cienega Valley produces the old vines riesling and Stampede in Clements Hills, Lodi produces 100-year-old zinfandel grapes from a vineyard that, until the present Perlegos family ownership, was sold out in bulk.

WINES - Guthrie picks early to make a racier style. The beautiful labels are all made by Blair, who has a background in graphic design. The wines are fresh, aromatic and acid-driven.

TOP **Calaveras County Faux Picpoul Blanc 2020**
EVERYDAY WINE ○ 200 cs; $ 22 - From the special Rorick Heritage Vineyard in the Sierra foothills, owned by Forlorn Hope's Matthew Rorick. Minerality and refreshing sea salinity, yet round and full with a lemon curd lushness.
Mendocino County Heirloom Grenache 2020 ● 200 cs; $ 28 - Guthrie set out to make this in a traditional style, but because of the wildfires, ended up doing it carbonic (the same way he does the Carignan). Offers bright cranberry and blood orange juiciness.
Mendocino Galaxy Carbonic Carignan 2020 ● 200 cs; $ 22 - 100% carbonic fermentation, with fruit coming from the very old vine, Testa family-owned vineyard Calpella in Mendocino County. Juicy strawberry, cranberry, cocoa and herbal notes prevail.

WINES - Chenin Blanc is the focus though some zinfandel, nebbiolo and riesling are also produced. Haarmeyer avoids sulfur completely. White and red grapes are processed whole cluster. The reds are bottled after malolactic conversion and the whites aged 10 months on lees.

TOP **Lodi Cresci Vineyard Chenin Blanc 2020** ○ 120 cs; $ 26 - Has a flinty nose with pure red apple. Its flavors are concentrated with apple, white peach and lemon. The wine is mouth-filling and long.
Cienega Valley Wirz Riesling 2019 ○ 25 cs; $ 30 - Destemmed and fermented on skins this wine shows yellow apple, flor and honey aromas with pear skin texture and tree fruit flavors.
Lodi Stampede Vineyard Zinfandel 2019 ● 25 cs; $ 35 - smells earthy with refined smokiness and dried strawberry giving way to a bright palate of strawberry and cherry.

acres 0 - **cases** 1,200
Fertilizers compost, cover crops, organic
Plant protection organic, sulfur
Weed control mechanical
Yeasts spontaneous fermentation
Grapes purchase 100%
Certification some of the vineyards are certified organic

acres 0 - **cases** 200
Fertilizers compost
Plant protection organic, sulfur
Weed control mechanical
Yeasts spontaneous fermentation
Grapes purchase 100%
Certification none

PASO ROBLES

HALTER RANCH

8910 Adelaida Road – tel. (805) 226-9455
www.halterranch.com – info@halterranch.com

PEOPLE - Founded in 2000 by Hansjorg Wyss, this 2700 acre west Paso Robles ranch has 180 acres of wine grapes, 15 acres of walnuts and 10 acres of olives along with a renovated Victorian farmhouse. With an eye towards environmental stewardship, the vineyards were originally SIP Certified Sustainable, but are now transitioning to organic. Winemaker Kevin Sass oversees the vineyards and new multilevel gravity flow production facilities onsite. Gracie Nino is Director of Marketing.

VINEYARDS - Dating back to the 1880's, this sprawling Central Coast ranch is sheltered from the ocean by the Santa Lucia Range. The focus on Rhone and Bordeaux varietals is not surprising given the daytime heat even here on the west side of Paso Robles. The "Ancestor Tree" is the largest known live oak tree on the Central Coast and the property has several wildlife corridors.

WINES - Kevin is not a fan of the classic Paso Robles style of "warm" high alcohol wines that are often and easily over-ripe. He says, "I try to be more restrained with lower alcohol and a longer aging potential.
Paso Robles Adelaida District Ancestor Estate Reserve 2018 ● Cabernet Sauvignon, Malbec, Petit Verdot; 3,000 cs; $ 75 - ⊞ - Powerful, chewy and dry with notes of cassis, mulberry, black peppercorn, cinnamon and nutmeg.
Paso Robles Adelaida District Cabernet Sauvignon 2018 ● 6,000 cs; $ 55 - ⊞ - Full bodied, chewy, gripping and dry with notes of blueberry, blackberry, vanilla, mocha and cedar.
Paso Robles Adelaida District CDP 2018 ● 4,500 cs; $ 46 - ⊞ - Very rich and chewy with notes of cherry, blackcurrant, mint leaf, cedar and game.

acres 180 - **cases** 25,000
Fertilizers organic-mineral
Plant protection copper, organic, sulfur
Weed control mechanical
Yeasts commercial cultured yeasts
Grapes 100% estate-grown
Certification converting to organics

SONOMA

HAMEL FAMILY WINES

15401 Sonoma Highway – tel. (707) 996-5800
www.hamelfamilywines.com – info@hamelfamilywines.com

PEOPLE - Hamel Family Wines was founded in 2006 with the first vineyard acquisition and realized when the Sonoma Valley winery and tasting room were completed in 2014. Managing Director John Hamel oversees winemaking and vineyard management and brother George Hamell III oversees the operations, sales and marketing aspects of the winery. The estate vineyards were CCOF certified organic in 2013 and 2016 for Demeter.

VINEYARDS - The estate's highest elevation site is the Nuns Canyon Vineyard which reaches 1400 ft. and is primarily basalt with dark, ferrous volcanic soils. Hamel Family Ranch sits on the valley floor at 500 to 1000 ft. and has alluvial and loam series soils. Within the last three years, the winery began transitioning to dry farming and the vines have been able to tolerate heat spikes and rebound successfully. To minimize risk from fire season, they are picking three weeks earlier compared to previous vintages.

WINES - Hamel has begun fermenting and aging in concrete tanks and eggs. A style shift is underway as Austrian cooperage has been introduced and the total time wines spend in oak has been dialed back.
Sonoma Valley Isthmus 2018 ● 2,000 cs; $ 90 - ◖ ⊞ - Dense and powerful with boysenberry, mulberry, savory umami and ferrous mineral notes, firm, resolved tannins showing dark spices and notes of cedar and tobacco.
Sonoma Valley Hamel Family Ranch Cabernet Sauvignon 2018 ● 500 cs; $ 160 - ⊞ - Bright red plum, dark cherry and red currant around a lean, muscular frame with thyme, coffee, clove and black pepper through a lengthy finish.
Moon Mountain District Nuns Canyon Vineyard Cabernet Sauvignon 2018 ● 600 cs; $ 160 - ⊞ - Mountain fruit power and finesse abound here with an abundance of red and black fruits scented with lavender, sage, black tea and umami.

acres 110 - **cases** 6,000
Fertilizers biodynamic compost, manure, organic-mineral
Plant protection biodynamic preparations, copper, organic, sulfur
Weed control mechanical
Yeasts selected indigenous yeasts
Grapes 100% estate-grown
Certification biodynamic, organic

HAMMERLING WINE $

1350 Fifth Street – tel. (510) 984-0403
www.hammerlingwines.co – hello@hammerlingwines.co

PEOPLE - Josh Hammerling plowed ahead into his traditional method sparkling wine project, in acceptance of the perils of the challenging style. Having spent time at Syncline in the Columbia Gorge and with future neighbors, Broc Cellars and Donkey and Goat Winery in Berkeley, he felt that 2018 was the time. But unique to most winemakers, Hammerling was able to quickly sell his product, courting wine club members and doing pop-ups with restaurateurs. The cashflow has allowed him to contend with the complexities of learning the sparkling game on the fly.

VINEYARDS - Observation grit and have landed Hammerling fine sources for California sparkling (and still) wine. They range from the Sierra Foothills to Mendocino and where he sources the most: the Cienega Valley.

WINES - Recently, Hammerling has made cuvées from many vineyards to understand what his options are. In the future, he intends to settle on a more limited portfolio, though with a resolve for experimentation. His wine names derive from film and literature expressing the desire to push boundaries.

El Dorado Wind, Sand & Stars Sparkling Gamay Noir 2020 ❄ 120 cs; $ 34 - ⊞ - Shows yellow apple and yeasty hints on the nose giving way to a burst of citrus and rounded tree fruit flavors. The perle twines effortlessly with the acidity.
Monterey Down by Law Solera Sparkling Riesling ❄ 100 cs; $ 38 - ⊞ - Shows a nose of yeast and citrus with a lush palate of nectarine and grapefruit pith, a combination 2018 and '19 wines.
Lime Kiln Valley Enz Vineyard Wild One Cabernet Pfeffer 2020 ● 200 cs; $ 34 - ⊞ - Cedar, red cherry, light rose aromas. Intense strawberry and peach flavors are bound with refined tannins.

acres 0 - cases 2,500
Fertilizers compost, green manure, mineral fertilizer, organic
Plant protection copper, organic, sulfur, synthetic pesticides
Weed control mechanical
Yeasts commercial cultured yeasts, spontaneous fermentation
Grapes purchase 100%
Certification none

HANDLEY CELLARS

3151 Highway 128 – tel. (707) 895-3876
www.handleycellars.com – handley.lulu@gmail.com

 In 1982, Milla Handley was the first female winemaker in the U.S. to establish a namesake winery in the fledgling Anderson Valley AVA.

PEOPLE - Lulu Handley, Milla Handley's younger daughter, has been managing the winery since 2016. Handley Estate was the first producer to certify an organic vineyard in Anderson Valley in 2005. Handley works with winemaker Randy Schock who joined winery in 2004 as cellarmaster and vineyard manager Jose Jimenez who has been with the winery since 1989.

VINEYARDS - The RSM Estate Vineyard which achieved certification in 2017 is named for Handley's late father, Rex Scott McClellan. At 1,000 ft., this steep hillside vineyard sits above the fog line and is sheltered from the wind by dense coastal redwood and fir forests. RSM is among the first to be harvested largely due to its shallow soils and the warmer nighttime temperatures. Water conversation practices have been a focus along with reduced tillage.

WINES - Founding winemaker Milla Handley whose wines put Anderson Valley on the map passed in 2020 but her legacy lives on. Lulu Handley notes that styles are evolving with the changing climate and she will continue to make wines that are true to the valley.

TOP **Anderson Valley Handley Estate Vineyard Pinot Noir 2017** SLOW WINE ● 325 cs; $ 50 - ⊞ - From the cooler end of the valley showing raspberry, blueberry and dark cherry with loam and herbal notes from the indigenous pennyroyal and a touch of caramel.
Anderson Valley Handley Valley Estate Vineyard Chardonnay 2018 ○ 1,928 cs; $ 28 - ⊞ - Partial ML keeps flavors of poached pears, Meyer lemon and green apples bright and intense with nutmeg and golden caramel extending the finish.
Anderson Valley Gewürztraminer 2020 ○ 200 cs; $ 26 - 🍷⊞ - Pronounced aromatics of rose, orange zest and white cardamom with lush white tree fruits, grapefruit, ginger and a tropical flourish of lychee on the finish.

acres 35 - cases 9,000
Fertilizers organic, cover crops, compost
Plant protection sulfur, organic
Weed control mechanical
Yeasts commercial cultured yeasts, spontaneous fermentation
Grapes purchase 50%
Certification some of the vineyards are certified organic

SONOMA

HANZELL VINEYARDS

18596 Lomita Avenue – tel. (707) 996-3860
www.hanzell.com – maildesk@hanzell.com

 Achieving organic certification in 2021 elevates the farming model at Hanzell to its apex.

PEOPLE - Winemaking at Hanzell is credited to a team that includes Jason, McNeill, Lynda, Cesar, Jim and Jose while Brandon Bredo and Jose Ramos Esquivel whose tenure at the winery spans 45 years do the farming. The winery won its reputation for being among the first to plant and produce world-class Chardonnay and Pinot Noir on the Mayacamas in the 1950s but isn't resting on its laurels. The wines are as authentic and interesting as the unique property itself.

VINEYARDS - Bredo posted a CCOF-certified sign for both the winery and the vineyards at the entrance of the estate this year and is now pursuing regenerative certification. The degree of biodiversity at the property is nothing less than astounding: a resident herd of sheep graze cover crops, chickens scratch, a drove of heritage hogs work on clearing underbrush and two placid Maremmano-Abruzzese sheepdogs manage the proceedings.

WINES - Never shouting, never shy, the balance and intensity of the wines continues to be a hallmark for this treasured estate.

🔝 **Sonoma Valley Hanzell Vineyards Chardonnay 2018** SLOW WINE ○ 1,336 cs; $ 78 - 🍷 ⊞ - An elevated Wente clone expression with lemon custard, nutmeg, lemon and orange zest, green tropical fruits and golden apples that's precise, balanced and sublime.
Sonoma Valley Hanzell Vineyards Pinot Noir 2018 ● 1,336 cs; $ 98 - ⊞ - Some whole cluster lends sapidity and cumin notes to the savory ground cherry, leather, tobacco and tangy blood orange and saline mineral flavors that make this so memorable.
Sonoma Valley Hanzell Vineyards Cabernet Sauvignon 2017 ● 255 cs; $ 125 - ⊞ - Roses and lavender dominate the aromas of spicy pomegranate, red plums, cassis, red cherries and leather of this truly elegant blend.

---

acres 46.1 - cases 10,000
Fertilizers green manure
Plant protection organic, synthetic pesticides
Weed control animal grazing
Yeasts spontaneous fermentation
Grapes purchase 20%
Certification some of the vineyards are certified organic

LOWER LAKE

HAWK AND HORSE VINEYARDS

13048 CA-29 – tel. (707) 696-4838
www.hawkandhorsevineyards.com
info@hawkandhorsevineyards.com

 Mitch and Tracey Hawkin's holistic approach at their Diamond B Ranch includes a natural compost factory – a herd of highland cattle. They were Certified Organic and are now Demeter Certified.

PEOPLE - In 2004 the Hawkins produced their first vintage on Diamond B Ranch, a former gold-mining, sight in Lake County's Red Hills AVA. The ranch was originally purchased by Tracey's stepfather David Boies as a family gathering place. In 2008 they hired legendary winemaker Richard Peterson and their Vineyard Manager of 20 years, Miquel Chavez, lives on the ranch.

VINEYARDS - This Demeter certified ranch has the classic silica "Lake County diamond" studded red volcanic soil and sits at an elevation of 1800'-2200, producing thick-skinned small berries and low yield. The area has the cleanest air in the nation and intense, sunshiny days with the nearest city, San Francisco, 130 miles away.

WINES - Focusing on Bordeaux varietals and French Oak-aged Petite Sirah, the wines are as rich and sumptuous as the best of Napa Valley but at 1/3 the price.

🔝 **Red Hills Lake County Petite Sirah 2017** SLOW WINE ● 150 cs; $ 65 - ⊞ - Full, chewy, gripping with an underlying juiciness and energy and notes of raspberry, blackberry, dried herbs, spearmint and vanilla.
Red Hills Lake County Cabernet Sauvignon 2017 ● 1,800 cs; $ 75 - ⊞ - Intense, powerful, gripping and dry with classic notes of cassis, fig, maple, vanilla and cedar.
Red Hills Lake County Cabernet Franc 2017 ● 150 cs; $ 65 - ⊞ - Rich, ripe, well-structured and lively with notes of cherry liqueur, shitake mushroom, tobacco, cedar, nutmeg and vanilla.

---

acres 18 - cases 2,800
Fertilizers biodynamic compost
Plant protection biodynamic preparations
Weed control mechanical
Yeasts commercial cultured yeasts
Grapes 100% estate-grown
Certification biodynamic

ST. HELENA

HEITZ CELLAR

436 St. Helena Highway – tel. (707) 963-3542
www.heitzcellar.com – info@heitzcellar.com

PEOPLE - Started in 1961, Heitz Cellars is one of Napa's most iconic wineries. The classic producer founded by Joe and Alice Heitz, has seen immense changes since Gaylon Lawrence, Jr., an Arkansas billionaire, purchased it in 2018. Former somms turned vintners Carlton McCoy, Jr. and Erik Elliott manage the estate. Vineyard and winemaking continuity is provided by long time vineyard manager Mark Neal and winemaker Brittany Sherwood. A luxury tasting room will open in 2021.

VINEYARDS - Acquired over 50 years, Heitz's vineyards include choice spots in Rutherford (132 acres) and Howell Mountain (200 acres), enabling it to select fruit from both valley and mountain vines. Its most famous wine, known internationally, comes from Martha's Vineyard in Oakville. All are currently certified organic and in transition to biodynamic certification.

WINES - The current vintages were made by David Heitz, aged in American oak barrels for one year and French barriques for three more years, and then bottle aged for four years before release, reflecting the unhurried pace and traditions of an old school, Napa family run winery.

Rutherford Trailside Vineyard Cabernet Sauvignon 2015 ● 24,000 cs; $ 214 - ⊕ - A Napa classic, it's a standout for its pure red and black fruit, elegance and complexity. Grown on Rutherford soils, this is a gorgeous expression of a classic Napa cab. A bit of herbaceousness adds to its allure. It comes from a mix of seven clones and eight soil types.

Oakville Martha's Vineyard Cabernet Sauvignon 2015 ● 30,000 cs; $ 427 - ⊕ - A stunning wine, the (2,500 cases, $250) offers up black fruit, herbs, and plum notes along with the unique menthol note the wine is famous for.

---

acres 450 - **cases** 420,000
Fertilizers biodynamic compost
Plant protection biodynamic preparations, organic
Weed control mechanical
Yeasts commercial cultured yeasts, spontaneous fermentation
Grapes purchase 15%
Certification converting to biodynamics, organic

SAN BERNARDINO

HERRMANN YORK WINES

440 East Caroline Street – tel. (951) 394-1755
www.herrmannyork.wine – taylor@herrmannyork.wine

PEOPLE - Brothers Garrett and Taylor York and friend Dustin Herrmann are Herrmann York. As dedicated desert dwellers from the 'Inland Empire', they wanted to make 'desert' wine. They are each married with one infant and this similarity extends into their decision-making as winemakers which is a product of their collective experimentation. There is something old world about them. As their winemaking came into focus, the vineyards that they source from became of primary importance and are highlighted on their labels.

VINEYARDS - A big day was when the men tore into the first wines produced by Abe Schoener's L. A. River Wine Company because it displayed the potential of local vineyards. The Munoa Lone Wolf vineyard is shared with Schoener and is mostly head trained mission. Until 2020, the vineyard had not been cared for for fifty years. Chavez vineyard in the Lancaster high desert is 23 years old and their 'grape superstore'.

WINES - From here, they select primarily muscat and alicante bouchet. Primitivo comes from a home vineyard in Redlands. Each Herrmann York wine possess an abundant mineral component.

California Munoa Ranch 2020 ● Grenache, Mission; 24 cs; $ 31 - ⊞ - Shows a nose of cherry and toasting sugar. On the palate is earth and spice blended with tart red cherry.

Antelope Valley Chavez Vineyard Amber Muscat 2020 ◎ 24 cs; $ 27 - 🗋 - This wine is made with skin contact and smells sweet with tree fruit and a bit of celery, while on the palate is pear and quince.

Antelope Valley Chavez Vineyard Alicante Bouchet 2020 ◍ 36 cs; $ 27 - 🗋 - Pressed as a rosé, shows a salty and mouth-watering Jolly Rancher watermelon palate while earthy red berries show on the nose.

---

acres 0 - **cases** 150
Fertilizers compost
Plant protection sulfur
Weed control mechanical
Yeasts spontaneous fermentation
Grapes purchase 100%
Certification none

CAZADERO

HIRSCH VINEYARDS

45075 Bohan Dillon Road – tel. (707) 847-3600
www.hirschvineyards.com – info@hirschvineyards.com

PEOPLE - David Hirsch famously planted Pinot Noir back in 1980 before the region was renowned as a great site for vineyards. Originally Hirsch sold grapes to wineries but by 2002 he started his own wine label. Today the region is a prime spot for Pinot Noir, having its own AVA designation - Fort Ross-Seaview. In 2015 Jasmine Hirsch (David's daughter) took over the helm as General Manager and in 2019 became Winemaker. A committed team runs this integrative farm with soil health as priority.

VINEYARDS - High in the coastal rainforest in an unpredictable climate sits the 1000 acre estate vineyard of Chardonnay and Pinot Noir. Lying on the San Andreas Fault, soils are sandstone-based with large rocks seemingly placed at random across the rolling hills. The vineyard blocks vary widely in water needs, exposure, rootstock, clonal selections and vine age, adding a lot of variety and blending choices in winemaking.

WINES - 2019 was notable for its wet winter, cold spring, mild summer, and was Jasmine's first vintage as Winemaker. The wines express exuberant fruits, complex aromatics and elegant tannins.

Fort-Ross Seaview San Andreas Fault Estate Pinot Noir 2019 ● 3,100 cs; $ 60 - ⊞ - A classic representation of the vineyard, aromas of cherry, licorice, wild earth and spices. The palate has a savory start followed by juicy cherry, red fruits, brambly earth and balanced tannins, giving a graceful finish, long and alive.
Fort-Ross Seaview Estate Chardonnay 2019 ○ 650 cs; $ 60 - ⊞ - Sunny, ideal growing conditions allowed the 3 acres of Chardonnay to exhibit a bold and luxurious vintage. With strong coastal influence the minerality plays with the complex aromatics lifting up ripe golden delicious apple, honey and coastal brush. The taste of pear, minerality, and salinity all lead to a long and supple finish. Drink now or age.

acres 72 - **cases** 9,700
Fertilizers biodynamic compost, green manure
Plant protection biodynamic preparations organic, sulfur
Weed control mechanical
Yeasts spontaneous fermentation
Grapes 100% estate-grown
Certification none

SANTA ROSA

HOBO WINE COMPANY

412 Timothy Road, Suite C – tel. (707) 595-3495
www.hobowines.com – info@hobowines.com

PEOPLE - Former skateboarder and Sonoma native Kenny Likitprakong and his wife Lynn Wheeler founded the winery in 2002. Today they release a wide range of approachable, consumer-friendly labels, including Folk Machine, Camp and Ghostwriter. Their earth-friendly approach includes using long-term renewable energy sources, geothermal energy, environmentally friendly label ink, recycled glass and natural corks.

VINEYARDS - Kenny and Lynn source fruit and work closely with a wide range of vineyards throughout Sonoma, Mendocino, Solano and Santa Cruz counties. Over 80% of the vineyards they work with are organic or biodynamic, including the old vine dry farmed organic Lolonis Family Vineyard in Redwood Valley, Mendocino. The vineyards they lease are all transitioning to organic with CCOF.

WINES - Their philosophy, perhaps best captured by their Ghostwriter label, is that the winemaker is "telling a story that is not entirely their own." The range of wines tends toward the lighter, fresher style and are priced for everyday enjoyment.

Redwood Valley Lolonis Family Vineyard Folk Machine Film & Camera Valdiguié 2019 EVERYDAY WINE ● 599 cs; $ 23 - 🍷 - Light, tart and dry with notes of raspberry, blueberry, pink rose and violet.
Mendocino County Camp Zinfandel 2020 ● 853 cs; $ 36 - 🍷 - Light, finely chewy, fresh and dry with notes of boysenberry, plum, fig, cocoa powder and toasted marshmallow.
Santa Cruz County Ghostwriter Pinot Noir 2019 ● 571 cs; $ 30 - 🍷 - Light, tart, crisp and dry with notes of pomegranate, cherry, mushroom, pumpernickel and sandalwood.

acres 60 - **cases** 2,500
Fertilizers compost
Plant protection sulfur
Weed control mechanical
Yeasts spontaneous fermentation
Grapes purchase 65%
Certification some of the vineyards are certified organic

SARATOGA

HOUSE FAMILY VINEYARDS

13336 Old Oak Way – tel. (800) 975-7191
www.housefamilyvineyards.com
info@housefamilyvineyards.com

PEOPLE - Dave House, family patriarch and proprietor, purchased the 73-acre property on the east side of the Santa Cruz Mountains AVA in 1998. He and his extended live on the property. Vines were planted in stages, first in 1998, then in 2000, and again in 2004. The first 12 vintages, the wines were made by the legendary Jeff Patterson of Mount Eden Vineyards. Today, Jim Cargill, Dave's son-in-law, manages winemaking and operations. Jonathan Goodling is the vineyard manager.

VINEYARDS - The Old Oak Vineyard, the estate vineyard, sits at 900 feet elevation. The 10-acre vineyard, located in the "Chaine d'Or" part of the Santa Cruz Mountains, is planted on very steep (25°) east-facing slopes. House Family meticulously maintains the vines by hand, harvests by hand, and incorporates organic farming practices. House Family also sources from other hand-selected vineyards.

WINES - Jim Cargill uses New World fruit to make Old World style wines with minimal intervention and native yeasts.

🔝 Petaluma Gap Saltonstall Vineyard Pinot Noir 2017 ● 300 cs; $ 66 - 🛢 - Fruit-forward Pinot with umami notes, blood orange, cola, and earl grey tea, the wine is complex and rich.
Santa Cruz Mountains Estate Chardonnay 2017 ○ 275 cs; $ 64 - 🛢 - A beautifully balanced Chardonnay with good fruit and fresh acidity, showing notes of lemon curd, vanilla, and pineapple.
Santa Cruz Mountains Estate Cabernet Sauvignon 2016 ● 800 cs; $ 78 - 🛢 - A bold mountain Cab with notes of blackberry, cassis, chocolate, cedar, tobacco, earth, and fresh forest.

acres 10 - **cases** 4,000
Fertilizers compost, green manure, humus, manure, mineral fertilizer, organic-mineral
Plant protection copper, sulfur, organic, synthetic pesticides
Weed control mechanical
Yeasts selected indigenous yeasts, spontaneous fermentation
Grapes purchase 50%
Certification none

NAPA

HYDE DE VILLAINE - HDV

588 Trancas Street – tel. (707) 251-9121
www.hdvwines.com – nate@hdvwines.com

PEOPLE - Hyde de Villaine is a French-American winery from two families—the Hydes of Napa, a family of Carneros growers, and the de Villaines of Burgundy, who make the most famous Pinot Noir wine in the world. They became connected by a 1973 marriage. In 2000, the two created HdV Wines, a Napa winery known mostly for its fine Chardonnays. Chris Hyde manages the vines. Guillame Boudet is the winemaker. Aubert de Villaine visits onsite each year.

VINEYARDS - Hyde Vineyards' best blocks, reserved for HdV, range in age from 11 to 42 years. The oldest 3 acres were planted in 1979. In 2012 after years of blind tasting Pinot from Hyde's grapes, de Villaine approved the release of an HdV Pinot Noir. It's sourced from a block planted in 2010 with seven of HdV's favorite clones. The vines grow in shallow Haire-clay loam soils in the Carneros, a cool climate region that borders the San Pablo Bay.

WINES - The house winemaking style shows its French heritage, creating wines that beautifully balance fruit and acid in fresh, lively wines that are unfined and unfiltered.

🔝 Carneros Hyde Vineyard Chardonnay 2018 ○ 2,275 cs; $ 75 - 🛢 - HdV's energetic flagship wine, it delivers a precise streak of citrus—notably Meyer Lemon—and green apple, in what may be Napa's finest Chardonnay. It's composed of 60 percent Wente clone (small berries) and 40 percent Calera (larger berries from Josh Jensen).
Carneros Ygnacia Pinot Noir 2017 ● 350 cs; $ 120 - 🛢 - A sublime wine—treated delicately with 20% new oak—it's a complex interweaving of 7 choice clones, unveiling beautiful aromas and flavors of cherries and strawberries with tea notes.
Carneros Californio Syrah 2017 ● 355 cs; $ 85 - 🛢 - Fresh and elegant, a delightful surprise—expressing a lighter, refined side of the variety with plums, violets and dark berries from a cool climate site.

acres 0 - **cases** 5,000
Fertilizers organic
Plant protection organic, synthetic pesticides
Weed control mechanical
Yeasts commercial cultured yeasts
Grapes purchase 100%
Certification none

SALINAS

I BRAND & FAMILY

1367 Dayton Street, Suite B – tel. (831) 212-3660
www.ibrandwinery.com – hello@ibrandwinery.com

PEOPLE - After a peripatetic early adulthood, Ian Brand found himself in the lab at Bonny Doon Winery in Santa Cruz. Today, he is a go-to man in greater Monterey County and his base in Carmel Valley, a region unknown to the general public that features the depleted soils of the west side of the San Andreas Fault and the majestic Monterey Bay with its enormous cooling effect.

VINEYARDS - When starting his winemaking project, Brand recognized that overdelivering to the public was crucial and in a region known for large bulk wine operations, his site-specific sourcing could be done economically. But it was the old vines plots such as Massi, Wirz and Enz nearby that were heart-stirring and needed a deep dive in understanding the past in order to optimize the present. Brand has had a positive hand in supervising organic farming in the region.

WINES - Buying grapes and supervising harvests for his labels, P'tit Paysan, La Marea and I Brand Family Wines Brand has become a student, historian and advocate for the terrains from where he acquires his 'competitive advantage'.

TOP **Arroyo Seco Zabala Vineyard P'tit Paysan Sauvignon Blanc 2020** EVERYDAY WINE ○ 1,500 cs; $ 22 - 🥂 - Shows a leafy and white flower nose giving way to green apple and melon on the palate. Zingy acidity is complemented by stream bed minerality.
Carmel Valley Massa Vineyard I Brand & Family Cabernet Sauvignon 2019 ● 208 cs; $ 75 - ⊞ - Displays 'Monterey Garrigue', aromas of bay and chapparal. Flavors of cherry, blackberry and mocha combine deftly with fine tannins and lively acidity.
San Benito County P'tit Paysan Cabernet Sauvignon 2019 ● 4,000 cs; $ 25 - ⊞ - Delivers aromas of cedar and red and dark cherry. On the palate, red and dark fruit flavors ride on earthy notes.

acres 0 - **cases** 12,500
Fertilizers compost, organic-mineral
Plant protection copper, organic, sulfur
Weed control mechanical
Yeasts spontaneous fermentation
Grapes purchase 100%
Certification some of the vineyards are certified organic, some of the vineyards are certified biodynamic

HEALDSBURG

IDLEWILD

132 Plaza Street – tel. (707) 385-9410
www.idlewildwines.com – info@idlewildwines.com

PEOPLE - Sam Bilbro is a 4th generation winemaker who grew up in the vineyards of Alexander Valley. After experiences in other wine regions of the world, Sam started Idlewild in 2012. His focus is on the grape varieties of Italy's Piedmont region, producing traditional varietal wines as well as affordable blends.

VINEYARDS - Bilbro sources his fruit from two vineyards in the Yorkville Highlands AVA. Lowell and Barbara Stone's 60 acre Fox Hill Vineyard is a living library of Italy's wine grape varieties. The site is on a warm, west-facing hillside in Ukiah on rocky, pebbly sandstone and quartz. The 724-acre Lost Hills Ranch, at 1500 ft elevation with steep slopes, is well-suited to Italy's cool climate grape varieties such as Nebbiolo, Dolcetto, Arneis and Cortese. Here, the soil is predominantly sandstone with schist veins.

WINES - Bilbro has a simple mission: To produce food-friendly wines of balance and beauty.

Mendocino Fox Hill Vineyard Nebbiolo 2017 ● 230 cs; $ 50 - 🍷 - Tart red fruit, floral aromas, tar and underbrush meet dusty tannins and medium acidity.
Mendocino County Flora & Fauna Rosé 2020 ● nebbiolo, Dolcetto, barbera; 1,000 cs; $ 25 - 🍷 - A lightly structured, food-friendly rosé delivering strawberry, blood orange and herbs on the palate.
Yorkville Highlands Lost Hills Ranch Arneis 2019 ○ 400 cs; $ 30 - 🍷 - Bright yet weighty on the palate, showing mineral, lemon, stone fruit, and blanched almond on the finish.

acres 15 - **cases** 5,000
Fertilizers compost, cover crops, green manure
Plant protection copper, sulfur
Weed control mechanical
Yeasts spontaneous fermentation
Grapes purchase 50%
Certification none

SANTA ROSA

INMAN FAMILY WINES

3900 Piner Road – tel. (707) 293-9576
www.inmanfamilywines.com – info@inmanfamilywines.com

 From grapegrowing to winemaking, the wines tell a story of place and taste.

PEOPLE - Kathleen Inman is a natural winemaker who harvests by feel and taste. "Acid is the skeleton on which all other things hang, and for me, acid is more important than sugar." She picks her grapes with natural acidity, producing elegant, low-alcohol wines. Each wine develops through its time on the fine lees, frequent stirring and hand punchdowns. Inman uses neutral oak to allow the fruit to come forward.

VINEYARDS - Olivet Grange Vineyard (OGV Estate), a 10.45-acre vineyard in the Russian River Valley, is certified sustainable and farmed organically. The winery, constructed of recycled materials, is energy-efficient and solar-powered. Inman feeds the vineyard worm castings and compost teas, plants cover crops and avoids tilling to encourage the natural soil biome. This regenerative farming produces high-quality fruit and supports the natural environment.

WINES - Handcrafted small lots of elegant, low-alcohol Pinot Noir, Pinot Gris, Chardonnay, Rosé and sparkling wines exhibit the singular characteristics of the Russian River Valley AVA and are alive with flavor.

🖤 **Russian River Valley Inman Family OGV Estate Pinot Noir 2018** SLOW WINE ● 583 cs; $ 75 - ⊞ - A battonage process and natural yeast fermentation produces aromas and flavors of dry rose petals, tart cherry, rhubarb, cranberry. The wine shows a medium body, long finish and great minerality.

🖤 **Russian River Valley Endless Crush Rosé of Pinot Noir 2020** ◉ 728 cs; $ 38 - ⊞ - An "intentional rosé," the wine has a lovely, natural acidity.
Russian River Valley Whole Buncha Love Pinot Noir 2019 ● 168 cs; $ 68 - ⊞ - Crafted from 100% whole clusters in small one-ton stainless steel fermenters, its structure and tannins come from grapes, not oak. A wild fermentation and the carbonic process adds savory and vibrant fruit flavors.

---

acres 8.3 - **cases** 4,167
Fertilizers compost, organic-mineral
Plant protection organic, sulfur
Weed control mechanical
Yeasts spontaneous fermentation
Grapes 100% estate-grown
Certification none

ESCONDIDO

J. BRIX WINES

298 Enterprise Street, Suite D – tel. (760) 994-8135
www.jbrix.com – emily@jbrix.com

PEOPLE - Emily and Jody Towe have been together since high school, benefiting from a spooky like-mindedness in their decision making. Perennial pet nats, rieslings and a red blend lead a unique line of other wines. They are always thought-provoking and tasty, utilizing skin contact, amphora aging and the delicate extraction of fruit. J Brix has weathered the pandemic year by recognizing quickly that sales were going off-premise and direct to consumer and actually ramped up production.

VINEYARDS - The focus is always on the expression of the grape and Jody goes to great lengths, driving all over California doing grape pick-ups from premier vineyards before returning to the winery in Escondido. The Rorick Heritage vineyard is known for rare limestone, organic farming and brilliant grapes. J Brix turns to quality San Diego vineyards for grenache blanc, picpoul from Rancho Guejito and vermentino from Pauma Vineyard farmed by conscientious Triple B Ranches.

WINES - The wines are native-yeast fermented, aged in neutral vessels, not fined, filtered or cold-stabilized and free of any additives, except for sulphites as necessary.

Calaveras County Rorick Heritage Vineyeard Limestone and Schist Chardonnay 2019 ○ 220 cs; $ 28 - ⊞ - Shows pure aromas of fennel, citrus and apricot. Palate adds lively pineapple and green herbs with a unique, exciting acid texture.
San Diego County Island of Souls 2020 ◎ 145 cs; $ 26 - 🍶 - The nose is peach, honey and green olive. A blend of grenache blanc, picpoul and vermentino, 30 day skin contact has imparted palate weight and a well-developed honied richness of peach and ginger.
San Diego County Rancho Guejito Vineyard Coucou Counoise 2019 ● 350 cs; $ 18 - ⊞ - Light bodied glou glou with enough ripeness to happily chill. Lots of earthy strawberry and cedar flavor, dry strawberry and cut herbs on the nose.

---

acres 0 - **cases** 3,500
Fertilizers compost
Plant protection sulfur
Weed control mechanical
Yeasts spontaneous fermentation
Grapes purchase 100%
Certification some of the vineyards are certified organic

HEALDSBURG

JOLIE-LAIDE WINES 🍾

202 Haydon Street – tel. (707) 501-7664
www. jolielaidewines.com – info@jolielaidewines.com

PEOPLE - Scott and Jenny Schultz's indie winery is celebrated for its love of whole cluster, foot stomped winemaking and for off beat varietals. Scott, a former restaurant wine guy (Bouchon), worked with Pax Mahle, while Jenny has a degree in winemaking from U.C. Davis. The couple produce 20+ wines each year–including novel Melon de Bourgogne, Gamay, and Trousseau Noir. Their hallmark: each wine is made from whole clusters, and each is foot trod.

VINEYARDS - The winery buys grapes from across the state. Clairette Blanche comes from Martian Ranch in Los Alamos in Santa Barbara County. Winemakers wait in line to get Gamay from Barsotti Vineyard in El Dorado, at 2,800 feet of elevation, where the vines sit on weathered and decomposed granite. A rare Cabernet Pfeffer–only 12 acres planted in the state–comes from the Enz Vinyerd in Lime Kiln Valley in San Benito County.

WINES - The house style often involves partial carbonic maceration, keeping aromatics high but tannins low, with texture coming from whole cluster fermentations.

🔵 **Los Alamos Clairette Blanche 2020** ○ n/a; $ 30 - 🍶 ⓐ - Bright and lively from Tablas clones imported from France: bursts of fruit–nectarines and lemons–beautifully balanced with acidity.
El Dorado County Barsoti Vineyards Gamay Noir 2020 ● n/a; $ 35 - 🍽 - Delicate plum aromatics get the party started on this fresh wine; then fragrant herbs, charming strawberry and cranberry notes kick in.
California Trousseau Noir-Cabernet Pfeffer-Gamay 2020 ● n/a; $ 34 - 🍽 - A crazy rock star combo that delivers Pinot Noir like lightness (Trousseau Noir) with slightly peppery notes (from the Cabernet Pfeffer), making it an utterly unique original–just what Jolie-Laide is going for. Fermented partially carbonic.

LOS OLIVOS

THE JOY FANTASTIC HOLUS BOLUS 🍾

2902 San Marcos Street, Unit B – tel. (805) 637-1005
www.thejoyfantastic.com – peter@thejoyfantastic.com

PEOPLE - Amy Christine and Peter Hunken met in 2004 when Peter assisted Sashi Moorman at Stolpman Vineyards and Amy was a sommelier at the legendary A.O.C. in Los Angeles. Not only did they get along but they quickly started making wine together. In 2016, wines were first released from Joy Fantastic, their estate vineyard which takes its name and inspiration from Prince. Christine is a Master of Wine while also working for Kermit Lynch Wine Merchant.

VINEYARDS - The couple's mission is to make classic wines from classic regions. This means pinot noir, chardonnay and syrah from the Sta Rita Hills and Santa Maria Valley. The Joy Fantastic's 5 acres sit on a south-facing slope in the far western reaches of the Sta Rita Hills AVA and is certified organic. Holus wines come from three additional vineyards, Bien Nacido and Presqu'il in the Santa Maria Valley and John Sebastiano on the eastern end of the Santa Rita Hills.

WINES - The philosophy is that cool weather and depleted soils = elegant varietal expression. Holus Bolus is the couple's 'negociant' brand.

🔵 **Sta. Rita Hills Holus Bolus Syrah 2019** SLOW WINE ● 200 cs; $ 35 - 🍽 - Shows effusive blackberry, olive and meaty aromas with fresh and dried black fruits flavors.
Santa Maria Valley Holus Bolus Syrah 2019 ● n/a; $ 40 - 🍽 - Built for aging with prominent tannins and wild peppery aromas. Palate shows potent red fruit with a bacon note.
Sta. Rita Hills The Joy Fantastic Estate Chardonnay 2019 ○ 130 cs; $ 50 - 🍽 - Elegant and focused with classic honeysuckle, yellow apple and a pretty, coniferous note. On the palate, it shows density and texture with lime rind, lemon curd and apple.

---

acres 0 - **cases** 4,000
Fertilizers n/a
Plant protection n/a
Weed control n/a
Yeasts spontaneous fermentation
Grapes purchase 100%
Certification some of the vineyards are certified organic

acres 5 - **cases** 700
Fertilizers compost, manure
Plant protection organic, sulfur
Weed control mechanical
Yeasts spontaneous fermentation
Grapes purchase 60%
Certification some of the vineyards are certified organic

CALISTOGA

KELLY FLEMING WINES

2339 Pickett Road – tel. (707) 942-6849
www.kellyflemingwines.com
welcome@kellyflemingwines.com

PEOPLE - In 2002 former restaurateur Kelly Fleming purchased a sustainably farmed hillside estate in Calistoga, and in 2010 added a stone winery. Her winemaker since 2013, UC Davis trained Rebecca George has experience at Domaine Meo Camuzet in Burgundy, in Australia, and locally at Marcassin, Williams Selyem and Schramsberg. Mike Wolf Vineyard Management has been with the winery since 2012 and Lili Shariati is Director of Sales & Marketing.

VINEYARDS - Located in Calistoga near Eisele Vineyard, the Simmons Canyon estate is tucked into a lateral canyon. Vineyards are planted exclusively to Cabernet Sauvignon. Block 1 was planted in 1999 on deep gravelly loam and is the core of Big Pour. Malbec from Chiles Valley and Syrah from the Farella Vineyard round out the blend. Block 3 and 4 were planted further into the canyon in 2005, where greater air flow and fewer light hours provide relief to the mid-day heat.

WINES - The wines showcase the sheer power and richness of happy Cabernet Sauvignon, lounging in the hot sun, with no ripening restraints whatsoever.

TOP **Napa Valley Estate Cabernet Sauvignon 2018** ●
1,072 cs; $ 165 - ⊞ - Very rich, intense, powerful and chewy with notes of mulberry, cassis, pancetta, soy sauce, cedar and cinnamon.
Napa Valley Big Pour 2018 ● Cabernet Sauvignon, Syrah, Malbec; 436 cs; $ 90 - ⊞ - Rich, bold, powerful and gripping with notes of cassis, fig, mushroom tar, vanilla and mocha.

acres 11 - cases 2,000
Fertilizers compost, mineral fertilizer
Plant protection sulfur, synthetic pesticides
Weed control chemical, mechanical
Yeasts commercial cultured yeasts
Grapes purchase 20%
Certification none

LOMPOC

KINGS CAREY WINES

1225 W Laurel Avenue – tel. (805) 680-7006
www.kingscarey.com – james@kingscarey.com

PEOPLE - James Sparks and Anna Ferguson-Sparks unveiled their micro-label, Kings Carey, in 2014 after some amazing Grenache grapes fell into their laps. The opportunity to produce this small-batch, single varietal wine launched a vision of showcasing fruit by doing as little as possible. Sparks is quick to say that wine is really about the vineyard, and that his job is to just strive for balance by picking at the right time.

VINEYARDS - As winemaker at Liquid Farm, Sparks uses preexisting relationships with vineyards and managers. He says that he has decided to work only with vineyards practicing organic farming methods. The goal is to utilize the Kings Carey label as a way to profile a lot of different varieties, to play around and experiment. Chardonnay comes from a terraced, old-vine vineyard that has been around since the 1800's. The Grenache vines are certified organic.

WINES - The approach is being patient and letting the fruit shine through with low intervention to achieve balance between freshness and ageability.

TOP **Sta. Rita Hills Spear Vineyard Grenache 2018** ●
140 cs; $ 38 - ⊞ - Unfiltered. Beautiful ruby color, light and bright in style with elegant, savory, herbal notes.
Cienega Valley Eden Rift Vineyard Chardonnay 2020 ○ 112 cs; $ 38 - ⊞ - The Gavilan mountain range foothills produce a super bright, clean and citrusy wine. Sparks employs neutral barrel aging and native yeasts, which leads to a leaner style Chardonnay, with some spice and minerality. "My goal is to not manipulate and just let it evolve," he explains.
Alisos Canyon Clos Mullet Cabernet Franc 2020 ●
112 cs; $ 34 - ⊞ - Made in a Loire style (harvested early, aged in neutral barrel). The tiny berries were intentionally foot stomped five times. It's a wild wine, with spice, peppercorns and lovely tannins and a deep purple ruby hue.

acres 0 - cases 350
Fertilizers compost, manure
Plant protection organic, sulfur
Weed control none
Yeasts spontaneous fermentation
Grapes purchase 100%
Certification some of the vineyards are certified organic

SOMERSET

LA CLARINE FARM

7721 Snowbird Lane – tel. (530) 306-3608
www.laclarinefarm.com – laclarinefarm@gmail.com

PEOPLE - Hank Beckmeyer makes wine in his miniscule facility in the hinterlands of El Dorado County. His goal is simply to make delicious wine. Though his philosophy is minimalist, he considers the winemaking effort a critical part of 'terroir' and the theoretically infinite number of choices in getting the grape into the bottle like a quantum field, always different according to perspective. This approach, Beckmeyer feels, allows experiments to occur each season.

VINEYARDS - Beckmeyer sources all of his grapes from nearby growers who execute his requests for non-chemical farming. The oak terrain and the pine environments at higher elevations which help constitute the vineyard topsoils are a distinct characteristic in La Clarine wines. From the organic Rorick Heritage Vineyard in Calaveras County, limestone soils are used as a lens for beautifully pure chardonnay.

WINES - Beckmeyer has his grapes picked on the early side which inclines his wines to a tart freshness with low alcohol. Inherent in his approach is the observation that wine tends to make itself if allowed to.

Sierra Foothills Chardonnay 2019 EVERYDAY WINE ○ 150 cs; $ 26 - Shows white flower, and a dairy tang on the nose with peach and apple on the palate moving to a crystalline minerality.
Sierra Foothills Cabernet Franc 2020 EVERYDAY WINE ● 105 cs; $ 26 - Brings florality, spice, herbaceousness and tart, dark cherry cola into one lifted package.
Sierra Foothills Angle of Repose Grenache/Tannat 2020 120 cs; $ 24 - Displays earth, dried rose and strawberry aromas and an herbal, strawberry/blackberry palate with youthful tannins.

ORCUTT

LAND OF SAINTS WINE COMPANY $

9550 San Antonio Road – tel. (805) 350-9638
www.loswines.com – info@loswines.com

PEOPLE - The Saints are the many Sans and Santas one finds in California as well as those from Cornwall England from where Jason, Angela Osborne's husband hails. Add Miguel Cuevas and you have the L O S team, with Cuevas assuming winemaking duties based at C2 Cellars, his crush facility. Land of Saints' first commission was supplying Norway's Vinmonopolet which continues to buy 40% of L O S output.

VINEYARDS - Being the owner of a crush facility, Manuel gives L O S the ability to establish relationships with clients which can also be leveraged in purchasing grapes. The vineyards sourced range from the Santa Barbara Highlands, a quite large high elevation vineyard, to small family vineyards who practice meticulous farming. Chris King's name comes up repeatedly with regard to L O S vineyard sources. He is a local vineyard manager associated with many organic farming projects, most notably Domaine de la Côte.

WINES - The concept is to produce region-specific, varietal wines from grape lots of high quality and moderate cost.

Santa Barbara County Sauvignon Blanc 2019 EVERYDAY WINE ○ 366 cs; $ 18 - Displays a serene nose of white flower, red apple and pear while on the tongue emerge assertive lemon and pineapple flavors.
Santa Barbara County Grenache Nouveau 2020 EVERYDAY WINE ● 200 cs; $ 20 - A revelation with a heady aroma of purple flowers and red currant and a rambunctious texture showing strawberry and loam flavors. Full carbonic maceration is used.
Central Coast Pinot Noir 2020 ● 1,300 cs; $ 22 - Shows red cherries and herbs on the nose with its flavors displaying a distinct earthiness and a maraschino note.

---

acres 0 - **cases** 2,000
Fertilizers compost
Plant protection copper, organic, sulfur
Weed control mechanical
Yeasts spontaneous fermentation
Grapes purchase 100%
Certification none

acres 0 - **cases** 8,300
Fertilizers compost, mineral fertilizer, organic-mineral
Plant protection copper, organic, sulfur, synthetic pesticides
Weed control mechanical
Yeasts spontaneous fermentation
Grapes purchase 100%
Certification none

CALISTOGA

LARKMEAD VINEYARDS

1100 Larkmead Lane – tel. (707) 942-0167
www.larkmead.com – reservations@larkmead.com

 A storied winery dedicated to fine winemaking, organic farming and a leader in on the ground climate research on its own estate.

PEOPLE - At an historic and iconic Napa winery, owners Cam and Kate Solari are converting to organics, culturing estate native yeasts for winemaking and establishing a research block of grapes for the warming future. This year winemaker Avery Heelan succeeded outgoing Dan Petroski. Her meteoric rise included stints in Western Australia, Meursault and at Screaming Eagle.

VINEYARDS - The estate sits in the narrow part of Napa Valley between the Mayacamas and Vaca mountain ranges in Calistoga, where soils are made of deposits from both ranges. The results is both gravelly soils (ideal for Cabernet Sauvignon) as well as clay soils (excellent for Merlot and Cabernet Franc). Compost is nutrient-fortified. Nabor Camarena leads the full time vineyard crew, with Kelly Maher as consultant.

WINES - Heelan continues with the visionary programs started by Petroski and the Solari's. Larkmead wines are remarkable for their freshness, their earthiness and the thorough culinary integration of their tannins. Aromas of bay, olive, smoke and hay are common to each wine.

Napa Valley Solari 2018 ● 700 cs; $ 200 - A powerful single block Cabernet Sauvignon with amaro aromas and a black raspberry and cassis palate.
Napa Valley Cabernet Sauvignon 2018 ● 1,200 cs; $ 125 - Shows a meaty, graphite nose with cranberry and blackberry fruit.
Napa Valley Firebelle 2018 ● 550 cs; $ 100 - A Merlot based blend that shows dried blue and red fruit with cocoa aromas while cherry and dried orange combine with gentian on the palate.

acres 110 - **cases** 5,050
Fertilizers compost
Plant protection organic, sulfur
Weed control mechanical
Yeasts selected indigenous yeasts
Grapes 100% estate-grown
Certification converting to organics

GLEN ELLEN

LASSETER FAMILY WINERY

1 Vintage Lane – tel. (707) 933-2800
www.lasseterfamilywinery.com

 The Lasseter Winery exemplifies the Slow Food Guide values: interpreting the sensory perceptions, territory, environment and identity in its wines.

PEOPLE - During their travels through the wine growing regions of France, John and Nancy Lasseter fell in love with the wines of the Southern Rhône and Bordeaux, and the art of blending, which became the template for Lasseter Family Winery's wines.

VINEYARDS - Rhône and Bordeaux varieties lead the way, on its 58 acres of certified organic vineyards, primarily in Sonoma Valley. The old vine Zinfandel block in Justi Creek Vineyard, has vines dating back to 1919, including rare varieties in a field blend. Striking single-varietal wines have also emerged from its newest vineyard atop the rugged, rocky, high elevation Trinity Ridge Vineyard on Moon Mountain.

WINES - The initial wines were a softer style, and over time, winemaking has evolved to focus more on increased depth, concentration, and structure.

Sonoma Valley Voilà White Bordeaux Blend 2019 ○ Sauvignon Blanc, Sémillon; 400 cs; $ 44 - Inspired by the wines of Southern Bordeaux region of Graves, this elegant blend reveals layers of ripe fruit, fig, spice with touches of vanilla.
Sonoma Valley Chemin de Fer Rhone Blend 2018 ● Grenache, Mourvèdre, Syrah; 280 cs; $ 56 - A small lot Rhone-inspired Grenache blend is complex with fruit forward notes of raspberry and spice, bursts of black fruit tamed by a lush soft finish.
Moon Mountain District Trinity Ridge Vineyard Cabernet Sauvignon 2017 ● 200 cs; $ 150 - The first vintage from Moon Mountain AVA, the small lot Trinity Ridge 100% Cabernet Sauvignon has pronounced black cherry, herbes de Provence and black olive notes giving way to rich black fruit with minerality and balanced tannins.

acres 58 - **cases** 5,000
Fertilizers compost, cover crops
Plant protection organic, sulfur
Weed control mechanical
Yeasts commercial cultured yeasts, selected indigenous yeasts, spontaneous fermentation
Grapes 100% estate-grown
Certification organic

GLEN ELLEN

LAUREL GLEN VINEYARD

13750 Arnold Drive – tel. (707) 933-9877
www.laurelglen.com – eric@laurelglenvineyard.com

PEOPLE - Celebrating 40 years, this iconic Sonoma Mountain winery was founded by Patrick Campbell in 1981. The land was originally planted to mixed agriculture in the late 19th century, replanted to grape vines in 1968 and expanded in 1977. General Manager and Partner Bettina Sichel has owned the estate since 2011. Her viticulturalist is Phil Coturri, who spearheaded and earned the 2014 CCOF Organic certification, and the winemaker is Randall Watkins.

VINEYARDS - This 14-acre organically farmed Sonoma Mountaintop estate sits 1,000 feet up from the valley floor is blocked from the Petaluma Gap to its east. The high altitude, eastern exposure and rocky soils provide favorable conditions for Cabernet Sauvignon, the exclusive planting. Biodiversity is a priority, with cycling cover crops, IPM and minimal outputs.

WINES - Considered one of California's iconic Cabernet Sauvignon producers, the small range of Cabernet Sauvignons are both elegant and powerful, showing their mountain heritage in concentration and structure.

(TOP) **Sonoma Mountain Lot 48 Cabernet Sauvignon 2016** ● 145 cs; $ 150 - ⊞ - Powerful, gripping, intense and dry with notes of cassis, tobacco, blood sausage, mushroom and bay leaf.
Sonoma Mountain Estate Cabernet Sauvignon 2017 ● 660 cs; $ 90 - ⊞ - This flagship wine is full-bodied and muscular, with grip and intensity and notes of cassis, black cherry, sage, turned earth and leather.
Sonoma Mountain Counterpoint Cabernet Sauvignon 2018 ● 1,550 cs; $ 55 - ⊞ - Rich and moderately chewy with notes of cherry, cassis, fennel seed, oregano, tobacco and vanilla bean.

acres 15 - cases 2,320
Fertilizers green manure, organic-mineral
Plant protection organic, sulfur
Weed control mechanical
Yeasts selected indigenous yeasts
Grapes purchase 29%
Certification some of the vineyards are certified organic

APTOS

LESTER ESTATE WINES

2000 Pleasant Valley Road – tel. (831) 728-3793
www.lesterestatewines.com – info@lesterestatewines.com

PEOPLE - In 1988, Dan and Patty Lester purchased the 200-acre Deer Park Ranch in Corralitos. Since 1998, Santa Cruz Mountains viticultural consultant Prudy Foxx manages the Lester Estate vineyard. After Dan's passing in 2014, the Lesters' daughter Lori Lester Johnson and her husband Steve Johnson developed a unique approach: to produce wines from the single vineyard for the Lester Estate Wines label made by some of the top winemakers in the region.

VINEYARDS - At 15 acres, the Lester Family vineyard is planted to Chardonnay, Syrah, and 8 different clones of Pinot Noir. The vineyard enjoys an excellent reputation for premium grapes, 75% of which are sold to other wineries. The gentle-sloping vineyard faces southwest on an ancient seabed and alluvial fans with diverse terroir. Prudy Foxx relies on organic and traditional practices to support and promote vineyard health.

WINES - John Benedetti, Ed Kurtzman, Joe Miller, Ian Brand all make wines for Lester Estate Wines using different clones and winemaking styles.

(TOP) **Santa Cruz Mountains Domingo Pinot Noir 2018** ● 135 cs; $ 55 - ⊞ - Made by Ed Kurtzman using clones Mt Edan, Swan, 667, and 777, this wine has a classic Pinot nose with raspberry, rose petal, forest floor, sweet tobacco, and brown spice.
Santa Cruz Mountains Mercurio Estate Pinot Noir 2018 ● 118 cs; $ 55 - ⊞ - John Benedetti makes Mercurio, a bolder, earthier Pinot expression from Mt Eden clones with 10 months lees contact in French and Chilean oak.
Santa Cruz Mountains Estate Chardonnay 2019 ○ n/a; $ 37 - ⊞ - Smooth and round, the wine presents pineapple, lemon, crème brulée, yuzu, and sandalwood along with judicious French oak notes, bright acidity, and long finish.

acres 15 - cases 978
Fertilizers compost, cover crops, humus, manure, mineral fertilizer, organic-mineral
Plant protection copper, organic, synthetic pesticides
Weed control mechanical
Yeasts commercial cultured yeasts, spontaneous fermentation
Grapes 100% estate-grown
Certification none

LICHEN ESTATE

LINDQUIST FAMILY WINES

11001 County Road 151 – tel. (707) 895-7949
www.lichenestate.com – info@lichenestate.com

130 West Branch Street – tel. (805) 270-4900
www.verdadwine.com – treeva@lindquistwine.com

PEOPLE - Douglas Stewart founded his first winery, Breggo, in 2005, achieving top marks from prominent wine critics for his Pinot Gris. He then moved into sparkling wines with the help of former Roederer Estate winemaker Michel Salgues. After selling Breggo, Stewart purchased 203 acres in Anderson Valley, planting his estate vineyard in 2008. Here at Lichen, Stewart's passion for making Pinot Gris and Pinot Noir – in as many combinations as possible – has found an ideal home.

PEOPLE - Bob Lindquist is a pioneer of the southern Central Coast. His trail-blazing brand, Qupé, helped put syrah on the wine map in the 1980s. Prior to covid, 65% of Lindquist Family sales were to restaurants, so there has been a scramble to pivot to retail sales. As of March 2020, some grape contracts were re-negotiated, temporarily delaying plans to grow the re-invented company which has taken the place of Qupé, with whom he parted ways in 2019.

VINEYARDS - The estate vineyard is beside Highway 128 in Mendocino's Anderson Valley. The soil consists mainly of sand, clay and loam. Lichen Estate grows Pinot Noir and Pinot Gris in the same meter-by-meter spacing as Burgundy and Champagne. Varied clonal and rootstock selections add complexity to the wines. Everything is farmed organically and by hand.

VINEYARDS - The Slide Hill (aka Sawyer Lindquist) Vineyard in Edna Valley is Demeter certified and though they have relinquished ownership, they continue to contract grapes from there. Bien Nacido in the Santa Maria Valley has been a central grape source since Lindquist persuaded the ownership to plant syrah there in the early 1980s. Regional and single block Syrahs as well as Viognier come from there.

WINES - Lichen Estate wines are made with balance and complexity in mind.

● **Anderson Valley Grand Cuvée 2012** ❄ n/a; $ 75
A complex sparkling wine, full on the palate, with good structure, a fine perlage and notes of brioche, lemon, violet, and apple.
Anderson Valley Pinot Gris 2019 ○ 615 cs; $ 29 - ☐ -
A round mouthfeel with flavors of candied lemon rind, ginger, pineapple and a mineral finish.
Anderson Valley Moonglow Pinot Noir 2019 ● 995 cs; $ 39 - ⊞ - Fresh fruit flavors of black cherry and blood orange, spices, and a vibrant acidity accompanied by light pleasing tannins.

WINES - Lindquist wines are known for exuberant fruit profiles.

● **Santa Maria Valley Bien Nacido Vineyard Z Block Syrah 2019** ● 72 cs; $ 60 - ⊞ - The quintessence of Central Coast syrah with its deep, earthy dark fruit beneath aromas of blackberry liqueur, smoke and black pepper. Finely knit tannins provide an elegant texture.
Edna Valley Marsanne 2019 ○ 96 cs; $ 38 - ⊞ - Has an inviting, musky nose of pear and green almond. On the palate is pear skin texture with peach and red apple.
Central Coast Viognier-Chardonnay 2020 ○ 200 cs; $ 28 - ☐ - Displays peach and citrus blossom aromas while showing hedonistic flavors of peach and pear pastry countered with a touch of bitterness.

acres 7 - **cases** 2,750
Fertilizers n/a
Plant protection copper, sulfur
Weed control mechanical
Yeasts commercial cultured yeasts, spontaneous fermentation
Grapes 100% estate-grown
Certification none

acres 0 - **cases** 2,000
Fertilizers compost, organic-mineral
Plant protection biodynamic preparations, organic
Weed control mechanical
Yeasts commercial cultured yeasts, spontaneous fermentation
Grapes purchase 100%
Certification organic, some of the vineyards are certified biodynamic

SEBASTOPOL

LITTORAI WINES

788 Gold Ridge Road – tel. (707) 823-9586
www.littorai.com – info@littorai.com

PEOPLE - Famous for their Pinot Noir, winemakers Heidi and Ted Lemon searched for months in 1992 for the best place to grow Pinot Noir and Chardonnay. Settling into the coastal hills of Sonoma County they began Littorai with purchased grapes. In 2003 they purchased a 30 acre estate atop Goldridge where they grow 3 acres of Pinot Noir using biodynamic and permaculture methods. They've built a solar, straw bale winery and constructed wetlands where plants recycle the winery water for irrigation.

VINEYARDS - Littorai sources from 12 prime vineyards (all farmed organically) in coastal regions and Anderson Valley. Littorai's estate, Pivot Vineyard, has Goldridge soils. Roman Vineyard (elevation: 1,150 feet), in Anderson Valley, a site cooled by coastal influences and grounded in sandstone soils sources Pinot Noir. B.A.Thieriot, (elevation: 900) grows Pinot Noir and Chardonnay on Goldridge loam and sandstone soils.

WINES - Committed to making wines of place, reflecting the authenticity of a site, comes through in Lemon's sought after Pinot Noir and Chardonnay.

Sonoma Coast The Pivot Vineyard Pinot Noir 2018 ● 515 cs; $ 90 - ▦ - Restrained dark red fruits, red apple, crunchy fresh leaves with lively acidity balances the richness and generous tannins. This structured wine could age for years, or enjoy now.
Anderson Valley Roman Vineyard Pinot Noir 2018 ● 210 cs; $ 95 - ▦ - Aromatic of dusty roses and juicy blackberry with a hint of orange peel. Delicate yet strong and present as good tannin density presents a long finish.
Sonoma Coast Thieriot Vineyard Pinot Noir 2018 ● 95 cs; $ 95 - ▦ - Candied notes of black and blue fruits, coffee bean, black pepper.

---

acres 6 - cases 6,000
Fertilizers biodynamic compost, compost, green manure, organic-mineral
Plant protection biodynamic preparations, organic, sulfur
Weed control mechanical
Yeasts spontaneous fermentation
Grapes purchase 50%
Certification some of the vineyards are certified biodynamic

LOS ALAMOS

LO-FI WINES $

448 Bell Street – tel. (805) 344-0179
www.lofi-wines.com – questions@lofi-wines.com

PEOPLE - Since 2014, Mike Roth and Craig Winchester have established Lo-Fi as a high quality, adventurous and egalitarian winery with attractive price points for the same reason that its specialties, chenin, gamay and cab franc are bargains in the Loire. So, when covid shutdowns occurred, they found consistent sales from their wine club and their distributors who devised some innovative sales incentives to compensate for the drop off in restaurant buyers. Their analogue, retro aesthetic fits perfectly with their brand.

VINEYARDS - Roth also makes the wine at Cocliquot Wines in Santa Ynez, whose organic home vineyard is a major source for Lo-Fi and qualifies as 'estate' along with Roth's own vineyard 'Clos Mullet' in Los Alamos. Grapes from these vineyards constitute 75% of Lo-Fi output. Other grapes are sourced from the organic Spear Vineyard in Sta Rita Hills, Oak Savannah in Santa Ynez and Tres Hermanos in Santa Maria Valley.

WINES - Roth has worked at a number of wineries in the region and has long-standing relationships with the growers he buys from, chosen in part, for their avoidance of synthetic inputs in their farming.

Santa Barbara County Clos Mullet Cabernet Franc 2020 SLOW WINE ● 388 cs; $ 32 - ▦ - Deeply savory with notes of asphalt beneath lively dark cherry aromas. The palate shows herbal amaro and salty minerals.
Santa Barbara County Gamay Noir 2020 EVERYDAY WINE ● 227 cs; $ 26 - ▦ - Made with carbonic maceration is redolent of almond and orange peel with an earthy cherry palate.
Santa Barbara County Sauvignon Blanc/Chardonnay 2020 ○ 245 cs; $ 28 - ▯ - With fourteen days on skins, produces a full-bodied wine, broad on the palate with tree fruit flavors and piney, spicy aromas.

---

acres 21 - cases 5,000
Fertilizers compost
Plant protection copper, organic, sulfur
Weed control mechanical
Yeasts spontaneous fermentation
Grapes purchase 25%
Certification some of the vineyards are certified organic

LOS ANGELES RIVER WINE CO.

4185 East Third Avenue
www.scholiumwines.com

PEOPLE - L.A. River Wine Company was conceived to be a hybrid facility; a winery and a tasting room that showcased grapes from southern California made in Abe Schoener's idiocyncratic style. Covid prevented this from taking place. The plan B was staying lean and mean as an operation by making the wines in rented warehouses and parking lots with rapid response teams of pickers and processors. Schoener shows that with basic tools and technology, compelling wines can be made.

VINEYARDS - L.A. River Wine Co. wines are mostly sourced from old and sometimes formerly neglected desert vineyards between Rancho Cucamonga and Temecula east of Los Angeles. The significance of these vineyards lies in their age and their survival. Grapes such as mission and palomino were planted many decades ago in the production of mostly fortified wine.

WINES - Today, Schoener makes table wines from these vines while accounting for the special requirements of the tannic mission or the low-acid palomino. Pecorino is sourced from a younger-vines vineyard. All fruit is foot treaded. No pumps are used. Pressing is generally in a manual press.

California Maglite Blanc 2020 ○ 9 cs; $ 100 - A Blanc de noir white wine made from grenache and rose of peru. The wine displays a curry nose which follows to a palate of tart fresh lemon and yellow apple. The depth of fruit is remarkable.
California Rancho California Flor 2019 ○ 13 cs; $ 50 - A pecorino made in a modified sherry style with fino and hazelnut aromatics and rich apple/pear fruit. Acidity and skin tannins make for a sizzling texture.
California Munoa Lone Wolf Red, 2020 ● 62 cs; $ 75 - Smells and tastes like an apple orchard, though on the palate more berry complexity is apparent, as well as an irony mineral presence.

acres 0 - cases 600
Fertilizers n/a
Plant protection n/a
Weed control n/a
Yeasts spontaneous fermentation
Grapes purchase 100%
Certification none

LOS PILARES $

1477 University Avenue – tel. (619) 709-0664
www.lospilareswine.com – michael@lospilareswine.com

PEOPLE - Los Pilares grew out of the friendship of wine lovers Michael Christian and Coleman Cooney who had spent extended time in France and Spain, respectively. Encouraged by early experiments with a home vineyard, they went commercial in 2010. What Europe taught them was that good wine expressed a sense of place- what they sought to bring out in San Diego County by simplifying fruit extraction in their winemaking. They repeatedly come back to muscat and grenache, though a newly planted vineyard with warm weather varieties is about to come on-line.

VINEYARDS - Los Pilares grapes come from McCormick Ranch in Pauma Valley as well as Highland Hills Vineyards and the Hunter and Mazzetti Vineyard on the Rincon Indian Reservation. Soils are mostly granite and clay. Coastal influence and elevation make for cool nights. Farming is done without chemical inputs.

WINES - The sparkling wine is crushed whole cluster while the red wine is left partly uncrushed accessing some carbonic effects.

San Diego County Grenache 2020 EVERYDAY WINE ●
105 cs; $ 23 - A screaming deal for a serious wine, showing red and dark cherry fruit, a full but effortless mid-palate and heady aromas of berries/cherries and violets.
San Diego County La Dona Sparkling Muscat 2019 EVERYDAY WINE 150 cs; $ 25 - In pet nat style, has citrus blossom, subtle spice and a fermented tang on the nose. The palate is broad with peach, pear, and a celery note. Fun and interesting.
San Diego County Nokoa Falanghina 2020 ○ 150 cs; $ 22 - Has a sweet, fermenty nose of ginger and yellow flower with a concentrated palate of pear, lemon and orange pulp.

acres 0 - cases 350
Fertilizers compost
Plant protection organic, sulfur
Weed control mechanical
Yeasts spontaneous fermentation
Grapes purchase 100%
Certification none

CAMINO

MADROÑA $

2560 High Hill Road – tel. (530) 644-5948
www.madronavineyards.com – winery@madronavineyards.com

PEOPLE - Dick Bush worked as a metallurgical engineer and his wife taught school, but starting in 1973, the family planted own-rooted vines on 32 acres surrounded by a diverse ecosystem including madrones. The winery followed in 1979. Paul Bush took over from his dad, and with wife Maggie, they grow organic grapes, make wine, and maintain the family values of environment, community, and education.

VINEYARDS - Located at 3000' elevation in the Sierra foothills above Placerville, Madroña Vineyards is in the heart of Gold Country where the 2021 vintage was disrupted by the Caldor fire. From the original 32 acres, Madrona added 250 in 1993, with 35 in vine, and the rest woodland, with 10 more acres of vines in 2001. Three vineyard sites provide various soils with over 26 varietals including Nebbiolo, Barbera, Cabernet Franc, Grenache, Syrah, Zinfandel, Riesling, Chenin Blanc, Gewürztraminer.

WINES - Madroña Vineyards makes remarkably affordable, high quality wines with acidity, elegance, and grace for three labels: Madrona, Rucksack, and M-Series which limits alcohols to 12.6 ABV. Yeast type depends on the grape and the vintage.

El Dorado County Signature Cabernet Franc 2017 ● 407 cs; $ 26 - 🍷 - With a strong backbone of tannin, texture, and tart cherry, the wine offers elegance, balance, and a dusty blackberry finish.
El Dorado Nebbiolo 2017 ● 372 cs; $ 26 - 🍷 - Planted in 1997, the wine's exotic aromas include violets, earth, spices, and raspberry, which is delivered on the palate along with pine, plum, and plenty of tannins.
El Dorado Signature Zinfandel 2016 ● 235 cs; $ 26 - 🍷 - A blend of two vineyards each located at 3,000', this expressive Zinfandel offers cool-climate tannins, and a complex balance of Sierra Spice, black pepper, bold fresh berry, tart cherry, plus violets and roses.

WATSONVILLE

MADSON WINES 🍾

153 Las Colinas Drive – tel. (831) 345-9834
www.madsonwines.com – info@madsonwines.com

PEOPLE - Madson Wines, located in the Corralitos area of the Santa Cruz Mountains AVA, was founded in 2016. The team consists of Cole Thomas, founder and winemaker, and Ken Swegles and Abbey Chrystal—viticulturists, partners, and Santa Cruz wine community "power couple.". Before his career in wine, Cole was an organic vegetable farmer and manager of the Demeter Seed Library. He found his passion in wine while working for Jeff Emery of Santa Cruz Mountain Vineyard. Ken and Abbey live on and farm the Ascona vineyard.

VINEYARDS - Madson Wines leases vineyards where they farm or consult directly with local Santa Cruz Mountain growers. Most of the vineyards are in the Santa Cruz Mountains (Ascona, Toyon, Arey, Legan, Red Tail, Hawk's Feather), and all of them have been converted to 100% organic farming practices. Regenerative agricultural farming practices are also employed.

WINES - A leader in the natural wine movement in the Santa Cruz Mountains, Madson Wines uses all native yeasts, no fining or filtration, neutral oak, and mostly 100% whole cluster. The wines are clean and fresh.

[TOP] Santa Cruz Mountains Toyon Vineyard Chardonnay 2019 ○ 75 cs; $ 40 - 🍷 - From a 3-acre vineyard grazed by sheep, this Chardonnay is balanced with refreshing acidity, bright citrus, apple, pineapple, ginger, white flowers, and vanilla cream notes.
Santa Cruz Mountains Pinot Noir 2019 ● 75 cs; $ 32 - 🍷 - Showcasing the cool coastal Santa Cruz Mountains terroir, the wine offers fresh raspberry, tart cherry, blood orange, spicy cinnamon, earth, and wet stone.
Santa Cruz Mountains Red Tail Vineyard Syrah 2020 ● 50 cs; $ 32 - 🍷 - Coming from a 2100-foot vineyard above the, this elegant Syrah presents notes of black fruit, meat, white pepper, mint, dark chocolate, and lilac.

---

acres 175 - **cases** 10,000
Fertilizers compost, mineral fertilizer
Plant protection sulfur
Weed control mechanical
Yeasts n/a
Grapes 100% estate-grown
Certification none

---

acres 0 - **cases** 1,500
Fertilizers compost, green manure, organic-mineral
Plant protection organic, sulfur
Weed control mechanical
Yeasts spontaneous fermentation
Grapes purchase 100%
Certification none

PASO ROBLES

MAHA | VILLA CREEK 🍾

5995 Peachy Canyon Road – tel. (805) 712-8038
www.villacreek.com – info@mahaestatewine.com

PEOPLE - Cris and JoAnn Cherry met in college, fell in love years later, and married at Cris's family's Villa Creek Ranch near Cayucas. Drawn to Paso Robles, they opened Villa Creek restaurant there and began making wine under the Villa Creek name, buying grapes from local growers. In 2004 they purchased a vineyard, naming it MAHA, and planted their own biodynamic vines, making wine in their own winery on site.

VINEYARDS - They appreciated the philosophy of biodynamics, but it was the quality of the grapes that won them over. With marine influence, high elevation, and steep hillsides of calcareous soils which reduce the need for irrigation, In 2012, they planted their first block of Grenache, followed by other Rhone varietals all surrounded by oak forests. Already Demeter certified biodynamic, they are currently pursuing regenerative organic certification.

WINES - Cris Cherry makes wines with minimal sulfur use and native yeasts.

🔵 **Paso Robles Before Anyone Else 2019** SLOW WINE ⚪ Clairette Blanche; 56 cs; $ 98 - 🔲 - This stunningly beautiful wine has complex aromas of gardenia, guava, and butterscotch, a visceral slickness that envelopes the palate, and lemon and butterscotch pudding with toast on the back palate.
Paso Robles Understory 2018 ● Grenache, Carignan, Mourvèdre; 60 cs; $ 98 - 🔲 - Densely plum in color, this complex wine has aromas of roses, carnations, baking spice, plum, raspberry, rhubarb, sarsaparilla with even more complexity on the palate including hibiscus and tart cherry.
Paso Robles Backlit 2018 ● Petite Sirah, Mourvèdre, Grenache, Carignan; 125 cs; $ 98 - 🔲 - An inky purple greets the eye with aromas of blueberry cobbler and a palate of black licorice and fresh raspberry, blueberry, and rhubarb.

---

acres 13 - **cases** 3,000
Fertilizers biodynamic compost, compost, cover crops
Plant protection biodynamic preparations, sulfur
Weed control mechanical
Yeasts spontaneous fermentation
Grapes purchase 60%
Certification some of the vineyards are certified organic, some of the vineyards are certified biodynamic

---

BERKELEY

MÂITRE DE CHAI 🍾

2315 4th Street – tel. (510) 616-1503
mdc.wine – info@mdc.wine

PEOPLE - Mâitre de Chai is Marty Winters and Alex Pitts, two friends and former cooks who were drawn into winemaking through Alex's internship with experimentalist Abe Schoener. Their facility is in West Berkeley where they process grapes with the help of Jessica and Stephanie, fiancé and wife, respectively. They have sought out older, preferably dry-farmed vineyards that receive no synthetic inputs. When the two were recruiting growers, these vineyards seemed a windfall as many other producers pursued higher yields and more fashionable varieties.

VINEYARDS - Since the goal at MdC is a wine's expression through its vineyard, nearly all of their wines come from single vineyards. Saini is chosen for chenin blanc; Gala for foresty, fresh Cabernet Sauvignon; Herron Vineyard Sauvignon Blanc is own-rooted old vine in a never tilled vineyard; Massa in Carmel Valley is certified organic and a source for old-vine Cabernet Sauvignon, and so on.

WINES - Winters represents MdC as specializing in white wine and, being happy to play the long game, refers to their chenin blanc as a 'gateway drug' leading younger customers to future pleasures.

🔵 **Napa Gala Vineyard Cabernet Sauvignon 2019** ● 650 cs; $ 49 - 🔲 - The nose displays an herbal overlay to aromas of glazed red and dark fruit. Red cherry and blackberry are inflected with savory leaf and earth flavors.
🔵 **Dry Creek Valley Kierkegaard Vineyard Chenin Blanc 2018** EVERYDAY WINE ⚪ 200 cs; $ 28 - 🔲 - Pays sly tribute to Dane and chenin expert, Leo Hanson. The wine shows pretty aromas of acacia, apple and pear. On the palate is an interplay of apple skin, orchard fruit and green herbs.
Sonoma Mountain Herron Reserve Sauvignon Blanc 2020 ⚪ 100 cs; $ 35 - 🔲 - Consists of ½ normally fermented and ½ skin contact wine which combines reductive and oxidative qualities of bruised apple, nuts and gunflint.

---

acres 0 - **cases** 3,000
Fertilizers compost
Plant protection organic, sulfur
Weed control mechanical
Yeasts spontaneous fermentation
Grapes purchase 100%
Certification some of the vineyards are certified organic

CALIFORNIA

DAVENPORT

MARGINS WINE $

P.O. Box 107 – tel. (925) 413-2654
www.marginswine.com – megan@marginswine.com

PEOPLE - Megan Bell launched her Margins Wine label in 2016 when she was just 25, with pure determination and a bootstrapping, kickstarter campaign to achieve her goal of showcasing wine varietals and vineyard sites that sit on the "margins." Low intervention, additive-free wines are what she produces. Chenin Blanc is Bell's signature wine. She recently expanded into a bigger facility.

VINEYARDS - Bell works with 10 vineyards, all of which she says are practicing organic as of the 2021 vintage. The source of her flagship wine, the Chenin Blanc from a Clarksburg vineyard (just south of Sacramento), is a unique site right on the water, with cool temperatures that produces grapes with high acid. Bell's "estate" site is the Makjavich vineyard in the Santa Cruz Mountains. Cabernet Franc, Merlot and Pinot Noir are grown here.

WINES - In 2020 Bell made a record (for her) 12 wines despite being evacuated from her home for seven weeks during the CZU Lightning Complex wildfire in the Santa Cruz Mountains.

⑩ Clarksburg Wilson Vineyard Chenin Blanc 2020
SLOW WINE ○ 218 cs; $ 26 - ⊞ - Bell's flagship wine, whose owners she nudged to convert to organic farming. Full of spring blossom and creamy lemon curd.

⑩ Santa Clara Valley Sattler's Family Vineyard Mourvèdre 2020 **EVERYDAY WINE** ● 190 cs; $ 28 - ⊞ - Fresh and juicy and ready to drink immediately. Belle buys the entire 2.7 acre lot from this backyard vineyard hot and dry foothill site. Tropical guava and passionfruit explode deliciously with each sip.
San Benito County Calleri Vineyard Négrette 2020 ●
74 cs; $ 30 - ⊞ - Showcases this lesser known, traditional blending grape from southern France. While being a super light wine, at only 11.5%, it is a deep red ruby color and full of fresh violets and a hint of black pepper.

acres 2 - **cases** 2,500
Fertilizers compost, cover crops, n/a, organic
Plant protection n/a, organic, sulfur, synthetic pesticides
Weed control mechanical
Yeasts n/a
Grapes purchase 85%
Certification none

MENDOCINO

MARTHA STOUMEN WINES   🍾

6780 McKinley Street, #170 – tel. (310) 923-1109
www.marthastoumen.com – info@marthastoumen.com

PEOPLE - During college, Martha Stoumen turned her interest in Italy and integrated farming and agriculture into an internship on a Tuscan farm. She came away with an interest in winemaking which prompted a masters at UC Davis which she furthered with internships in Germany, France and at COS in Sicily whose co-founder, Giusto Occhipinti, pestered her to make her own wine. She did so with friends for a few years before starting her own brand based in Sonoma.

VINEYARDS - Stoumen focuses on hot weather grapes from Mendocino: Zinfandel, Carignan, Petite Sirah and particularly, the rarely grown Nero d'Avola. For white grapes, she gets 73 year old, dry farmed Colombard from Mendocino and other varieties from Contra Costa and Suisun Valley. She farms and holds long term leases on 25% of her vineyard sources. Most are dry-farmed. Nearly all her grapes are organic or farmed without chemical inputs.

WINES - Vintage after vintage, Stoumen derives the most from her sites producing wines with delicate precision and marked varietal typicity.

⑩ California Post Flirtation White Blend 2020
EVERYDAY WINE ○ 755 cs; $ 29 - 🍷 - An inviting blend of Roussanne, Colombard, Marsanne and Muscat with floral, yellow apple and yuzu aromas, mandarin and pear flesh flavors and powerful lime rind acidity.
Mendocino Benchlands Red Blend 2020 ● 759 cs; $ 32 - ⊞ - A blend of Petite Sirah, Zinfandel and Nero d'Avola is good a bit chilled. Aromas of red berry, cedar and dried rose give way to a dried cherry palate with soft tannins.
Mendocino County Nero d'Avola 2019 ● 504 cs; $ 44 - ⊞ - Shows a nose of dried rose and earth notes. On the palate: structure with smooth tannins supporting rich dark fruit–but with a streak of red fruit freshness.

acres 7 - **cases** 7,000
Fertilizers compost, cover crops, mineral fertilizer, organic
Plant protection organic, sulfur, synthetic pesticides
Weed control mechanical
Yeasts spontaneous fermentation
Grapes purchase 75%
Certification some of the vineyards are certified organic

MASSICAN

MATTHIASSON

P.O. Box 86
www.massican.com – hello@massican.com

3175 Dry Creek Road – tel. (707) 637-4877
www.matthiasson.com – info@matthiasson.com

PEOPLE - Dan Petroski drew on his experiences in Sicily when he started Massican. The custom there was to drink refreshing wines informed by the sea. Upon arriving in California, he was impressed by the lack of thirst-quenching wines made in an area purported to be "Mediterranean". So, though he himself was now an agent of red wines at DuMol and then at Larkmead, he set about starting the only white wine brand in Napa Valley.

VINEYARDS - Petroski uses a handful of Italian varieties including ribolla gialla, friulano, greco and pinot bianco. Sourcing them is a challenge. Most of his vineyards are certified organic or avoid chemical inputs. They include the esteemed Hyde and Hudson Vineyards in Carneros, The Vare Vineyard planted by George Vare, the Friulian grape apostle, as well as other high-quality sites in Napa and Sonoma such as Rudd and Clos du Val.

 San Francisco Chronicle's Winemaker of the Year Steve Matthiasson and his wife Jill share a rich history of sustainable agriculture and the local food movement.

PEOPLE - They launched their wine brand in 2003, sourcing fruit locally. They acquired their estate vineyard in 2006 and winery in 2017. The estate includes their organic garden, olive groves, and production of peaches, plums and nectarines and is visited by their children, coyotes, owls and bees.

VINEYARDS - Linda Vista Vineyard is behind the family home across a creek in West Oak Knoll. Cooled by the San Pablo Bay, their flagship Chardonnay's natural acids are retained while hot sun provides ripe fruit. Certified organic Phoenix, for Cabernet Sauvignon, is at the base of Mt. Veeder in the Oak Knoll District with rare shale soil. Matthiason Vineyard is planted on the family estate in West Oak Knoll to Refosco, Ribolla Gialla, Tocai Friulano and more.

WINES - Petroski is a celebrity in the winemaking community, conducting online wine-topical 'salons' while using social media to spread a message of sustainability.

Napa Valley Hyde Vineyard Chardonnay 2020 O 200 cs; $ 50 - Shows elegant aromas of white flower, honeysuckle and lemon rind while the palate displays racy lemon and slate broadening to mandarin and nectarine flavors.

Napa Valley Annia 2020 EVERYDAY WINE O 1,500 cs; $ 30 - Made from 61% friulano, 27% ribolla gialla and 12% chardonnay this white is redolent of jasmine and citrus blossom with a palate of tangerine and melon disciplined with chiseled acidity.

Napa Valley Sauvignon Blanc 2020 O 1,200 cs; $ 32 - Shows musky, piney aromas with a hint of paprika. The palate is electric with lime rind, green mango and grapefruit. Extravagant flavors cinched with acidity.

WINES - Light, expressive of origin and grape character, fresh and lively with natural acidity and very lightly oaked has long been the style preferred by sommeliers as they pair so beautifully with food. This style is getting more mainstream every day.

Napa Valley Phoenix Vineyard Cabernet Sauvignon 2018 ● 300 cs; $ 125 - Mid-weight, finely gripping and dry with notes of cassis, blueberry, black peppercorn, seared game and cedar.

Napa Valley Linda Vista Vineyard Chardonnay 2020 O 2,876 cs; $ 34 - Light, delicate, crisp and dry with notes of dried pineapple, peach sorbet, vanilla and buttercream.

Napa Valley Matthiasson Vineyard Ribolla Gialla 2018 ◎ 293 cs; $ 45 - Light, supple, finely textured and dry with notes of almond sliver, honeycomb, brown mushroom and dried flowers.

acres 0 - cases 4,200
Fertilizers compost, manure, mineral fertilizer, organic
Plant protection copper, sulfur, organic, synthetic pesticides
Weed control mechanical
Yeasts commercial cultured yeasts, spontaneous fermentation
Grapes purchase 100%
Certification some of the vineyards are certified organic

acres 50 - cases 8,334
Fertilizers compost, green manure, organic-mineral
Plant protection organic, sulfur
Weed control mechanical
Yeasts spontaneous fermentation
Grapes purchase 25%
Certification some of the vineyards are certified organic

MEDLOCK AMES

3487 Alexander Valley Road – tel. (707) 431-8845
www.medlockames.com – info@medlockames.com

 Using farming to improve carbon sequestration in the land as well as creating a supportive work environment for all employees.

PEOPLE - College friends Christopher Medlock James and Ames Morison shared wine and dreamed of making Bordeaux style wines in California. In 1998 they searched over 100 properties until they found their ideal site in Sonoma County, a 338 acre estate on Bell Mountain straddling Alexander Valley and Russian River AVAs. Julie Rothberg is President and Abby Watt is the new winemaker.

VINEYARDS - Soils are gravelly-clay with volcanic ash on 47 acres growing seven varietals. Most land is wild, supporting habitats of flora and fauna. Vineyards are organic and in a pilot program for Climate Adaptation Certification raising carbon sequestration. A Regenerative Organic Certification (for soil health, animal welfare and social fairness) is expected in 2022. Agustin Santiago is vineyard manager.

WINES - Quality through mindful and organic farming along with a light touch in the cellar brings about these elegant wines made to drink now or age.

● **Alexander Valley Bell Mountain Estate Sauvignon Blanc 2020** ○ 600 cs; $ 32 - Showcasing Bell Mountain, picked with 6 passes and fermented separately with a small percentage in barrel, the dedication is obvious in the glass. Alluring tropical fruits, white flower, pear, tangy mouthfeel with a creamy finish. barrel/stainless
Alexander Valley Bell Mountain Estate Red 2018 ●
4,727 cs; $ 48 - Cabernet Sauvignon, Merlot, Cabernet Franc, Petite Verdot and Malbec blend with layers of cherry, plum, earth, sweet tobacco, chocolate and forest floor. Strong structure and bold tannins. barrel
Alexander Valley Bell Mountain Estate Cabernet Sauvignon 2018 ● 1,200 cs; $ 60 - Wild blackberry, warm spice, cigar box with strong tannins and matching acidity made to age or decant and drink now.

acres 47 - **cases** 6,500
Fertilizers compost, cover crops, organic
Plant protection copper, organic, sulfur
Weed control mechanical
Yeasts commercial cultured yeasts, spontaneous fermentation
Grapes 100% estate-grown
Certification organic

MIA BEA WINES $

P.O. Box 371 – tel. (707) 485-8606
www.miabeawines.com – miabea@barrafamilyvineyards.com

PEOPLE - In 1967 Pete Barra and his wife Bea purchased land in rural Redwood Valley, built a home, raised three girls and planted an income vineyard. Pete, a descendant of Italian vineyard workers since the 1800's, worked the vineyard and sold the grapes until he was nearly 90 years old with the help of Bud Thompson who has continued to oversee the estate. Now grown, daughters Lori, Cyndi and Christina created "Mia Bea" to honor their late parents with wines made from the family vineyard.

VINEYARDS - Surrounded by oaks and redwoods, Barra Family Vineyard (organically farmed) sits 200 ft. above the valley floor near the headwaters of the Russian River. Days are warm, nights cool where a gradual ripening creates complex and refined flavors. The Redwood Valley 30 acre estate formerly sold all of the Pinot Noir, Chardonnay and Petite Syrah until recently. Now some of the grapes are held back to make the family tribute wine.

WINES - Reflecting the love of land and family, Winemaker Chris Nelson uses a light hand in the cellar, allowing the Petite Syrah and Chardonnay to express their unique characteristics. Pinot Noir will be added to their line-up in 2022.

● **Redwood Valley Petite Sirah 2016** EVERYDAY WINE ●
106 cs; $ 28 - Deep rich flavors of candied plum, licorice, dark chocolate with a long, broad light pepper finish. Aged 20 months in 80% French and 20% American Oak. Fruit, acid and tannins are well balanced. Drink now or save.
Redwood Valley Chardonnay 2020 ○ 220 cs; $ 22 - Emitting ripe pear, chalk and honeysuckle with fresh melon, minerality and a light salinity. Friendly balance between acidity with fruity structure offering a long subtle finish. Drink now or save.

acres 30 - **cases** 326
Fertilizers green manure, manure pellets, organic-mineral
Plant protection organic, sulfur
Weed control mechanical
Yeasts commercial cultured yeasts, selected indigenous yeasts
Grapes 100% estate-grown
Certification converting to organics

SANTA ROSA

MORA ESTATE

414 Buena Vista Drive – tel. (707) 328-5617
www.moraestate.com – fabiano@moraestate.com

PEOPLE - Sicilian native Fabiano Ramaci grew up in his family's restaurant business, La Traviata, and began making wine in his early 20s. He started with Barbera from Lodi and is now pioneering the production of Amarone-style wines made with Corvina, Rondinella, Molinara, Corvinone and others grown in Sonoma County's Alexander Valley and Russian River AVAs. Ramaci spent time in Valpolicella working with producers to learn the art of appassimento production and his passion for the wine style has proved fruitful.

VINEYARDS - By convincing growers to over graft from sites once planted to Merlot to the indigenous grape varieties needed for authentic Valpolicella-style wines, Ramaci only works with these varieties that improve in flavor during withering. The amount of which depends up on vintage conditions. The appassimento technique informs each of the wine styles which rely more on the expression of the varieties themselves than of terroir.

WINES - Ramaci's wines are listed by Michelin-starred restaurants and his bottles are individual works of abstract art; each hand painted to express the soul of the wine.

TOP Valporone 2015 ● 2,400 cs; $ 85 - 🍴 - A contemporary Amarone in style with just 14.5 abv, the character of Corvina, Rondinella, Molinara and Negrara varieties is undeniable in the macerated cherries, sweet spices and complex tertiary flavors.
Valpo 2018 ● 2,700 cs; $ 55 - 🍴 - A ripasso technique wine that referments the base wine on amarone pommace and uses 30 percent appassimento for savory aromas of dark berries and cinnamon with earthy red fruit and spicy tannins.
Retico 2016 ● 1,200 cs; $ 90 - 🍴 - A tawny dessert wine made from Port varieties that have undergone appassimento and aged in solera showing roasted figs, hazelnuts, dried cherries and caramel.

acres 0 - **cases** 800
Fertilizers green manure
Plant protection sulfur, synthetic pesticieds
Weed control mechanical
Yeasts commercial cultured yeasts, selected indigenous yeasts, spontaneous fermentation
Grapes purchase 100%
Certification none

SARATOGA

MOUNT EDEN VINEYARDS

22020 Mount Eden Road – tel. (408) 867-5832
www.mounteden.com – info@mounteden.com

PEOPLE - The longest lineage of Chardonnay and Pinot Noir in the United States is at Mount Eden Vineyards, the estate property founded in 1945 by Martin Ray. This historic site holds a storied past full of intrigue, drama and shocking tales. Yet at the root is always great wine. In 1981, a young Jeffrey Patterson came on as assistant winemaker, and over the next thirty years, he and his wife Ellie became the majority shareholders of this historic estate.

VINEYARDS - There are few sites in the Santa Cruz Mountains that grow Chardonnay, Pinot Noir and Cabernet Sauvignon on one single estate property. Mount Eden is one of these, in which the elevation, clonal selections and soil structure allow for ageable wines. Patterson's philosophy of making "vineyard wines" as opposed to "winemaker wines" means that his direct involvement in the vineyard results in low volume, high quality, consistent wine year after year.

WINES - The Patterson's son and daughter have recently begun stepping into leadership roles as the next generation of Mount Eden.

TOP Santa Cruz Mountains Estate Cabernet Sauvignon 2017 ● 1,285 cs; $ 100 - 🍴 - In line with the previous outstanding Mount Eden Cab vintages. This one is inky and aromatic, full of cassis, spice, and tobacco.
Santa Cruz Mountains Estate Pinot Noir 2018 ● 944 cs; $ 65 - 🍴 - Made without fining, filtration or additions, with 35% whole cluster fermentation. It is a dark ruby beauty, with rich, spice box notes and gentle blackberry and cocoa flavors.
Santa Cruz Mountains Estate Chardonnay 2018 ○ 1,288 cs; $ 60 - 🍴 - Has the astounding acidity, structure and minerality that Mount Eden is known for, with pretty floral aromas and a tropical, nutty, citrus burst. The 2014 vintage of this wine was poured at the most recent royal wedding, so some would say there are high expectations here.

acres 32 - **cases** 3,161
Fertilizers green manure
Plant protection sulfur
Weed control mechanical
Yeasts commercial cultured yeasts, selected indigenous yeasts, spontaneous fermentation
Grapes 100% estate-grown
Certification none

CALIFORNIA

PLACERVILLE

NARROW GATE VINEYARDS

4282 Pleasant Valley Road – tel. (530) 664-6201
www.narrowgatevineyards.com
wine@narrowgatevineyards.com

PEOPLE - In 2000 Frank and Teena Hildebrand moved their family to a cattle ranch in the Sierra Foothills to plant a vineyard and make wine, eventually becoming one of the only fully biodynamic wineries in the state. Selling completely direct-to-consumer, their tasting room harkens to more rustic times, repurposing wood from the original ranch. Teena uses her cooking skills to help attract a solid customer base. They raise animals and practice restorative stewardship of their land while producing a diverse line of wines.

VINEYARDS - For the 15 acres that the Hildebrands farm, their forest soils have been enriched compost and biodynamic amendments. Vineyards are in former pastures and a dry streambed. The soils are based on decomposed iron-rich Sierra granite and volcanic ash. Flora such as the surrounding ponderosa pine and chapparal inform the flavors of Narrow Gate wines.

WINES - Rhône varietals are the specialty with gamay recently added. White wines are pressed whole cluster while reds are destemmed and experience a short carbonic pre-fermentation.

🔝 **El Dorado Dunamis Block Head-Trained Grenache 2017** ⬤ 24 cs; $ 36 - 🛢 - Bursts with woodsy, buckbrush aromas while the flavors are lively dried cherry/strawberry with a singular hazelnut streak.

🔝 **El Dorado Roussanne 2020** EVERYDAY WINE ◯ 70 cs; $ 28 - 🛢 - Co-fermented with 10% viognier shows aromas of pretty white flower and a hint of nuts while the palate is broad with dried fig, pear and pineapple.

El Dorado Primitivo 2017 ⬤ 150 cs; $ 32 - 🛢 - Smells brambly and spicy over dried dark cherry and blackberry. Flavors display darks fruits and orange peel with an herbal undercurrent.

---

acres 15 - cases 1,800
Fertilizers biodynamic compost
Plant protection biodynamic preparations
Weed control mechanical
Yeasts spontaneous fermentation
Grapes purchase 10%
Certification spme of the vineyards are certified biodynamic

ANGWIN

NEAL FAMILY VINEYARDS

716 Liparita Avenue – tel. (707) 965-2800
www.nealvineyards.com – info@nealvineyards.com

 Mark Neal has converted more than 1,000 acres of Napa's vineyards to organic farming and certification. His own wines cover the spectrum from affordable to prestigious, ageworthy and collectible.

PEOPLE - Mark Neal's day job is being one of Napa's top organic vineyard managers, farming world class wines for his clients (including Demeine Estates). But he makes superb wine under his own brand–known mostly to insiders. Martin Mackenzie makes the wines; Tony Biagi is the consulting winemaker. Jessica Neal, Mark's daughter, manages sales and marketing.

VINEYARDS - Neal's two estate vineyards encompass the alpha and omega of Napa: valley and hillside. The 17 acres of valley vines in Rutherford are planted on a site Mark's parents purchased in 1966, growing Cabernet Sauvignon, Petite Syrah, and Zinfandel on loam soils known for their fine tannins. The iron rich, 10 acre Howell Mountain vineyard, at 1,800 feet of elevation, has four different soil types. Its tiny berries add intensity.

WINES - Soil geek that he is, Neal has his wine labels made in the color of Aiken Loam, the soil type of his Howell Mountain vineyard.

🔝 **Howell Mountain Cabernet Sauvignon 2017** ⬤ 2,000 cs; $ 100 - 🛢 - Grown on volcanic and slate soils, the wine is deep and vibrant, with red and blue fruits–cassis, blackberry, plum and dark cherries, and a touch of spice.

Napa Valley Cabernet 2017 ⬤ 560 cs; $ 55 - 🛢 - A steal at this price–a blend from both Rutherford and Howell Mountain, aged 60 percent in new French oak, it's full of cherry, blackberry, and cassis.

Rutherford Rutherford Dust Zinfandel 2019 ⬤ 500 cs; $ 32 - 🛢 - Blended with Petite Sirah (9%), juicy, with blueberry notes, a food friendly demeanor and well balanced fruit and acidity.

---

acres 27 - cases 6,000
Fertilizers compost, cover crops
Plant protection organic, sulfur
Weed control mechanical
Yeasts commercial cultured yeasts, spontaneous fermentation
Grapes 100% estate-grown
Certification organic, biodynamic

NEWTON VINEYARD

NICHOLSON RANCH

1040 Main Street Suite, #201 – tel. (707) 204-7423
www.newtonvineyard.com – winery@newtonvineyard.com

4200 Napa Road – tel. (707) 938-8822
www.nicholsonranch.com – guestservices@nicholsonranch.com

PEOPLE - A winery with a legacy of very talented winemakers, a lavish estate, and luxurious English gardens, Newton celebrated its 40th vintage in 2019 only to be devastated in the 2020 Glass Fire, which destroyed the winery, 73 acres of its main Bordeaux vineyard (on Spring Mountain), and elaborate English gardens. Today it is replanting and building with support from parent company LVMH. French born Jean-Baptiste Rivail is the estate director.

VINEYARDS - Newton grows both Bordeaux and Burgundian varietals on its remaining 53 acres on three diverse estate sites that were unaffected by the fire in the Carneros, Mount Veeder and Yountville. All but the Yountville site were certified organic in 2020-21. It also purchases grapes (non-organic). Soils range from volcanic (red pumice to white ash), loam and shale. Vineyard manager Laura Deyermond oversaw replanting at Spring Mountain's 67 acres in 2021.

 The all organic, all estate winery uses regenerative and eco-friendly practices in the vineyards as well as minimal intervention in the cellar.

PEOPLE - The winery is the creation of Mumbai born computer scientist Deepak Gulrajani who came to the U.S. for a tech job and fell in love with wine, gradually trading one for the other. After first making wine in his garage, in 1995 he bought a former cattle ranch from a Greek immigrant family. In 2003, he launched his own wine brand, building a winery, tasting room and a gracious, open air Mediterranean style courtyard on a hillside in the Carneros.

VINEYARDS - The dry farmed vines sit at the southern tip of the Mayacamas Range. There volcanic slopes and marine sedimentary soils meet, cooled by breezes from nearby San Pablo Bay. The 27 acres grow mostly Chardonnay and Pinot Noir (on the 40 acre property). In 2014, Gulrajani began to farm organically, certifying the vines in 2020.

WINES - Milan-born winemaker Alberto Bianchi made the current releases through 2020, followed by his former assistant Andrew Hoyle in 2021. Philippe Melka is the winemaking consultant. Its earlier renowned winemakers–John Kongsgaard, Aaron Pott, and Andy Erickson—later catapulted into the ranks of Napa indie rock stars.

WINES - All wines are unfined and unfiltered. The whites are whole cluster. Gulrajani says his wine club members noticed an improvement in wine quality when he switched to organic farming.

Carneros Spring Hill Chardonnay 2015 ○ 212 cs; $ 111 - ⬜ - Opens with lemon notes on the nose, then into green apple and pear notes on the palate.
Carneros Cactus Hill Pinot Noir 2015 ● 688 cs; $ 128 - ⬛ - From a select block on the property, it's floral with cherry, raspberry and pomegranate notes.

TOP **Napa Valley The Puzzle Bordeaux Blend 2018** SLOW WINE ● 1,200 cs; $ 125 - ⬛ - Bottled unfiltered, this flagship wine is a three vineyard blend of Cabernet (77%), Cabernet Franc (11%), Merlot (8%), Petit Verdot (2%) and Malbec (2%). It's aged in 40 percent new oak for a year, blended and aged for 8 more months. Medium bodied, enjoy plums, black currants, allspice and tobacco.
Mount Veeder Cabernet Sauvignon 2016 ● 350 cs; $ 210 - ⬛ - Grown on sedimentary soils at 750 and 1250 feet of elevation on Mount Veeder from 18 year old (average age) vines. Powerful and intense and ageworthy, this single vineyard bottling is herbaceous on the nose, with a complex blend of plums, cassis and herbs on the palate.

acres 53 - **cases** 15,000
Fertilizers compost, cover crops, mineral fertilizer, organic
Plant protection organic, sulfur, synthetic pesticides
Weed control chemical, mechanical
Yeasts spontaneous fermentation
Grapes purchase 50%
Certification some of the vineyards are certified organic

acres 31 - **cases** 5,000
Fertilizers compost, cover crops, organic
Plant protection organic
Weed control mechanical
Yeasts spontaneous fermentation
Grapes 100% estate-grown
Certification organic

OAKVILLE RANCH

7781 Silverado Trail – tel. (707) 944-9665
www.oakvilleranch.com – info@oakvilleranch.com

 A spectacular site known for making great wines is tended with care, embodying ecofriendly practices in Napa's top tier.

PEOPLE - Now one of Napa's most sought after vineyards (growing grapes that others buy to make 100 point wines), Oakville Ranch was originally purchased by British born Mary Miner and her husband, Robert Miner, co-founder of Oracle Corporation, in 1989 as a weekend getaway home. After Bob died in 1994, Mary assembled an A-list team to convert it to organic farming and makes wines with top tier talent.

VINEYARDS - Perched on a dramatic Vaca Mountains site on the east side of Napa Valley, overlooking the valley, the 330 acre ranch sits on shallow, red, volcanic soils at 1,100-1,300 feet of elevation. It grows Cabernet Sauvignon, Merlot and Cabernet Franc. About 15 percent is reserved for the house brand. The rest is sold for top dollar. Organic vineyard guru Phil Coturri converted it to organic certification in 2009.

WINES - Jennifer Rue makes the wines with Mark Herold as consulting winemaker.

🔵 **Oakville Oakville Ranch Bordeaux Blend 2016** ●
109 cs; $ 190 - ⊞ - Multi layered and gorgeously perfumed showcases the estate's best barrels, offering a symphony of cassis, blackberries and chocolate notes. Ageworthy, it is a classic from a great vintage.
Oakville Oakville Ranch Chardonnay 2020 ○ 100 cs; $ 55 - ⬜ ⊞ - From a selection of 3 clones, barrel fermented and aged in 35 percent new oak, it's bright and fresh with lemon and stone fruits enveloped by a gentle, plush, round texture.
Oakville Oakville Ranch Robert's Cabernet Franc 2016 ● 50 cs; $ 110 - ⊞ - An aromatic blend of two very different blocks that become one spectacular wine, juicy and rich, opening with aromas of violets and herbs, leading to a sumptuous midpalate of plums and black currants, and a long, long finish.

acres 66 - cases 750
Fertilizers compost, cover crops
Plant protection organic, sulfur
Weed control mechanical
Yeasts commercial cultured yeasts
Grapes 100% estate-grown
Certification organic

OAKVILLE WINERY

7830-40 St. Helena Highway – tel. (800) 848-9630
www.ghostblockwine.com – drinkcab@ghostblockwine.com

 A family owned winery for decades, its large acreage shows how producers can scale up organic farming, promoting healthy practices and clean water for residents. It also makes fine wines at remarkable prices.

PEOPLE - This is one of three brands from Napa's oldest and biggest organic grape growing family—the descendants of the Pelissa family—who've farmed in Napa for more than 100 years. In 1993, they bought an historic winery (built in 1877), launched custom crush services to boutique wineries and opened a tasting room in 2006 selling the family's three brands.

VINEYARDS - Land rich from purchases made in 1938, their Oakville vineyards border renowned sites sandwiched between the east side of Highway 29 and the Napa River. One vineyard is the former BV7–BV stands for Beaulieu Vineyard—known for its fine Cabernet. Their Pelissa vineyard, which preserves the last Zinfandel vines in Oakville, is next to famed Opus One and fabled To Kalon vineyard.

WINES - The family owns 557 acres of vines in Yountville and Oakville, prompting locals to nickname the sites as "the Pelissa Hills." Lynn Watanabe makes the wines.

🔵 **Oakville Zinfandel 2018** SLOW WINE ● 800 cs; $ 30 - ⊞ - Light on its feet, delivers lovely berry and cherry notes on the palate.
Oakville Oakville Winery Malbec 2017 ● 130 cs; $ 45 - ⊞ - Debuting this year in its inaugural vintage, this is richly rewarding, displaying cassis and spices, with dark fruits.
Oakville Oakville Winery Cabernet Sauvignon 2017 ●
1,510 cs; $ 60 - ⊞ - The flagship wine is a steal—a Napa Cab that overdelivers for the price (and sells out often), offering up velvety red and black currants and elegant tannins.

acres 557 - cases 2,300
Fertilizers compost, cover crops, organic
Plant protection organic, sulfur
Weed control mechanical
Yeasts commercial cultured yeasts
Grapes 100% estate-grown
Certification organic

THE OJAI VINEYARD

109 S Montgomery Street – tel. (805) 649-1674
www.ojaivineyard.com – help@ojaivineyard.com

PEOPLE - A pioneer in Santa Barbara winemaking, Adam Tolmach began making wine withpurchased fruit over 40 years ago. In 1981, he planted vines in Ojai on property hisgrandfather bought in 1933, and where Tolmach grew up playing in the creek. His wifemanages the operation, and his brother helps with the farm.General manager FabienCastel grew up in Paris, studied biology and advertising, and joined the operation 20years ago as an intern.

VINEYARDS - Tolmach planted vines in 1981 near Creek Road, the sycamore-lined route that leadsfrom Ventura on the coast to inland Ojai. Unfortunately, the vines were hit with Pierce'sdisease, so he removed them in 1995.With new resistantgrape varieties, in 2017 heplanted 1800 hybridized cuttings. Tolmach embraces organic; most of the fruitpurchased is farmed organically but not certified. In January 2021 he purchased Fe Ciega which means "Blind Faith."

WINES - The aesthetic pursuit is to find subtle delicacy in a climate that is quite warm and hot especially at harvest but also hit with cold fog and winds. Minimal intervention and native yeasts express place.

(TOP) Santa Barbara County Puerta Del Mar Chardonnay 2018 ○ 442 cs; $ 34 - 🍴 - They didn't think grapes this far west of the Sta. Rita Hills appellation could ripen, yet this chardonnay proves otherwise with its striking salinity, bracing acidity, lemongrass, and lingering Eureka lemon.

(TOP) Santa Barbara County Duvarita Vineyard Syrah 2017 SLOW WINE ● 165 cs; $ 45 - 🍴 - This cool climate syrah comes from Demeter certified Duvarita vineyard west of the Sta. Rita Hills AVA and offers intriguing aromas of blueberries, incense and a finish of fresh blue fruit.

Sta. Rita Hills Fe Ciega Pinot Noir 2016 ○ 301 cs; $ 45 - 🍴 - This pure essence of pinot noir brings earthy, woodsy, spicy, cherry cola,rhubarb, and sage to the nose with more of the same savoriness on the palate.

acres 1.2 - cases 7,000
Fertilizers biodynamic compost
Plant protection biodynamic preparations
Weed control mechanical
Yeasts spontaneous fermentation
Grapes purchase 90%
Certification some of the vineyards are certified biodynamic, some of the vineyards are certified organic

---

OLD WORLD WINERY

850 River Road – tel. (707) 490-6696
www.oldworldwinery.com – info@oldworldwinery.com

PEOPLE - Darek Trowbridge started Old World Winery over 20 years ago, after learning the skills of a farmer and winemaker by working alongside his grandfather, Lino Martinelli. His passion is combining old farming traditions with more modern ones such as regenerative farming. To make plants more resilient to climate events Darek applies inoculated and composted mulch made from charred trees from the wildfires which are rich in species of fungal mycorrhizae and nutrient cycling bacteria.

VINEYARDS - Darek has brought new life into the old vineyards which have been in the family for 3 generations. In the idyllic Martinelli Valley lies the 1890 Block, a field blend of Muscadelle, Abouriou, Zinfandel, Mondeuse Noire, Trousseau Gris, and Palomino which he co-ferments. Soil is a layer of loam over shale providing minerality and drainage. The last block of Abouriou in the USA grows in the Sherry Martinelli Vineyard on gnarly head-trained vines planted in 1930.

WINES - Darek finds footstomping the gentlest way to juice whole clusters and uses neutral barrels along with spontaneous wild yeasts to allow the curious flavors to evolve with minimal sulfur added at the end.

Russian River Valley Sherry Martinelli Vineyard Early Harvest Sparkling Abouriou 2018 ⊛ 112 cs; $ 35 - 🍴 - Sparkling Lambrusco style fermented with apples adding sweetness to the strawberry and rhubarb flavors, tart, dry finish.

Russian River Valley Sherry Martinelli Vineyard Luminous Abouriou 2013 ● 125 cs; $ 45 - 🍴 - This red has a tannic grip with intense dark fruits and spice on the nose and palate followed by bright acidity alongside bold tannins leaving a long earthy finish.

Russian River Valley A.J.Duckhorn Vineyard Abundance Red 2014 ● 90 cs; $ 45 - 🍴 - A field blend from the 120-year-old 1890 Block, this chillable red lifts off with bright cherry, grass and artichoke with a warm spice finish.

acres 10 - cases 2,000
Fertilizers biodynamic compost, compost
Plant protection organic
Weed control mechanical
Yeasts spontaneous fermentation
Grapes purchase 10%
Certification none

GLEN ELLEN

ONCE & FUTURE WINE

P.O. Box 164 – tel. (855) 566-3946
www.onceandfuturewine.com – info@onceandfuturewine.co

PEOPLE - Joel Peterson, the "godfather of Zinfandel," began making small-lot Zinfandel in 1976. In 2001, his popular Ravenswood label was acquired by Constellation Brands. In 2016, Peterson started Once and Future, crafting wines in an old-world style, from unique vineyards using his original California redwood fermenters and indigenous yeasts. Says Peterson, "My wines are a reflection of the people and the places that made them."

VINEYARDS - Peterson sources grapes from dry farmed vineyards, that use cover-crop and crimping techniques to build the soil, resulting in high-quality fruit. The Old Hill Ranch and Bedrock Estate Vineyards in Sonoma Valley were planted in the 1880s and are traditional "field-blend" vineyards. Petite Sirah from Palisades Vineyard was planted in the mid-1970s and produces low yields with small clusters, resulting in an exceptional, perfumed grape.

WINES - Using indigenous yeasts on historic field blends in open-top redwood fermenters, Peterson creates bold wines exploding with flavor.

TOP **Sonoma Valley Bedrock Vineyard Zinfandel 2019** SLOW WINE ● 275 cs; $ 50 - ▦ - Morgan Twain-Peterson is the grower at his family's 1886 estate vineyard, one of the state's oldest. The field-blend of 26 varietals produces a complex wine with spicy aromas and dark fruit flavors.
TOP **Sonoma Valley Old Hill Ranch Zinfandel 2019** ●
302 cs; $ 55 - ▦ - Will Bucklin grows Zinfandel, Grenache and other varietals used in this "flavor fusion" Zinfandel, a balanced wine with complex aromatics and a long, moderately astringent finish.
Napa Valley Palisades Vineyard Petite Sirah 2019 ●
252 cs; $ 65 - ▦ - The grapes for this structured Petite Sirah are grown by Felicia Woytak and Steven Rasmussen. Fragrant and intense, white and black pepper, spice and balanced tannins lead to the long finish.

acres 75 - **cases** 2,000
Fertilizers compost, green manure, mineral fertilizer, organic
Plant protection sulfur, synthetic pesticides
Weed control chemical, mechanical
Yeasts spontaneous fermentation
Grapes purchase 60%
Certification none

OAKVILLE

OPUS ONE

7900 St. Helena Highway – tel. (707) 944-9442
www.opusonewinery.com – info@opusonewinery.com

PEOPLE - An internationally known brand beloved by fans in Asia and the rest of the world, Opus One solidified Napa's international reputation as on par with Bordeaux. Founded in 1978 by wine scions Baron Philippe de Rothschild of Bordeaux and Robert Mondavi of Napa united a French First Growth winery and Napa's renowned To Kalon vineyard. Michael Silacci has led the winery since 2003. In 2021 it set a new standard in high end hospitality.

VINEYARDS - Mondavi famously sold Opus One 100 acres of his finest vineyard, To Kalon, a treasured spot first planted by visionary viticulturist H. W. Crabb in 1872 . "To Kalon" means "the call of beauty." Another 70 acres of vines surround the winery site, bordered by the banks of the Napa River with abundant wildlife. The soils are primarily bale clay loam and gravel. Farmed organically for more than a decade, the winery certified its vines in 2021.

WINES - All organic and all estate only, the winery uses native yeasts selected from many strains on the property.

Opus One Bordeaux Blend 2017 ● 25,000 cs; $ 623 - ▦ - The flagship wine, it's a seamlessly integrated, plush blend of Cabernet Sauvignon (8%), Petit Verdot (9%) and 5 percent each of Cabernet Franc and Merlot plus one percent Malbec. Aged 17 months in new French oak, it's silky yet concentrated, it reveals layers of classic black and red fruits–cassis, raspberries, black cherries and blackberries–in a structured wine with a long finish.
Overture Bordeaux Blend NV ● n/a; $ 239 - ▦ - The estate's second wine, a nonvintage wine, is a graceful blend of Cabernet Sauvignon, Petit Verdot, Cabernet Franc, Merlot and Malbec made in a softer, rounder style–designed to be consumed when released.

acres 170 - **cases** 300,000
Fertilizers compost
Plant protection organic, sulfur
Weed control mechanical
Yeasts selected indigenous yeasts
Grapes 100% estate-grown
Certification organic

KELSEYVILLE

OVIS

4350 Thomas Drive – tel. (707) 281-6780
www.shannonfamilyofwines.com/wine_producer/ovis/

 A leading winery in Lake County that's just gone organic in the vines–with the help of 600 sheep.

PEOPLE - In 2019, Clay Shannon, a prominent Lake County vintner, launched an ambitious project converting 900 acres to organic certification. But he's doing it in a unique way–letting his flock of 600 ewes fertilize and sucker the vines. In addition to his high end Ovis brand–Ovis is Latin for sheep–Clay's launching a line of organically grown wines in the $20 price range in 2022.

VINEYARDS - Ovis' wines come from the best blocks on its Home Ranch in the High Valley AVA, first farmed by the Ogulin family in the 1890's. It's planted mostly to Cabernet, but includes 5 test acres of Nero d'Avola, a Sicilian variety that can be dry farmed and withstands high temperatures–a good choice for resilience in a time of drought and heat from climate change. The windy site borders wildlands where bears and coyotes roam, amid oak trees and madrone.

WINES - In the vineyards 345 acres were certified organic. By the summer of 2022, it will have a total of 908 acres make it the fourth largest organic vineyard in the country and the largest that pastures its sheep year round. Joy Merrilees makes the wine.

Lake County Cabernet Sauvignon 2019 ● 2,980 cs; $ 60 - ⊞ - A selection from the best blocks at the Home Ranch. it's aromatic and full bodied, with plum, cherries, black currant and black fruits coupled with a long finish. Aged 24 months in 40% new French and American oak. A drought year brought smaller berries and more intense fruit.
High Valley Petit Verdot 2019 ● 396 cs; $ 60 - ⊞ - Brimming with black cherries and plums, this full bodied wine sports a juicy mid palate and a tiny cinnamon note.
High Valley Betsy's Vineyard Petite Sirah 2019 ● 580 cs; $ 60 - ⊞ - Intensely fruitful, and overflowing with blueberries and rich black fruits.

acres 908 - **cases** 1,000
Fertilizers compost, cover crops, manure, organic
Plant protection organic, sulfur
Weed control animal grazing, mechanical
Yeasts commercial cultured yeasts
Grapes 100% estate-grown
Certification converting to organics, some of the vineyards are certified organic

PENNGROVE, CALIFORNIA

PANTHER RIDGE

5252 Lichau Road – tel. (970) 379-1217
www.pantherridgevineyard.com
info@pantherridgevineyard.com

PEOPLE - When she moved from Colorado to Sonoma seven years ago, Suzanne Farver was a white collar worker, having taught sustainability at Harvard Extension and running the Aspen Art Museum. After finding her perfect house in the country, she transformed a boulder strewn, rocky hillside into a Pinot Noir vineyard. She assembled a team–Daniel Chavez as the vineyard manager and Adrian Manspeaker as the winemaker–to produce quality fruit and her estate wine.

VINEYARDS - In the Petaluma Gap, cooling winds flow through a 15 mile gap, reducing mildew pressures. Night time warmth and daytime coolness makes it a bright spot for Pinot Noir, which ripens well here. After clearing hay and thistle from the site, Calera and 115 were planted here. Farver sells 75 percent of her grapes to other wineries, retaining 25 percent for her own Panther Ridge wine. The vineyard was certified organic in 2019.

WINES - Biodynamic consultants Philippe Corderey and Natalie Winkler bring their expertise to improve vineyard health and grape quality.
Petaluma Gap Pinot Noir 2019 ● 45 cs; $ 116 - ⊞ - The winery's inaugural vintage, an elegant wine with delicate cherry notes and a beautiful complexity that portends much from this vineyard site and producer.

acres 7 - **cases** 250
Fertilizers biodynamic compost, cover crops
Plant protection biodynamic preparations, sulfur
Weed control mechanical
Yeasts spontaneous fermentation
Grapes 100% estate-grown
Certification organic

SEBASTOPOL

PAX WINES

6780 McKinley Street, Suite 170 – tel. (707) 310-2743
www.paxmahlewines.com – pam@paxmahlewines.com

PEOPLE - The intention of Pax wines was to produce Rhône varietals. Iconoclasm led Pax Mahle to making handfuls of different expressions of syrah in the early 2000s. More recently, it was the same urge that led to diversifying into less well-known grapes such as trousseau gris, valdigué and gamay. In each case, there seemed to be both a unique intentionality and a deft touch in expressing elegance and at times, hedonism. Mahle's facility in Sebastopol also serves as a crush pad for several other well-regarded winemakers.

VINEYARDS - Having often long relationships with vineyard owners that he sources from, he has been beating the no-chemical-input drum for years and has helped normalized organic practices, if not certification among them. Buddah's Darma Vineyard belongs to a nearby Buddhist community and is dry farmed on volcanic soils. Armagh Vineyard's iron-rich soils and chilly climate produce unique, savory qualities in the syrah farmed there.

WINES - A background as a sommelier has finetuned Mahle's sensitivity to aromatics and texture and it shows in these wine.

TOP Sonoma Coast Armaugh Vineyard Syrah 2018 ●
165 cs; $ 60 - 🍽 - Expressive in the extreme with elements of gaminess, lavender, black pepper and culinary smokiness carried in a tart blackberry medium. Fine tannins help engineer an effortless and lingering finish.
Mendocino County Buddha's Dharma Vineyard Chenin Blanc 2019 ○ 300 cs; $ 38 - 🍽 - The nose shows gunflint, white flower and green apple which carries to the palate expanded by white peach; linear and pure.
Sonoma Coast Gamay 2019 ● 400 cs; $ 40 - 🍽 - Puts gamay in the big leagues. It shows aromas of rose, subtle lavender sachet and red cherry while a sapid mineral palate blends with raspberry and cranberry.

ANNAPOLIS

PEAY VINEYARDS

33201 Annapolis Road – tel. (707) 864-8720
www.peayvineyards.com – info@peayvineyards.com

PEOPLE - In 1996, brothers Andy and Nick Peay purchased the 280-acre Peterson Ranch in Annapolis, in what is now the Sonoma Coast AVA. Only 4 miles from the Pacific Ocean, they were drawn to the cool marine influence and were one of the first in the industry to set up shop here, planting 52 acres to vines. Soon they met Hirsch and Peter Michael winemaker Vanessa Wong, and the trio was formed. Nick is the Winegrower, his wife Vanessa is the winemaker and Andy runs Sales & Marketing.

VINEYARDS - Cooling ocean breezes and fog provide ideal, if challenging, environments for Chardonnay and Pinot Noir. They experiment with multiple clones planted in thin, eroded sandstone soils that were once part of the ocean floor. They also grow Rhone varietals Viognier and Syrah. Peay is the only CCOF Certified organic vineyard in the Sonoma Coast AVA and the only one in Annapolis.

WINES - Peay's Burgundian Chardonnays and Pinot Noirs and cool climate Rhone varietals are all about lightness, tartness, site expression, energy and tension.

TOP Sonoma Coast Pomarium Estate Pinot Noir 2019 ● 575 cs; $ 60 - 🍽 - Light, tart, bone dry and lively with notes of raspberry, blackberry, fennel seed and sundried tomato.
Sonoma Coast Estate Chardonnay 2019 ○ 400 cs; $ 55 - 🍽 - Silky, fresh and dry with notes of green apple, grilled peach, banana bread, nutmeg and yellow rose.
Sonoma Coast La Bruma Estate Syrah 2018 ● 475 cs; $ 56 - 🍽 - Light-bodied but full-flavored, juicy, tart and dry with notes of boysenberry, dried herbs, dark, bitter greens and pink rose.

---

acres 0 - **cases** 3,000
Fertilizers compost, cover crops, manure
Plant protection organic, sulfur
Weed control mechanical
Yeasts spontaneous fermentation
Grapes purchase 100%
Certification some of the vineyards are certified organic

acres 52 - **cases** 5,000
Fertilizers compost
Plant protection organic
Weed control mechanical
Yeasts spontaneous fermentation
Grapes purchase 20%
Certification some of the vineyards are certified organic

PIEDRASASSI

1501 E Chestnut Avenue – tel. (805) 736-6784
www.piedrasassi.com – melissa@piedrasassi.com

PEOPLE - Piedrasassi was started in 2003 by Sashi Moorman and his wife Melissa as a wine company specializing in Syrah and a bakery producing bread utilizing heritage grain they grow themselves. To make the most aromatically lifted Syrah possible has led him to the principle of picking his grapes earlier than most with a low alcohol potential. He notes that a natural ferment is easiest and shortest when there is less alcohol to discourage healthy yeasts.

VINEYARDS - A limited yield per vine creates concentration and complexity. This is accomplished by planting on depleted soils and in cool condition. Moorman notes, vine age is a great asset. Bien Nacido vineyard has such old vines and a cool climate in the Santa Maria Valley. Patterson and John Sebastiano vineyards in Sta. Rita Hills are windy and at elevation while Rim Rock vineyard, Arroyo Grande, Moorman's 'estate' wine, gets a strong Pacific influence.

WINES - Moorman's Syrahs achieve intensity and lift without too much fruit density. Fermentation is done with whole clusters to enhance aromatics and add flavor elements.

Arroyo Grande Valley Rim Rock Vineyard Syrah 2019 ● 150 cs; $ 50 - 🍷 - Leaps from the glass with purple flowers and fresh black fruit. The blackberry palate is refined but a little wild with notes of iodine and smoked meat.
Santa Barbara County Syrah 2019 ● 200 cs; $ 50 - 🍷 - Shows a mineral streak underneath blackberry fruit with generous wafts of grilled meat, rose and blackberry liqueur.
Sta. Rita Hills Syrah 2019 ● 150 cs; $ 50 - 🍷 - Chewy and textured with dark berries and olive aromas giving way to a palate of tart blackberry with smoky notes.

acres 3 - cases 1,000
Fertilizers compost, cover crops, manure, mineral fertilizer
Plant protection organic, sulfur
Weed control mechanical
Yeasts spontaneous fermentation
Grapes purchase 85%
Certification none

PORTER CREEK VINEYARDS

8735 Westside Road – tel. (707) 433-6321
www.portercreekvineyards.com
info@portercreekvineyards.com

Being one of the few estates that carries both Organic and Biodynamic Certification, Alex shows that fine wines can be grown in the vineyard.

PEOPLE - Alex Davis was 8 years old when he and his father, George, moved to the Russian River Valley property in 1978. George became part of the early Pinot Noir movement. Alex went on to work in France and specialize in Pinot, eventually taking over the winery. The wines and the estate vines are both certified organic and biodynamic.

VINEYARDS - Alex stewards the steep hillside vineyards with keen observation, soil regeneration and low-impact farming. This past year of historic drought challenged him to cut back on water usage and by leaning on his intimate knowledge and intuition Alex manipulated irrigation to keep the hilly vineyards hydrated enough to sustain the Pinot Noir, Chardonnay and Viognier vines and ultimately produce fruit.

WINES - Davis uses neutral barrels, presoaking and less than 30 percent new wood guide for wines that will age in order to bring out the vineyard character.

Russian River Valley George's Hill Vineyard Old Vine Chardonnay 2018 SLOW WINE ○ 500 cs; $ 46 - 🍷 - Juicy and fresh golden delicious pear with wet stone and hints of grass and vanilla. Offers a creamy mouthfeel with balanced acidity. Drink now or age.
Russian River Valley Fiona Hill Vineyard Pinot Noir 2017 ● 600 cs; $ 58 - 🍷 - This flagship wine smells of forest floor and red fruit. The delicate use of barrels allows the herbaceous, cherry and light tannins to pop on the palate with a balanced long finish. Drink now or age.
Mendocino County Old Vine Carignane 2018 ● 650 cs; $ 32 - 🍷 - Rich in purple fruits and spice, supple mouthfeel with structured tannin and silky with a unique taste of black currants, plum and spice. Drink now or age.

acres 22 - cases 4,000
Fertilizers biodynamic compost, compost, manure
Plant protection organic, sulfur
Weed control mechanical
Yeasts spontaneous fermentation
Grapes purchase 20%
Certification some of the vineyards are certified biodynamic, some of the vineyards are certified organic

PORTOLA VALLEY

PORTOLA VINEYARDS

850 Los Trancos Road – tel. (650) 906-1059
www.portolavineyards.com – len@portolavineyards.com

This regenerative small family winery is a treasure, producing exceptional wines of value.

PEOPLE - Since 2005, Len Lehmann and his family have been producing hand-crafted wines that reflect the unique terroir of the Peninsula foothills. Lehmann farms sustainably and regeneratively, with minimal disturbance to the soil. The winery uses organic fruit in all its wines and all wines are certified kosher. His goal is to "integrate with community" and he offers harvest opportunities, yoga, art in the vineyards and a jazz series.

VINEYARDS - Portola Vineyards straddles the border of the Santa Clara Valley and Santa Cruz Mountains AVAs. The certified organic Pinot Noir vineyard is dry- and hand-farmed, using no-till, compost and minimal additions – just one tablespoon of potassium per vine, annually. Lehmann sources his Cabernet grapes from the historic Cooper-Garrod Estate high in the famed Santa Cruz Mountains.

WINES - Using native fermentations on organically farmed grapes, Lehmann produces refined wines of value and distinction in the foothills of the Santa Cruz Mountains.

TOP **Santa Clara Valley Estate Pinot Noir 2015** SLOW WINE ● 175 cs; $ 38 - A complex and refined Pinot Noir, with aromas of mulberry and dried violet. Rose, dried cranberry and spice on the palate. Native yeast fermentation and aged 16 months in French oak.

TOP **Santa Clara Valley Rosé of Pinot Noir 2020** EVERYDAY WINE 76 cs; $ 20 - A refreshing, fruit-forward rosé with dry, crisp notes of strawberry.

Santa Cruz Mountains Cooper-Garrod Estate Cabernet Sauvignon 2016 ● 95 cs; $ 38 - Lehmann has been buying grapes from this CSWA certified sustainable vineyard since 2010. Spicy aromas and flavors of fine leather, blackberry and blueberry, plus a satiny, vibrant, medium-to-full body with silky tannins and moderate oak. A youthful and bright Cabernet.

acres 2 - cases 750
Fertilizers compost, organic-mineral
Plant protection organic
Weed control mechanical
Yeasts spontaneous fermentation
Grapes 0
Certification organic

NAPA

POTT WINES

2272 Mt Veeder Road – tel. (707) 967-9378
www.pottwine.com – claire@pottwine.com

Going the extra mile, Pott requires his growers to be organic, paying them extra fees to ensure the farming is free from synthetics.

PEOPLE - Named Winemaker of the Year by Food and Wine in 2012, Aaron Pott is one of Napa's winemaking rockstars, famous first for the wines he makes for others and now for his own.He worked toward his current superstar status in the usual manner–by starting at the bottom. Lucky breaks sent him to Saint-Emilion, then to flying winemaker gigs. Back in Napa, he bought land in 2004, releasing his own wines in 2015.

VINEYARDS - Pott sources from a number of organically farmed sites but focuses on his five acre Mount Veeder estate on the east facing side of a steep ridge at 1,400 feet, on rocky sandstone soils that were once sea floor beds. Planted in 2010, it's nicknamed Chateauneuf-du-Pott. Pott uses dehydrating teas made of yucca and kelp extract to slow ripening, enhancing flavor development.

WINES - Pott uses clay amphora imported from Italy for Viognier and Cabernet Franc. The other estate wines are aged in 225L barriques (33 percent new).

TOP **Mount Veeder Space & Time Cabernet Franc Blend 2019** ● 125 cs; $ 175 - A master Cab Franc lover's homage to his favorite grape variety. The blend is Cabernet Franc (70%), Cabernet Sauvignon (20%) and Merlot (10%). Vibrant aromas and tastes of violets, blueberries, and plums.

Mount Veeder Incubo Cabernet Sauvignon 2019 ● 125 cs; $ 299 - Collectors' gold, this sought after wine has complexity and structure that reward, yet freshness and nimbleness that bely its ageworthiness.

Mount Veeder 20M3 Viognier 2020 ○ 125 cs; $ 102 - Focused yet complex with notes of lychee, honeysuckle, peach and citrus.

acres 5 - cases 1,450
Fertilizers compost, cover crops, organic
Plant protection organic, sulfur
Weed control mechanical
Yeasts spontaneous fermentation
Grapes purchase 65%
Certification some of the vineyards are certified organic

WOODSIDE

PRECEDENT WINE $

tel. (415) 342-7324
www.precedentwine.com – nathan@precedentwine.com

PEOPLE - Michigander Nathan Kandler became exposed to wine while working in restaurants, having soured on a potential career in government. He settled in Sonoma continuing at various wine-related jobs. A winemaking degree at Fresno State was followed by internships and a stint at Torbreck in the Barossa Valley. He then returned to a job at Thomas Fogarty Winery where he remains as winemaker. Kandler is fond of old vines and seeks them out.

VINEYARDS - Massa in Carmel Valley is at high elevation and benefits from its coastal proximity. It has been certified organic since the '80s. Lodi's Mokelumne River subregion is a favorite source with the ancient vineyards of Spenker Ranch (1900) and Kirchenmann (1915) both consisting of sand of unlimited depth and the latter owned by old vines specialist, Tegan Passalaqua who, according to Kandler, farms it with 'Napa Valley' fastidiousness.

WINES - Precedent is Kandler's personal passion project, where he seeks to 'foster the voice of the soil to (the) glass'.

🔴 **Mokelumne River Kirschenmann Vineyard Zinfandel 2019** SLOWWINE ● 110 cs; $ 36 - ⬚ - Displays effusive and exotic aromas of incense, dried flowers and dark cherry. The palate shows smooth tannins with light spice and vanilla over dried cherry fruit.
Mokelumne River Spenker Ranch Carignan 2019 ● 120 cs; $ 22 - ⬚ - Shows heady aromas of earth, red cherry and flowers and a crunchy palate of cherries, cranberries and dusty tannins, doubling down on earthiness.
Carmel Valley Massa Vineyard Chenin Blanc 2019 O 140 cs; $ 22 - ⬚ - Displays an assertive nose with piquant nectarine and beeswax while on the palate are yellow apple, stone fruit and lemon flavors.

---

acres 0 - **cases** 400
Fertilizers compost, cover crops
Plant protection organic, sulfur
Weed control mechanical
Yeasts spontaneous fermentation
Grapes purchase 100%
Certification some of the vineyards are certified organic

HEALDSBURG

PRESTON FARM & WINERY

9282 W Dry Creek Road – tel. (707) 433-3372
www.prestonfarmandwinery.com – mail@prestonvineyards.com

 A long time exemplary winery that shows the beautiful marriage of farm and fine wine, and embodies the living history of Sonoma wine traditions.

PEOPLE - Lou and Susan Preston purchased a sprawling 145-acre ranch in Dry Creek Valley in the 1970's and quickly began producing 30,000 cases of wine a year. Soon they realized they wanted to down-size and farm organically, diversifying so that only 63 acres remain planted to grapes. Grayson Hartley is Winemaker and Viticulturalist, Susan creates artwork for the labels and their son makes bread for sale in the tasting room from home grown grain.

VINEYARDS - With well-draining partly gravelly soil, these warm, sunny upper Dry Creek Valley floor vineyards are planted to Rhone varieties – mostly Grenache, Mourvèdre, and Zinfandel. There are a few blocks of head-trained century-old Carignane and Zinfandel and as of 2018, Italian varietals including Nero d'Avola, Ribolla Gialla and Tocai Friulano.

WINES - Grayson aims for "high palate energy, vigorousness, seamlessness and liveliness." While the Zins are still 14.5% abv and above, the other wines are below 14% abv, a rarity in this hot area of Sonoma.

🔴 **Dry Creek Valley Carignane 2018** ● 294 cs; $ 38 - Ⓒ - Supple, fresh, tart and dry with notes of mulberry, blackberry, mushroom and pink peppercorn.
Dry Creek Valley Zinfandel 2018 ● 830 cs; $ 38 - ⬚ - Full, gripping and dry with notes of black cherry, blackberry, black licorice, cedar and clove.
Dry Creek Valley White Wine 2019 O Sauvignon Blanc, Ribolla Gialla, Friulano; 450 cs; $ 38 - 🍷 - Light, supple, crisp and dry with notes of apricot, peach, lemongrass, celery, pink peppercorn and honeycomb.

---

acres 63 - **cases** 8,334
Fertilizers compost
Plant protection organic, sulfur
Weed control mechanical
Yeasts commercial cultured yeasts, selected indigenous yeasts
Grapes 100% estate-grown
Certification organic

OAKLAND

PRIMA MATERIA VINEYARD AND WINERY $

482 #B 49th Street – tel. (510) 920-0327
www.prima - materia.com – info@prima-materia.com

PEOPLE - Viticulturist, winemaker and chef Pietro Buttitta makes wine from Kelseyville Bench AVA in Lake County, with a passionate focus on Italian varieties. A philosopher at heart, the Prima Materia name references the theories of alchemy, the first element that everything is based upon for transformation and evolution, which is reflected in the Prima Materia winemaking process.

VINEYARDS - The 12 acre estate in the Kelsey Bench AVA sits at 1,500 ft. elevation between the Mayacamas Mountain and the extinct Mt. Konocti volcano. The soils are rich, red Forbesville, high in iron, obsidian and volcanic rock. personally tends the vines using traditional agricultural techniques and produces terroir-driven wines that capture the essence of the high-elevation mountain site and red volcanic soils.

WINES - From Aglianico to Sangiovese, the well-structured, terroir-driven wines using traditional techniques show balanced acidity.

Kelsey Bench Sangiovese 2018 ● 216 cs; $ 30 - ⬚ - This estate grown, hand harvested fruit comes from higher elevations producing a ripe red and blue fruit-forward wine, with vivid notes of cherry, good structure with balanced acidity.

Kelsey Bench Barbera 2018 ● 200 cs; $ 30 - ⬚ - This old-world classic reflects its Italian heritage while embracing the local growing region. A versatile pairing wine with notes of pomegranate, blackberry fruit, tea leaf with low tannins, high acidity with good minerality makes this a fan favorite.

Kelsey Bench Aglianico 2018 ● 150 cs; $ 30 - ⬚ - This long aging bold red with black fruits and cherry offers a medium acidity with elegant tannins, leathery earth notes and good structure.

acres 10 - **cases** 1,600
Fertilizers compost, cover crops, organic-mineral
Plant protection organic
Weed control mechanical
Yeasts commercial cultured yeasts, selected indigenous yeasts
Grapes 100% estate-grown
Certification none

RICHMOND

PURITY WINE $

1401 Marina Way S #280 – tel. (510) 295-5442
www.puritywine.net – purity.wine@gmail.com

PEOPLE - Community minded and creative, natural wine vintner Noel Diaz's winery is the East Bay epicenter of the unpretentious, good vibes, zero zero movement—a natural wine offshoot that worships at the altar of "nothing added and nothing taken away." In a warehouse near the Richmond waterfront, he and fellow winemakers, many of whom he mentors, are discovering new flavors, making crazy blends, and blurring boundaries—redefining wine.

VINEYARDS - Committed 100 percent to organically farmed vineyards, Diaz reads each grower's pesticide use report to verify their farming. He also farms a few acres organically himself. Grapes come from seven sites. A few are in Contra Costa County. Syrah comes from Oakstone Farm and Vineyard in the town of Rough and Ready, outside Nevada City in the Sierra Foothills. Wines come and go quickly, depending on grape finds.

WINES - The wines are unfined, unfiltered and un-sulfited—i.e. zero zero—and fermented in a variety of vessels, from plastic carboys and stainless steel to neutral oak. Diaz rotates wines often, typically offering 20 different bottles at any given moment, but each is subject to disappear (with a few regular wines that don't roll off the list).

🔝 **Contra Costa County Rosehaze Pinot Gris 2021** EVERYDAY WINE ◍ 200 cs; $ 24 - A skin contact natural wine (not a ramato) this is light and fruity.

Nevada County Strawberry Daze Red Rhone Blend 2020 ● 130 cs; $ 24 - Best served chilled, the bright, juicy, glou glou, a GSM blend, shows strawberries and herbs.

Nevada County Henry's Cuvee Syrah 2018 ● 50 cs; $ 24 - Minerality notes with leather and cherries.

acres 0 - **cases** 2,500
Fertilizers n/a
Plant protection organic
Weed control mechanical
Yeasts spontaneous fermentation
Grapes purchase 100%
Certification none

RUTHERFORD

QUINTESSA

1601 Silverado Trail S – tel. (707) 286-2730
www.quintessa.com – rebekah@quintessa.com

 The winery's top tier wines are produced solely from their certified organic and biodynamic vineyards.

PEOPLE - Chilean vintner Agustin and his wife Valeria Huneeus founded this brand in 1989. Their career in wine started in Chile where Agustin worked at Concho y Toro. They have also been active in the U.S. and famously acquired and then sold other brands, including The Prisoner. The two also own many estates in Chile. They recently brought their Chilean estate director Rodrigo Soto to Quintessa. Rebekah Wineburg is the winemaker.

VINEYARDS - The 280 acres of Rutherford estate vines in Napa span five hillsides. Each block offers its own unique soil type and exposures that contribute tremendous diversity. In 2018 the team oversaw a winery redesign and an intense mapping and analysis of each of the estate's vineyard blocks to get a deeper understanding of the estate's soil characteristics.

WINES - Careful blending brings out the unique chararacteristics of their blocks.

Rutherford Quintessa 2018 ● Cabernet Sauvignon, Merlot, Cabernet Franc, Carmenère, Petit Verdot; 10,000 cs; $ 210 - 🍷 - A beautifully balanced estate blend offering layers of intense cassis, black cherry, and raspberry with savory notes of sage and thyme, with lingering hints of dark chocolate, graphite and fresh tobacco.
Illumination Sauvignon Blanc 2019 ○ n/a; $ 50 - 🍷🍷 🍷 - Illumination is the partner wine of Quintessa. Lively and expressive with grapefruit, kumquat, and guava, layered floral notes of peach blossom and fresh herbs on the nose followed with flavors of stone fruit, lemon zest with a fresh and flavorful finish.

acres 160 - **cases** 12,000
Fertilizers biodynamic compost, compost, cover crops, mineral fertilizer, organic-mineral
Plant protection biodynamic preparations, organic, sulfur
Weed control mechanical
Yeasts spontaneous fermentation
Grapes 100% estate-grown
Certification biodynamic, organic

HEALDSBURG

QUIVIRA VINEYARDS

4900 W Dry Creek Road – tel. (800) 292-8339
www.quivirawine.com – info@quivirawine.com

 Quivira is committed to long-term health of the land and vineyards with gardens, fruit trees, animals and organic farming in order to create complex and balanced wines.

PEOPLE - Holly and Henry Wendt began Quivira in Dry Creek Valley in 1981. They restored nearby Wine Creek and began converting the vineyards to organic farming. Pete and Terri Kight bought the property in 2006 and completed the conversion. Hugh Chappelle joined as winemaker in 2010 bringing decades of experience.

VINEYARDS - Quivira's vineyards are all within Dry Creek. Wine Creek Ranch is 55 acres of Sauvignon Blanc, Rhône varieties and Zinfandel on gravelly and sandy loam. Anderson Ranch is 9 acres of Zinfandel as is the 2 acre Katz Vineyard, planted in 1900. All sites boast a hot and sunny climate. Biological diversity with native plants and fauna are an integral part ensuring health and vitality to the vineyards and environment.

WINES - Chappelle uses phased picking, making several passes in the vineyard and picking by hand when fruit has the desired level of ripeness, bringing complexity and layers into the bottle.
🅣 **Dry Creek Valley Anderson Ranch Zinfandel 2017** ● 497 cs; $ 50 - 🍷 - Their "Grand Cru" , deep garnet with aromatics of juicy dark fruits and brambles. Blackberry, cherry cola, pomegranate, violet, herbs and finishing with cocoa exhibit the complexity acheived from precision-picking. Drink now or age 10 years.
🅣 **Dry Creek Valley Fig Tree Vineyard Sauvignon Blanc 2019** EVERYDAY WINE ○ 1,247 cs; $ 28 - 🍷 🍷 - Aromatics of crisp citrus, grass and white flowers. Mineral freshness lifts up white fig, green apple, melon and citrus rind with a mouth-watering and refreshing finish.Drink now or age 7 years.
Dry Creek Valley Wine Creek Ranch Rosé 2020 ◖ 1,136 cs; $ 26 - 🍷🍷 - Grenache as a base, balanced and crisp with nectarine, strawberry flavors and aromas with a smooth finish.

acres 66 - **cases** 16,000
Fertilizers compost, green manure
Plant protection n/a
Weed control mechanical
Yeasts commercial cultured yeasts, selected indigenous yeasts, spontaneous fermentation
Grapes purchase 10%
Certification some of the vineyards are certified organic

RADIO-COTEAU

RAEN

2040 Barlow Lane – tel. (707) 823-2578
www.radiocoteau.com – clientservices@radiocoteau.com

6780 McKinley Avenue – tel. (707) 633-3016
www.raenwinery.com/ – info@raenwinery.com

 Eric Sussman creates highly sought after coastal climate wines with regenerative farming and little intervention in the cellar and vineyards.

PEOPLE - After studying agriculture, Eric Sussman worked in Burgundy and the West Coast before launching Radio-Coteau in 2002, and becoming known for fine Pinot Noir. In 2012 he bought an historic 42 acre farm and estate and began rejuvenating the land through organic and biodynamic farming. Eric works collectively with a winegrowing team, instilling a collaborative work culture. The label makes sought after wines.

VINEYARDS - Purchased grapes come from coastal vineyard sites in Sonoma and Mendocino that have been farmed organically since 2002. The 42 acre, certified biodynamic estate sits on Goldridge soils, with 22 acres planted to Zinfandel, Pinot Noir and Chardonnay, a vegetable farm, honey bees, chickens, goats, fruit trees and wild lands.

WINES - Aging in large-format barrels results in wines that are fruit-forward and less influenced by wood. The wines are also Demeter certified.

Sonoma Coast Belay Estate Pinot Noir 2018 ● 200 cs; $ 74 - ⊞ - Finely nuanced expressions of cherry, cranberry, strawberry, green leaves followed by lively acidity and fine tannins with an elegant presence. Drink now or age.
Sonoma Coast SeaBed Estate Chardonnay 2019 ○ 130 cs; $ 70 - ⊞ - Aromatics of lemon curd and white flowers and takes a turn on the palate with crisp fresh pear, woody spice, full bodied with potent acidity and salinity in a lingering smooth finish. Drink now or age to 20 years.
Sonoma Coast Harrison Grade Estate Syrah 2018 ● 150 cs; $ 70 - ⊞ - First vintage from the estate rich black and blue fruits with plum, white pepper and savory spice finishing with a lengthy chocolate finish.

 Though RAEN farms organically, it also requires its suppliers to do the same, ensuring healthier vines and better wines. Chief farming officer at Monarch Tractor, Carlo is also leading the movement to electrify tractors and reduce carbon emissions in ag.

PEOPLE - When Carlo and Dante Mondavi, of the illustrious Mondavi family started a new winery in 2013, it was one few might have predicted. RAEN carries on the Mondavi's lesser known tradition of making fine Pinot but sources it from Pinot's new epicenter–the Sonoma Coast.

VINEYARDS - The duo source from a trio of organically farmed vineyards, keeping their central focus on their 7 acre Freestone Occidental estate. There the soils on two separate terraces are Goldridge sandy loam and iron rich Franciscan. In the Fort Ross-Seaview AVA, RAEN buys Chardonnay from the sought after Charles Ranch vineyard, farmed by the Martinelli family, as well as Pinot from the Sea Field.

WINES - The house style is whole cluster vinification, a restrained use of oak (less than 15% new) and native yeast fermentations.

Fort Ross-Seaview Charles Ranch Vineyard Chardonnay 2019 ○ 250 cs; $ 111 - ⊞ - Elegant, with delicate stone fruits, whispering peach and nectarine notes.
Sonoma Coast Royal St. Robert Pinot Noir 2019 ● 1,800 cs; $ 102 - ⊞ - RAEN's delicate, floral flagship wine, sourced half from Sea Field and half from the Freestone Occidental estate, is unfined and unfiltered offering up plums and red cherries on the nose, and black cherries with tea and herbs on the palate.
Freestone Occidental Bodega Vineyard Pinot Noir 2019 ● 350 cs; $ 162 - ⊞ - From three clones, this is a treasure, filled with delicate wild strawberry and cherries on the palate. Gorgeous and complex.

acres 22 - **cases** 4,000
Fertilizers compost, cover crops, organic, organic-mineral
Plant protection organic, sulfur
Weed control mechanical
Yeasts spontaneous fermentation
Grapes purchase 50%
Certification some of the vineyards are certified biodynamic, some of the vineyards are certified organic

acres 17 - **cases** 3,000
Fertilizers compost, cover crops, organic
Plant protection organic, sulfur
Weed control mechanical
Yeasts spontaneous fermentation
Grapes purchase 50%
Certification none

SANTA ROSA

RAFT WINES $

1160 Hopper Avenue – tel. (707) 477-2172
drink.raft.wine

PEOPLE - Jennifer Reichardt is one of the new generation of small wine producers who have sprung up in the fertile soil of Sonoma's informal indie incubator community. She works days in her family's business—they raise gourmet Liberty Ducks for restaurants and consumers—while growing her wine label, Raft (the word means a group of ducks). Reichardt came to wine through harvest experiences in New Zealand and Sonoma and winemaking under Pax Mahle.

VINEYARDS - Raft finds organically farmed grapes from far flung counties across the state, ranging from Sonoma to Chico (north of Sacramento), El Dorado County (in the Sierra Foothills) and Madera (in the Central Valley). Viognier comes from Love Ranch (certified organic) with granitic schist soils at 1,350 feet of elevation on a site 35 miles south of Yosemite National Park. Sangiovese comes from Nascere Vineyard in Chico where the no till vines are dry farmed.

WINES - Raft's wines are fresh and juicy, made for everyday drinking. Each is fermented in stainless steel and aged in neutral oak.

Madera Jonquille Viognier 2020 `EVERYDAY WINE` ○
108 cs; $ 25 - ▦ - Gently aromatic, bright, lively and well balanced. This is a Viognier that doesn't scream Viognier (as many Viogniers do) but seduces you with a more delicate, lighter fruit style making it a very food friendly wine.
California Sangiovese 2019 ● 250 cs; $ 23 - ▦ - This Sangiovese is fresh and juicy and has cherries written all over it. A versatile wine, it can pair easily with a wide variety of everyday dishes, including those from Italy, of course. Think pizza and pasta but also omelets, quiche, and other light fare.

acres 0 - **cases** 14,400
Fertilizers n/a
Plant protection n/a
Weed control n/a
Yeasts spontaneous fermentation
Grapes purchase 100
Certification some of the vineyards are certified organic

SONOMA

RAM'S GATE WINERY

28700 Arnold Drive – tel. (707) 721-8700
www.ramsgatewinery.com – concierge@ramsgatewinery.com

PEOPLE - Under the direction of winemaker Joe Nielsen, Ram's Gate's estate wines have come in to focus. While the winery sources fruit from status vineyards including Hyde, Durell, Gap's Crown, El Diablo and others, the radiant quality of the wines produced from this cool maritme Carneros site is undeniable. The winery's location at the gateway to Sonoma and Napa counties means the Backen & Gillam designed tasting room is never still.

VINEYARDS - The estate is planted to Chardonnay, Pinot Noir, Syrah, Grenache, Grenache Blanc, Sauvignon Blanc and Pinot Blanc with the white wines stealing the show in 2020. The winery lists Certified Sustainable Vineyard and Fish Friendly Farming® certifications but has not yet achieved organic certification. Nielsen is also making a light, spicy Rhone blend of Grenache and Syrah sourced from Estate vineyards.

WINES - Windy, fog and aspect inform the estate wines in ways that can't be disguised in the winery and Nielsen knows how to make them shine.

Carneros Estate Pinot Blanc 2020 ○ 421 cs; $ 38 - ▦ - Delicately floral aromas of acacia and chamomile with creamy, vanilla-spiced pear and refreshing acidity from this windswept site.
Carneros Estate Chardonnay 2019 ○ 776 cs; $ 78 - ▦ - Gorgeous Chablis-like acidity with Meyer lemon custard, orange blossom and stone fruit reflecting the ripeness of warmer lots through a saline mineral finish.
Carneros Estate Sauvignon Blanc 2020 ○ 587 cs; $ 38 - ▯ ▦ - One of the latest-ripening sites in Carneros, the addition of Musque elevates aromas of lemongrass, passionfruit and white peach that are mirrored on the palate.

acres 28 - **cases** 10,000
Fertilizers compost, mineral fertilizer
Plant protection organic, sulfur, synthetic pesticides
Weed control mechanical, chemical
Yeasts commercial cultured yeasts, selected indigenous yeasts
Grapes purchase 69%
Certification converting to organics

RAMBLE WINES

P.O. Box 846 – tel. (707) 512-0111
www.billydwines.com – info@billydwines.com

 Committed to organics (he was formerly on the board of the organic certifier CCOF), Billy D's passion for simple and more fresh, youthful and affordable wines—on the natural side—is finding a home.

PEOPLE - What's old is new again. Billy D., the oldest son of Jack and Jamie Davies (the famous founders of the sparkling wine house Schramsberg in Napa) grew up in the wine world, foot stomping grapes with the greats—with Robert Mondavi and the like. His new wine label, Ramble, was inspired by time spent in Brooklyn's natural wine bars. Now he's making fresh, young wines from organic vines.

VINEYARDS - The warm inland Ukiah area in Mendocino is the source for his Ramble wines which come from a certified organic vineyard called Buddha's Dharma. There Davies buys old vine, dry farmed Carignan, Charbono, Chenin Blanc, and Valdiguié. Planted in 1944, the vines sit on gravelly, volcanic soil at the foot of Enlightenment Mountain.

WINES - The wines are all foot trod, vinified with native yeast, and limited to 50 ppm of sulfites, which means they qualify as natural wines. They are food friendly and low in alcohol. Billy D's daughter Abbie is responsible for the wines' arty labels.

TOP Mendocino County Buddha's Dharma Vineyard Carignan 2019 EVERYDAY WINE ● n/a; $ 30 - 🍷 - Half of this wine goes through carbonic maceration, making it a bit like a Beajolais. Fresh and lively, with lovely cherry zing notes.
Mendocino County Buddha's Dharma Vineyard Rose of Valdiquié 2019 🍷 n/a; $ 25 - 🍷 - A versatile choice for food pairings.
Mendocino County Buddha's Dharma Vineyard Chenin Blanc 2019 ○ n/a; $ 28 - 🍷 - Aromatic, filled with a bit of spice and lots of stone fruit.

---

acres 0 - **cases** 1,000
Fertilizers compost, cover crops, organic
Plant protection organic
Weed control mechanical
Yeasts spontaneous fermentation
Grapes purchase 100%
Certification organic

RIDGE VINEYARDS

17100 Monte Bello Road – tel. (408) 867-3233
www.ridgewine.com

 As the largest organic winegrower in Sonoma and Santa Cruz counties, land stewardship a priority.

PEOPLE - 2021 was a year of milestones for John Olney who was promoted to head winemaker at the Ridge Lytton Springs estate where he has been chief operating officer since 1999. Under Olney's guidance, Ridge has evolved founding winemaker Paul Draper's legacy to become a model for organic and regenerative winegrowing in Sonoma and Santa Cruz counties. As a member of the International Wineries for Climate Action (IWCA), an association of wineries dedicated to decarbonizing the global wine industry, the winery is committed to reducing carbon emissions to zero by 2050.

VINEYARDS - As of 2021, Ridge received organic certification for a collective 379 acres of vines at the Monte Bello, Lytton Springs, Geyserville, and East Bench vineyards. In response to drought, Olney reduced yields in 2021 with a more aggressive green harvest.

WINES - Founder Paul Draper's "pre-industrial" approach to winemaking has never faltered and, as such, wine style has remained true to form at Ridge.
TOP Santa Cruz Mountains Monte Bello Estate Cabernet Sauvignon 2018 SLOW WINE ● 4,050 cs; $ 230 - 🍷 - Black and red currant finely laced with black tea and a medley of brown spices progress to firm, darker fruits on the palate driven by ample acidity and tannins through a savory finish.
Alexander Valley Geyserville Zinfandel 2019 ● 10,000 cs; $ 45 - 🍷 - A field blend of 71% Zinfandel, 19% Carignane, 7% Petite Sirah and 3% Alicante Bouschet with bright red cherry, raspberry with star anise and resinous, dried herbs through a lengthy, saline finish.
Dry Creek Valley Lytton Springs Zinfandel 2019 ● 11,000 cs; $ 45 - 🍷 - This blend of 73% Zinfandel, 16% Petite Sirah, 9% Carignane, 2% Mataro shows generous amounts of red-fruited tannin and acidity with complex lavender notes deepening to peppery blue and black fruit

---

acres 450 - **cases** 80,000
Fertilizers compost, humus, mineral fertilizer
Plant protection copper, organic, sulfur, synthetic pesticides
Weed control mechanical, chemical
Yeasts spontaneous fermentation
Grapes purchase 30%
Certification some of the vineyards are certified organic

ROBERT SINSKEY VINEYARDS

6320 Silverado Trail – tel. (707) 944-9090
www.robertsinskey.com

 Producing beautiful fruit and wines, this producer embodies ecofriendly practices and makes deeply satisfying wines.

PEOPLE - In 1982, Bob Sinskey, a retired eye doctor, followed his nose for Pinot to the Carneros and bought land. Today his son Robert and his wife Maria Helm Sinskey, a renowned chef, run the family winery. Maria brings a foodie perspective, cultivating relationships with top chefs, growing organic produce at the winery, and pioneering the farm to table movement with chef made food pairings at the winery.

VINEYARDS - In 1990, Sinskey became concerned about the effects of pesticides on soil health and began experimenting with organic farming. They found it improved wine quality and by 2003 all was certified organic. The current wine grower is Kari Flores. Pinot Noir predominates (70 acres), alongside 60 acres of Bordeaux varieties and 30 acres of Alsatian varieties.

WINES - A who's who of organic viticulturists including Kirk Grace and Debbie Zygielbaum—and now Cari Flores— have tended the vines at the estate. Jeff Virnig is the winemaker since 1991

Los Carneros Scintilla Sonoma Vineyard Abraxas 2018 O 2,150 cs; $ 36 - 🍷 - A one of a kind Alsatian blend, and beautifully textured, it is lively, crisp, and refreshing. Floral on the nose with tropical fruits on the palate. Extremely versatile, it pairs handily with a wide variety of foods.
Los Carneros Pinot Noir 2017 ● 5,920 cs; $ 50 - 🛢 - A broad mix of clones and grapes from all 24 estate parcels: red fruits and roses shine through. Aged 30% in new French oak.
Napa Valley Marcien 2013 ● 1,340 cs; $ 110 - 🛢 - Sinskey describes this as a "right bank" Bordeaux blend, with Merlot, Cabernet Franc and Cabernet Sauvignon in the mix. Aged for 8 years (30% in new French oak), the 2013 offers up complex, integrated notes of plum, brambly fruit and herbs.

acres 178 - **cases** 20,000
Fertilizers compost, cover crops
Plant protection organic, sulfur
Weed control animal grazing, mechanical
Yeasts commercial cultured yeasts, spontaneous fermentation
Grapes 100% estate-grown
Certification organic

ROCCA FAMILY VINEYARDS

129 Devlin Road – tel. (707) 257-8467
www.roccawines.com – hello@roccawines.com

 This family run, eco friendly winery in Napa makes an extra effort to promote health locally and internationally.

PEOPLE - Medical professionals as well as growers and vintners, Mary Rocca, a Santa Rosa native, and her husband Eric Grigsby started their wine label in 2000. Their 2002 wines, by Celia Welch, won top prizes in prestigious blind tastings, surprising many. Welch's assistant Paul Colantuoni then made the wines until 2021, when Tom Sherwood became the new winemaker. The Rocca's donate winery profits to medical research and international health projects.

VINEYARDS - Two estate vineyards grow Cabernet Franc, Cabernet Sauvignon, Merlot, Petit Sirah, and Syrah. The 21 acre Grigsby vineyard in Yountville sits on Bale clay loam soils. Their 10 acre Collinetta vineyard in Coombsville was planted on virgin Sobrante loam and Hambright-Rock outcrop soils a site that's cooler than Grigsby.

WINES - The estate wines offer a lesson in terroir, providing an excellent comparison of the soil types and climate of each site. Current releases were made by outgoing winemaker Paul Colantuoni.

🔝 **Sonoma Coast UV Chardonnay 2019** SLOW WINE O 313 cs; $ 65 - 🛢 - From the coveted UV Vineyard in Sebastopol: complex and rounded, it's barrel fermented, giving it a plush texture, with lively citrus notes, hazelnuts and oak notes from 15 months in French oak (30 percent new).
Yountville Cabernet Sauvignon 2018 ● 228 cs; $ 95 - 🛢 - The wine spends 21 months in French oak barrels (70% new), showing plums and red, blue and black fruits—cherries, raspberries, red currants, and blackberries.
Coombsville Collinetta Cabernet Sauvignon 2018 ● 251 cs; $ 95 - 🛢 - Pure Coombsville (a site with cooler temperatures and a longer ripening season than Grigsby), leading to a more savory and herbaceous notes of red fruits and tobacco. It's aged 21 months in French oak barrels (80% new).

acres 31 - **cases** 2,000
Fertilizers compost, cover crops, organic
Plant protection organic, sulfur
Weed control mechanical
Yeasts spontaneous fermentation
Grapes purchase 10%
Certification organic

HEALDSBURG

RUTH LEWANDOWSKI WINE $

132 Plaza Street – tel. (707)385-1797
www.ruthlewandowskiwines.com
evan@ruthlewandowskiwines.com

PEOPLE - Evan Lewandowski started his label intending to make wine in Utah. The state is near and dear to his heart, and after viticulture school and international internships, he saw its potential. He set out to source fruit from California and then bring it back to Utah to ferment but pivoted to using the grapes he helps manage in California to make wine at a cooperative with other natural winemakers.

VINEYARDS - Lewandowski leases land in Boulder, Utah, with the goal of planting a vineyard there. But in the meantime, 98% of the fruit he uses comes from Mendocino County, from five varied sites. Two are managed by him completely, and the other three are farmed by friends or long-time farmers that he trusts. The one non-Mendicino source of fruit comes from the esteemed Rorick Heritage Vineyard in the Sierra Foothills of Calaveras County.

WINES - The wines are varied and diverse in each release, but often feature unusual blends using obscure Italian varieties.

🔝 **Mendocino Testa Vineyard Boaz 2019** SLOW WINE ●
230 cs; $ 40 - 🏠 - A flagship wine, this blend of 78% Carignan, 13% Cabernet Sauvignon and 9% Grenache is foot trod and basket pressed. It appeals to traditional palates as well as die-hard natural wine fans. Sourced from the historic, organically certified Testa Ranch.

🔝 **Mendocino Fox Hill Vineyard Feints 2020**
EVERYDAY WINE ● 1,250 cs; $ 26 - 🍶 - The most recognizable wine, its sales took off in 2013, with the swelling of the natural wine tide in the U.S. It is a chillable, summer red, lighthearted and easy breezy, a co-fermentation of all the Piedmontese varieties found at Fox Hill Vineyard: Dolcetto, Barbera, Nebbiolo, Arneis and Montepulciano. "Feints" is a fencing term, a maneuver designed to throw off your opponent, like a fake.

acres 0 - **cases** 5,000
Fertilizers compost, cover crops, manure, organic
Plant protection organic, sulfur
Weed control mechanical
Yeasts spontaneous fermentation
Grapes purchase 100%
Certification some of the vineyards are certified organic

LOMPOC

SANDHI WINES   🍾

1712 Industrial Way, Suite B – tel. (805) 500-8337
www.sandhiwines.com – tasting@sandhiwines.com

PEOPLE - Sandhi is one of three projects that Sashi Moorman and Raj Parr collaborate on. It focuses on grapes from the Santa Rita Hills. Though the two are fascinated by single vineyard chardonnay and pinot noir and produce some of the best examples, the company's bread and butter are medium production regional wines, particularly chardonnay, of which former somm, Parr has been able to make internationally popular by means of its extensive placement in restaurants.

VINEYARDS - Much of Sandhi wine is sourced from Domaine de la Côte, the duo's estate vineyards for the eponymous brand which is farmed according to biodynamic principles. The larger production wine is sourced from various growers mostly in San Luis Obispo County. Single vineyard sources such as Sanford and Benedict and Bentrock Vineyards are at the heart of Sandhi's terroir-driven project for chardonnay and pinot noir.

WINES - Moorman and Parr access elevation, the diatomaceous soils and northern exposures for maximum expression.

🔝 **Sta. Rita Hills Bentrock Vineyard Chardonnay 2018** ○ 100 cs; $ 50 - 🏠 - Extraordinary in its intensity. Concentrated but delicate apple and citrus fruit are at play with pronounced acidity and mineral flavors supported by a trace of nuttiness.
Sta. Rita Hills Sanford and Benedict Chardonnay 2018 ○ 200 cs; $ 50 - 🏠 - Shows mineral qualities on display under yellow apple and white peach fruit. Elegant white flower combines with yellow apple on the nose.
Sta. Rita Hills Sanford & Benedict Vineyard Pinot Noir 2018 ● 200 cs; $ 50 - 🏠 - Shows pretty aromas of dried flowers, strawberry and orange. The palate is of red cherry and strawberry with earth undercurrents.

acres 17 - **cases** 11,000
Fertilizers compost, green manure, mineral fertilizer
Plant protection copper, organic, sulfur, synthetic pesticides
Weed control mechanical
Yeasts spontaneous fermentation
Grapes purchase 30%
Certification none

APTOS

SANTE ARCANGELI FAMILY WINES $

154 Aptos Village Way C-1 – tel. (831) 207-6048
www.santewinery.com – aptos@santewinery.com

PEOPLE - Owner and winemaker John Benedetti was influenced by his great grandfather's wine cellar. Some would say he has wine in his blood. Homebrewing beer led to hobby winemaking, before he turned pro. He also makes wines at Lester Vineyard. On his own, Benedetti is known for his Santa Cruz Mountain Pinot Noirs. In 2019, his wife tragically passed away, leaving him as a single dad to a young son. The wildfires in 2020 were an additional stressor.

VINEYARDS - Benedetti sources most of his fruit from small vineyards in the Corralitos area. In 2020, he did not make any wine from his former "signature" vineyard, Split Rail, due to smoke damage. He collaborates with Prudy Fox, a respected local viticulturist and has started putting her name on the back of his bottles. He also sources fruit from Sonoma and Mendocino.

WINES - Benedetti wants his wines to be clean and precise, and have the vineyard site show through more than the cellar.

🔟 **Santa Cruz Mountains Split Rail Vineyard Pinot Noir 2019** SLOW WINE ● 400 cs; $ 49 - ⊞ - Amazingly lighbodied, lively and floral. "It's not me, it's the site...It's such a unique place," explains Benedetti. This vineyard holds the true history of the Santa Cruz Mountains, captured in this bottle. Split Rail is the last of the purely original Paul Masson massale cuttings, and the rose and forest floor notes are gorgeous.
🔟 **Santa Cruz Mountains Lester Family Vineyard Chardonnay 2019** ○ 150 cs; $ 32 - ⊞ - Bright and acid-driven, with a nod to Burgundy stylistically, a creamy backnote and lovely minerality. Benedetti was worried about this wine because PG&E cut the power during fermentation due to a heat wave, but that slipup ended up changing his approach, leading to a lesson in fluidity.

---

acres 7 - cases 833
Fertilizers compost, green manure
Plant protection organic, sulfur
Weed control mechanical
Yeasts selected indigenous yeasts
Grapes purchase 40%
Certification none

HOPLAND

SARACINA VINEYARDS

11684 US 101 – tel. (707) 670-0199
www.saracina.com – amacgregor@saracina.com

PEOPLE - John Fetzer and Patty Rock, husband and wife team, originally founded Saracina Estate in 2001, built a winery and wine cave and set to making top-rated wines in Mendocino County. In 2018, the 110 acre estate was sold to the Taub family and CEO Marc Taub, took over stewardship. Founding winemaker, Alex MacGregor, who began as a sommelier in Canada, studied enology and viticulture in the US has continued to craft wine at Saracina.

VINEYARDS - Saracina is home to vineyards (under conversion), 140 year old olive trees, vegetable gardens, bee hives, domestic and wild animals, keeping diversity at the forefront. Historic Casas Verde Vineyard (certified organic) was planted with Carignane, Grenache and French Colombard in 1945 and is dry farmed. Lolonis Vineyard (certified organic) has the oldest Sauvignon Blanc vines in the country, planted in 1942 at 200 ft. elevation in a cooler climate with longer time to ripen.

WINES - Using bâtonnage, newer and older oak barrels, MacGregor has passion and skill for creating single variety and red blends from old vines in Mendocino.

Redwood Valley Lolonis Vineyard Sauvignon Blanc 2020 ○ 200 cs; $ 34 - ⊞ - White peach, white flowers, sweet hay, balanced acidity mid- palate with creamy long finish. Drink now or age to 10 years.
Redwood Valley Winter's Edge 2018 ● 200 cs; $ 30 - ⊞ - Old vine field blend presents ripe red fruit, dried cranberry, brambly, bay laurel with dusty rose and spice. LIghter red with noticeable tannin. Drink now or age
Mendocino County Sauvignon Blanc 2020 ○ 1,000 cs; $ 20 - ⊞ - Enters crisp and bright, juicy mouth-watering lime, minerality and a lively acidic structure. Drink now.

---

acres 30 - cases 7,000
Fertilizers compost, green manure
Plant protection organic, sulfur
Weed control mechanical
Yeasts commercial cultured yeasts, spontaneous fermentation
Grapes purchase 40%
Certification some of the vineyards are certified organic

SCHOLIUM PROJECT 🍾

4185 East Third Avenue
www.scholiumwines.com

PEOPLE - Abe Schoener was a professor of philosophy when, on a sabbatical year, he interned with the legendary winemaker, John Kongsgaard, learning his unorthodox protocols which allowed more oxygen and less SO2 exposure to his wine than most. When Schoener made his own wine, he pushed the protocols to the extreme. His results included failures, but his successes resulted in his recognition as an innovator making thrilling bottles.

VINEYARDS - Though Schoener makes varietal wines, he is less concerned with the grape grown than with the terroir and conditions. When his experimentalism leads to riding a fine line between success and failure, perfect grapes are the best hedge; that is, grapes without chemical inputs or preferably none at all. Sources include the Farina Vineyard in Sonoma, the ancient Bechthold vineyard and Tegan Passalaqua's Kirschenmann old vine vineyards in Lodi.

WINES - While admired for his mostly sulfurless wines, Schoener, does not shy away from sulfur when hygienically necessary or used as a wine making tool. His love of travel and his gentle but absolute candor have gained him a devoted following.

🔴 **California The Prince In His Caves 2018** SLOW WINE ◎ 342 cs; $ 50 - A skin-contact Sauvignon Blanc with refined tannins, a caramel apple nose and a rich apple/pear palate.
California Bechthold Ranch 1MN 2019 ● 342 cs; $ 38 - A cinsault which shows deep dark cherry and orange fruit suffused with earth and mineral qualities.
California Kirchenmann On The Molekumne FTP-C 2018 ○ 66 cs; $ 36 - An old vine chenin blanc with concentrated green fruit and almond on the nose and a palate showing pear, apple and a mouth-watering acid structure.

acres 0 - **cases** 1,500
Fertilizers none
Plant protection organic, sulfur
Weed control mechanical
Yeasts spontaneous fermentation
Grapes purchase 100%
Certification none

SCRIBE 🍾
🍽️

2100 Denmark Street – tel. (707) 939-1858
www.scribewinery.com – frontdesk@scribewinery.com

PEOPLE - The Mariani brothers hail from a family of Italian nut farmers in Winters. Adam and Andrew came to Sonoma in 2007, purchasing a crumbling 1858 hacienda and transforming it into a David Ireland inspired architectural wow—a super chic food and wine Mecca—it's even mentioned by Goop—serving estate grown vegetables and wines in an arty, indoor-outdoor setting. Slow Food trained chef Kelly Mariani, their sister, runs the impressive culinary program.

VINEYARDS - The estate has 60 acres of vines in Sonoma Valley. The estate emphasis is on Chardonnay (24 acres) and Pinot Noir (27 acres). As an homage to the German immigrant Dresel brothers, who owned the property in the 1850's, the winery grows Riesling and Sylvaner as well as the Mission grape, which were historically grown here. Additional grapes are sourced from 8-10 growers and help to fuel production of 3,000 cases of their popular rosé each year.

WINES - Gustavo Sotelo-Miller uses partial whole cluster inclusion and a bit of concrete aging. He's working on making the Mission grape into something delectable.

🔴 **Sonoma Valley Estate Pinot Noir 2018** ● 1,800 cs; $ 50 - Six different clones of Pinot give this unfined and unfiltered wine purity and complexity. It gets partial whole cluster inclusion (10% max) and 8 months of aging in oak (12% new) and 1% in concrete egg.
Sonoma Valley Estate Chardonnay 2020 ○ 1,100 cs; $ 48 - Whole cluster pressed, fermented cold in a concrete egg and stainless steel tanks for 17 days and then aged for an additional 5 months in concrete. Bright, lively and elegant.
Sonoma Valley Sparkling Mission 2020 ❄ 100 cs; $ 48 - An ongoing experiment, this inaugural vintage is an ode to the first variety planted in California, the Mission grape, originally planted by Spanish missionaries in California. This vintage is 30% whole cluster inclusion. Tastes of sour cherries and cranberries.

acres 53 - **cases** 15,000
Fertilizers compost, cover crops, mineral fertilizer, organic
Plant protection organic, synthetic pesticides
Weed control chemical, mechanical, n/a
Yeasts commercial cultured yeasts, spontaneous fermentation
Grapes purchase 50%
Certification none

MARINA

SEABOLD CELLARS

3348 Paul Davis Drive #100
tel. (831) 641-7730 - (831) 288-2730
www.seaboldcellars.com – chris@seaboldcellars.com

PEOPLE - Master Sommelier Chris Miller and beloved California enologist/viticulturalist Peter Figge, a graduate of the master's program at UC Davis, founded Seabold Cellars as custom crush facility in 2014. When Figge passed away unexpectedly in 2017, Miller took over as winemaker. Today, with Operations Director Lucas Orme, Miller continues to produce wines under Seabold, BOLD, and Adroît labels in part to honor the legacy of his dear friend, one of Monterey's most respected winemakers.

VINEYARDS - Miller sources grapes from select vineyards in Monterey/San Benito in the Central Coast and from Sonoma, including Olson in Prunedale, Zabala and Mission Ranch in Arroyo Seco, Siletto Estate (CCOF transitioning 2nd year) in San Benito, Pelio (CCOF transitioning 1st year) in Carmel Valley, Paraiso in Santa Lucia Highlands, Brousseau and Rodnick Farm (both CCOF Certified organic) in Chalone AVA, Four Sisters in Paso Robles and Simpatico Ranch in Sonoma's Bennett Valley.

WINES - Chris is a pioneering spirit who ardently pursues his mission of producing non-interventionist Burgundy and Rhone varieties from iconic yet not well-known or recognized legacy vineyards.

Chalone Brousseau Vineyard The Swale Pinot Noir 2018 ● 98 cs; $ 56 - ⓦ - Medium-bodied, classically delicate, tart and dry with notes of cherry, red plum, mushroom and sandalwood.
Monterey Pelio Vineyard East Ridge Pinot Noir 2017 ● 275 cs; $ 49 - ⓦ - Layered, complex, light, tart and dry with notes of cherry, sarsaparilla, mushroom, tar and dried herbs.
San Benito Siletto Vineyard Adroît Trousseau 2020 ● 168 cs; $ 28 - ⓦ - Light, energetic, crisp and dry with notes of meyer lemon, blood orange, cranberry and dried herbs.

acres 0 - cases 4,000
Fertilizers compost, organic-mineral
Plant protection organic, sulfur
Weed control mechanical
Yeasts spontaneous fermentation
Grapes purchase 100%
Certification some of the vineyards are certified organic

NAPA

SEAN WALKER MCBRIDE $

45 Enterprise Court, #6 – tel. (707) 258-8599
www.seanwmcbride.com – info@crosbyroamann.com

PEOPLE - Sean Walker McBride founded his eponymous brand in 2016, setting out to make handmade, single vineyard bottlings from choice vineyards. A lawyer by training, he works with many vintners on the business side of things from his office and winery in an industrial office complex south of Napa called the Crusher District. He also makes wine under the Crosby Roamann label. The winery makes affordable, hand crafted wines.

VINEYARDS - Farmed by Chris and Stephanie Tebbutt, Filigreen Farm is a certified biodynamic 87 acre farm and vineyard with 17 acres of Pinot Noir and Pinot Gris and additional acres devoted to heritage fruits, olives and vegetable crops. Fertilizer comes solely from azolla, a tiny fern that grows in the farm's ponds. It efficiently sequesters large amounts of carbon and eliminates the need for compost from animals. The farm is surrounded by redwood forests.

WINES - The two Pinot Noirs are made with 50 percent whole cluster and aged in 25 to 50 percent new oak. They are hand pressed and hand bottled.

ⓣⓞⓟ **Anderson Valley China Block Pinot Noir 2018** EVERYDAY WINE ● 108 cs; $ 28 - 🍷 - From vines planted in 2005: brims with ripe cherry and red berry notes.
Anderson Valley Old St. George Pinot Noir 2018 ● 134 cs; $ 32 - 🍷 - From slower ripening, Old St. George rootstock blocks, originally planted in 1951 (and later grafted over to Pinot Noir): cherries on the nose followed by dark red fruits.

acres 0 - cases 1,000
Fertilizers biodynamic compost
Plant protection biodynamic preparations, organic
Weed control mechanical
Yeasts spontaneous fermentation
Grapes purchase 100%
Certification biodynamic

SANTA CRUZ

SILVER MOUNTAIN VINEYARDS

1146 Soquel Avenue – tel. (408) 353-2278
www.silvermtn.com – info@silvermtn.com

PEOPLE - Silver Mountain Vineyards, a leader in organic farming in the Santa Cruz Mountains for over 40 years, was founded by Jerold O'Brien in 1979 with environmental stewardship his top priority. In addition to the certified organic estate vineyard, sustainable practices at the winery feature the largest solar array in the Mountains, a vast rain catchment system, and a concrete wine cave for barrel storage. Anthony Craig is lead winemaker.

VINEYARDS - Jerold revived grape growing on the 10-acre estate he bought in 1973. The site had been a vineyard from 1870 to 1920, but was planted to fruit trees during Prohibition. He certified the vines organic in 1980. Chardonnay vines are own-rooted Mount Eden clones; Pinot Noir are Swan clones. The vineyard sits at 2,100 feet on a southwest-facing hillside above the fogline surrounded by redwood forest. Additional fruit comes from local growers.

WINES - Wines are made in the Old World style using minimal intervention and a gravity fed system, and released after 3 to 6 years bottle age.

TOP Santa Cruz Mountains Estate Chardonnay SLOW WINE ○ 100 cs; $ 34 - Showcasing the terroir and Mr. Craig's skilled winemaking, this elegant Chardonnay offers lemon tart, yuzu, pineapple, mango, sandalwood, baking spice, and vanilla, refreshing acidity and a long silky finish.
Santa Cruz Mountains Estate Pinot Noir 2015 ● 60 cs; $ 44 - Dark cherries, damson plum, licorice, and powdered nutmeg notes followed by tobacco, potpourri, black tea, and cola.
Santa Cruz Mountains Alloy 2015 ● 300 cs; $ 34 - A classic Bordeaux blend with aromas of blackberry, shishito pepper, mint, violet, and graphite, and a complex explosion on the palate of black fruits, earth, clove, cedar, coffee, and mint.

acres 10 - **cases** 2,000
Fertilizers compost, cover crops, organic-mineral
Plant protection organic, sulfur, synthetic pesticides
Weed control chemical, mechanical
Yeasts commercial cultured yeasts
Grapes purchase 60%
Certification some of the vineyards are certified organic

AVILA BEACH

SINOR-LAVALLEE

550 1st Street – tel. (805) 459-9595
sinorlavallee.com – wineclub@sinorlavallee.com

PEOPLE - When Mike Sinor was confronted with the covid closures of 2020 he reached into his inventory of past vintages, offering discounts to wine club members. The response was positive and business was only slightly off from 2019. Sinor is the founding winemaker at the much larger Ancient Peaks which allows him to observe mass market tendencies.

VINEYARDS - Sinor purchased the 30 acre Bassi vineyard in 2013 and all his wines are from the estate. A mere 1.2 mile from the Pacific, the vineyard consists of decomposed marine sandstones over a shallow bedrock. A prevailing north wind reduces disease pressure. With little organic material in the soil, grape yields tend to be low. Slopes are dramatic and exposures varied which has drawn in some of the best producers in the region as customers for grapes. Farming uses no synthetic inputs and employs homeopathic tea sprays.

WINES - Sinor releases two lines of wine for his company, one with grapes picked earlier with lower alcohols and the other riper and more fruit driven.

TOP San Luis Obispo Bassi Vineyard Whole Cluster Pinot Noir 2018 SLOW WINE ● 72 cs; $ 50 - Releases extravagant floral and Indian masala aromas while flavors show a dark cherry and deeply mineral palate.
San Luis Obispo Bassi Vineyard White Label Chardonnay 2016 ○ 50 cs; $ 40 - Wears its maturity with a burnt butter and ripe yellow apple nose while the palate displays pure, rich apple and lemon rind.
San Luis Obispo Bassi Vineyard White Label Syrah 2018 ● 50 cs; $ 48 - Shows meat smoke, baking spice and amaretto on the nose with blackberry and an oceanic mineral vein on the palate.

acres 30 - **cases** 1,000
Fertilizers organic-mineral
Plant protection organic
Weed control mechanical
Yeasts commercial cultured yeasts, spontaneous fermentation
Grapes 100% estate-grown
Certification none

SNOWDEN VINEYARDS

490 Taplin Road – tel. (707) 963-4292
www.snowdenvineyards.com – office@snowdenvineyards.com

 Deeply rooted in Napa, this family run operation makes classic, terroir driven wines in the hands of a third generation family winemaker.

PEOPLE - When Randy Snowden was a child, he suffered from sickliness. The family doctor told his parents, Wayne and Virginia, to take him to a hot and sunny locale which led to buying 160 acres in 1955. They developed into growers, selling to a who's who of pioneering Napa wine legends—Warren Winiarski and Joe Heitz. In 1993, Randy and his brother expanded into estate winemaking. In 2005 third generation Diane Snowden-Seysses became the winemaker.

VINEYARDS - The 23 acres of vines are above Auberge du Soleil at 600 feet of elevation. Soils are light tufa–volcanic rhyolite—with a variety of exposures. Most is planted to Bordeaux varieties. Abundant wildlife and forests of oak, madrone, bay and fir occupy 137 acres of the property. The vineyard is in the first year of the three year path to organic certification.

WINES - Diane Snowden-Seysses married a Frenchman and lives in the Bourgogne. In Napa, she began making the family's wines using classic, traditional French techniques.

Napa Valley Sunninghill Sauvignon Blanc 2018 ○ 550 cs; $ 30 - 🍷📦 - The only U.S. wine to take a gold medal in the Concours Mondial du Sauvignon in 2018 (in a previous vintage), it's lively, with delicate citrus flavors; pressed whole cluster, barrel fermented by wild yeasts, and creamy from sur lee aging.
Napa Valley The Ranch Cabernet Sauvignon 2018 ● 1,800 cs; $ 55 - 📦 - Clean, pure, fresh 100 percent Cabernet, offering up black fruits and fine tannins.
Napa Valley Brothers Vineyard Cabernet Sauvignon 2018 ● 708 cs; $ 90 - 📦 - From an outstanding vintage, this ageworthy wine show dark fruits, refined tannins and beautifully balanced acidity.

acres 23 - cases 2,083
Fertilizers compost, cover crops, organic-mineral
Plant protection organic
Weed control mechanical
Yeasts spontaneous fermentation
Grapes 100% estate-grown
Certification converting to organics

SPEAR VINEYARDS & WINERY

6700 E Highway 246 – tel. (805) 735-2190
www.spearwinery.com – visit@spearwinery.com

PEOPLE - With high demand for their certified organic fruit from Sta. Rita Hills, Spear will add vines on 1100 acre former cattle ranch property which ranges from near sea level to 900'. Guided by Ofer Shepher, Ben Merz, and Shannon Gledhill, Spear maintains wildlife corridors and habitat along with nourishing soils, enriching diversity, and providing for the vitality of microorganisms to continually improve vine health and vineyard expression. Winemaker Sonja Medeski joined in 2021

VINEYARDS - Located along the Highway 246 corridor in the heart of Sta. Rita Hills AVA, Spear has some of the highest elevation plantings. On 38 acres in 2012 they began planting: 15 acres with 7 clones Pinot noir, 10 acres with 5 clones Chardonnay, 4 acres Syrah, 4 acres grenache, and 1.5 acres of Grüner Veltliner all grown with diverse rootstock, orientation, elevation, soils, and with a commitment to sustainable and organic farming; no trees removed!

WINES - Spear crafts wines that clearly communicate the voices of the vineyard by highlighting the various blocks in small, intimate lots.

Sta. Rita Hills Gnesa Chardonnay 2018 ○ 350 cs; $ 45 - 🍷 -Grown on its own roots, this daffodil colored chardonnay has freesia, pineapple, nutmeg, and toasted hazelnut aromas with light, crisp refreshing fruits of lemon and apple.
Sta. Rita Hills Estate Pinot Noir 2019 ● 420 cs; $ 45 - 📦 - Sourced from every block on the estate and made with 15% whole cluster, a very pale raspberry pinot noir greets the eye with aromas of roses, raspberries, and cola while earth, pomegranate, cranberry, and a mineral finish delight the palate.
Sta. Rita Hills 943 Pinot Noir 2019 ● 75 cs; $ 60 - 📦 - Sourced from the 943 block and 100% destemmed, delicate aromas of fruit and florals with a touch of violets belie the tart bright fruits of cranberry, wild strawberry, and cherry.

acres 38 - cases 1,500
Fertilizers compost, humus
Plant protection n/a
Weed control mechanical
Yeasts spontaneous fermentation
Grapes 100% estate-grown
Certification some of the vineyards are certified organic

ST. HELENA

SPOTTSWOODE ESTATE VINEYARD & WINERY

1902 Madrona Ave – tel. (707) 963-0134
www.spottswoode.com – estate@spottswoode.com

 Spottswoode was among the first wineries in Napa Valley to champion organic certification which it has held since 1992.

PEOPLE - Spottswoode was originally founded in 1882 by George Schonewald and the winery celebrates its 50th anniversary under the ownership of the Novak family in 2022. This multigenerational family business is led by Beth Novak Milliken who manages the winery, and sister Lindy Novak serves as the winery's marketing ambassador. Novak Milliken is an ardent advocate for the planet and the winery's One Earth philosophy encompasses her holistic approach.

VINEYARDS - The winery uses neither synthetic or organic herbicides and enriches their alluvial, clay loam soils with vetch, peas, clover, oats and California grasses in the cover crop. Modified trellising, tighter vine spacing and state-of-the-art drainage systems have furthered both vine health and wine quality. The Estate Vineyard is both CCOF and Demeter certified.

WINES - The winery is B Corp certified and is working toward LEED certification. Winemaker and vineyard manager Aron Weinkauf implements the myriad holistic practices that guide both the estate farming and wine production.

TOP **St. Helena Napa Valley Spottswoode Estate Cabernet Sauvignon 2018** SLOW WINE ● 4,278 cs; $ 235 - 🍷 - A deep black core built around mulberry, blackberry, clove and black pepper expand to tertiary notes of mushroom and dense, mouthcoating tannins.
Napa Valley Lyndenhurst Cabernet Sauvignon 2018 ● 2,966 cs; $ 85 - 🍷 - Cassis, dusty cocoa and toasty sandalwood enrich the red plum and red currant fruit of this spectacular blend of all five Bordeaux varieties.
Spottswoode Sauvignon Blanc 2020 O 3,000 cs; $ 42 - 🍷 - Blended with small amounts of Sémillon and Sauvignon Musque that add green tea aromas, zippy lime and topical notes of coconut, green mango and apricot.

WATSONVILLE

STIRM WINE CO.

65 Rogge Lane – tel. (831) 854-7611
www.stirmwine.com – ryan@stirmwine.com

PEOPLE - Ryan Stirm grew up in a garden and exploring nature which led him to Cal Poly-San Luis Obispo, he got a degree in viticulture and enology. His lo-fi approach has made him very popular in the natural wine movement. In September of 2020, Stirm and his wife welcomed a son, moved close to the winery, where he is playing around with a huge range of hard to find varieties, as well as custom crush work that helps pay for the space and equipment.

VINEYARDS - Stirm sources grapes from six different sites, including one in the Santa Cruz Mountains that he farms himself practicing no-till, dry-farming. His signature Riesling comes from Wirz Vineyard, a very hot site in the Cienega Valley. He also made Syrah from a friend's tiny Miers-Kuenster Vineyard in Sonoma. Stirm just planted Vermentino and Albarino grapes at the property surrounding his winery which he plans to pick in 2024.

WINES - Due to wildfires, Stirm did not make a 2020 vintage of his Santa Cruz Mountains Pinot Noir. Instead, he distilled it and aged it slightly in oak, which created a nutty, intense sip for the lucky few who might inquire about it at a tasting onsite.

TOP **San Benito County Siletto Cabernet Pfeffer 2020** SLOW WINE ● 240 cs; $ 33 - 🍷 - A rarely grown variety originally from Bordeaux, but marketed as from Saratoga–and given the last name Pfeffer. It's now only planted in San Benito County. Reminiscent of Nebbiolo. Full of dusty rose and dried flower notes.
TOP **Los Chuchaquis Champelli Sparkling Albariño 2020** EVERYDAY WINE ☼ 700 cs; $ 26 - 🍷 - Made en triage, with zero sulfites, it is bright and effervescent, with grapefruit and crisp lime salinity.
Cienega Valley Calcite White 2020 O 340 cs; $ 18 - 🍷 - A barrel fermented, organic blend of Riesling, Chardonnay and Scheurebe, a German hybrid grape.

---

acres 46 - **cases** 10,244
Fertilizers compost, cover crops, organic-mineral
Plant protection biodynamic preparations, organic
Weed control mechanical
Yeasts commercial cultured yeasts
Grapes purchase 10%
Certification some of the vineyards are certified organic, some of the vineyards are certified biodynamic

acres 0 - **cases** 2,000
Fertilizers compost, cover crops, organic
Plant protection organic, sulfur
Weed control mechanical
Yeasts spontaneous fermentation
Grapes purchase 100%
Certification none

SONOMA

STONE EDGE FARM

5700 Cavedale Road – tel. (707) 935-6520
www.stoneedgefarm.com – concierge@stoneedgefarm.com

PEOPLE - Former bank executive and wine lover, Carmenet founding partner Mac McQuown and his wife Leslie returned to Moon Mountain in 2004 they created Stone Edge Farm, a 16-acre site with culinary gardens, olive groves and 5 acres of the area's famous Cabernet Sauvignon. In 2012 he purchased 160 acres on the eastern slope of Mount Veeder near Glen Ellen, Silver Cloud.

VINEYARDS - The 1800' 18-acre vineyard at Silver Cloud is the main estate. Soil here is the thin volcanic typical of the steep, craggy Mayacamas range that forms a barrier between Napa and Sonoma valleys. The 5-acre valley floor site has alluvial soil, and the third source is founding winemaker Jeff Baker's Mount Pisgah vineyard farmed by founding viticulturalist Phil Coturri. All three are CCOF Certified organic.

WINES - Winemaker Alejandro Zimman and the culinary team work closely together to create exceptional food and wine experiences.
Sonoma Valley Cabernet Sauvignon 2016 ● 1,002 cs; $ 130 - 🛢️ - Full, chewy, vibrant and dry with notes of cherry, cassis, black olive, oregano and cedar.
Sonoma Valley Sauvignon Blanc 2019 ○ 638 cs; $ 50 - 🛢️ - Both creamy and crisp like a good white Bordeaux with notes of papaya, basil, lemon grass and cardamom.
Sonoma Valley Surround ● Cabernet Sauvignon, Malbec; 658 cs; $ 84 - 🛢️ - Rich, chewy and dry with notes of black cherry, game, mushroom, cedar and cigar box.

acres 24 - cases 1,800
Fertilizers green manure
Plant protection organic
Weed control mechanical
Yeasts commercial cultured yeasts, spontaneous fermentation
Grapes 100% estate-grown
Certification organic

ST. HELENA

STONY HILL VINEYARD

P.O. Box 308 – tel. (707) 963-2636
www.stonyhillvineyard.com – info@stonyhillvineyard.com

 A talented team is transitioning the winery to a new era while also protecting biodiversity and wildlands that surround the estate.

PEOPLE - A Napa classic, Stony Hill is in the midst of a grand transformation. Founded by the McCrea family in the 1940's, Stony Hill was for decades the benchmark for Napa's white wines. In 2020, Demeine Estates purchased it from the Ted Hall family (the McCrea's friends who'd bought it in 2018), pivoting to a youthful management team—estate director Michaela Kelly and indie winemaker Jaime Motley—with fresh ideas and a growing focus on red wines.

VINEYARDS - The Halls converted the vines to organics. Demeine Estates nearly doubled the planted acreage, focusing on red wine vines. They also restored nine acres of 40 year old Chardonnay vines to their original head trained form. The estate's rocky slopes in the Mayacamas face north and northeast—reducing vigor—at 800 to 1,500 feet of elevation (above the fogline).

WINES - The estate's previous winemakers, Mike Chelini and Stephan Vivier, made the current release vintages, all aged in neutral oak under Chelini (through 2018) and whites in stainless steel by Vivier (2018-2020).
Napa Valley Chardonnay 2018 ○ 1,200 cs; $ 54 - 🛢️ - One of Napa's Chardonnay stars, this barrel fermented wine comes from eight acres of 40 year old vines, brilliantly balancing fruit and acid in a wine that's fresh, bright and slightly creamy.
Spring Mountain District Gewürztraminer 2018 ○ 2,000 cs; $ 48 - 🍶 - A classic Stony Hill white with a devoted following, the wine offers up stone fruit and floral notes.
Spring Mountain District Cabernet Sauvignon 2017 ● 325 cs; $ 150 - 🛢️ - Light on its feet with fresh berry and red currant notes, emblematic of Stony Hill's Cabernet future, it's aromatic with a flavor profile that leans towards the herbaceous and nuanced.

acres 30 - cases n/a
Fertilizers compost, cover crops
Plant protection organic, sulfur
Weed control mechanical
Yeasts commercial cultured yeasts
Grapes 100% estate-grown
Certification organic

APTOS

STORRS WINERY & VINEYARDS

1560 Pleasant Valley Road – tel. (831) 724-5030
www.storrswine.com – pamelas@storrswine.com

PEOPLE - Pamela and Stephen Storrs have built a highly regarded label in Santa Cruz County ever since harvesting their first vintage together in 1988. In 2010, the couple began comprehensive construction on their net-zero estate winery and tasting room completed in 2018. Pamela sees a quality difference from using biodynamic and regenerative practices. They have employed sheep grazing for over ten years and are devoted to being a wildlife friendly zone.

VINEYARDS - The estate Hidden Springs Vineyard is in the south-western foothills of the Santa Cruz Mountains known as the Pleasant Valley region. The Storrs purchased the property in 2001 and finally planted Chardonnay and Pinot Noir in 2007. They grow five Dijon clones of Pinot Noir at the estate. They purchase additional fruit from local growers.

.....

WINES - Storrs is known for their Chardonnay, earning countless awards for it over the years.

⬤ **Santa Cruz Mountains Hidden Springs Chardonnay 2017** SLOW WINE ◯ 168 cs; $ 44 - ⊞ - Aged in oak, this wine has a great profile of acid coalescing with lush and lively pear notes.
Santa Cruz Mountains Christy Vineyard Chardonnay 2019 ◯ 694 cs; $ 33 - ⊞ - A gold winner at the Sunset International Wine Competition, it's balanced and integrated, with a bit of butter, yet a strong mineral backbone and crisp green apple snap.
Santa Clara County Rusty Ridge Zinfandel 2017 ⬤ 260 cs; $ 34 - ⊞ - From a tiny, 110-year old vineyard with very low yields in the Gilroy area on the easter slopes of Mount Madonna. The first vintage that they made of this was in 1993, so it is very near and dear. It is bursting with red berries, spice and pretty, dark flowers.

.....

acres 13 - **cases** 10,000
Fertilizers biodynamic compost, compost, green manure
Plant protection organic, synthetic pesticides
Weed control mechanical
Yeasts commercial cultured yeasts, selected indigenous yeasts
Grapes purchase 86%
Certification some of the vineyards are certified organic

CALISTOGA

STORYBOOK MOUNTAIN VINEYARDS

3835 CA-128 – tel. (707) 942-5310
www.storybookwines.com

 For excellence in farming, biodiversity and wine-making the winery's been a Wine & Spirits Top 100 winery, a prestigious honor, 16 times.

PEOPLE - Unique in Napa for its focus on Zinfandel, Storybook was built in 1883 by the Grimm brothers from Germany, with Chinese laborers digging caves still used today. In 1976, former history professor Jerry Seps purchased the 120 acre property, planting Zinfandel on the advice of legendary wine expert Andre Tchelistcheff. Nicknamed the Zin master, Seps led the Zin fine wine renaissance in the U.S..

VINEYARDS - Seps initially planted the best Zinfandel clones from across California and a few from Croatia for his red clay loam soils. He also added Viognier and Bordeaux grapes and just planted Touriga Nacional, a drought and heat tolerant variety. The vines were organically farmed from the start and certified organic in 2008. About a quarter of the vines date back to 1976.

.....

WINES - Seps was among the first to treat California Zinfandel as a fine wine in the cellar. All the wines are barrel selections; they are not chosen by vineyard blocks.

⬤ **Napa Valley Mayacamas Range Zinfandel 2018** SLOW WINE ⬤ 2,000 cs; $ 42 - ⊞ - The flagship wine, known for its delicately perfumed nose, bramble, raspberry and red fruit flavors, and Pinot-esque lightness.
Napa Valley Eastern Exposures Zinfandel 2018 ⬤ 588 cs; $ 55 - ⊞ - Fragrant with aromatics from the addition of about 6 percent Viognier. A slightly richer wine, it offers a smooth, silky mouthfeel and plush texture with subtle cherries and raspberries.
Napa Valley Bottled Poetry Red Blend 2018 ⬤ 400 cs; $ 50 - ⊞ - A new red blend of Zinfandel, with Cabernet Sauvignon, Merlot, and Petit Verdot–a bigger, juicier wine that takes lightness and red fruits to delicious, new heights.

.....

acres n/a - **cases** n/a
Fertilizers compost, cover crops
Plant protection organic, sulfur
Weed control mechanical
Yeasts selected indigenous yeasts
Grapes 100% estate-grown
Certification organic

PASO ROBLES

TABLAS CREEK VINEYARD

9339 Adelaida Road – tel. (805) 237-1231
www.tablascreek.com – info@tablascreek.com

PEOPLE - Tablas Creek, one of California's most acclaimed wineries, was founded by two famous wine families: the Perrins of Château de Beaucastel in Châteauneuf-du-Pape and their American distributor, the Haas family. In 1989, after a four year search, the families found their ideal spot in Adelaida District. Jason Haas, founder Robert Haas' son, runs the estate with the Perrins.

VINEYARDS - The certified organic, biodynamic 125-acre estate grows 16 varieties from cuttings from Château de Beaucastel in France. The dry farmed vineyards sit on rolling hills comprised of calcareous soils in a mild climate at 1500 feet altitude. A flock of 100 sheep work the land year round to fertilize, gently till, and chew down forest fire fuel. In 2020, Tablas became the first winery in the US to be Certified Regenerative Organic, a farming practice focused on soil health.

WINES - Tablas, a leader of the California Rhône movement, focuses on Rhône blends and varietal bottlings from their estate made in the Rhône tradition with native yeast and large neutral oak foudres.

🔴 **Adelaida District Paso Robles Esprit de Tablas 2019** SLOW WINE ● 3,650 cs; $ 60 - 🍽 ⚫ - Mourvèdre-based (39%) with Grenache, Syrah, and Counoise, this flagship red shows dark fruit, earth, baking spice, dark chocolate, and meat, with good acidity and firm tannins. Ageworthy.
Adelaida District Paso Robles Grenache 2019 ● 455 cs; $ 35 - ⚫ - Translucent ruby red, the wine has purity of fruit character (wild strawberries) and spice along with good acid and soft tannin.
Adelaida District Paso Robles Esprit de Tablas Blanc ○ 2,121 cs; $ 50 - 🍽 ⚫ - Rich, round, honeyed qualities from the Roussanne (63%) blend with citrus and minerality from the Picpoul (14%) and Picardan (3%) and lovely orchard fruit and floral characteristics from Grenache Blanc (20%).

acres 125 - **cases** 30,000
Fertilizers biodynamic compost, cover crops, manure
Plant protection biodynamic preparations, sulfur
Weed control mechanical
Yeasts spontaneous fermentation
Grapes purchase 35%
Certification some of the vineyards are certified organic, some of the vineyards are certified biodynamic

SANTA MARIA

TATOMER

2705 Aviation Way – tel. (805) 325-5612
www.tatomerwines.com

PEOPLE - Graham Tatomer started his career at 16 working at the Santa Barbara Winery with Greg Brewer and Bruce McGuire. He took to riesling and an odd plot of sylvaner which seemed to seal his orientation to Germanic varietals. He returned from multiple years with Weingut Knoll in the Wachau armed with the sensibility he has been carrying out ever since: exploiting the cool weather of the region to produce elegant multiple cuvées of riesling, grüner veltliner and pinot noir. He is singular in this pursuit and in his success at it.

VINEYARDS - Vineyards for Tatomer wines range up the Central Coast. Favorite sites are John Sebastiano in Sta Rita Hills which receives ample ocean influence from its elevation and Kick-On Ranch which is a straight shot of a few miles to the ocean. Both vineyards feature sandy soils.

WINES - When harvesting the white grapes, multiple picking stages take place, sometimes a month apart, which produce complexity. The wines successfully express this regimen in youth, but also may have many years to age.

🔴 **Santa Barbara County Kick-On Ranch Clone 239 Riesling 2019** ○ 100 cs; $ 50 - 🥛 - Full-bodied with ample texture and minerality. Aromas of sweet grass, white flower, peach and mango give way to flavors of lime rind, stone fruit and pineapple.
Sta. Rita Hills John Sebastiano Vineyard Grüner Veltliner 2019 ○ 52 cs; $ 35 - 🥛 🍽 - Electric on the palate with unripe pear, peach and lime while the nose invites with lime rind and maraschino cherry.
Santa Barbara County Kick-On Ranch Pinot Noir 2019 ● 48 cs; $ 50 - 🍽 - Complex and hits notes of dried herbs, dark cherry and strawberry with deep salty minerality and smooth, slightly bitter tannins perfumed with rose, cedar bark and dried strawberry.

acres 0 - **cases** 4,500
Fertilizers green manure, manure
Plant protection copper, sulfur
Weed control mechanical
Yeasts selected indigenous yeasts
Grapes purchase 100%
Certification none

PLYMOUTH

TERRE ROUGE/EASTON WINES

10801 Dickson Road – tel. (209) 245-4277
www.terrerougewines.com – info@terrerougewines.com

PEOPLE - Unlike most of his fellow Rhône Rangers, Bill Easton headed to the Sierra Foothills to grow grapes. His familiarity with the real Rhône as a wineshop owner had taught him the value of the region's granitic and volcanic soils for grape growing. The Easton brand is for non-Rhône wines, primarily Zinfandel. For the covid year, Easton says that business was off 10%. Considering that 80% of his sales are through distribution, half of that from mostly closed restaurants - not so bad. Years of establishing sales channels was key, he says.

VINEYARDS - Easton's estate grapes are spread over two ranches in the Fiddletown AVA. He has concentrated on viognier, syrah and zinfandel but he is keeping an eye on the changing climate. Vermentino was produced this year for the first time and a newly acquired family vineyard will be coming on-line next year growing other warmer weather varietals.

WINES - As a winemaker concerned with authenticity, Easton's farming is traditional and pure and even his entry-level wines can experience extended élevage to be best represented.

🔴 **Fiddletown Terre Rouge Syrah 2014** [SLOW WINE] ●
400 cs; $ 45 - 🔲 - Displays inviting smoky black olive and blackberry aromas with an earthy, blackberry and pomegranate palate. Refined tannins combine to show the virtue of the wine's time in the bottle.

🔴 **Sierra Foothills Saureel Vineyard Easton Vermentino 2020** [EVERYDAY WINE] ○ 150 cs; $ 25 - 🔲 - has aromas of lemon verbena, yellow apple and pear with a broad palate with flavors of anise and pineapple.
Fiddletown Easton Zinster Lot 1852 Zinfandel 2019 ●
350 cs; $ 25 - 🔲 - A chillable grown-up summer red that shows floral notes and an earthy dried strawberry/cherry palate.

acres 25 - cases 18,000
Fertilizers cover crops, organic
Plant protection organic, synthetic pesticides
Weed control chemical, mechanical
Yeasts commercial cultured yeasts, selected indigenous yeasts
Grapes purchase 85%
Certification none

WOODSIDE

THOMAS FOGARTY

19501 Skyline Boulevard – tel. (650) 851-6777
www.fogartywinery.com – info@fogartywinery.com

PEOPLE - Dr. Thomas Fogarty established his winery in 1980 after relocating to the bucolic Santa Cruz Mountains for professional reasons. In 1981 he hired Michael Martella as vineyard manager and winemaker. In 2004 current winemaker Nathan Kandler began to work with Michael and learn the ins and outs of the property and wines, concentrating especially on the various unique estate vineyards.

VINEYARDS - Of the 350 acres here in the remote northern end of the Santa Cruz Mountains, much of it wild, protected forested land, only 30 are planted to grapes. The team has been farming in accordance with organic practices since the late 1970's. Kandler is looking at increasing soil health of these 40-year old vines and using spontaneous fermentation to highlight individual terroir.

WINES - Both the namesake line and the new Lexington Wine Co. line offer a direct line to the wild, rugged, remote atmosphere of the vineyards. Struggling to ripen brings added character and a bit of old world earthiness shines through as well.

🔴 **Santa Cruz Mountains Rapley Trail Vineyard Pinot Noir 2017** ● 175 cs; $ 82 - 🔲 - Ripe, juicy, bright and dry with notes of raspberry, mint, Campari, cedar and lavender.
Santa Cruz Mountains Langley Hill Vineyard Chardonnay 2019 ○ 250 cs; $ 60 - 🔲 - Silky and dry with a crisp finish and notes of lemon pound cake, toasted wheat bread and honey-crisp apple.
Santa Cruz Mountains Walker's Vineyard Nebbiolo 2018 ● 325 cs; $ 60 - 🔲 - Full gripping, tart and dry with notes of cherry, cedar, mushroom, green peppercorn and fennel seed.

acres 35 - cases 6,250
Fertilizers compost, manure
Plant protection organic
Weed control mechanical
Yeasts spontaneous fermentation
Grapes purchase 5%
Certification none

HEALDSBURG

THUMBPRINT CELLARS

102 Matheson Street – tel. (707) 433-2393
www.thumbprintcellars.com – lounge@thumbprintcellars.com

PEOPLE - Scott Lindstrom-Dake, founder and winemaker, and co-founder Erica Lindstrom-Dake respect the land and people, providing their team with a living wage, insurance and an investment plan. Their production facility uses barrel steamers for cleaning, night-time air fans for cooling and LED lighting. Their recyclable bottle closures are made from molasses, designed to minimize resources and eliminate waste.

VINEYARDS - All Thumbprint wines are sourced from 10 growers within a 10- to 15-mile radius of the winery including Dry Creek, Knights, Alexander, and Russian River Valley AVAs. Throughout his career, Lindstrom-Dake has only sourced from sustainably farmed vineyards and has worked to educate growers and help them switch from conventional to sustainable practices.

WINES - Thumbprint Cellars' portfolio includes masterful Rhône- and Bordeaux-influenced blends. The award-winning Sculptured Cellars offerings are the result of experimentation with fermentation techniques and use of special limited-production artisan barrels that give unique and exciting nuances to these wines. A total of 22 different blends and varietals make up Thumbprint's wide-ranging portfolio of wines.

TOP Knights Valley Lisa's Vineyard Cabernet Sauvignon 2017 ● 325 cs; $ 65 - ⊞ - Deep black/purple hue. Bold black and blue fruit with exotic spice aromas and flavors.
Alexander Valley Four Play Red Blend 2017 ● 275 cs; $ 52 - ⊞ - From four Sonoma County sustainable vineyards in Alexander Valley AVA. Malbec-based Bordeaux-style blend with immense depth and character.
Alexander Valley López Family Vineyard Rosé of Cabernet Franc 2021 ● 120 cs; $ 32 - 🍷 - Pale pink hue, aromas and flavors of ripe fall watermelon, thyme, and strawberry.

acres 0 - **cases** 4,500
Fertilizers compost, mineral fertilizer, organic-mineral
Plant protection organic, sulfur, synthetic pesticides
Weed control chemical, mechanical
Yeasts spontaneous fermentation
Grapes purchase 100%
Certification none

ST. HELENA

TRES SABORES

1620 S Whitehall Lane – tel. (707) 967-8027
www.tressabores.com – visitus@tressabores.com

PEOPLE - Owner/winemaker Julie Johnson, husband Jon and her son Rory oversee 35 acres of pristine natural beauty just five minutes from Highway 29. There is nothing manicured or curated for tourists here. It feels like a visit to a nature lover's home and garden. She says, "we are a dog park with a wine bar." Animals graze, heritage pomegranates, pink roses and Petite Sirah thrive, and native birds have returned along with bees to this farm and winery.

VINEYARDS - In 1987 Julie began farming 12 acres of historic Zinfandel as well as Cabernet Sauvignon, Petite Sirah and Petite Verdot. By 1991 the estate vineyards were certified organic. She experiments with no till to build soil quality, manages the canopy meticulously and makes multiple passes through the vineyard at harvest. She sources Sauvignon Blanc from the Farina Vineyard on Sonoma Mountain and St. Laurent from Los Carneros-Sonoma.

WINES - The estate wines are rich, ripe, and lavishly oaked - quintessential Napa Valley. There is an underlying energy as well, perhaps reflective of the thriving terroir.

TOP Rutherford Napa Valley Zinfandel 2019 ● 500 cs; $ 50 - ⊞ - Full, finely chewy and dry with notes of boysenberry, green peppercorn, dark chocolate and cedar.
Sonoma County Headline Red 2018 ● 300 cs; $ 32 - Ⓠ - Light, juicy, tart and refreshing with notes of strawberry, cherry, blueberry and cumin. Made from Saint Laurent with a tiny portion of greneache and syrah.
Napa Valley Ingrid & Julia Rosé 2020 ● 586 cs; $ 28 - 🍷 - Delicate, silky, tart and dry with notes of apricot, raspberry, haybale and dried herbs.

acres 12 - **cases** 3,000
Fertilizers compost, cover crops, organic
Plant protection organic, sulfur
Weed control mechanical
Yeasts commercial cultured yeasts, spontaneous fermentation
Grapes purchase 30%
Certification some of the vineyards are certified organic

UKIAH

TRINAFOUR 🍾

832 Alice Avenue – tel. (707) 228-5440
www.trinafourcellars.com – alexmacgregor@sbcglobal.net

PEOPLE - Alex's path to winemaking began at restaurants in his native Toronto, before he moved to California to study at Fresno and Santa Rosa. Working in vineyards, cellars and alongside some of the best winemakers—David Ramey–, enabled him to become a skilled winemaker. Head winemaker for Saracina, he launched his own label, Trinafour, named after his father's hometown in Scotland. He focuses on old vine blends from choice spots.

VINEYARDS - Alex crafts his wines from 3 historic vineyards in Mendocino. The Casa Verde Vineyard (certified organic), a field blend planted in 1942, where Alex cherrypicks the French Colombard vines. Dry farmed Nieme Vineyard has old Carignane vines planted over 60 years ago, excellent for blends. Lolonis Vineyard in Redwood Valley grows vines planted over 70 years ago, including the oldest Sauvignon Blanc vines in the country.

WINES - Using old world techniques combined with carefully selected vineyards these wines are of exceptional quality and craftsmanship.

🔵 **Redwood Valley Lolonis Vineyard Sémillon 2020** ⚪ 50 cs; $ 24 - 🔲 - Using bâtonnage makes for smooth lemon curd and stone fruit followed by a slightly waxy experience midpalate with a long supple finish. 5% Savignon Blanc brings acid and some zest for a delightful balance. Drink now.
Redwood Valley Casa Verde Vineyard Rosso Misto 2017 ⚫ 75 cs; $ 28 - 🔲 - Dark raspberry, cherry, delights with warm spices, licorice followed with violet and lovely tannin structure. Delicious with mushroom risotto and harvest foods.
Redwood Valley Casa Verde Vineyard French Colombard 2020 ⚪ 50 cs; $ 24 - 🔲 - Peach and melon combined with white flowers offers fruit then lively acidity and well-balanced. Drink now.

acres 0 - **cases** 300
Fertilizers compost, cover crops, green manure, manure
Plant protection organic, sulfur
Weed control mechanical
Yeasts spontaneous fermentation
Grapes purchase 100%
Certification some of the vineyards are certified organic

TEMPLETON

TURLEY WINE CELLARS 🍾

2900 Vineyard Drive – tel. (805) 434-1030
www.turleywinecellars.com
pasorobles@turleywinecellars.com

PEOPLE - The Turley family will long be known for setting the global standard for Zinfandel. Founded in Napa Valley by former Emergency Room physician Larry Turley in 1993, and now joined by two of his four daughters, Turley and his long-time Director of Winemaking Tegan Passalacqua produce over 50 wines across the state of California, mostly Zinfandel and Petite Sirah. They are dedicated to buying and preserving heritage Zinfandel blocks.

VINEYARDS - Turley and Passalacqua work with over 50 vineyards, many with old vines dating back to the late 1800's, that are head-trained and dry-farmed. Amador County, Contra Costa County, Paso Robles, Sonoma, Mendocino, Napa Valley and Lodi are top sources. While most are farmed organically/transitioning, not all are certified. Hayne in Napa Valley and most of the Sonoma vineyards are CCOF Certified organic.

WINES - Bold, powerful, richly extracted and lavishly oaked, this iconic style harnesses exquisite ripeness, old vine complexity and a deft use of barrel. The result is spectacular and moving.

🔵 **Paso Robles Pesenti Vineyard Zinfandel 2019** ⚫ n/a; $ 50 - 🔲 - Rich, intense, chewy and dry with notes of blueberry, blackberry, bacon, rose and black pepper.
Lodi Dogtown Vineyard Zinfandel 2019 ⚫ n/a; $ 70 - 🔲 - Bold, chewy, earthy and dry with notes of cassis, plum, fig, date, Ragu, cream of mushroom and nutmeg.
Contra Costa County Salvador Vineyard Zinfandel 2019 ⚫ n/a; $ 65 - 🔲 - Sumptuous and glossy with notes of raspberry, cherry, sundried tomato, fennel, menthol and dark chocolate.

acres 220 - **cases** 58,000
Fertilizers compost
Plant protection organic
Weed control mechanical
Yeasts spontaneous fermentation
Grapes purchase 30%
Certification converting to organics, some of the vineyards are certified organic

WINDSOR

TWO SHEPHERDS $

7763 Bell Road – tel. (415) 613-5731
www.twoshepherds.com – william@twoshepherds.com

PEOPLE - William Allen was a garagiste before his first well-received commercial release in 2010. In 2015, partner and wine industry veteran Karen Daenen joined the company, now with a production facility in Windsor. In 2017, a combination of the comradery of the natural wine world, and the decision to make early release styles like carignan and vermentino took the company in its present direction. Previous experiments in skin contact wines were suddenly in demand.

VINEYARDS - By doubling down on some of their grape orders which others had abandoned among heat spikes and terrifying fires, Two Shepherds expanded in 2020. Even with a larger than typical harvest, they were forced to process their grapes in half the normal time period. A lot of the effort was used to fetch fruit from the organic Windmill Vineyard in Yolo county with fires burning nearby. Trimble Vineyard in Mendocino, also organic, is where the carignan originates.

WINES - Allen's wines navigate a path incorporating quality and fun. Production has doubled in three years with 20% of the output released in cans.

TOP **Yolo County Windmill Vineyard Natty Pets Picpoul 2020** EVERYDAY WINE ○ 3,600 cans; $ 11 - 🥤⊞ - surprisingly intense and tasty with peach, orange pulp, and almond flavors and bubbles complementing a bit of grip.
Yolo County Windmill Vineyard Vermentino 2020 ○ 175 cs; $ 26 - 🥤⊞ - Shows yellow flower on the nose along with lively peach and grapefruit. Pineapple and peach land on the palate with an apple skin texture.
Mendocino Trimble Vineyard Old Vine Carignan 2018 ● 175 cs; $ 40 - ⊞ - Has a nose of smokey flint overlaying concentrated florals and berry aromas. Tart and earthy cranberry and strawberry are on the palate.

---

acres 0 - cases 3,400
Fertilizers compost, cover crops
Plant protection organic, sulfur
Weed control mechanical
Yeasts spontaneous fermentation
Grapes purchase 100%
Certification some of the vineyards are certified organic

ARROYO GRANDE

VERDAD WINE CELLARS   🍾

130 W Branch Street – tel. (805) 270-4900
www.verdadwine.com – treeva@lindquistwine.com

PEOPLE - Verdad is Louisa Sawyer Lindquist. Its focus is on Spanish grape varieties. Lindquist developed her tastes working in wine retail, eventually bringing those tastes to eventual husband, Bob Lindquist who helped introduce the Iberian sister to his own brand, Qupé. Not only was Louisa an early adopter of albariño and tempranillo, she, along with Bob, established the Sawyer Lindquist Vineyard in Edna Valley in 2005, one of the first biodynamic vineyards in the U. S., (they are no longer owners).

VINEYARDS - The Sawyer Lindquist Vineyards (now known as Slide Hill), where Lindquist still gets most of her fruit, consists of well drained clay-loam and limestone soils. The climate is influenced by the nearby Pacific. The albariño plant material, obtained from Galicia, was some of the first in the U. S. Both albariño and tempranillo plantings date from 2005. Garnacha and graciano are also planted, with additional grapes sourced regionally.

WINES - Verdad is setting the bar high for Iberian varieies which are California's new shining stars.

TOP **Edna Valley Sawyer Lindquist Vineyard Albariño 2019** SLOW WINE ○ 225 cs; $ 28 - 🥤⊞ - A serious wine with mineral depth showing a nose of white peach and anise and a palate of concentrated peach and pear.
Edna Valley Tempranillo Reserva 2016 ● 72 cs; $ 50 - ⊞ - Has a layered nose of leather, smoke and tobacco giving way to flavors of cherry, plum and mocha with discreet, dusty tannins.
Paso Robles Pine Hawk Vineyard Cabernet Sauvignon 2018 ● 450 cs; $ 38 - ⊞ - Sourced from biodynamic Pine Hawk Vineyard in Paso Robles, this Cab displays an intense, bright core of red and dark fruit flavors and nose of cedar and dried herbs woven into a cherry perfume with hints of oak.

---

acres 0 - cases 2,000
Fertilizers biodynamic compost
Plant protection biodynamic preparations, organic
Weed control mechanical
Yeasts commercial cultured yeasts, spontaneous fermentation
Grapes purchase 100%
Certification some of the vineyards are certified organic, some of the vineyards are certified biodynamic

VILUKO VINEYARDS

VOLKER EISELE FAMILY ESTATE

5005 Alpine Road – tel. (707) 490-6708
www.vilukovineyards.com – relations@vilukovineyards.com

PEOPLE - Pedro Arroyo, born in Chile, and his wife Karen Arroyo continue their passionate commitment to making wines and working to restore the beautiful nature of their mountain site in the Mayacamas, a family retreat as well as a vineyard. Since the 2017 Tubbs Fire, which burned their steep hillsides and historic barn, the couple along with family and team have been working hard to restore life to the property. Tim Milos makes the wines.

VINEYARDS - Founded in 2006 on 22 acres, the estate grows classic Bordeaux and Burgundy varietals that thrive in the region's unique terroir composition of alluvial and volcanic soils. Certified organic and a member of the Real Organic Project, the vineyards range from 600 and 1100 feet and include Cabernet Sauvignon, Sauvignon Blanc and Chardonnay, as well as Malbec, inspired by the Pedro's Chilean heritage.

WINES - The small-lot, limited production allows each micro-terroir to be fully expressed, producing balanced, rich, complex wines.

TOP **Sonoma County Split Rock Cabernet Sauvignon 2016** SLOW WINE ● 323 cs; $ 45 - ⊞ - This wine is very approachable now and promises with time to be undeniably rewarding with soft tannins and expressive ripe fruit notes, a lively mid palate and a finish that lingers of sweet cocoa and spice.
Sonoma County Estate Cabernet Sauvignon 2016 ● 431 cs; $ 55 - ⊞ - Their benchmark wine, it's complex, with notes of brown spice and clove, giving way to reveal a core minerality layered with rich ripe red fruit and cocoa powder. Worthy of aging 8-10 years.
Sonoma County Estate Malbec 2016 ● 151 cs; $ 56 - ⊞ - Grown at higher elevations producing a rich complex wine with notes of ripe fruit, exotic spices with bright acidity. A family and fan favorite.

acres 22 - **cases** 900
Fertilizers compost, green manure, organic-mineral
Plant protection organic
Weed control mechanical
Yeasts commercial cultured yeasts, selected indigenous yeasts
Grapes 100% estate-grown
Certification organic

3080 Lower Chiles Valley Road – tel. (707) 965-9485
www.volkereiselefamilyestate.com
info@volkereiselefamilyestate.com

 An historic winery that has continually led environmental preservation initiatives to preserve the natural ecosystem of the entire Napa Valley.

PEOPLE - Alexander and Catherine Eisele run the winery that Alexander's parents, Liesel and Volker Eisele, started in 1991. The parents became Cabernet growers (starting in 1974). Jose Neverez (from Durango, Mexico) arrived on horseback from a neighboring farm in 1974, too. The two families have worked together ever since. Volker Eisele was an important figure in the movement to preserve agricultural land in Napa and a key activist against overdevelopment.

VINEYARDS - The 400 acre ranch has 60 acres of vines (certified organic since 1997) at 900 to 1,100 feet of elevation in Chiles Valley District. The 2020 Hennessey Fire came a mere 100 yards away from the 1870's winery, but the historic structures and all but the oldest vines survived. Cooler than on the valley floor, grapes ripen a bit slower—a plus for flavor development.

WINES - Molly Lippitt is the winemaker.

TOP **Napa Valley Las Flores Cabernet Sauvignon 2013** ● 1,200 cs; $ 95 - ⊞ - Named Los Flores because it comes from a single block where mustard plants flower with more vibrant yellow hues in the winter than the rest of the vineyard. Dusty rose notes on entry open into plum and dark red and blue fruits—cherries, black currants, blueberries and cassis—on the palate.
Napa Valley Cabernet Sauvignon 2015 ● 30,000 cs; $ 65 - ⊞ - Blended with 25% Merlot, opens with roses on the nose, this wine offers up plum notes before settling into the cherry and blackberry heartbeat of the wine.
Napa Valley Sauvignon Blanc 2019 ○ 8,088 cs; $ 30 - ⏷ - Co-fermented with Sémillon (19%), for extra body and complexity, whole cluster pressed, and fermented cold and slow, giving it more texture, nuanced flavors, and a remarkable elegance.

acres 60 - **cases** 5,000
Fertilizers compost, cover crops
Plant protection sulfur
Weed control mechanical
Yeasts commercial cultured yeasts
Grapes 100% estate-grown
Certification organic

LOMPOC

WENZLAU VINEYARD 🍶

25 Mail Road – tel. (626) 695-9240
www.wenzlauvineyard.com – info@wenzlauvineyard.com

PEOPLE - The covid year quickly forced Cindy and Bill Wenzlau to up their yearly releases from twice to four times. Wine club subscribers responded and salvaged the year somewhat. In the meantime, the company busied itself dispensing 75 cases to first responders. Wenzlau is a tiny estate/producer born out of the owners' passion for the terroir of the Sta. Rita Hills.

VINEYARDS - The 2013-15 drought has taken its toll with virus and insect problems on the Wenzlau lower vineyards. Willet and Etienne de Montille (Domaine de Montille) directed layered replanting with multiple clones chosen for diversity and drought resistance. 2021 is the first productive vintage of the new vines, since the grubbing up of 2017. The lower vineyards border the Santa Ynez River with clay and diatomaceous earth. A pinot noir vineyard set on a bluff (the Perch) is subjected to brutal Sta Rita Hills winds.

WINES - Local vigneron, Justin Willet (Tyler) has been the winemaker and Cedric Bouchard (Roses de Jeanne) has advised on their sparkling wine.

TOP **Sta. Rita Hill Estate Pinot Noir 2016** ● 200 cs; $ 50 - 🔲 - Wafts of rose, orange pulp and smoked sausage emerge, with a smooth palate of rich red berries, orange rind and sweet herbs. Potent acidity and fine-grained tannins flesh things out.
Sta Rita Hills Estate Blanc de Blancs Cuvée L'Inconnu 2014 ✵ 107 cs; $ 54 - 🍾 - This traditional méthode sparkling wine is driven and pure. Honeysuckle, apricot and brulée on the nose with biscuit, citrus and a load of minerality on the palate.
Sta. Rita Hill Estate Chardonnay 2016 ○ 150 cs; $ 45 - 🍾🔲 - Shows toast and honeysuckle on the nose with a refined palate of creamy white peach braced by lemon acidity.

acres 12.5 - cases 1,200
Fertilizers none
Plant protection copper, sulfur
Weed control mechanical
Yeasts commercial cultured yeasts, spontaneous fermentation
Grapes 100% estate-grown
Certification none

CAZADERO

WILD HOG VINEYARD $

30904 Bohan Dillon Road – tel. (707) 847-3687
www.wildhogvineyard.com – info@wildhogvineyard.com

PEOPLE - Back in the 70's Daniel Schoenfeld bought land in the wilds above the Sonoma Coast to homestead and become an organic vegetable farmer. He and his wife, Marion, planted a small vineyard in 1981 and began making wine. They then built a winery all with solar, becoming the first all solar winery in California, and launched their first wines by 1990. As a trained volunteer firefighter and EMT for 40 years Schoenfeld was put to task last year as multiple wildfires surrounded the area.

VINEYARDS - The vineyard sits amidst forested hills, five miles from the Pacific Ocean at 1,400 feet, catching the sun above the coastal fog. Here Daniel grows Petite Sirah, Pinot Noir, Syrah and Zinfandel on Wild Hog Creek where bobcats and wild hogs roam. Certified organic since 1983, they are one of the first certified organic vineyards in both Sonoma County and California. The vines are, on average, 30 years of age.

WINES - Part of the Fort Ross-Seaview AVA, the wines are characteristically coastal of this extreme winegrowing region with bold, fruity and complex flavors with the help of aged oak barrels. Wines are made to drink now or age to 10 years.

Fort Ross-Seaview Estate Syrah 2017 ● 100 cs; $ 30 - 🔲 - Black raspberry, blueberry, star anise, lavender, with a spicy mocha finish. Tannin and acid get along well.
Fort Ross-Seaview Estate Pinot Noir 2015 ● 500 cs; $ 35 - 🔲 - Rich and dark cherry fruit with plenty of oak flavors, this coastal Pinot brings forest and brambles with a full mouth feel and a smooth finish.
Fort Ross-Seaview Estate Zinfandel 2015 ● 400 cs; $ 35 - 🔲 - Fruit forward with purple berries, spice, forest floor, sweet tobacco, baking spices and oak overtones with medium acid and light tannins.

acres 6 - cases 1,200
Fertilizers compost, green manure
Plant protection copper, organic, sulfur
Weed control mechanical
Yeasts commercial cultured yeasts
Grapes purchase 10%
Certification some of the vineyards are certified organic

CORRALITOS

WINDY OAKS

550 Hazel Dell Road – tel. (831) 724-9562
www.windyoaksestate.com – info@windyoaksestate.com

PEOPLE - While they were living in France, proprietors Jim and Judy Schultze love for wine, particularly Burgundy, was born. Shortly after buying a home in California, undeveloped adjacent land became available and they planted it to vines, with their first vintage in 1999. Windy Oaks is a family operation: Jim oversees winemaking and the vineyard, Judy oversees daily operations, and both sons, Spencer and James, work alongside them.

VINEYARDS - Located in the Santa Cruz Mountains, the estate sits at 1000 feet on a ridge 6 miles inland overlooking Monterey Bay and its deep underwater canyons. The altitude and cooling coastal influence afford the 27 acre vineyard a very long growing season—one of the longest of any Pinot Noir in California—with many microclimates within it. They practice biodynamic and organic methods. They also work with 5 acres of non-estate vineyards that Schultze oversees.

WINES - Windy Oaks takes a hands-off approach to winemaking: no filtering, no fining, no racking, all gravity fed, and the use of whole cluster fermentation.

🔝 **Santa Cruz Mountains Estate Cuvée Pinot Noir 2019** ● 416 cs; $ 39 - ⊞ - A blend of Pinot Noir clones, this elegant wine presents crushed red cherries, raspberry, cranberry sauce with some umami notes, spice, sandalwood, and fine grain tannin.
Santa Cruz Mountains Wild Yeast Estate Pinot Noir 2019 ● 195 cs; $ 58 - ⊞ - After a long 35-40 day fermentation on native yeasts, the wine yields a pale garnet color with aromas of bright cherry, redwood duff, umami, cumin, and blood orange peel.
Santa Cruz Mountains One-Acre Estate Chardonnay 2018 ○ 160 cs; $ 45 - ⊞ - Apple tart, lemon curd, dried pineapple and French oak notes balanced by bright acidity, minerality and sea spray.

acres 27 - **cases** 5,000
Fertilizers compost, mineral fertilizer, organic-mineral
Plant protection organic, sulfur, synthetic pesticides
Weed control mechanical
Yeasts commercial cultured yeasts, selected indigenous yeasts, spontaneous fermentation
Grapes purchase 40%
Certification none

SONOMA

WINERY SIXTEEN 600

589 1st Street W – tel. (707) 721-1805
www.winerysixteen600.com – sam@winerysixteen600.com

🌿 *An organic local hero in Sonoma, Phil-Coturri-farmed wines showcase the family's dedication to authentic flavors.*

PEOPLE - Sonoma's leading organic vineyard manager Phil Coturri and son Sam create wine from grapes Phil farms for clients—everything from white Rhones to high end Cabs. It's Grenache that Coturri adores, recommending that his prestigious clients plant it for resilience in the face of climate change and for pure deliciousness. In 2019, he launched a second label, A Deux Tetes, with Rhone winemaker Philippe Cambie.

VINEYARDS - All but one wine come from certified organic sites Phil farms in Sonoma and Napa. Primitivo comes from 25 year old own-rooted, dry farmed vines. Rhone grapes from 100+ year old vines at historic Rossi Ranch in Kenwood are a mainstay. Dos Limones, an east facing site at 500 feet of elevation on Sonoma Mountain is the source for Syrah and was the first vineyard Phil converted to organic viticulture back in 1979.

WINES - Terroir driven, the winemaking techniques all focus on bringing out the site specific qualities from each vineyard.

🔝 **Sonoma Mountain Mountains of Sonoma-Dos Limones Syrah 2018** SLOW WINE ● 125 cs; $ 46 - ⊞ - Complex and multifaceted, it stands out for spice and baking spice notes on the nose, a textured mid palate, and gorgeous black fruits.
Sonoma Valley Homage a Val Ross White Rhone Blend 2019 ○ 400 cs; $ 35 - ⊞ - Lively and bright, this is a testament to love. Phil met his wife Arden in this vineyard during harvest in 1978. The blend that is 66% Roussanne, 17% Grenache Blanc and 17% Marsanne–a food friendly, refreshing wine.
Sonoma Valley Canard Family Vineyard Rosé of Primitivo 2020 ◗ 280 cs; $ 22 - 🥫 - Dry with just a touch of sweetness, with raspberry and cherry notes; comes in 250ml cans, perfect for picnicking.

acres 2 - **cases** 8,300
Fertilizers compost, cover crops
Plant protection organic, sulfur
Weed control mechanical
Yeasts spontaneous fermentation
Grapes purchase 95%
Certification organic

SANTA ROSA

WINESMITH

411 Beaver Street – tel. (707) 237-7000
www.winesmithwines.com – clark@winemaking411.com

PEOPLE - Wine-renaissance man Clark Smith's has over 60 vintages for the WineSmith brand and is the noted author of "Postmodern Winemaking." Smith's vibrant down to earth nature is an invitation to share his passion for all things wine and music. His latest project, co-authoring "A Practical Guide to Pairing Wine and Music" reveals the significant effect that music can have on our perception of wine. "When the wine and the music match, both improve."

VINEYARDS - Smith sources grapes from Adobe Creek Vineyard located in the Northern Mayacama mountain range, Prudy Foxx's Bates Ranch in the Santa Cruz Mountains, Ibo Tejada's Tempranillo and Garnacha vineyard in Lake County along with sites in the Hoopa Valley on the lower course of the Trinity River in Northern Humboldt County.

WINES - Smith's believes that "living soil matters" and employs techniques for using oxygen to build structure, avoiding sulfur and extended aging in old French oak barrels.

Santa Cruz Mountains Grenache 2017 ● 212 cs; $ 40 - ⊞ - Beyond the strawberry profile, complex aromas of melon, saddle leather, "garrigue" herbs and Asian spices. Medium-bodied with refined tannins and a lively minerality.
Humboldt County The Lost Chord Syrah 2013 ●65 cs; $ 75 - ⊞ - The Ishi Pishi vineyard, surrounded by forested mountains near Hoopa in Northern Humboldt County, produces perfectly complex Syrah with unrivaled characteristics, without the use of sulfites. Aged 78 months, the indescribable aroma profile is profound with once dense tannins turned silky soft.
Santa Clara Adobe Creek Sangiovese 2020 ● 135 cs; $ 40 - ⊞ - Adobe Creek Vineyard, located in the Mayacamas mountain range in Lake County, produced vibrant wine with alluring notes of cherry and dried roses, oregano and fig undertones. The mouth is silky and ethereal.

acres 0 - **cases** 12,000
Fertilizers compost
Plant protection sulfur, synthetic pesticides
Weed control chemical, mechanical
Yeasts spontaneous fermentation
Grapes purchase 100%
Certification some of the vineyards are certified organic

SOLEDAD

WRATH WINES

35801 Foothill Road – tel. (831) 678-2212
www.wrathwines.com – info@wrathwines.com

PEOPLE - In 2007, the San Saba vineyard was purchased by Barbara Thomas and her son Michael, the team behind Wrath Wines. Michael's love of Italy and wine inspired him to embark on a large vineyard rejuvenation program. Winemaker Sabrine Rodems is now in her 18th harvest, starting as an assistant winemaker and moving into the leading role. Her belief in experimentation has created a label with exciting results year after year.

VINEYARDS - The focus is on its estate Pinot Noir, Chardonnay, and Syrah, from a slope in the Santa Lucia benchlands and Arroyo Seco riverbench. It is a special site that has been farmed since the late 1970's by the same vineyard management company and has been sustainable since the early days. Rodems says that San Saba is "like picking from a spice rack. It's like a good curry."

WINES - Wrath primarily makes nine different Pinots, focusing on differences in block elevation, clonal selection, and location in each wine.

(TOP) Monterey Swan/828 Pinot Noir 2018 ● 685 cs; $ 35 - ⊞ - A blend of two clones, Swan is a little cherry and berry and 828 is more earthy. This is 20% whole cluster, with a bit of stem component, with loads of black cherry, spice, spruce and juniper.
Monterey San Saba Vineyard Chardonnay 2018 ○ 262 cs; $ 49 - ⊞ - Rodems calls this their "biggest" Chardonnay though it is pretty lean. A nice balance of acid with creamy fruit. Lemon zest up front, then brulee in the middle and a clean finish. The barrel brings in some nutmeg, peppercorn and clove.
Monterey Destruction Level 2017 ● 107 cs; $ 39 - ⊞ - The inaugural vintage of this 50-50 blend of estate Syrah with Grenache from the Ventana property. Displays a nice balance of spices–white pepper, coriander and cumin –with iron, currant, and purple fruit notes.

acres 68 - **cases** 10,000
Fertilizers compost, cover crops, mineral fertilizer
Plant protection sulfur, organic, synthetic pesticides
Weed control chemical, mechanical
Yeasts commercial cultured yeasts
Grapes purchase 30%
Certification none

YORKVILLE

YAMAKIRI WINES $

P.O. Box 93 – tel. (510) 495-7224
www.yamakiriwines.com – info@yamakiriwines.com

PEOPLE - Retired after a career in recycling at U.C. Berkeley, Lisa Bauer named her tiny brand Yamakiri after the legendary Japanese farmer Masanobu Fukuoka from Yamakiri. He wrote the book The One-Straw Revolution, a book that expresses the way Bauer farms her Slippery Slope vineyard—with little effort, letting nature dictate the path. She sells wholesale to upscale restaurants and a few wine shops who treasure the unique flavors of her wines

VINEYARDS - Located in Mendocino County, near Anderson Valley, Bauer gets her grapes locally. Pinot Gris is from the biodynamic Filigreen Farm in Boonville. Bauer farms a 2 acre site in Yorkville–Slippery Slope—calling it basically untended and describing her role simply as "pruning and picking." A one acre vineyard of Albarino, organically farmed, in the Wentzel Vineyard, is another source, although this may be the last vintage (possible owner retirement).

WINES - It's minimal intervention all the way in these handmade wines made in tiny lots by winemaker Alex Crangle. Bauer's second label, Sin Eater, is for her popular pet nats and hard ciders.

Anderson Valley Sin Eater Pét-Nat of Pinot Gris 2019 O 131 cs; $ 39 - 🍶 - Delicately fizzy with straight ahead citrus flavors and balanced acidity: a satisfying wine that pairs well with seafood and salad alike.
Yorkville Highlands Sauvignon Blanc 2020 O 112 cs; $ 39 - 🍶 - Citrus comes to the fore accompanied by delicate green apple and pear notes.
Anderson Valley Wentzel Vineyard Albariño 2020 O 89 cs; $ 39 - 🍶 - A food friendly, lipsmacking combo of fruit and acid that delivers oversized pleasure. Oranges and apricots.

---

acres 0 - **cases** 700
Fertilizers compost, cover crops
Plant protection organic, sulfur
Weed control mechanical
Yeasts spontaneous fermentation
Grapes purchase 100%
Certification some of the vineyards are certified organic

NAPA

ZD WINES   🍾

8383 Silverado Trail – tel. (707) 963-5188
www.zdwines.com – info@zdwines.com

PEOPLE - Third-generation winemaker Brandon deLeuze continues the family legacy as winemaker at ZD Wines. The name ZD comes from 'Zero Defects,' a philosophy that's evident in all aspects of their business. Recycling, water reclamation and solar power have been essential to operations at ZD for decades. The winery leads by example and all of their contract growers have been certified organic since 2018. They successfully blend across AVAs for their California-appellation Chardonnay.

VINEYARDS - The winery's 3.2-acre Napa Valley vineyard lies on the eastern edge of the Rutherford AVA along the Silverado Trail and the tasting room terrace overlooks the estate vineyards and the Mayacamas to the west. A 29-acre site in Carneros is where the reserve Chardonnay and Pinot Noir grapes are grown. Biodiversity on the estate is abundant with honey bees, owl boxes, chickens, and organic gardens and longstanding organic winegrowing practices.

WINES - Wine style at ZD has remained steadfast in eschewing ML, the use of American oak and a solera aging approach to its pinnacle wine Abacus.

🔝 **California Chardonnay 2020** SLOW WINE O 3,000 cs; $ 42 - 🍷 - A barrel sample showed delicate chamomile, pineapple and yellow peaches laced with nutmeg and precise acidity.
Napa Valley Sauvignon Blanc 2020 O 1,800 cs; $ 30 - 🍶🍷 - Sourced from an old vine vineyard in Yountville, it's tropical on nose with flavors of bright lemon and grapefruit, green apple and a lip-smacking mineral expression.
Napa Valley Reserve Cabernet Sauvignon 2018 ● 445 cs; $ 230 - 🍷 - A combination of estate and Coombsville, Carneros, and Rutherford sites showing red plum and blackberry with savory camphor, star anise and black tea.

---

acres 34 - **cases** 30,000
Fertilizers compost
Plant protection organic, sulfur
Weed control mechanical
Yeasts commercial cultured yeasts
Grapes purchase 75%
Certification organic

OREGON

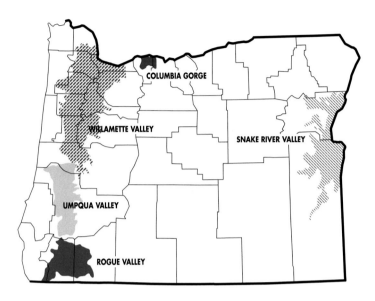

Snail 🐌

Coin $

Bottle 🍾

CARLTON

ABBOTT CLAIM VINEYARD 🍾

11011 NE Bayliss Road - tel. (503) 687-3839
www.abbottclaim.com – taste@abbottclaim.com

PEOPLE - Antony Beck of South Africa's Beck Family Estates founded Abbott Claim Vineyard on a former 1855 land claim skirting the Savannah Ridge in Carlton. Here, French-trained winemaker Alban Debeaulieu, assistant winemaker David Martinez, and viticulturist Heath Payne balance diverse nature and agriculture in harmony to produce wines Debeaulieu calls "vectors of terroir."

VINEYARDS - The 170 acre estate includes 49.1 acres of dry-farmed, mixed-clone chardonnay and pinot noir planted on ancient marine sandstone ranging between 330-480 feet, with south, southeast and southwest exposures. The balance of land supports natural habitats, cover crops, pollinator corridor, fallow mixes, and heirloom wheat. Payne employs regenerative, no-till agriculture to balance nitrogen, increase and maintain humidity, and nurture complex microbiome habitats. Other sustainable practices include solar panels, rainwater catchment, and worms to recycle grey water.

· ·

WINES - Ethereal, elegant, seamless wines evocative of place, with a timeless purity of expression.

🔵 Yamhill-Carlton Due North Pinot Noir 2019 ●
145 cs; $ 115 - ⊞ - Ethereal red-fruited core, effortless body, refined tannins, lilting finish. Sublime.
Yamhill-Carlton Pinot Noir 2019 ● 808 cs; $ 75 - ⊞ - Lovely, lithe mèlange of floral (rose, violet) red fruit (pomegranate, tart red cherry, currant, raspberry), and sous bois.
Yamhill-Carlton Orientate Pinot Noir 2019 ● 173 cs; $ 115 - ⊞ - Seamless structure, intense red and dark fruit notes, underpinnings of forest floor echo on the finish.

acres 49 - **cases** 1.675
Fertilizers biodynamic compost, compost, cover crops, humus, mineral fertilizer, organic-mineral
Plant protection biodynamic preparations, organic, sulfur
Weed control mechanical
Yeasts spontaneous fermentation
Grapes purchase 85%
Certification none

SHERWOOD

ALLORO VINEYARD 🍾

22075 SW Lebeau Road - tel. (503) 625-1978
www.allorovineyard.com – info@allorovineyard.com

PEOPLE - David Nemarnik's vision to find a special place in Oregon's north Willamette Valley for a sustainable vineyard and integrated farm came true in 1999 when he purchased his 110-acre property. At Alloro, he works with a passionate and dedicated team that includes winemaker Tom Fitzpatrick, cellarmaster Andrew Ward, sales/marketing manager Eric Ploof and field foreman David Lopez. Nemarnik is also the CEO of Pacific Coast Fruit Company and founder/owner of Rose City Transportation.

VINEYARDS - Loess soil, a variety of aspects and elevations, and a prime location on the eastern flank of the Chehalem Mountains AVA combine to make a perfect spot to grow Pinot Noir, Chardonnay, Riesling, Muscat and Nebbiolo. The property is dry farmed, no till and managed with a sustainable focus. Sheep and pigs lend a hoof in controlling the cover crop. A new tasting room is currently offering light snacks such as charcuterie and house-cured olives.

· ·

WINES - Nemarnik believes that by paying attention to the health of the plants and soil, you can produce beautiful wines of place. That is the focus at Alloro.

Chehalem Mountains Justina Pinot Noir 2018 ●
200 cs; $ 95 - ⊞ - The Justina Pinot Noir highlights the favorite barrels from a given year and includes wine with notable weight and structure; this year's offering is redolent of spiced cherry jam and fresh cooking herbs.
Chehalem Mountains Chardonnay 2019 ○ 200 cs; $ 39 - ⊞ - Creamy and rich, with aromas of baked apple and barrel spice and flavors of lemon zest and salted caramel.
Chehalem Mountains Bianco de Nero 2020 ● 680 cs; $ 37 - 🍷 - Made in the style of a white Pinot Noir but with the color of a rosé, this bottling exhibits strawberry shortcake, melon and white flowers on the nose and palate.

acres 35 - **cases** 4,000
Fertilizers humus, manure, mineral fertilizer
Plant protection organic, sulfur, synthetic pesticides
Weed control mechanical
Yeasts spontaneous fermentation
Grapes 100% estate-grown
Certification none

MOSIER

ANALEMMA WINES

1120 State Road - tel. (541) 478-2873
www.analemmawines.com – cellardoor@analemmawines.com

 Biodynamic® grower-producer Analemma Wines fosters a healthy, sustainable community for its workers and the environment through thoughtful stewardship of the land and property using regenerative agriculture.

PEOPLE - Analemma Wines, a partnership between vigneron Steven Thompson and Kris Fade, sits amidst the Mosier Valley, part of the Columbia River Gorge National Scenic Area in Mosier, Oregon. Founded in 2010, Analemma employs biodynamic farming, composted teas and herbs and manure derived from their 4-cow herd. Analemma also encourages biodiversity, incorporating a sweet cherry orchard, grasslands, and oaks amidst the vines.

VINEYARDS - Analemma Wines source from three sites: Mosier Hill Estate, their own 52-acre biodynamic vineyard planted on river stones and granitic glacial erratics. They also source from Oak Ridge Vineyard which has alpine and volcanic soils. Since 2010, the winery also leases and grows Gewürztraminer and Pinot Noir on historic, high-altitude Atavus Vineyard.

WINES - Thoughtfully crafted, deftly balanced still and sparkling wines, some wrought from unconventional varieties and aging vessels, all alive with an energetic core reflective of the region's craggy clash between maritime and continental climates.

TOP **Columbia Gorge Mosier Hills Estate Blanco 2019** SLOW WINE O Viognier, Albariño, Godello; 350 cs; $ 36 - A masterful balance between seductive orange blossom, jasmine, and yellow fruit notes, and a flinty stone, star fruit, and mineral core.
Columbia Gorge Mosier Hills Estate Mencia 2019 ● 250 cs; $ 42 - A lean, exotic wine redolent with notes of cinnamon, allspice myrrh, nutmeg and red currant
Columbia Gorge Mosier Hills Estate Syrah 2019 ● 180 cs; $ 48 - A surprising, light-bodied wine, replete with heady aromatics, and notes of rich red fruit, baking spices, and savory white pepper that linger on the finish.

acres 15 - **cases** 1,200
Fertilizers compost, cover crops, manure, organic
Plant protection biodynamic preparations, organic, sulfur
Weed control mechanical
Yeasts spontaneous fermentation
Grapes 100% estate-grown
Certification some of the vineyards are certified organic or biodynamic

JUNCTION CITY

ANTIQUUM FARM

25075 Jaeg Road - tel. (541) 998-3153
www.antiquumfarm.com – info@antiquumfarm.com

 Antiquum Farm was founded by Stephen and Niki Hagen in 1996 as a model of sustainable agriculture and an all-encompassing food system.

PEOPLE - The Hagen family keeps dogs, sheep, pigs, goats, geese, ducks, turkeys, and chickens. All aid with grape growing in one form or another, and some of the animals also provide meat that is available through a farm share and will eventually be available for consumption in the property's charming tasting room.

VINEYARDS - A former garden designer who grew up on a farm near his present-day home, Stephen started farming the property with draft horses to keep his carbon footprint low and lower soil compaction. He has since moved to a grazing-based viticulture system, where a series of hooved and feathered animals work together to maintain a permanent cover crop. This system requires no tilling, which stabilizes the microbiome of individual plants and the property as a whole. The result is fruit with incredible acid retention and low pH levels that reaches phenolic ripeness at consistent times from year to year.

WINES - Antiquum Farm's grazing-based viticulture program makes it a model of carbon sequestration and sustainable agriculture, while also allowing winemaker Andrew Bandy-Smith to creatively showcase the beauty and terroir of the estate's fruit.

Passiflora Pinot Noir 2019 ● 250 cs; $ 68 - Made with 667 and Wadenswil clones planted at the highest reaches of Antiquum's vineyard, this exceptional wine exhibits flavors of dried mango, red plum, cranberry, blueberry and rose.
Willamette Valley Luxuria Pinot Noir 2019 ● 150 cs; $ 85 - This wine comes from lower-elevation fruit that produces a dark, brooding drink full of blackberry, new leather, pepper and clove.
Willamette Valley Aurosa Pinot Gris 2019 ● 320 cs; $ 30 - After spending 72 hours on the skins, this blushing wine explodes with aromas of apple blossom, melon, lemon skin and gravel.

acres 20.5 - **cases** 3,000
Fertilizers green manure
Plant protection organic, sulfur
Weed control mechanical, none
Yeasts spontaneous fermentation
Grapes 100% estate-grown
Certification none

AUTHENTIQUE WINE CELLARS

BECKHAM FAMILY ESTATE

5100 SE Rice Lane - tel. (503) 307-1593
www.authentiquewinecellars.com nicholas@authentiquew-inecellars.com

PEOPLE - Nicholas Keeler has two jobs: U.S. sales director for the renowned French cooperage Tonnellerie Allary and winemaker at Authentique Wine Cellars. Keeler's experience with the cooperage allows him to get creative in the cellar by using unique-forest-origin French oak barrels and fermenters. In the past year, he's added oval and egg concrete vessels, jacketed stainless steel and ovoid French Oak foudre to his operations. Assistant winemaker Jose Arguelles, who started at Authentique in 2015, also plays a critical role at the brand.

VINEYARDS - While much of Authentique's fruit comes from Keeler's parents' biodynamic vineyard, Keeler Estate, he also works with a variety of well-respected properties all over the Willamette Valley. Other partners include Ridgecrest, Bois Joli, Murto and, coming soon, Temperance Hill. Keeler also makes excellent wines under two other brands: The Corridor (a nod to the Van Duzer Corridor, where much of his fruit comes from) and Leisure.

WINES - Diligence in the cellar, excellent fruit and thoughtfully-selected fermentation and aging containers make for beautiful, expressive wines. Watch for Gamay Noir, Riesling and methode champenoise sparkling wines in the coming years

TOP **Eola-Amity Hills Eola Springs Vineyard Pinot Noir 2017** ● 150 cs; $ 75 - With aromas of strawberry jam, blueberry, baking spice, lavender and leather, this wine is like drinking Oregon from a bottle.
Eola-Amity Hills Fond Marin Chardonnay 2017 ○ 300 cs; $ 65 - Caramelized pineapple, lime and apple joins intensive minerality for a wine with outstanding flavor and lovely texture.
Eola-Amity Hills Keeler Estate Vineyard Pinot Noir 2017 ● 350 cs; $ 60 - Cranberry, raspberry, baking spice and cedar are prominent in this wine, with a touch of smoke and lavender adding additional interest.

30790 SW Heater Road - tel. (971) 645-3466
www.beckhamestatevineyard.com
annedria@beckhamestatevineyard.com

PEOPLE - Andrew and Annedria Beckham remain committed to making wines inspired by their travels and creating bottlings that push the boundaries of tradition—without pushing those boundaries too far. To keep up with the success of their brand and wine club, the couple is in the process of converting their home on the property to a tasting room so they can accommodate bigger groups. Construction is expected to wrap up in April.

VINEYARDS - In total, the Beckhams have 35 varieties planted on the estate's three contiguous vineyards on Parrett Mountain. While all vineyards have Jory soil, the conditions between each vary. Some have rockier, more cobble-laden dirt, while others have deeper layers of clay. In addition to growing the grapes of their beloved Jura region (Trousseau, Poulsard and Savagnin), they have increased the number of Gamay vines on the estate and continue to invest in aromatic whites and lesser-known Italian grapes.

WINES - Beckham maintains its focus on amphorae-aged and skin-contact wines that are full of life, energy and outstanding acid profiles.
Chehalem Mountains A.D. Beckham Trousseau Noir 2019 ● 200 cs; $ 65 - An exceptionally fresh and bright wine. Watch for red cherries, dried raspberries, lilac and decomposing leaves.
Chehalem Mountains A.D. Beckham Creta Pinot Noir 2018 ● 200 cs; $ 65 - This wine is made with the same fruit and fermentation process as the Estate Pinot Noir, but ages in amphorae instead of oak, and showcases dark cherries, stone fruit and pleasing minerality.
Chehalem Mountains Estate Pinot Noir 2018 ● 350 cs; $ 30 - This wine shows red fruit, spice and fresh earth.

Andrew is still providing lovers of amphorae with vessels they can use in their winemaking efforts through Novum Ceramics.

---

ac 0 - cases n/a
Fertilizers n/a
Plant protection n/a
Weed control n/a
Yeasts spontaneous fermentation
Grapes purchase 100%
Certification none

acres 20 - cases 2,600
Fertilizers biodynamic compost, compost
Plant protection organic, sulfur
Weed control mechanical
Yeasts spontaneous fermentation
Grapes purchase 10%
Certification none

CARLTON

BELLE PENTE VINEYARD & WINERY

12470 NE Rowland Road - tel. (503) 550-6312
www.bellepente.com – wine@bellepente.com

 Belle Pente (which means 'beautiful slope') Vineyard and Winery espouses sustainable farming in gentle harmony with the surrounding environment, producing affordable wines of exceptional quality.

PEOPLE - New York native Brian O'Donnell and wife Jill jettisoned Silicon Valley for Oregon to pursue full-time winemaking in 1992. There, they purchased a 70-acre historic hillside homestead in Carlton, where they established Belle Pente Vineyard and Winery in 1994, celebrating their first harvest in 1996. The estate embraced organic farming in 2000, later incorporating biodynamic techniques in 2005. Brian O'Donnell and foreman Marcial Gonzales manage the vineyard.

VINEYARDS - Located in the middle of horseshoe-shaped Yamhill-Carlton AVA, estate elevations range between 240-550 feet, with southeast, south and southwest exposures. Dry-farmed varieties include Pinot Noir, Pinot Gris, Chardonnay, and Gamay Noir planted on sedimentary Willakenzie soils.

WINES - O'Donnell also oversees winemaking at the gravity-flow facility, along with assistant Lisette Hrapmann, producing new world wines with an old-world feel that offer exceptional quality and value and a distinct sense of place.

TOP Yamhill-Carlton Belle Pente Vineyard Chardonnay 2017 EVERYDAY WINE O 134 cs; $ 20 - ⊞ - Sunny disposition of a white floral, golden-fruited Mâconnais, but with delicate citrus notes, and the complex texture of a Bourgogne Côte d'Or blanc.
Yamhill-Carlton Belle Pente Vineyard Pinot Noir 2018 ● 446 cs; $ 45 - ⊞ - A ruby-robed, well-constructed wine flush with notes of dark berry, raspberry, cherry, clove and evergreen, and a persistent, lilting finish

acres 18 - cases 4,167
Fertilizers compost, cover crops, manure
Plant protection biodynamic preparations, copper, organic, sulfur
Weed control mechanical
Yeasts spontaneous fermentation
Grapes purchase 20%
Certification none

NEWBERG

BERGSTRÖM WINES

18215 NE Calkins Lane - tel. (503) 554-0463
www.bergstromwines.com
reservations@bergströmwines.com

PEOPLE - Swedish immigrant Dr. John Bergström and wife Karen founded Bergström Wines in 1999 in the Dundee Hills. After studying Viticulture and Enology in Beaune, FR., son Josh and his Burgundian wife Caroline joined the family winery. Today, Josh serves as owner, general manager, and winemaker, and Caroline oversees sales. As winemaker, Bergström weaves a deft, 'vinous roadmap' of the region through minimal manipulation and extraction, whole cluster fermentation, and less than 10% new oak.

VINEYARDS - Bergström farms 70 acres of Pinot Noir and Chardonnay on five properties in three appellations (Dundee Hills, Chehalem Mountains, and Ribbon Ridge), most planted on ancient, sandy marine soils. He also produces "gargantua" Syrah. Bergström uses homeopathic teas and biodynamic sprays, and brews biodynamic compost from locally sourced organic manure, local organic straw, and recycled vineyard grapes, skins, seeds, stems, and pruned vine canes.

WINES - Complex, masterful single vineyard expressions of regionality, brimming with bright fresh fruit, succulent acidity, and salty, saline notes.

TOP Dundee Hills Bergström Vineyard Chardonnay 2018 O 68 cs; $ 80 - ⊞ - A creamy, complex chardonnay with heft and balance. Zesty, Meyer lemon attack, subtle golden apple mid palate, appealing salty, mineral finish.
Dundee Hills Bergström Vineyard Pinot Noir 2019 ● 428 cs; $ 110 - ⊞ - Intense blue and red fruit riven with savory, baking spice notes, and a brooding dark mineral finish.
Ribbon Ridge La Spirale Vineyard Pinot Noir 2019 ● 511 cs; $ 80 - ⊞ - A supple, ruby-robed stunner awash with dried florals, subtle baking spices, and bright red currant, cherry, and raspberry.

acres 70 - cases 10,000
Fertilizers compost, cover crops, humus
Plant protection biodynamic preparations, organic
Weed control mechanical
Yeasts commercial cultured yeasts, spontaneous fermentation
Grapes 100% estate-grown
Certification none

BETHEL HEIGHTS VINEYARD

6060 Bethel Heights Road NW - tel. (503) 581-2262
www.bethelheights.com – info@bethelheights.com

PEOPLE - Started by five members of the Casteel and Dudley families in 1977, Bethel Heights remains a preeminent spot for Oregon Chardonnay and Pinot Noir. The whole family is still involved at the board level, but three manage the day-to-day operations: president/general manager Pat Dudley, vineyard manager Ted Casteel and head winemaker Ben Casteel.

VINEYARDS - Bethel Heights includes the original estate property, which has some of the oldest own-rooted Pinot Noir and Chardonnay in the Eola-Amity AVA, and neighboring Justice Vineyard and Lewman Vineyard. The former two properties are certified organic; Lewman should be certified by 2023. Lewman came with greenhouses, which are being used to grow fresh produce for a fledgling culinary program at the winery. In keeping with their belief that "island viticulture" is not healthy, the family maintains diverse plantings and wildlife corridors on its properties. Goats help keep weeds and invasives under control.

....

WINES - Bethel Heights was one of the early champions of Oregon Chardonnay and produces elegant yet powerful wines from this grape and Pinot Noir. Ben Casteel has also worked at Domaine de Perdrix in Burgundy, and at Rex Hill under the tutelage of Lynn Penner-Ash.

Eola-Amity Hills Casteel Pinot Noir 2019 ● 166 cs; $ 75 - ⊞ - A nose full of blackberry and pipe tobacco give way to flavors of dark fruit, lavender, baking spice and black pepper.
Eola-Amity Hills Estate Chardonnay 2018 ○ 208 cs; $ 32 - ⊞ - This mineral-driven Chardonnay features beautiful aromas and flavors of baked apple, pineapple and thyme.
Eola-Amity Hills Justice Pinot Noir 2019 ● 177 cs; $ 56 - ⊞ - Made exclusively with grapes from the Justice Vineyard, this wine shows cranberry, lavender and nectarine skin.

---

acres 83 - cases 9,000
Fertilizers compost
Plant protection organic, sulfur
Weed control mechanical
Yeasts selected indigenous yeasts, spontaneous fermentation
Grapes 100% estate-grown
Certification converting to organics, some of the vineyards are certified organic

BRICK HOUSE WINES

18200 Lewis Rogers Lane - tel. (503) 538-5136
www.brickhousewines.com – info@brickhousewines.com

 Biodynamically farmed Brick House produces wines that are among the most elegant in the Willamette Valley and offer excellent value.

PEOPLE - In their fourth decade in the Oregon Wine Industry, former news people and married couple, Doug Tunnell and Melissa Mills, continue to produce some of the most elegant wines in the Willamette Valley. Tunnell is a native Oregonian and returned home after traveling the world. Melissa Mills is a former Portland television newscaster.

VINEYARDS - After clearing a hazel nut orchard and beginning a soil rehabilitation program, Tunnell planted the first Pinot Noir in 1990 at his 40 acre estate in the Ribbon Ridge AVA. These were followed by more Pinot, Chardonnay, and Gamay. Halliday Hill vineyard which abuts the estate and is farmed by Brick House supplies Pinot Noir for a single vineyard bottling. Since 2005, all the vines are certified biodynamic by Demeter.

....

WINES - Graceful and beautifully balanced with structure to ensure a long life, each offering reflects the vintage and displays a purity one can expect from a biodynamically farmed vineyard. The couple's love of white Burgundy influences the Cascadia Chardonnay while Bandol serves as a model for their Rosé

🔝 **Ribbon Ridge Pinot Noir Les Dijonnais 2019** ● 650 cs; $ 54 - ⊞ - From a cooler vintage, this lovely bottling from a mixture of Dijon clones offers floral aromas with a hint of citrus and a juicy palate with unobtrusive tannins.
🔝 **Ribbon Ridge House Red Pinot Noir** EVERYDAY WINE ● 945 cs; $ 29 - ⊞ - This multivintage blend exudes intense aromas of roses and subtle fruit; the palate is elegant with great acidity and good tannins.
Ribbon Ridge Intentional Rosé of Pinot Noir 2020 🌸 220 cs; $ 28 - 🍷 🌀 - This mouthwatering, food friendly beauty is pale salmon, with an interesting forward nose of herbal wrapped fruit that bursts from the glass and medium delicate palate with an unusually long finish.

---

acres 30 - cases 4,000
Fertilizers compost, cover crops
Plant protection organic, sulfur
Weed control mechanical
Yeasts spontaneous fermentation
Grapes 100% estate-grown
Certification biodynamic

MCMINNVILLE

BRITTAN VINEYARDS $

829 NE 5th Street, Suite 700 - tel. (971) 241-8228
www.brittanvineyards.com – info@brittanvineyards.com

PEOPLE - UC Davis and Stags' Leap Winery alum Robert Brittan leads winemaking and growing efforts at the brand he started in 2004. His associate winemaker Emily Terrell worked at Erath Winery and several spots before joining in 2013. Together, they craft wines that express clarity of place and clarity of fruit, with a special focus on wines that develop texture and shape in the mouth. Ellen Brittan, Robert's wife, oversees sales and marketing.

VINEYARDS - The couple's 128-acre property in the McMinnville AVA focuses on Pinot Noir and Chardonnay. A passion project is a small Rhône block on the eastern side of the property, where they grow Syrah and Grenache. The site is a challenging one, with relatively cold temperatures due to a location in the Coast Range foothills and strong winds from the Van Duzer corridor.

WINES - Brittan Vineyard has relatively diverse soil conditions and elevations for a property of its size, allowing it to produce wines that are noticeable different from block to block.
McMinnville Estate Chardonnay 2019 O 492 cs; $ 45 - ▦ - Bruléed lemon tart, white peach, barrel spice and distinct minerality make this wine a real stunner.
McMinnville Cygnus Block Pinot Noir 2018 ● 234 cs; $ 60 - ▦ - One of four single block Pinot Noirs, expect this selection to showcase a complex combination of tobacco, mint, baking spice, red plum, cranberry and blueberry.
McMinnville Estate Syrah 2017 ● 179 cs; $ 50 - ▦ - Made in the style of a Northern Rhône Syrah, looks for a nose with smoked bacon and dark cherry that adds fresh oregano, plum and blackberry on the palate.

acres 30 - cases 2,000
Fertilizers compost, organic-mineral
Plant protection organic, sulfur
Weed control mechanical
Yeasts commercial cultured yeasts
spontaneous fermentation
Grapes 100% estate-grown
Certification converting to organics

AMITY

BROOKS WINE

21101 SE Cherry Blossom Lane - tel. (503) 435-1278
www.brookswine.com – info@brookswine.com

PEOPLE - Established in 1998 by Jimi Brooks who had an intense commitment to organic and biodynamic farming. He passed away far too early in 2004 at age 38 from a sudden illness. His son Pascal inherited the property and Jimi's sister Janie Brooks Heuck took on the managing role. Chris Williams (who worked with Jimi) took over the winemaking role in 2005. Claire Jarreau is the associate winemaker and grower liaison.

VINEYARDS - Brooks sources from a number of growers as well as its 18 acre, certified biodynamic estate with own-rooted vines planted in 1974. They also source fruit from other organic and sustainably farmed Willamette Valley AVA vineyards. They make Pinot Noir, Riesling and Pinot Gris, as well as Tempranillo, Syrah, Petite Syrah, Melon de Bourgogne, and Orange Muscat.

WINES - Their environmental and social commitments include biodynamic certification, 1% For the Planet, and being a certified B Corporation.
● **Eola-Amity Hills Brooks Estate Riesling 2018** SLOW WINE O 200 cs; $ 34 - 🍶 - Aromas of tree fruits and wet stone lead to Ambrosia apples, ripe summer peaches, fresh apricot, minerality, quince glaze, and a touch of seashore salinity. Creamy and mouthfilling with brisk acidity.
● **Eola-Amity Hills Rastaban Pinot Noir 2018** ● 500 cs; $ 65 - ▦ - A gorgeous medley of Bing cherries, black licorice, wild mushrooms, black raspberry jam, herbs, earthy elements, subtle oak, and savory spice with brisk acidity. Polished and pure with a memorable finale.
Eola-Amity Hills Old Vine Pommard Pinot Noir 2018 ● 300 cs; $ 51 - ▦ - A fragrant cherry aroma, then a satin smooth, earth-tinged palate brimming with concentrated fruit at the core. Black cherries, spiced berry chutney, marionberries, join toasty oak.

acres 18.5 - cases 18,000
Fertilizers biodynamic compost, compost
Plant protection sulfur
Weed control mechanical
Yeasts commercial cultured and selected indigenous yeasts
Grapes purchase 80%
Certification biodynamic, some of the vineyards are certified organic and/or biodynamic

BRYN MAWR VINEYARDS

5935 Bethel Heights Road NW - tel. (503) 581-4286
www.brynmawrvineyards.com
rachel@brynmawrvineyards.com

PEOPLE - Bryn Mawr is owned by Kathy and Jon Lauer, who purchased the rundown property in 2009 and lovingly transformed it into an outstanding destination for fine wine. Visitors who want to come and stay a while can now sleep over in a two-bedroom guest houses that provide expansive views of the surrounding area. For years, the pair and winemaker/vineyard director Rachel Rose had talked about increasing sustainability practices, and the COVID-19 pandemic gave them the time they needed to make some exciting changes.

VINEYARDS - Bryn Mawr's estate now encompasses 40 acres and has 26 acres under vine. In addition to Pinot Noir and Chardonnay, there are plantings of Riesling, Dolcetto, Tempranillo and Pinot Blanc. The site is now LIVE certified. Rose is moving to an all-organic spray program, planting wildflowers and building rock piles to encourage biodiversity. The property will be a test area for a predatory wasp program that aims to provide natural pest control.

WINES - Bryn Mawr means "high hill" in Welsh, a fitting name for this steep, rocky site that produces wines with expressive terroir. Lighter bottles (beginning in 2020) mean fewer carbon emission when the wines are shipped.

Willamette Valley Sparkling Rosé 2020 EVERYDAY WINE 300 cs; $ 28 - This outstanding blend of Pinot Noir, Pinot Gris and Chardonnay exhibits a winning combination of apple, strawberry, apricot, apple blossom and thyme.
Eola-Amity Hills Estate Riesling 2020 O 150 cs; $ 25 - A medium dry Riesling with a highly pleasing nose and palate of petrol, pineapple, apple blossom and leafy herbs.
Eola-Amity Hills Estate Dolcetto 2019 ● 150 cs; $ 35 - This lighter-bodied Dolcetto shows a combination of prune, blueberry, rose and dried oregano.

acres 26 - **cases** 6,500
Fertilizers organic-mineral
Plant protection organic
Weed control mechanical
Yeasts commercial cultured yeasts
spontaneous fermentation
Grapes purchase 25%
Certification none

CHEHALEM WINERY

106 S Center Street - tel. (503) 538-4700
www.chehalemwines.com – visit@chehalemwines.com

PEOPLE - Chehalem Winery was founded by Oregon wine legend Harry Peterson-Nedry, the current owner of Ribbon Ridge Winery. Bill Stoller was an early investor in the company and purchased it outright in 2018. The team there is led by Katie Santora, a UC-Davis grad who worked with other top Oregon wineries (including Domaine Serene) before coming to Chehalem in 2008. Director of hospitality Dave Rice has been leading in-person tastings for over a decade.

VINEYARDS - Chehalem sources grapes from three Willamette Valley vineyards with a fourth on the way. Stoller Vineyard is its estate vineyard and was first planted in 1995. Ridgecrest Vineyard was the first vineyard planted in the Ribbon Ridge AVA. Corral Creek was planted in 1983. A newly planted site with Laurelwood soil will grow Pinot Noir, Chardonnay, Pinot Gris, Pinot Blanc, and Gruner Veltliner.

WINES - The company is currently planting a new 140-acre estate vineyard that will more than double its vineyard acreage.

Chehalem Mountain Reserve Pinot Noir 2018 ● 600 cs; $ 70 - Redolent of cherry, tobacco, fennel and charcuterie, this wine also has great structure and balance.
Dundee Hills Reserve Chardonnay 2018 O 207 cs; $ 40 - A nose of mineral-rich lemon verbena and oak spice is followed by a palate of Meyer lemon tart and parmesan.
Ribbon Ridge Grüner Veltliner 2019 O 238 cs; $ 30 - Flavors and aromas of unripe mango, bay leaf and green pepper.

acres 225 - **cases** 30,000
Fertilizers compost, humus, cover crops
Plant protection organic, sulfur, synthetic pesticides
Weed control mechanical
Yeasts commercial cultured yeasts, selected indigenous yeasts
Grapes purchase 50%
Certification none

BEAVERTON

COOPER MOUNTAIN VINEYARDS

20121 SW Leonardo Lane - tel. (503) 649-0027
www.coopermountainwine.com – info@coopermountain-
wine.com

 *The iconic status of this pioneering biodynamic
producer grows with each passing year.*

PEOPLE - Founded in 1978 by Dr. Robert Gross
and his wife Corrine in Beaverton, OR., today
Gross and his daughter Barbara oversee 160 estate acres in northern Willamette Valley. Certified
biodynamic since 1999, the winery also achieved
carbon neutrality in 2010. Cooper Mountain Vineyards lowers their carbon dioxide (CO_2) outputs
via renewable solar energy, biodiesel, electrical
outlet retrofitting, and ongoing employee energy
conservation education.

VINEYARDS - Cooper Mountain Vineyards was
the first certified biodynamic vineyard in the Pacific Northwest. Vineyard manager Geraldo San-
chez oversees five vineyards planted to volcanic,
sedimentary, and windblown soils, with elevations
ranging from 300-650 feet. All are dry farmed and
most are self-rooted.

WINES - Winemaker Gilles de Domingo of Bordeaux aims for pure, lively, balanced wines true to
their diverse terroir. Varieties include Pinot Noir,
Pinot Gris, Pinot Blanc, Gamay Noir, Chardonnay,
Gewürztraminer, and Tocai Friulano.

TOP Willamette Valley Life Pinot Noir 2019 SLOW WINE
● 450 cs; $ 40 - ⊞ - A light-bodied, organic wine, sans
additives, chemicals, and sulfites, bursting with blue and
black fruits, and a brambled finish.
**TOP Willamette Valley Cooper Mountain Pinot Noir
2018** EVERYDAY WINE ● 4,520 cs; $ 28 - ⊞ - An elegant,
even-keeled wine with lovely, textured red and dark ber-
ry notes and fillips of sous bois.
**Willamette Valley Cooper Mountain Meadowlark
Pinot Noir 2018** ● 250 cs; $ 50 - ⊞ - Dark-robed,
light-bodied, and artfully balanced. A wine bursting with
notes of blackberry, raspberry, and exotic baking spices.

---

acres 160 - **cases** 18,000
Fertilizers biodynamic compost, cover crops, organic
Plant protection biodynamic preparations, organic, sulfur
Weed control mechanical
Yeasts spontaneous fermentation
Grapes 100% estate-grown
Certification biodynamic, organic

JACKSONVILLE

COWHORN VINEYARD & GARDEN

1665 Eastside Road - tel. (541) 899-6876
www.cowhornwine.com – tastingroom@cowhornwine.com

 *Under new leadership, Cowhorn has fully em-
braced and is demonstrating the ten points of the
Slow Wine Manifesto.*

PEOPLE - At age 26, Katherine "Mini" Banks purchased the winery in 2021, with the intention of
deepening the farming and holistic approach at the
biodynamic winery and farm founded by the Steeles.
She hired Sarah Thompson (from Troon) as the new
head winemaker. Banks' plan is to leverage the team's
rich and varied experiences to build and improve upon Cowhorn's existing reputation for regenerative
farming and superb wines in southern Oregon.

VINEYARDS - The property is a 117 acre, Demeter
certified biodynamic perennial polyculture farm
with an onsite winery. It was the first winery to receive a Living Building Certification for its tasting
room. In addition to the 25 acres of vineyards, Cowhorn grows lavender and asparagus. It also has hazelnut trees inoculated with Périgord black truffle.

WINES - The Rhône style wines are made with
100% estate fruit and have received more than one
hundred 90+ scores over the years.

TOP Applegate Valley Spiral 36 2020 SLOW WINE ○ 350 cs;
$ 32 - ⊞ - This spirited blend of 45% Roussanne, 30%
Marsanne and 25% Viognier kicks off with a fragrant
jasmine aroma. Mouthwatering flavors of star fruit,
poached pear, minerality, lemon custard and hints of
flintiness weave through the richly textured palate.
TOP Applegate Valley Sentience Syrah 2016 ● 150 cs;
$ 56 - ⊞ - Forest berries and savory spice on the nose
open to well-defined flavors of plum chutney, grilled
meat, huckleberry jam, and crushed herb accents. Complex with chalky tannins, deep fruit, and nice acids ideally
balanced, and the finish just keeps on going.
Applegate Valley Syrah 2016 ● 150 cs; $ 45 - ⊞ -
The expressive fruit forward aroma gives a clue as to what's
to come. A juicy mouthful of fresh blackberries, a pinch of
multi-colored peppercorns, dark plums, and a touch of va-
nilla. Well-balanced and velvety smooth through the close.

---

acres 25 - **cases** 2,500
Fertilizers biodynamic compost, cover crops, manure,
organic-mineral
Plant protection biodynamic preparations, organic, sulfur
Weed control mechanical
Yeasts spontaneous fermentation
Grapes 100% estate-grown
Certification biodynamic, organic

CRAMOISI VINEYARD

8640 NE Worden Hill Road - tel. (503) 583-1536
www.cramoisivineyard.com – info@cramoisivineyard.com

PEOPLE - Mexico City native Sofia Torres McKay and Oregonian Ryan McKay dreamed of someday owning a vineyard. In 2011, the techie couple bought land on the Dundee Hills. Sofia oversees everything from farming and winemaking, to sales and marketing. Consulting winemaker Drew Voit and vineyard manager Jessica Cortell assist. Named a Wine Business Weekly 2020 Industry Leader, she co-founded AHIVOY (Asociación Hispana de la Industria del Vino en Oregon Y Comunidad), and Celebrating Hispanic Roots.

VINEYARDS - South-facing Cramoisi Vineyard rises between 500-650 feet in the heart of the Dundee Hills AVA, with rocky, deep volcanic soils planted to Pinot Noir. Torres McKay follows biodynamic principles, including camomile tea sprays during heat spikes, all guided by seasonal and celestial cycles.

WINES - Torres McKay's wines reflect her fierce yet nurturing spirit - simultaneously elegant, plush, perfumed, intense, and terroir-expressive.

Dundee Hills Cramoisi Estate Pinot Noir Cuvée 2018 ● 200 cs; $ 55 - ⊞ - Deep ruby robe. Plush, Pommard-like texture, with lovely violet, dark raspberry, sous bois, and spice box aromatics.
Dundee Hills Sofia's Block Estate Pinot Noir 2018 ● 175 cs; $ 65 - ⊞ - Lots of blackberry, raspberry, baking spice (cinnamon, clove, mace) and smooth, red fruit finish.
Dundee Hills Cramoisi Estate Reserve Pinot Noir 2018 ● 100 cs; $ 75 - ⊞ - Attractive wild rose, bramble berry, wild raspberry notes, lithe body, lengthy finish.

acres 7 - **cases** 700
Fertilizers biodynamic compost, compost, cover crops, humus, manure
Plant protection biodynamic preparations, organic, sulfur
Weed control mechanical
Yeasts spontaneous fermentation
Grapes 100% estate-grown
Certification none

DANCIN

4477 South Stage Road - tel. (541) 245-1133
www.dancin.com – info@dancin.com

PEOPLE - There's a sweet fairy tale story behind DANCIN Vineyards, named after owners Dan and Cindy Marca. After a meeting by chance, they married in three months and remain happily paired now, 25 years later. Wine, a key interest early in their relationship, led Dan and Cindy into the study of viticulture at U.C. Davis, and in 2008 DANCIN Vineyards was established. Chris Jiron is the winemaker.

VINEYARDS - The estate is 27 acres planted Chardonnay and Pinot Noir vines at elevations of 1,710 to 1,960 feet, primarily on northeast facing slopes. Their site is situated above the rolling tree-lined foothills overlooking southern Oregon's Rogue Valley. The team considers nature as their managing partner. They are converting to becoming certified organic by 2024.

WINES - At harvest time, grapes are hand sorted twice (sometimes three times) prior to cold soak and native yeast fermentation.

⊕ Rogue Valley Ecarté Pinot Noir 2018 ● 125 cs; $ 45 - ⊞ - Stunning earthy, dusty cherry aroma. Well-structured and integrated as layers of forest floor, cola, black raspberries, dark cherries, anise, and subtle oak spice on the palate.
Rogue Valley Plié Pinot Noir 2019 ● 158 cs; $ 42 - ⊞ - The aroma and entry of sun ripened cherries and earthiness create a delicious melding of old world and new world Pinot Noir. Grilled plums, cherry cobbler, nutmeg, and earthy tones supported by balancing acidity interlace in harmony, and the finish is vivid.
Rogue Valley Capriccio Chardonnay 2019 ○ 150 cs; $ 32 - ⊞ - This beautifully scented Chardonnay is vibrant and lively. Crunchy Honeycrisp apples, lemon ice, honeysuckle, hints of fresh chopped herbs, and underlying oak interlace from first sip through tingling finish.

acres 27 - **cases** 3,300
Fertilizers compost, manure, organic-mineral
Plant protection organic, sulfur
Weed control mechanical
Yeasts spontaneous fermentation
Grapes purchase 20%
Certification converting to organics

FOREST GROVE

DAVID HILL
VINEYARDS AND WINERY

46350 NW David Hill Road - tel. (503) 992-8545
www.davidhillwinery.com – mike@davidhillwinery.com

PEOPLE - In 1965, Charles Coury, one of the pioneers of the Willamette Valley wine industry, resurrected a pre-Prohibition vineyard planting a variety of red and white grapes including Gewürztraminer, Pinot Noir, and Riesling. After several ownership changes, Milan and Jean Stoyanov purchased the property in 1991 and later acquired a nearby vineyard. Mike Kuenz serves as managing partner and is responsible for the vineyards. Chad Stock joined as winemaker in 2019.

VINEYARDS - David Hill estate vineyard sits on loess, which has discouraged phylloxera from infesting the self-rooted vines. They continue to produce Pinot Noir, Gewürztraminer, Sylvaner, Sémillon, Pinot Blanc, and Riesling. Chardonnay and various Dijon clones of Pinot Noir were added later. The Wirtz Vineyard, planted beginning in 1974, was purchased recently adding Muscat, Chasselas, and Pinot Gris as well as more Pinot Noir and Gewürztraminer.

WINES - The wide selection of grapes available including some rare and unusual varieties allows for both traditional and experimental winemaking, the latter, a specialty of Chad Stock.

Tualatin Hills Black Jack Estate Block 21 Pinot Noir 2019 ● 200 cs; $ 60 - ⊞ - The nose is lovely, subtle and elegant with floral and fruit notes while the palate is tight but nicely balanced with good acidity, vanishingly fine tannins and medium long finish.
Tualatin Hills Discovery Series Riesling Pétillant Naturel 2020 ❋ 140 cs; $ 34 - ⬚ - Yeasty nose with hints of tropical fruit and lime; lots of fun on the lemony palate with a nice balance of flavor and acidity and a pleasant mouthfeel.
Tualatin Hills Estate Gewürztraminer 2019 ○ 220 cs; $ 28 - ⬚ - The nose is untypical with oak apparent and elusive aromas of rose; dry to the point of austere on the palate but with an attractive savoriness.

NEWBERG

DOMAINE DIVIO

16435 NE Lewis Rogers Lane - tel. (503) 334-0903
www.domainedivio.com – info@domainedivio.com

PEOPLE - After growing vines and making wines worldwide, fourth-generation, Burgundy-born vigneron Bruno Corneaux bought land on Ribbon Ridge AVA in 2014. Domaine Divio means "gathering place" in Gaelic, and the ancient Latin name for Dijon - both nods to his heritage. Here, Corneaux seeks to practice his own winemaking vision and philosophy, centered around organic and biodynamic farming principles designed to produce the purest fruit possible.

VINEYARDS - Estate vineyard Clos Gallia contains marine sedimentary and clay soils reminiscent of Corneaux's family vineyards in Burgundy, planted to Pinot Noir, Chardonnay and Aligoté. The 23-acre property also supports biodiverse grasslands, native growth buffers, and wildlife habitats. Additionally, the winery sources from a number of renown non-estate vineyards, including Prince Hill, Kalita, Cedar Hills, Shea, Janice, Westmount, Hyland, Zena Crown, Loubejac, Hirshy, Perlstadt, and Tresori.

WINES - Traditional Burgundian methods rooted in minimal intervention, coupled with Oregon innovation yield transparent, polished, terroir-driven wines.

Willamette Valley Chardonnay 2019 ○ 250 cs; $ 50 - ⊞ - Pear, quince, lemon zest attack, mineral core, caramel and crème brûlée mid palate, lingering vanilla finish.
Ribbon Ridge Clos Gallia Estate Pinot Noir 2018 ● 180 cs; $ 50 - ⊞ - Ruby robe, light body, pomegranate, red plum, floral notes, elegant balance, silky tannins, soft finish.
Ribbon Ridge Pinot Noir 2018 ● 140 cs; $ 48 - ⊞ - Bright spice and floral attack, well-integrated tannins, dark cherry, berry, currant and plum mid palate, and a brawny, black tea finish.

---

acres 57 - **cases** 7,400
Fertilizers compost, cover crops, organic-mineral
Plant protection organic, sulfur
Weed control mechanical
Yeasts spontaneous fermentation
Grapes 100% estate-grown
Certification

acres 13 - **cases** 3,200
Fertilizers cover crops
Plant protection copper, organic, sulfur
Weed control mechanical
Yeasts spontaneous fermentation
Grapes purchase 25%
Certification none

DOMAINE DROUHIN OREGON 🍾

6750 NE Breyman Orchards Road - tel. (503) 864-2700
www.domaindrouhin.com – info@domainedrouhin.com

PEOPLE - Domaine Drouhin Oregon was founded in 1987 in Dundee Hills AVA by Robert Drouhin of 142-year old Maison Joseph Drouhin in Burgundy. Drouhin first learned of the Willamette Valley's potential as a wine region after tasting David Lett's wines from Eyrie at the 1979 Gault-Millau Wine Olympics. A family enterprise, fourth-generation Véronique Boss-Drouhin helms winemaking, and brother Philippe Drouhin oversees the vineyards.

VINEYARDS - Viticulturalist Philippe Drouhin farms the Oregon estate organically. Over the past two to three years, he's moved towards organic certification. He and his team opt for proactive, rather than reactive methods in the vineyard, especially important as climate change increasingly impacts harvest.

WINES - Véronique Boss-Drouhin and assistant winemaker Arron Bell produce elegant wines imbued with "French Soul, Oregon Soil," rich with Dundee's notable spice and red fruit notes.

🔝 **Dundee Hills Pinot Noir 2019** SLOW WINE ● 15,000 cs; $ 45 - 🍱 - Masterful balance, supple body, attractive dried rose petal, dark cherry, raspberry, allspice, and sous bois notes, lingering finish.

🔝 **Dundee Hills Cuvée Laurène Pinot Noir 2018** ● 2,800 cs; $ 75 - 🍱 - A graceful, garnet robed beauty with seamless structure, refined tannins, elegant spice (nutmeg, clove,) vanilla, and red fruit notes, and melodious finish.

Dundee Hills Arthur Chardonnay 2019 ○ 2,200 cs; $ 40 - 🍶🍱 - A golden-robed wine of elegant structure and mellow, creme brûlée, lemon curd, vanilla, white blossom, and golden fruit note

acres 135 - cases 25,000
Fertilizers cover crops, humus, organic-mineral
Plant protection organic, sulfur
Weed control mechanical
Yeasts selected indigenous yeasts spontaneous fermentation
Grapes 100% estate-grown
Certification converting to organics

DOMAINE NICOLAS-JAY 🍾

11905 NE Dudley Road - tel. (971) 412-1124
www.nicolas-jay.com – info@nicolas-jay.com

PEOPLE - A project founded in 2012 by longtime friends Jean-Nicolas Méo of Burgundy, and music impresario Jay Boberg. Méo assumed winemaking at his family's illustrious Vosne-Romanée estate in 1989. In Oregon, Méo's savoir faire informs every aspect of production. Associate winemaker Tracy Kendall collaborates with him on winemaking, while Boberg adds valuable marketing expertise. In 2021, they opened a new state-of-the-art tasting room and winery facility in Dundee Hills.

VINEYARDS - Vineyard manager Ryan Wilkinson farms organically at both 53 acre volcanic red soiled Nicolas-Jay Estate, purchased in 2019 on the north side of the Dundee Hills, and Bishop Creek Estate in Yamhill-Carlton, acquired in 2014. Since its inception, the winery also sources from premium valley vineyards, including Momtazi, Nysa, Hyland, Hopewell, La Colina, and Knight's Gambit.

WINES - A meticulous, old-world approach respectful of tradition, coupled with new world innovation and verve.

🔝 **Yamhill-Carlton Bishop Creek Chardonnay 2018** ○ 120 cs; $ 75 - 🍱 - Seductive acacia, citron, and waxy yellow and white flower aromas, with a slight, tangy back note. Poised, subtle, nuanced, complex, with a refined finish.

Yamhill-Carlton Bishop Creek Pinot Noir 2018 ● 290 cs; $ 100 - 🍱 - A forest of intricate, brooding aromatics and and flavors - earthy red berry and cherry and lush layers of blackberry, bramble berry, baking spice, dried florals that linger on the finish.

Willamette Valley L'Ensemble Pinot Noir 2018 ● 1,145 cs; $ 70 - 🍱 - True to its name, a super-blend of rich red fruit, spice and sous bois sourced from Willamette Valley's best Bio-dynamic, organic and LIVE certified vineyards.

acres 18.7 - cases 2,920
Fertilizers compost, green manure, manure, organic-mineral
Plant protection organic, sulfur
Weed control mechanical
Yeasts spontaneous fermentation
Grapes purchase 50%
Certification some of the vineyards are certified organic and/or biodynamic

DUNDEE

DOMAINE ROY & FILS

8351 NE Worden Hill Road - tel. (503) 687-2600
www.domaineroy.com – hospitality@domaineroy.com

PEOPLE - Domaine Roy et fils combines scions from two celebrated wine families into one premium project. In 2012, Jared Etzel and father Mike Etzel of Oregon's Beaux Freres, along with Marc-Andre Roy and father Robert Roy of Quebec, established a winery on the site of a former hazelnut orchard on Dundee Hills. Mike Etzel bring his considerable winemaking talents, while partner Marc-Andre advances the winery's mission to produce "Grand Cru"-style wines from Oregon terroir.

VINEYARDS - Iron Filbert Vineyard rises 300-500 feet on the Dundee Hills. Organically dry-farmed, it slopes south, its 15 acres of iron-rich Jory soils peppered with basalt erratics runs north-south, planted to high-density Pinot Noir and Chardonnay. Organically farmed Quartz Acorn Vineyard on Yamhill-Carlton comprises 21 acres of Pinot Noir and three acres of Chardonnay planted on marine sedimentary soils flecked with rare crystalline quartz.

....

WINES - A time-intensive, bespoke approach in both the vineyard and cellar, intent on coaxing the finest Pinot Noir and Chardonnay wines possible.

Dundee Hills Incline Pinot Noir 2019 ● 700 cs; $ 64 - ⊞ - A cooler vintage, yielding light body, bright acidity, and dark fruit notes.
Yamhill-Carlton Incline Pinot Noir 2019 ● 600 cs; $ 64 - ⊞ - Savory, earthy, cherry notes and mineral core, with a super-silky finish.
Willamette Valley Pinot Noir 2019 ● 1,000 cs; $ 42 - ⊞ - A ballerina-like wine with diaphanous body, deft structure, and lovely dried rose petal and red fruit notes.

CARLTON

DOMINIO IV

11570 NE Intervale Road - tel. (971) 261-7781
www.dominiowines.com – info@dominiowines.com

PEOPLE - Winemaker Patrick Reuter and vineyard manager Leigh Bartholomew, who manages some of the valley's most esteemed vineyards, founded Dominio IV in 2002. Initially, the charismatic husband-and-wife team planted vines in Oregon's Columbia River Gorge near Mosier, later adding another property in Yamhill-Carlton in 2016. Reuter pioneered "Shape Tasting," a pictorial representation of wine aromas and shapes depicted on their "Imagination Series" labels.

VINEYARDS - Warm and sunny "Three Sleeps" in Columbia Gorge AVA comprises 10 acres of Tempranillo, Syrah, Viognier, Cabernet Franc, Malbec and Petit Verdot planted on ancient flood soils. "Shallow-blue-sea" in Yamhill-Carlton features marine sedimentary soils planted to Pinot Noir, Chardonnay, hazelnuts, and cherries, and charming tasting areas tucked throughout the property.

....

WINES - Easy-going, well-balanced, food-friendly wines with bright, natural acidity, vibrant fruitiness, and artistic appeal.

Yamhill-Carlton Imagination Series no.19 Wahle Vineyard Chardonnay 2017 ○ 124 cs; $ 38 - ⊞ - Lush jasmine, almond, citron, and golden apple notes, plush body, and an opulent finish.
Dundee Hills Bella Vida Vineyard The Violet Hour Pinot Noir 2016 ● 97 cs; $ 58 - ⊞ - Savory, umami notes unfold into lilting violet and black fruit layers.
Eola-Amity Hills Temperance Hill Vineyard Slow Walk of the Wind Pinot Noir 2017 ● 73 cs; $ 48 - ⊞ - Ethereal dried floral, lavender, bergamot and evergreen aromatics, rich red and blue fruit notes, lithe body, and exquisite balance.

---

acres 40.5 - **cases** 5,000
Fertilizers none
Plant protection organic
Weed control mechanical
Yeasts spontaneous fermentation
Grapes 100% estate-grown
Certification organic

acres 19 - **cases** 4,000
Fertilizers compost, compost, manure, organic-mineral
Plant protection biodynamic preparations, organic, sulfur
Weed control mechanical
Yeasts commercial cultured yeasts, spontaneous fermentation
Grapes purchase 35%
Certification converting to organics and biodynamics

DUNDEE

ÉLEVÉE WINEGROWERS

9653 NE Keyes Lane - tel. (503) 840-8448
www.eleveewines.com – tom@eleveewines.com

PEOPLE - Tom Fitzpatrick's mission is to present a study in Oregon terroir by producing wines made with the same processes but grapes from different vineyards around the Willamette Valley. Historically, he has worked with his estate vineyard in the Dundee Hills, Madrona Hill Vineyard in the new Laurelwood AVA and Björnsen Vineyard in the Eola-Amity AVA. In 2019 he added biodynamic certified Meredith Mitchell Vineyard in the McMinnville AVA.

VINEYARDS - Élevée's estate vineyard has a permanent cover crop and is farmed using no till agriculture. Besides Pinot Noir, Fitzpatrick makes one bottling of Riesling each year. In 2021, he began working with Gruner Veltliner. It and Riesling are sourced from Ridgecrest Vineyard, the famed estate planted by Harry Peterson-Nedry in what is now the Ribbon Ridge AVA. Fitzpatrick is in the beginning stages of a similar terroir experiment with Oregon Riesling.

WINES - Fitzpatrick's site-specific Pinot Noirs live up to their goal of showcasing the differences between vineyards. His other wines are well worth a try too.

Willamette Valley Departure Pinot Noir 2018 ● 200 cs; $ 90 - 🍷 - This wine is a blend of the best barrels from all the sites Fitzpatrick works with; expect cherry, game, oregano, lavender and baking spice in this wine with great structure and balance.
Dundee Hills Élevée Vineyard Pinot Noir 2018 ● 400 cs; $ 52 - 🍷 - Made with a combination of 777, 115 and Pommard clones, this excellent wine exudes pomegranate, cherry pie, potpourri and black tea on the nose and palate.
Ribbon Ridge Ridgecrest Vineyard Riesling 2018 ○ 400 cs; $ 33 - 🍷 - A dry Riesling that sings with juicy peach, petrol, spiced pear and honeysuckle.

acres 5 - **cases** 1,200
Fertilizers n/a
Plant protection organic, sulfur, synthetic pesticides
Weed control mechanical
Yeasts spontaneous fermentation
Grapes purchase 60%
Certification none

GASTON

ELK COVE VINEYARDS

27751 NW Olson Road - tel. (503) 985-7760
www.elkcove.com – info@elkcove.com

PEOPLE - Joe and Pat Campbell founded the winery in 1974. They were among early grape growing pioneers in the state. Their son Adam Campbell began winemaking in 1995 and is now head Winemaker. Heather Perkin, who studied winemaking in her home country of Australia, is the associate winemaker. Travis Watson has been the team's vineyard manager since 2002. Cellar master José Sotto joined the team in 2003.

VINEYARDS - In 1974 Pat and Joe planted their first vineyard, The Elk Cove Winery Estate with 5 acres of Pinot Noir. They added more acres of Pinot Noir, Riesling, Gewurztraminer, Chardonnay and Pinot Gris. Their Pinot Gris vines are among the oldest planted in Oregon (some up to 35 years old). They use only organically approved materials on their estate.

WINES - Fruit from each vineyard block is fermented separately in small, temperature-controlled steel tanks and hand punched down prior to aging in French oak barrels.

🔝 **Yamhill-Carlton Mount Richmond Pinot Noir 2019** ● 709 cs; $ 60 - 🍷 - From a steep-sloped vineyard comes this earth-toned, dusty cherry fragranced Pinot Noir. A bowlful of black cherries, Santa Rosa plums, mushrooms, licorice, black raspberries, and Asian spices swirl delectably on the palate. Refined tannins and a forever finish cap off the striking package.
🔝 **Willamette Valley Estate Pinot Gris 2020** EVERYDAY WINE ○ 13,470 cs; $ 20 - 🍷 - Fragrant white flowers on the nose followed by layers of creamy pear, summer melon, lemon cream pie, and hints of fresh cut herbs.
Willamette Valley Estate Pinot Noir 2019 ● 15,195 cs; $ 32 - 🍷 - Mixed berries and earthy aromas, with flavors of cherry pie, toasted marshmallows, nutmeg, tayberries and tinges of licorice.

acres 400 - **cases** 45,000
Fertilizers compost, cover crops, organic-mineral
Plant protection organic, sulfur
Weed control mechanical
Yeasts commercial cultured yeasts, spontaneous fermentation
Grapes 100% estate-grown
Certification none

CARLTON

EST

10501 NE Abbey Road - tel. (503) 522-2481
www.estwines.com – info@stateracellars.com

PEOPLE - The ability to combine science, agriculture, art and other such beautiful disciplines slowly drew Meredith Bell to the world of wine. After earning a graduate degree in viticulture and enology at UC Davis, she returned home to the Portland area to begin her career. While working as an assistant winemaker at Craft Wine Company, she connected with Bruce Weber, a family friend with a 4-acre vineyard planted in the 1980s. She and Weber now farm the property together with the idea that she will eventually become the property's vigneron.

VINEYARDS - EST is about farming and celebrating wine as an agricultural product, so all of the fruit comes from Weber's property near Oregon City. The property is all organic short a few anti-mildew sprays used up to three times annually. For years, Dick Erath purchased all of the fruit and used it for a single-vineyard designate. Some still goes to Erath Winery, but Weber is proud to have Bell using much of it to make natural wines.

WINES - EST means "east" in French and draws attention to the beautiful Pinot Noir that grows on the eastern side of the Willamette Valley. In line with the idea that wine is food, Bell makes EST wines with as little intervention as possible. Bottles are labeled with all ingredients (typically just grapes and sulfites).

Willamette Valley Sparkling 2019 ⚬ 75 cs; $ 30 - 🛢 - Made with the methode ancestrale process, this wine shows cherry, raspberry and forest floor.
Willamette Valley Swirl Rosé 2018 ● 97 cs; $ 26 - 🛢 - Inspired by piquette, this wine is made from Pinot Noir fermented on the skins of Sauvignon Blanc and has flavors of mango, strawberry and lychee.
Willamette Valley Pinot Noir 2019 ● 47 cs; $ 31 - 🛢 - Cherry, brambly raspberry, dried mango and rose are a few of the flavors in this wine made with one-third whole cluster fruit.

---

acres 4 - cases 300
Fertilizers none
Plant protection sulfur
Weed control mechanical
Yeasts spontaneous fermentation
Grapes 100% estate-grown
Certification converting to organics

DUNDEE

EVENING LAND 🍾
SEVEN SPRINGS ESTATE

1326 N Highway 99W, Suite 100 - tel. (503) 538-4110
www.elvwines.com – oregonhospitality@elvwines.com

PEOPLE - Owners and vintners Sashi Moorman and Raj Parr struggled in 2020, as did many winemakers in the Willamette Valley, with the toxic environment due to smoke from nearby forest fires. Evening Land released 2000 cases of a rosé of pinot noir and Salem, an adjunct brand, released 2500 cases of chardonnay. Moorman points out that the major issue today is not chemical farming, though Evening Land farms with biodynamic-style practices, it is reducing one's carbon footprint more directly.

VINEYARDS - Unfortunately, smoke taint was the story in 2020. Normally, Seven Springs Estate is a Willamette grand cru vineyard. Moorman talks of squeezing out half of normal production in 2020. Separating the juice from the skins was of primary importance with pinot noir, as was positioning the wines to be for immediate consumption. For 2021, estate production will be down due to record heat spikes and some rain during flowering. But quality will be high, especially for the resilient chardonnay.

WINES - Moorman and Parr have tinkered with production to get it to their current satisfaction.

Eola-Amity Hills Seven Springs Estate La Source Pinot Noir 2018 ● 465 cs; $ 75 - 🛢 - Lavender sachet and exotic spice are on the nose with a palate of concentrated cherry, blackberry and blood orange flavors. Dusty tannins breathe with each sip, spreading on the palate, contracting on the finish.
Eola-Amity Hills Seven Springs Chardonnay 2019 ○ 660 cs; $ 35 - 🛢 - Shows a nose of mandarine, nougat and lemon pith with textured acidity and flavors of pineapple and green mango.
Eola-Amity Hills Seven Springs Pinot Noir 2019 ● 1,721 cs; $ 35 - 🛢 - Shows aromas of rose, cherry cobbler and cedar, while on the palate are rhubarb, blood orange and peat with a delicately tannic finish.

---

acres 35 - cases 5,000
Fertilizers compost
Plant protection biodynamic preparations
Weed control mechanical
Yeasts spontaneous fermentation
Grapes 100% estate-grown
Certification none

SALEM

EVESHAM WOOD

3795 Wallace Road NW - tel. (503) 371-8478
www.eveshamwood.com – info@eveshamwood.com

PEOPLE - Evesham Wood was founded by Russ and Mary Raney in 1986. Russ attended winemaking school in the Nahe region of Germany but was also a fan of Burgundy, and both serve as an inspiration. Erin Nuccio purchased the winery in 2010 and continues to make wines of place fermented with a yeast culture Russ captured over 20 years ago. Erin's wife Jordan, a veterinarian by trade, is using her science background to help explore new sustainability measures, including no-till and regenerative agriculture. Watch for owl and other raptor boxes in the vineyard to help with natural pest control.

VINEYARDS - Evesham Wood's estate vineyard near the southern edge of the Eola-Amity Hills is 80% Pinot Noir. There are also small plantings of Pinot Gris, Gewürztraminer and other Alsatian varieties and a few newly-grafted rows of Chardonnay.

WINES - The winery's remaining fruit comes from Temperance Hill (organic), Mahonia (transitioning to organic with help from Evesham Wood's staff), Sojeau (organic methods) and Illahe (organic methods). Between its commitment to organic growing, use of selected yeast, high quality and great hospitality, Evesham Wood is a place not to be missed on any wine excursion.

Eola-Amity Hills Le Puits Sec Vineyard Pinot Noir 2018 ● 525 cs; $ 40 - ⊞ - Hailing from the estate vineyard, this wine shows rose, baby powder, red plum and Bing cherry.
Eola-Amity Hills Mahonia Vineyard Pinot Noir 2018 ● 175 cs; $ 36 - ⊞ - Aromas and flavors of cherry vanilla cola, raspberry, earth, baking spice and rose.
Eola-Amity Hills Cuvee Pinot Noir 2018 ● 825 cs; $ 26 - ⊞ - Made with fruit from six vineyards around the region, this wine expresses ripe cherry, lavender and a touch of orange zest.

acres 12.5 - cases 6,000
Fertilizers none
Plant protection organic, sulfur
Weed control mechanical
Yeasts selected indigenous yeasts
Grapes 100% estate-grown
Certification some of the vineyards are certified organic

MCMINNVILLE

THE EYRIE VINEYARDS

935 NE 10th Avenue - tel. (503) 472-6315
www.eyrievineyards.com – info@eyrievineyards.com

 Jason Lett's motto "We tread best when we tread lightest" is the guiding principle of farming an estate that has never seen herbicides, pesticides, tillage or irrigation.

PEOPLE - Affectionately referred to as "Papa Pinot," David Lett and wife Diana planted vines on Dundee Hills in 1965 with plant material he'd propagated temporarily in Corvallis the year prior. They bottled their first vintage in 1970, naming it "The Eyrie" after an ever-present pair of resident red-tail hawks. David Lett passed away in 2008, leaving respected son Jason Lett to tend the estate and winemaking.

VINEYARDS - The Eyrie Vineyards comprises five sites on the Dundee Hills totaling 115 acres, 57 acres planted to vines. Non-vineyard lands include pastures, forests and native habitat. The Eyrie boasts the original vines planted in 1965. Others include Daphne, Roland Green Farm, Sisters, and Outcrop.

WINES - Respectful, gentle traditional methods like native yeast fermentations, full malo, extended lees contact, no fining, and minimal racking or filtration.

🔝 **Willamette Valley The Eyrie Pinot Noir 2017** ● 445 cs; $ 80 - ⊞ - An 'old soul' that fulcrums between celestial structure, effortless balance and earthy, brambled berry notes.
Dundee Hills Outcrop Vineyard Pinot Noir 2017 ● 188 cs; $ 50 - ⊞ - Tangled evergreen, sous bois, peat, spice box, and red fruit notes, delicate as bone-china. Lovely acids and ultra-fine tannins support long-term cellaring.
Dundee Hills Trousseau 2018 ● 259 cs; $ 35 - ⊞ - Organic, estate-grown fruit, wild yeasts, and no fining, filtering, or sulfur at bottling. Translucent ruby robe, with savory notes of red plum, cherry, currant, and eglantine.

acres 57 - cases 8,333
Fertilizers manure pellets, organic
Plant protection organic, sulfur
Weed control mechanical
Yeasts commercial cultured yeasts, selected indigenous yeasts, spontaneous fermentation
Grapes 100% estate-grown
Certification organic

GROCHAU CELLARS $

HADEN FIG $

9360 SE Eola Hills Road - tel. (503) 522-2455
www.grochaucellars.com – info@gcwines.com

3795 Wallace Road - tel. (503) 371-8478
www.hadenfig.com – info@eveshamwood.com

PEOPLE - Former European amateur cyclist and seasoned fine-dining professional John Grochau founded Grochau Cellars in 2002. Together with associate winemaker Aurelien Labrosse, the pair run a lean, mean operation and tasting room in Amity. Working mostly by hand among the vines, Grochau paying acute attention each site's needs. "Minimum intervention requires maximum attention," he says. "We don't do anything prescriptively."

PEOPLE - Evesham Wood winemaker Erin Nuccio uses Haden Fig as his playground, a chance to express himself through winemaking and experiment with things like whole-cluster fermentation, spontaneous fermentation and extended elevage. Nuccio began his career working in retail and distribution, then attended Napa Valley College to study enology and viticulture. He is a steward of good fruit, allowing it to show season and place.

VINEYARDS - Grochau Cellars currently owns no estates, but draws upon 17 vineyards stretching from the Willamette Valley to the Rogue River. Many hold Sustainable, Salmon-Safe, and L.I.V.E certifications, such as Björnson Vineyard in Eola-Amity AVA and Carlton Hill in Yamhill-Carlton AVA. Redford-Wetle Vineyard in Eola-Amity Hills AVA farms certified Organic. Varieties include Pinot Noir, Pinot Blanc, Chardonnay, Melon de Bourgogne, Gamay Noir, and Syrah.

VINEYARDS - Nuccio works with a variety of vineyards, most of which are located in the Eola-Amity Hills. Cancilla, located near Gaston, is a certified Organic vineyard growing on Melbourne soil, a mixture of decomposing mud stone and basalt. Croft Vineyard (certified organic) has a mix of bellpine and Jory soil. Freedom Hill is also on bellpine soil. Bjornson Vineyard has Nekia and Jory soils.

WINES - Intentionally crafted, affordable, approachable, low sulfur wines designed for enjoyment with friends and family over warm, inviting meals.

🔵 **Willamette Valley Melon de Bourgogne 2020**
EVERYDAY WINE ○ 250 cs; $ 22 - ▢⊞ - Aged for 8 months on the fine lees, a light, lithe lemon and white flower stunner with intriguing texture and bright acids.
Eola-Amity Hills Vivid Vineyard Pinot Noir 2019 ● 0;
$ 40 - ⊞ - Vivid ruby robe, with dusky minerality, pungent black pepper, and inky blue fruit notes reminiscent of a cru Beaujolais.
Eola-Amity Hills Redford Wetle Vineyard Pinot Noir 2019 ● 100 cs; $ 25 - ⊞ - Violets, dried florals, dark red and blue fruit nose. Light body, lovely acids, silky tannins. Florals, cherry & raspberry notes.

WINES - Though Nuccio's occasionally makes Pinot Gris and rosé, his main focus is Pinot Noir and Chardonnay.
Willamette Valley Cancilla Vineyard Pinot Noir 2019 ● 35 cs; $ 36 - ⊞ - Showcasing the quality of high-acid Pinots, this wine expresses delicious flavors and aromas of cranberry, cherry and clove.
Willamette Valley Freedom Hill Vineyard Pinot Noir 2019 ● 0; $ 36 - ⊞ - A powerful nose of red cherry and cedar gives way to flavors of lavender, cranberry and raspberry on the palate.
Willamette Valley Croft Vineyard Pinot Noir 2019 ● 40 cs; $ 36 - ⊞ - A lovely combination of cherry, raspberry and lavender.

acres 0 - cases 9,833
Fertilizers compost, manure, organic-mineral
Plant protection organic, sulfur
Weed control mechanical
Yeasts selected indigenous yeasts
Grapes purchase 100%
Certification some of the vineyards are certified organic

acres 12.5 - cases 2,000
Fertilizers compost, cover crops, n/a, organic
Plant protection organic, sulfur, synthetic pesticides
Weed control mechanical
Yeasts selected indigenous yeasts
Grapes purchase 65%
Certification some of the vineyards are certified organic

ROSEBURG

HILLCREST VINEYARD

240 Vineyard Lane - tel. (541) 673-3709
www.hillcrestvineyard.com – info@hillcrestvineyard.com

PEOPLE - Dyson DeMara has been steering the ship at HillCrest Vineyards since 2003. DeMara and his wife Susan do all of the winemaking and other work for the brand. In 2021, the couple's daughter, Hanna, officially joined the team. Hanna is a recent graduate of the viticulture, oenology and marketing program at the Universitá Degli Studi di Udine in northeastern Italy. She brings an exceptional palate and new skills and ideas to the storied winery.

VINEYARDS - HillCrest's original vineyard is 25 acres and planted to Tempranillo, Chardonnay, Riesling, Pinot Noir and Malbec (a southern Oregon standout, in DeMara's opinion). DeMara has added two additional vineyards to the portfolio. The 15-acre Pazzo Collina Vineyard is near Sutherlin is planted to a range of Italian varietals, including favorites like Sangiovese and unusual choices like Friesa. The 13-acre 707 Vineyard is home to Chenin Blanc and Sémillon.

....

WINES - In the winery, the DeMaras use the lightest touch possible because they believe low intervention techniques produces the most interesting end results. DeMara is also deeply committed to extended aging, traditional vessels such as botti, and other tools for creating richer, more complex expressions of terroir.

🔺 **Umpqua Valley Petit Blanc 2017** EVERYDAY WINE ○150 cs; $ 28 - 🍷 - This blend of two grapes has Pinot Blanc texture and Chardonnay flavor: caramel ice cream topping, yellow apple, lemon zest and more.
Umpqua Valley HillCrest Pinot Noir 2017 ● 100 cs; $ 75 - ▦ - Aromas of plum, coffee grounds and rose give way to blackberry, vanilla and baking spice on the palate.
Umpqua Valley Old Stones Teroldego 2016 ● 200 cs; $ 38 - ▦ - This Italian grape is doing well in southern Oregon, where it produces a nicely balanced and textural wine with aromas of dark cherry, blackberry and leafy herbs.

acres 53 - cases 2,000
Fertilizers none
Plant protection sulfur
Weed control mechanical
Yeasts commercial cultured yeasts, selected indigenous yeasts, spontaneous fermentation
Grapes 100% estate-grown
Certification none

DALLAS

ILLAHE VINEYARDS

3275 Ballard Road - tel. (503) 831-1248
www.illahevineyards.com – karen@illahevineyards.com

PEOPLE - Brad Ford joined his family's wine business in 2005 and became its first winemaker. He and his wife Bethany, who handles sales and marketing, have been running Illahe on their own since 2015. Ford has stepped back from daily winemaking and is now focused mainly on vineyard management. Nathan Litke, who has worked at Illahe for many years, is now the winemaker. Ford is a student of history who is always trying something new and interesting as he hones the art and science of winemaking.

VINEYARDS - Twelve acres at Illahe's estate are farmed organically. The remainder are LIVE certified. In the past year, Illahe added 21 acres of Pinot Noir and Chardonnay. Traditionally, Ford has bought fruit from sustainably-farmed Goschie Farms and Ash Creek Vineyards. New in 2021, some grapes are coming from Pauline Vineyard, an organic property that Illahe bought from Croft Vineyard. Illahe will be building a tasting room in 2022.

....

WINES - For now, tastings take place in the winery or on a patio overlooking the proposed Mt. Pisgah Polk County AVA, for which Ford authored the application. Illahe's wines sometimes take some time to open up, but when they do, both the texture and flavor are thought-providing and awe-inspiring.

🔺 **Willamette Valley 1899 Pinot Noir 2019** SLOW WINE ● 300 cs; $ 75 - ▦ - Made entirely without electricity or other conveniences that existed before the 20th century, this elegant wine has aromas and flavors of cherry, cocoa, lavender, anise and cinnamon.
Willamette Valley Bon Sauvage Estate Pinot Noir 2019 ● 1,300 cs; $ 35 - ▦ - Expect wild blueberries, cranberry, baking spice and vanilla.
Willamette Valley Tempranillo Rosé 2019 ◐ 300 cs; $ 19 - ▦ - This mineral-driven, bright rose is flush with flavors of white peach, red current, fresh flowers and leafy herbs.

acres 65 - cases 15,000
Fertilizers manure pellets
Plant protection organic, sulfur
Weed control mechanical
Yeasts commercial cultured yeasts, selected indigenous yeasts, spontaneous fermentation
Grapes purchase 30%
Certification none

CARLTON

J.C. SOMERS VINTNER

258 N. Kutch Street, Suite A - tel. (503) 502-1641
www.jcsomers.wine – hello@jcsomers.wine

PEOPLE - In 2021, Jay Christopher Somers "graduated" after 2 years from The Carlton Winemakers Studio incubator into his own facility. Together with his wife Ronda Newell-Somers, he continues to develop his latest brand which he started after selling his interest in J. Christopher which he founded in 1996. Newell-Somers has been an important part of both the previous and new ventures involved in all aspects of the business including harvest, cellar work, marketing and sales.

VINEYARDS - Somers has no vineyards and sources from several in the Willamette Valley. Corinne vineyard in the Chehalem Mountains American Viticultural Area (AVA) is the source of Chardonnay. It at 300 to 450 feet elevation and the soils are volcanic and sedimentary. The Sauvignon Blanc comes from the organically farmed Croft Vineyard which was established in 1983 in the Willamette Valley AVA. The soil is ancient marine sediment.

....

WINES - Somer's approach to winemaking reflects the styles of several regions in France including Sancerre, Cote D'or and Chablis and encourages excellent acidity.

Willamette Valley Croft Vineyard Sauvignon Blanc 2020 O 180 cs; $ 28 - 🗇 🔔 - An aroma of grapefruit jumps from this wine. With air, some pyrazine emerges. The palate is rounded showing the effects of the concrete aging, then tapers to great acidity in the long finish.
Chehalem Mountains Corrine Vineyard Chardonnay 2020 O 94 cs; $ 40 - ◍ - Tasted two days after bottling, this wine exhibited a complex nose featuring lemon curd. True to Somers preference for Chablis, the palate shows great balance and a long finish with excellent acidity.

NEWBERG

J.K. CARRIERE

9995 NE Parrett Mountain Road - tel. (503) 554-0721
www.jkcarriere.com – linda@jkcarriere.com

PEOPLE - J.K. Carriere owner and Oregon native Jim Prosser had worked in wine for nearly a decade when he bought 40 acres of land in the Chehalem Mountains AVA to bring his winemaking vision to life. He focuses on crafting high acid, ageworthy Pinot Noirs – wines of substance, he explains further, that only go in the bottle if they're undeniable delicious. He is assisted in this effort by general manager (and sister) Linda Crabtree, cellarmaster Lucas Ehrhard and vineyard manager Drew Herman.

VINEYARDS - In line with his long-held belief that vineyards should be dry farmed, Prosser's St. Dolores Vineyard receives no irrigation. The exceptionally dry year in 2021 tested the veracity of this idea, and he is confident the vineyard will pass. Prosser has been making his own biochar and compost to improve soil health and is moving to a no-till system with the goal of minimizing disturbance to the soil. The vineyard is organic save the certification.

....

WINES - In addition to St. Dolores Vineyard, J.K. Carriere buys fruit from the organic Temperance Hill Vineyard and LIVE certified Gemini Vineyard. Prosser makes small lots of Chardonnay with fruit sourced from Temprance Hill, but Pinot Noir is the star here.

Willamette Valley Vespidae Pinot Noir 2019 ● 759 cs; $ 42 - ▦ - This wine exemplifies Prosser's goal of making wines that are seamless and tell the story of the vintage year by blending vineyard sites, and exudes blackberry, dark cherry, leaf mold, coffee grounds and talc minerals.
Willamette Valley Provocateur Pinot Noir 2019 ● 2,220 cs; $ 28 - ▦ - Expect flavors and aromas of tart cherry, smoked blueberries, dusty rose and vanilla.
Willamette Valley Lucidité Chardonnay 2017 O 143 cs; $ 32 - ▦ - This mineral-driven Chardonnay also features fresh caramel, lemon peel, tart apple and grapefruit pith.

---

acres - cases 1,500
Fertilizers biodynamic compost, compost, cover crops
Plant protection organic
Weed control mechanical
Yeasts n/a
Grapes purchase 100%
Certification some of the vineyards, are certified biodynamic, some of the vineyards are certified organic

acres 26 - **cases** 5,000
Fertilizers compost, humus, manure
Plant protection organic, sulfur
Weed control mechanical
Yeasts spontaneous fermentation
Grapes purchase 20%
Certification some of the vineyards are certified organic

RICKREALL

JOHAN VINEYARDS

4285 N Pacific Highway 99 W - tel. (503) 623-8642
www.johanvineyards.com – info@johanvineyards.com

PEOPLE - Norway resident Dag Johan Sundby started Johan Vineyard on 175 acres at the mouth of the Van Duzer Corridor in 2005. It is now owned by Katherine Banks, who also owns Cowhorn Vineyard in southern Oregon and has a stellar reputation for managing biodynamic properties. Morgan Beck has been the head winemaker since 2018. Elise Hansen is now the vineyard manager, a task she fully took over in 2021 after being mentored by longtime employee Dan Rinke.

VINEYARDS - Johan's organic and biodynamic vineyard grows 16 different types of grapes, including Oregon standards Pinot Noir and Chardonnay and more unusual varieties such as Zweigelt, Mondeuse, Grüner Veltliner and Blaufränkisch (the latter two, plus Chardonnay, have a growing presence in the vineyard thanks to a grafting project last year). Hansen has introduced hair sheep, chickens and ducks to help keep the vineyard healthy and thriving.

WINES - 2021 was the driest year ever in Oregon, surpassing 2018, but Beck is confident the vineyard produced beautiful fruit with great ripeness and balanced pH levels.

Willamette Valley Van Duzer Corridor Jazzy Juice 2020 ● 438 cs; $ 30 - ⊞ ◎ - Beck blended Blaufränkisch, Zweigelt, St. Laurent, Grüner Veltliner and Kerner to make this savory, light-bodied, chillable red.
Willamette Valley Van Duzer Corridor Pinot Noir 2019 ● 714 cs; $ 30 - ⊞ - Includes fruit from all 10 clones of Pinot from the estate, making a wine that is representative of the entire farm; flavors include blackberry, black pepper, fresh herbs and rose.
Willamette Valley Van Duzer Corridor Pet Nat of Pinot Noir 2020 ❋ 583 cs; $ 27 - ⊞ - This lightly fizzy drink shows bright flavors of red fruit and savory yeast.

---

acres 88 - cases 5,000
Fertilizers compost
Plant protection organic
Weed control mechanical
Yeasts spontaneous fermentation
Grapes 100% estate-grown
Certification biodynamic, organic

AMITY

KEELER ESTATE VINEYARD

5100 SE Rice Lane - tel. (503) 687-2618
www.keelerestatevineyard.com
info@keelerestatevineyard.com

Through their practices, the Keelers exemplify the ten points of the Slow Wine Manifesto.

PEOPLE - Craig and Gabriele Keeler planted a vineyard on their family's property in 2007. Growing biodynamically and making low-intervention wine has always been a goal, and they've found their perfect partner in Kevin Healy, who started with the brand in 2017 but became head winemaking in 2019. He enjoys using unusual vessels, including a new beehive amphorae and concrete eggs and dolia, and experimenting with new methods.

VINEYARDS - Keeler Estate is certified biodynamic and committed to increasing biodiversity through maintaining natural areas and implementing best practices. Currently, the site is planted with Pinot Noir, Pinot Gris, Riesling and Chardonnay, but the Keelers have added Blaufrankisch and Gamay to increase the variety of available grapes. Soils are Amity and sedimentary. The Van Duzer Corridor helps keep the vineyard cool in the afternoon.

WINES - A focus on biodynamic agriculture, natural techniques and vessels, and the joie de vivre that is winemaking makes Keeler a special place for vinophiles. Keeler tends to produce a lot of small lots so the team can experiment with different techniques, blends and ideas.

Eola Amity Hills Skin Contact Pinot Gris 2019 ◎ 144 cs; $ 24 - ⋀ - This wine spent 15 days on the skins, so it has beautiful texture along with enticing aromas of strawberry, papaya and orange blossom
Eola Amity Hills Field Blend 2019 ● 75 cs; $ 38 - ⋀ - A blend of all the varieties currently in production at Keeler Estate, this wine is vibrant, alive and full of flavors such as red plum, rose, strawberry and white flowers.
Eola-Amity Hills Clone 943 Pinot Noir 2019 ● 29 cs; $ 100 - ⊞ - This no-added-sulfite wine is more on the traditional end of the wine spectrum and has old-world character, with blackberry, cherry, tobacco and vanilla apparent on the nose and palate.

---

acres 50 - cases 2,500
Fertilizers biodynamic compost, compost
Plant protection organic
Weed control mechanical
Yeasts spontaneous fermentation
Grapes 100% estate-grown
Certification biodynamic, organic

KELLEY FOX WINES

KING ESTATE WINERY $

26421 Highway 47 - tel. (503) 679-5786
www.kelleyfoxwines.com – kelley@kelleyfoxwines.com

80854 Territorial Highway - tel. (541) 942-9874
www.kingestate.com – info@kingestate.com

PEOPLE - Kelley Fox arrived in the Willamette Valley in 2000, working with respected wineries like Eyrie and Scott Paul before founding Kelley Fox Wines in 2007. "I feel almost like this is something I was I felt like it was a calling in a way," says Fox. "And so, there's some some spiritual aspects to this work also, and maybe some monastic qualities, to the way I do things." Fox imbues a gentle grace to every aspect of her vine tending and winemaking - all guided by celestial rhythms.

PEOPLE - King Estate is led by Ed King, who founded the winery with his father in 1991. Over time, he has a built a steady team committed to making Pinot Gris and other wines from biodynamic and sustainably-farmed grapes. COO and winemaker Brent Stone, a chemist with a long history in the food and beverage industry, came on board in 2011. Director of viticulture Ray Nuclo worked as a consultant to King Estate before becoming a full-time employee. Vineyard manager Meliton Martinez has been maintaining the vineyards for almost 30 years.

VINEYARDS - Fox owns no vineyards, but sources from Willamette Valley's finest, many 'franc de pied,' or own-rooted. On Dundee Hills AVA, Maresh Vineyard provides old-vine Pinot Noir, and neighboring Weber Vineyard Pommard and Pinot Gris, while Durant Vineyard offers Chardonnay. Hyland Vineyard in McMinnville AVA supplies Coury Pinot Noir. In Eola-Amity Hills AVA, Ken and Karen Wright's Carter Vineyard proffer own-rooted Wädensvil, and Freedom Hill Vineyard furnishes Pinot Blanc.

VINEYARDS - King Estate's 470-acre vineyard is certified organic and biodynamic. The newest addition to the property is a small planting of Pinot Meunier, which will be used for an estate-only sparkling program. King Estate also has long-term relationships with numerous vineyards in Oregon and Washington to source grapes each year. Several, including Temperance Hill Vineyard and Croft Vineyard, are certified organic.

WINES - Part fairy dust, part alchemist's elixir, Fox's wines capture an ineffable 'lightness of being,' "bringing Earth and humanity together" in the process.

WINES - Ed King's passion is Pinot Gris, which he firmly believes can be aged. King Estate also produces a wide range of other fine, affordable wines.

Dundee Hills Maresh Vineyard Pinot Noir 2019
● 213 cs; $ 75 - From own-rooted vines planted in 1970. An ethereal, ruby-robed shapeshifter. Savory, crunchy red berries, black pepper and sous bois aromas presage an aromatic, evergreen attack, mid palate savory, smokey notes, and profound raisin and red cherry finish.
Eola-Amity Hills Carter Vineyard Pinot Noir 2019 ●
144 cs; $ 75 - Inaugural vintage from this renown vineyard planted in 1983. Elusive, effortless, endlessly unfolding layers of forest floor, mushroom, violet, wild rose, raspberry, and dark red fruit make this wine to savor.

Willamette Valley Domaine Pinot Gris 2019 O 2,200 cs;
$ 29 - This wine sits on the lees for six months, giving it creamy notes of brioche and lemon tart alongside fresher flavors of pear and apple blossom.
Willamette Valley Four Nobles Cuvée Blanc 2019 O
100 cs; $ 30 - Made with Pinot Gris, Gewürztraminer, Muscat and Riesling, this refreshing blend is packed with orange and apple blossoms, pineapple, peach and gravely minerals.
Willamette Valley Domaine Pinot Noir 2017 ● 875 cs;
$ 70 - Picked from the highest-elevation estate vineyard, this wine has aromas of cherry, black pepper and fresh turned soil and adds cranberry, raspberry and rose on the palate.

acres - cases 3,400
Fertilizers cover crops
Plant protection sulfur
Weed control mechanical
Yeasts spontaneous fermentation
Grapes purchase 100%
Certification none

acres 470 - cases 150,000
Fertilizers compost, mineral fertilizer, organic-mineral
Plant protection organic, sulfur
Weed control mechanical
Yeasts commercial cultured yeasts, spontaneous fermentation
Grapes purchase 60%
Certification some of the vineyards are certified biodynamic, some of the vineyards are certified organic

KRAMER VINEYARDS

26830 NW Olson Road - tel. (503) 662-4545
www.kramervineyards.com – becky@kramervineyards.com

PEOPLE - Trudy and Keith Kramer produced their first wine in 1971–50 years ago. Drawn to Pinot Noir, they dreamed of owning a vineyard in the Willamette Valley. In 1983 their dream came true when they purchased their Gaston property in the Yamhill-Carlton AVA. Keith worked as a pharmacist and Trudy ran the winery until Keith retired. In 2008, their daughter Kim Kramer joined the winemaking team, along with general manager Becky Kramer in 2017.

VINEYARDS - The vines were initially planted to Pinot Noir, Chardonnay and Riesling in 1984. In 1986 they added Pinot Gris and Muller Thurgau. Their plantings currently span 22 acres. The well-drained soils here are composed of sedimentary rock-based Peavine and Willakenzie soil deposits over ancient seabeds. Their first commercial vintage was released in 1998, and the Kramers became Salmon Safe in 2000 and LIVE certified in 2005.

WINES - The Kramer family farms sustainably farming their 22-acre site in the Yamhill-Carlton AVA.

TOP Yamhill-Carlton Estate Pinot Gris 2018 ○ 300 cs; $ 18 - 🍷 - Citrus blossom and white fruits on the nose followed by bright flavors of tropical star fruit, creamy pear, and hints of chopped herbs. The viscous texture offers a beautiful mouthfeel, and lively acidity carries the wine to a vivacious finish.

TOP Yamhill-Carlton Estate Müller-Thurgau 2019 EVERYDAY WINE ○ 200 cs; $18 - 🍷 - Deliciously fruity, it kicks off with a heady aroma of tropical fruit and gardenias. It's bright and multilayered with mango, yellow apple and peach fruit joining lemon basil and lime ice.

Yamhill-Carlton Estate Pinot Noir ● 500 cs; $ 28 - 🛢 - A basketful of red fruits sweetheart cherries, allspice, raspberry-pomegranate compote, subtle oak elements, and a touch of anise seed. A clean, quaffable wine.

acres 22 - **cases** 2,500
Fertilizers compost, cover crops
Plant protection sulfur, synthetic pesticides
Weed control mechanical
Yeasts commercial cultured yeasts
Grapes 100% estate-grown
Certification none

LARES WINES

10501 NE Abbey Road - tel. (310) 985-5853
www.lareswines.com – luk@lareswines.com

PEOPLE - Luke Wylde (he/they) began his career in theater and live TV. When that work dried up in the 2008 recession, he landed in the wine section of a Whole Foods. The experience sparked a passion for wine and a desire to farm. Wylde worked harvests in numerous places, including New Zealand, Germany and Oregon. He made the latter his permanent home in 2011. To continue to flex his artistic muscles, he designs all of Lares's labels himself, drawing inspiration from the artist Gustave Doré. The name Lares is a Latin word that references the gods people would pray to for protecting of their home, hearth and harvest.

VINEYARDS - Lares Wines has traditionally sourced fruit from organic and biodynamic vineyards around Oregon, including Jubilee and Covey Ridge. Wylde is also very committed to partnering with vineyard owners who pay all of their workers a living way.

WINES - Wylde's goal is to craft the kinds of wines they and their wife like to drink on a Tuesday night, including bubbly whites, chillable reds and glou glou wines of any color. In future years, the majority of the wines are likely to be made with fruit from the five-acre Gillirose Vineyard in Elkton, where they recently acquired a long-term lease.

Tyroma 2020 ● 325 cs; $ 25 - 🛢 - A blend of 77% Gamay Noir and 23% Pinot Noir, this smoky, earthy Passe-tout-grains-style blend sings with notes of cherry, raspberry and violets.

Wicked Liquid 2020 ⟐ 175 cs; $ 23 - 🛢 - A force carbonated mix of Pinot Gris, Riesling, Chardonnay, Pinot Noir and Aligote. Watch for salty, umami flavors alongside aromas of melon, pear and strawberry.

Babel 2020 ⟐ 100 cs; $ 23 - 🛢 - Honey mango, raspberry and earth are prominent on the nose and palate of this blend of Pinot Noir, Riesling and Chardonnay.

acres 0 - **cases** 850
Fertilizers n/a
Plant protection n/a
Weed control n/a
Yeasts spontaneous fermentation
Grapes purchase 100%
Certification

RICKREALL

LEFT COAST ESTATE

4225 N Pacific Highway 99W - tel. (503) 831-4916
www.leftcoastwine.com – hospitality@leftcoastcellars.com

PEOPLE - Family-owned Left Coast Estate was established in 2001, when Bob Pfaff and his wife Suzanne Larson Pfaff purchased their original 200-acre site in the Willamette Valley. In 2016 son Taylor took the helm. His wife Christina heads up their Run for the Oaks to preserve old-growth white oak trees. Daughter Cali Pfaff, a Landscape Architect, is the Creative Director. Founder Bob takes on the role of Chef and Master Gardener, while wife/co-founder Suzanne enjoys her role as Brand Ambassador.

VINEYARDS - The Pfaff's 142 acres of vines are planted in the well-drained marine sedimentary soils of the Van Duzer Corridor AVA. A 100-acre oak forest, including trees that are 300+ years old, decorates the property. The Pfaffs collaborate with Winemaker Joe Wright and Assistant Winemaker Mark Rutherford. Joe has crafted award-winning wines from fruit planted on the steep hills of Left Coast Estate for more than 11 years.

WINES - The winery's been awarded 2020 Oregon Winery of the Year and Top 100 Best Fan Favorite Destinations in Oregon.

Ⓣ Van Duzer Corridor Estate White Pinot Noir 2020 ○ 9,069 cs; $ 24 - ⊞ - A crystalline pale pink hue and mouthwatering aroma engage the senses. Captivating flavors of raspberries, Rainier cherries, Gala apples, citrus accents, and watermelon framed by crisp acidity simply dance on the palate. Vibrant, perfectly balanced, and irresistible.

Ⓣ Van Duzer Corridor Cali's Cuvée Pinot Noir 2018 EVERYDAY WINE ● 6,759 cs; $ 25 - ⊞ - The earthy, raspberry aroma segues to flavors of cherry pie, baking spices, forest floor, exotic tea, and a thread of minerality coating the palate. Silky and well balanced through the bright finish.

Van Duzer Corridor Truffle Hill Estate Chardonnay 2019 ○ 1,969 cs; $ 24 - ⊞ - Summer florals on the nose lead to a lively palate of nectarines, crisp pears, a pinch of white pepper, lemon gelato, and hints of fresh mint. Well integrated oak adds a nice textural quality, and the finish lingers.

acres 142 - **cases** 22,000
Fertilizers compost, cover crops, manure
Plant protection organic, sulfur
Weed control animal grazing, mechanical
Yeasts commercial cultured yeasts
spontaneous fermentation
Grapes 100% estate-grown
Certification none

CARLTON

LEMELSON VINEYARDS

12020 NE Stag Hollow Road - tel. (503) 852-6619
www.lemelsonvineyards.com
info@www.lemelsonvineyards.com

 An ecofriendly pioneer, it makes organically grown fine wines at affordable prices.

PEOPLE - Inspired by his passion for Burgundy wine, Eric Lemelson established Lemelson Vineyards in 1999, farming organically from the start and building a gravity-flow winery for gentle processing. Ben Kaehler is the general manager. Matt Wengel makes the wines, Ashley Campion is the Associate Winemaker. The team makes blends and single vineyard designates from its 140 acres of certified organic estate vineyards in three regions.

VINEYARDS - Its six estate vineyards are the sole source for its wines. Four–Stermer Vineyard, Johnson Vineyard, Rocky Noel Vineyard and Briscoe Vineyard–are in the Yamhill-Carlton District AVA. The other two are Chestnut Hill Vineyard in the Chehalem Mountains AVA, and Meyer Vineyard situated in the Dundee Hills AVA.

WINES - These terroir driven wines showcase excellent balance and classic earthiness entwining with vibrant fruit, and the varietal truth is noteworthy.

Ⓣ Willamette Valley Thea's Selection Pinot Noir 2018 SLOW WINE ● 9,700 cs; $ 34 - ⊞ - Floral scents on the nose lead to a juicy mouthful of wild cherries, plum jam, cocoa powder, strawberry pie, baking spices and classic earthiness on the palate. This graceful and well-balanced wine speaks clearly of the Willamette Valley AVA.

Ⓣ Willamette Valley Tikka's Run Pinot Gris 2019 EVERYDAY WINE ○ 730 cs; $ 22 - ⊞ - A pleasing citrus blossom fragrance leads to a burst of flavor on the palate. Stone fruit, pear chutney, a splash of Meyer lemon and tinge of sweet herbs traverse the palate, beautifully textured and bright all the way through the close.

Willamette Valley Meyer Vineyard Pinot Noir 2017 ● 375 cs; $ 48 - ⊞ - Aromas of forest floor and allspice engage the senses. Layers of red fruit, striking spice and ideally managed oak meld seamlessly. This complex wine is pure and rich while maintaining fine balance.

acres 140 - **cases** 15,000
Fertilizers cover crops, manure
Plant protection organic, sulfur
Weed control mechanical
Yeasts commercial cultured yeasts
spontaneous fermentation
Grapes 100% estate-grown
Certification organic

SALEM

LINGUA FRANCA

9675 Hopewell Road NW - tel. (503) 687-3005
www.linguafranca.wine – hospitality@linguafranca.wine

PEOPLE - Master sommelier Larry Stone is the driving force behind Lingua Franca, which started as a grape-growing operations but has transformed into a highly-regarded Oregon house for Pinot Noir and Chardonnay. Winemaker Thomas Savre, a protégé of Burgundy winemaker Dominique Lafon, interned at estates such as Domaine de La Romanée-Conti and Dujac before joining Stone's passion project in 2015.

VINEYARDS - Lingua Franca's east-facing vineyard gets plenty of sun, but in the afternoon, cooling winds from the Van Duzer Corridor come in and lower the temperature. Stone has always had faith in this site and feels like each vintage further cements his belief that it can produce exquisite wines. He keeps plenty of natural space on the property to support the macrobiome of birds, animals and beneficial insects. Vineyard managers employ many regenerative and organic practices, including dry farming.

WINES - 2018 is the current vintage. This very dry year produced wines with great fruit, tannin and structure.
Eola Amity Hills The Plow Pinot Noir 2018 ● 400 cs; $ 65 - Drawn from some of the best land on the property, this wine exudes brambly raspberry, cherry, black tea, rose and gingerbread spice.
Willamette Valley Sisters Chardonnay 2018 ○ 290 cs; $ 100 - Caramel, Meyer lemon tart, apple blossom, wet stone and a touch of oak spice shows up on the nose and again in the mouth.
Eola-Amity Hills Estate Pinot Noir 2018 ● 760 cs; $ 56 - Look for flavors of raspberry, rose, gravel and fresh oregano.

Lingua Franca began taking extra steps to lower its carbon footprint in 2020, including purchasing carbon offsets for all consumer wine shipments.

acres 66.5 - **cases** 9,500
Fertilizers compost, manure pellets
Plant protection organic, sulfur
Weed control mechanical
Yeasts spontaneous fermentation
Grapes purchase 20%
Certification converting to organics

PHILOMATH

LUMOS WINE CO. $

24000 Cardwell Hill Drive - tel. (541) 929-3519
www.lumoswine.com – lumos@lumoswine.com

PEOPLE - Award-winning vineyard manager Dai Crisp and wife PK McKoy founded Lumos Wine in 2000 in Philomoth, OR. Since 1999, Crisp also claims fame as manager at iconic Temperance Hill, earning it Wine & Spirits Magazine's 2014 "Grower of the Year." Third-generation Lumos Wines, a 16-acre estate planted in 1985 by Crisp's parents, overlooks a National Fender's Blue Butterfly and Kincaid Lupine Reserve.

VINEYARDS - Lumos Wines sources from three certified organic and Salmon-Safe vineyards: Temperance Hill in Eola-Amity Hills AVA for Pinot Noir, Chardonnay, Pinot Gris, and Gewürztraminer and low-elevation Logsdon Ridge Vineyard near Corvalis offers Pinot Gris. The winery's estate Wren Vineyard in southern Willamette Valley grows Pommard Pinot Noir, Pinot Gris, and Dijon clone Chardonnay. To combat frost, the south-facing, 300-500 feet elevation site employs an overhead frost protection system.

WINES - Award-winning winemaker Julia Cattrell offers energetic, affordable wines reflective of the winery's low impact, minimalist, natural approach.
● Willamette Valley Wren Vineyard Chardonnay 2018 SLOW WINE ○ 60 cs; $ 34 - A pristine, light bodied, golden-fruited beauty brimming with rich creme brûlée aromas, and hints of yellow apple and lemon.
● Eola-Amity Hills Temperance Hill Vineyard Aligoté 2019 EVERYDAY WINE ○ 65 cs; $ 30 - Burgundy's 'other' white variety, this Oregon iteration pours out bright gold, with slightly yeasty, toasty, citron aromas, with a nervy lemon core.
Eola-Amity Hills Temperance Hill Vineyard The G Pinot Noir ● 75 cs; $ 56 - A black-fruited, bramble berry brooder, slipstreaming into deep eddies of blackberry, raspberry, and dark cherry.

acres 16 - **cases** 3,000
Fertilizers compost, cover crops, humus, organic-mineral
Plant protection copper, organic, sulfur
Weed control mechanical
Yeasts commercial cultured yeasts, spontaneous fermentation
Grapes purchase 80%
Certification organic

MCMINNVILLE

MAYSARA WINERY

15765 SW Muddy Valley Road - tel. (503) 843-1234
www.maysara.com – tastingroom@maysara.com

 The Momtazi family pursues holistic and bio-dynamic practices with extraordinary passion, commitment and success.

PEOPLE - Persian immigrants Moe Momtazi and wife Flora fled post-revolutionary Iran in 1982 for Oregon's Willamette Valley, where they planted Pinot Noir in 1998. Oldest daughter Tahmiene Momtazi is the winemaker, while sisters Naseem and Hanna handle sales and accounting. Maysara means "House of wine" in Persian.

VINEYARDS - Biodynamic certified since 2005, the vast vineyard faces the Coast Range's Van Duzer corridor. Basalt bedrock supports sedimentary and volcanic soils planted to Pinot Noir, Pinot Gris, Pinot Blanc, and Riesling. They maintain an ecosystem of forests, pastures, meadows, and reservoirs. They also harvest medicinal and dynamic herbs and flowers for homeopathic teas and spray, and tend a herd of cows for manure and compost.

WINES - "In our old culture, wine was construed as a liquid embodiment of the sun's radiance," says Moe Momtazi. Each wine name honors the winemaker's Persian heritage.

McMinnville Asha Pinot Noir 2015 SLOW WINE ●
630 cs; $ 45 - 🍴 - 'Asha' means someone with a clean conscience and pure demeanor in ancient Persian. An elegant, sensory magic carpet ride of savory red raspberry and cherry, black tea, leather, and truffle notes, and dulcet finish.
McMinnville Arsheen Pinot Gris 2020 EVERYDAY WINE
○ 1,429 cs; $ 18 - 🍷 - Named for Arsheen, a legendary Archeamenian Princess, a veiled Shahezarade in a glass, this fresh, lively, straw-robed enchantress pulses with lively lemon, stone fruit, and mineral notes.
McMinnville Jamsheed Pinot Noir 2017 ● 4,649 cs; $ 30 - 🍴 - Fabled Persian King Jamsheed could observe his entire kingdom in a full wine chalice. This ruby-bright, other-worldly wine radiates with fragrant notes of dried roses, white pepper, truffle, raspberry and cherry.

acres 260 - cases 10,000
Fertilizers compost, cover crops, humus, manure
Plant protection biodynamic preparations, organic, sulfur
Weed control mechanical
Yeasts selected indigenous yeasts, spontaneous fermentation
Grapes 100% estate-grown
Certification biodynamic

FOREST GROVE

MONTINORE ESTATE $

3663 SW Dilley Road - tel. (503) 359-5012
www.montinore.com – info@montinore.com

PEOPLE - Founded in 1982, forty-year wine industry veteran Rudy Marchesi joined Montinore Estate in 1998, purchasing it in 2005. He converted the conventionally farmed estate to organics in 2001, and to Demeter USA certified biodynamics® in 2008. First introduced to wine as a child through his grandfather Carlo Marchesi, a native of northern Italy's Oltrepò Pavese region, the Slow Food and Wine Movements resonate deeply with Marchesi.

VINEYARDS - The Demeter USA Certified Biodynamic and CCOF Certified Organic dry-farmed Montinore Estate in northern Willamette Valley comprises 200 acres planted to Pinot Noir, Pinot Gris, Riesling, Gewürztraminer, Müller-Thurgau, Lagrein, Teroldego, Muscat and Sauvignon Blanc. Montinore also owns a 30-acre biodynamic® site in western Yamhill-Carlton AVA, and a 176-acre site in Yamhill-Carlton - future home of new a vineyard, winery facility and hospitality center.

WINES - Affordable, approachable, yet complex wines with an unmistakeable purity, clarity, and bright energy from start to finish.

Tualatin Hills Pinot Gris 2019 EVERYDAY WINE ○7,608 cs;
$ 20 - 🍷 - Seven various estate blocks, pressing cycles, fermentation protocols, and lees aging lends complexity to this refreshing, light-bodied vin de soif brimming with golden fruit, pineapple, ginger, mango, green gage plum, and citrus notes.
Tualatin Hills Reserve Pinot Noir 2018 ● 2,083 cs; $ 40 - 🍴 - A fresh, easy-quaffing wine full of crunchy red cherry, florals and aromatic evergreen notes that pairs well with roasted meats and vegetables.
Tualatin Hills Teroldego 2018 ● 73 cs; $ 40 - 🍷 - An Italian varietal grown on the warmest vineyard site yields notes of plush Italian plum, dried violet, and savory black pepper.

acres 220 - cases 40,000
Fertilizers cover crops, humus, manure, organic-mineral
Plant protection biodynamic preparations, organic, sulfur
Weed control mechanical
Yeasts commercial cultured yeasts, selected indigenous yeasts, spontaneous fermentation
Grapes purchase 15%
Certification organic and biodynamic for estate vineyards

OPEN CLAIM VINEYARDS

PORTLAND WINE COMPANY

2795 Ballard Road - tel. (949) 338 3343
www.openclaimvineyards.com
info@openclaimvineyards.com

3201 SE 50th Avenue - tel. (503) 320-9956
www.portlandwinecompany.com
info@loveandsqualorwine.com

PEOPLE - Marnie and Brett Wall followed a fascinating, circuitous route becoming vineyard and winery owners. After meeting in Atlanta, they followed career paths across three continents. One of the countries they lived and worked in was France. While dining in Paris, that they decided to plant a vineyard. Now winery owners in the Willamette Valley, they make wine with superstar winemaker Tony Rynders. Alex Cabrera is the vineyard manager.

VINEYARDS - Open Claim's first Mount Pisgah plantings were planted in 2012. Their marine sedimentary soils sit atop some of the oldest geological formations in the Willamette Valley at an elevation of 470 feet. Ten clones are planted in an intentional array (10 blocks on 20.78 acres, vine space 4', row space 6', 1815 vines per acre). They dry farm sustainably and became LIVE Certified in 2019.

PEOPLE - Matt Berson learned about wine in the school of hard knocks – not that it was too hard working side-by-side with people like Patricia Green, Jay Somers and Jimi Brooks. Given that he was mentored by some of the biggest names in Oregon Pinot Noir and Riesling, it's no surprise these grapes continue to be his passion, although he also enjoys working with other varieties. Berson's wife, Angela Reat, plays an instrumental role as general manager.

VINEYARDS - Berson likes his vineyard a little bit wild, farmed with no chemical herbicides, and maintained by growers he can communicate with so he can understand what choices they're making in the vineyard and why. The LIVE-certified Sunnyside Vineyard, located just outside of Salem, is a long-term partner. So is Salmon Safe and organic-certified Temperance Hill Vineyard. He also sources from Sunny Mountain near Corvallis, LIVE-certified Gemini in Sherwood and organic-certified Ribbon Ridge Vineyard.

WINES - The Walls are the 50th to sign the Accord, a group of landowners working to protect native Oregon white oak habitats.

TOP Willamette Valley Estate Pinot Noir 2018 ●
216 cs; $ 75 - ⊞ - The mind-blowing forest floor and wild cherry aroma leaves no doubt what's in the glass. This finely tuned, deeply flavored, sensuous Pinot Noir boasts blueberries, exotic spice, tayberries, underlying earthiness, black cherries, sandalwood, black tea, and well managed oak, while the silky texture carries it to a remarkable, savory close.
Willamette Valley Estate Chardonnay 2018 ○ 67 cs; $ 75 - ⊞ - The sparkling clear pale yellow hue and expressive aromatic captures your attention. On the palate creamy pears, citrus blossom, a touch of herbs, Meyer lemon tart, flintiness, spiciness, and gentle toasted oak tones interlace in harmony. Exquisitely defined and precisely balanced through the lasting finish.

WINES - Berson and Reat's main label is Love & Squalor. Their goal is to make wines that are highly aromatic and have cut, and to be a part of the history and ongoing story of wine in the Willamette Valley.
Willamette Valley A Frayed Knot Rosé of Gewürztraminer 2020 ◎ 65 cs; $ 20 - ⊞ - Flavors and aromas of lychee, white peach and white cherry.
Willamette Valley Gamay Noir 2019 ● 120 cs; $ 28 - ⊞ - Berson believes in making Gamay like a Gamay, not a Pinot Noir, so this wine has classic flavors such as raspberries, blueberries, smoke and violets.
Eola-Amity Hills Temperance Hill Pinot Noir 2017 ●
50 cs; $ 62 - ⊞ - Pleasing flavors of dark cherry, raspberry, baking spice and oregano on the palate.

---

acres 21 - **cases** 350
Fertilizers compost, cover crops
Plant protection organic, sulfur, synthetic pesticides
Weed control mechanical
Yeasts commercial cultured yeasts, selected indigenous yeasts
Grapes 100% estate-grown
Certification none

acres 0 - **cases** 3,000
Fertilizers n/a
Plant protection n/a
Weed control n/a
Yeasts commercial cultured yeasts, spontaneous fermentation
Grapes purchase 100%
Certification none

QUADY NORTH 🍾

RÉSONANCE 🍾

255 East California Street - tel. (541) 702-2123
www.quadynorth.com – info@quadynorth.com

12050 NW Meadow Lake Road - tel. (971) 999-1603
www.resonancewines.com – info@resonancewines.com

PEOPLE - Herb Quady grew up at the family winery in California, but moved to Oregon after purchasing 100 acres in Applegate Valley in 2005. There he and his wife Meloney planted wines and founded Quady North. Winemaker Brian Gruber joined Quady North in 2009, and Associate Winemaker Nichol Schulte joined the team in 2012.

VINEYARDS - Both the estate vineyard and winery are certified organic. Mae's Vineyard is planted to Syrah, Viognier, Cab Franc, Grenache, Tannat, Malbec and Orange Muscat. In 2011 the Eevee Vineyard was planted to Grenache Blanc, Marsanne, Roussanne, Cab Franc, Grenache Noir and Malvasia Bianca. Fruit also comes from other, non-organic vineyards in Applegate Valley, including Steelhead Run, and Layne Vineyard, each with unique characteristics.

PEOPLE - Founded in 2013 by Maison Louis Jadot, Résonance resides in Yamhill-Carlton AVA. Winemaker Jacques Lardiere jettisoned retirement to join Jadot's first project beyond Burgundy; colleague Guillaume Large joined him in 2017 to oversee the entire project. As stewards of their Oregon estate vineyards and winery, the Résonance team shares a deep emotional and physical connection to its land, its people, its culture, and its history. "This place, its harmony, inspires us."

VINEYARDS - Résonance Vineyard estate in the Yamhill Carlton AVA produces Pinot Noir. Planted in 1981, the 20-acre, organically dry-farmed vineyard of mostly submarine, silty, basaltic sediment soils slopes south at 262 - 492 foot elevations. The second estate, Découverte Vineyard, lies 10 miles away in the Dundee Hills AVA, where red, volcanic Jory soils studded with golden-colored stones predominate. The 18-acre property rises 600 to 690 feet in elevation, planted to Pinot Noir and Chardonnay.

WINES - Quady North aims for minimal intervention in the winemaking process, focusing on varieties that naturally yield balanced fruit.

WINES - Résonance crafts wines of impeccable structure, balance, and nuance, revealing the soul of each vineyard with clarity, poetry, and precision.

🔴 **Applegate Valley Mae's Vineyard Cabernet Franc 2019** ● 120 cs; $ 39 - ▦ - Earthy tones join boysenberry jam, tobacco, purple plums, and graphite framed by well-structured tannins fully engaging the palate. Impressive depth and balance.
Applegate Valley Mae's Vineyard Syrah 150 cs; $ 32 - ▦ - Lush and balanced with a velvety texture. Integrated tannins and acids support a delicious core of red and black berries, toasted marshmallows, peppercorns, and underlying grilled meat.
Applegate Valley Cabernet Franc Sparkling Q-Vée 2019 ☀ 120 cs; $ 39 - 🍸 - Snappy and dry, made in the traditional method. Red raspberries, strawberries, fresh baked pie crust, and spiced blackberry-rhubarb compote prevail, and the finish shows off a drop of fresh squeezed orange.

Yamhill-Carlton Résonance Vineyard Pinot Noir 2017 ● 2,066 cs; $ 65 - ▦ - Limoges-thin body, with complex notes of dried florals, tangled bramble, wild raspberry, and dark cherry, harmonious balance, and an energetic, mineral finish.
Dundee Hills Découverte Vineyard Pinot Noir 2017 ● 875 cs; $ 65 - ▦ - A luminous, silky wine expressive of dark berry, cherry, exotic spices, haunting florals, and mineral verve.
Willamette Valley Pinot Noir 2018 ● 7,733 cs; $ 35 - ▦ - An earthy, well-constructed wine bursting with red and blue fruits, and intoxicating notes of cinnamon and allspice.

acres 25 - **cases** 7,000
Fertilizers compost, cover crops
Plant protection organic, sulfur, synthetic pesticides
Weed control chemical, mechanical
Yeasts selected indigenous yeasts
Grapes purchase 60%
Certification some of the vineyards are certified organic

acres 95 - **cases** 10,000
Fertilizers compost
Plant protection organic
Weed control mechanical
Yeasts spontaneous fermentation
Grapes 100% estate-grown
Certification organic

ROOTS WINE CO.

19320 NE Woodland Loop Road - tel. (503) 662-4652
www.rootswine.com – info@roots.wine

PEOPLE - Chris and Hilary Berg celebrated their 20th vintage in 2021 at their winery. Aiming to become more holistic, Chris seeks to "keep in tune" with the vines and the fruit in the cellar. Ever the experimenter, Chris has made several versions of Sauvignon Blanc and is looking forward to working with Trousseau which he planted in a new part of his estate vineyard.

VINEYARDS - The Bergs recently planted the Estate East vineyard to Trousseau, Sauvignon Blanc, and the Coury clone of Pinot Noir, adding 3 acres to their estate holdings. The Roots Estate Vineyard sits at 625 feet and is comprised of WillaKenzie soil and a broad vein of iron oxide. Grapes are sourced from a number of Yamhill-Carlton vineyards including Cancilla, Saffron Fields, Fairsing, Carlton Hill, and Oak Grove and Ninebark Vineyard in the Chehalem Mountains AVA. All are organically farmed.

WINES - Berg looks to several regions in France including Jura for examples of taking a holistic approach in action and does nothing to interfere with the flow of the grapes from vine to bottle.

🔝 **Yamhill-Carlton Roots Estate Vineyard Pinot Noir 2019** SLOW WINE ● 50 cs; $ 44 - 🍴 - Lovely cherry-tarragon nose with some spice and floral notes and a delicate and elegant palate.
Chehalem Mountains Ninebark Vineyard Chardonnay 2019 ○ 60 cs; $ 35 - 🍴 - Exhibits a creamy lemon curd, nutty nose with some oak and a nicely balanced palate with good acidity a creamy finish.
Yamhill-Carlton Cluster Pinot Noir 2018 ● 24 cs; $ 75 - 🍴 - Grapes from Saffron Fields, Fairsing and Carlton Hill vineyards are co-fermented and aged in a single new oak barrel yielding a dark brooding cherry-tarragon nose and immature palate that will need several years to show its stuff.

acres 11 - **cases** 5,000
Fertilizers compost, organic-mineral
Plant protection organic, sulfur
Weed control mechanical
Yeasts spontaneous fermentation
Grapes purchase 25%
Certification none

RUBY VINEYARD & WINERY

30088 SW Egger Road - tel. (503) 628-7829
www.rubyvineyard.com – info@rubyvineyard.com

PEOPLE - Owner Stephen Hendricks and his wife Flora Habibi purchased the Beran Vineyard in the Chehalem Mountains AVA in 2012. Its history goes back to 1843, when Steve's great-great-grandfather Abijah Hendricks traveled to the Willamette Valley on the first wagon train of the Oregon Trail and built a homestead there. Winemaker Andrew Kirkland joined Ruby Vineyard in 2016. Their first commercial wine was released in 2015.

VINEYARDS - The estate vineyards of own-rooted Pinot Noir are LIVE certified and dry farmed. Some of the plantings in the Ruby Vineyard are 40-year-old own rooted vines. Flora's Reserve comes from silty, basalt based Laurelwood District soils. In 2016, more than a century and a half later, Steve purchased Pinot Noir grapes from Timbale and Thyme Vineyard, the land once owned by his great-great grandfather. The winery also buys grapes from local growers.

WINES - Steve and Flora are keenly involved with all aspects of the business, from farming, to consulting with Winemaker Andrew, to greeting visitors. Ruby Vineyard represents a return to Steve's familial roots in the Willamette Valley.

🔝 **Chehalem Mountains Laurelwood District Flora's Reserve Pinot Noir 2015** ● 45 cs; $ 125 - 🍴 - The alluring aroma of fresh turned earth wafts from the glass. Mouthfilling and vibrant with a silky texture, it displays dusty cherry, earthiness, cranberry sauce, sandalwood, hints of anise, blueberry, and well-integrated oak, and a pinch of spice enhances the long finish.
Chehalem Mountains Laurelwood District Old Vine Estate Pinot Noir 2019 ● 500 cs; $ 50 - 🍴 - Cherry cola and fresh cut herbs on the nose segue to a succulent palate of raspberries, huckleberries, earthy undertones, marionberries, and toasty oak in the background. Satin smooth and well-balanced all the way through the last swallow.

acres 9 - **cases** 3,500
Fertilizers compost, cover crops, organic-mineral
Plant protection organic, sulfur, synthetic pesticides
Weed control mechanical
Yeasts spontaneous fermentation
Grapes purchase 50%
Certification some of the vineyards are certified organic

SOKOL BLOSSER WINERY

ST. INNOCENT WINERY

5000 NE Sokol Blosser Lane - tel. (503) 864-2282
www.sokolblosser.com – info@sokolblosser.com

10052 Enchanted Way SE - tel. (503) 378-1526
www.stinnocentwine.com – mark@stinnocentwine.com

PEOPLE - Co-Founders Bill Blosser and Susan Sokol Blosser were among early pioneers in the Oregon wine industry, establishing the winery in 1971. Early adopters of eco friendly practices, they built the first LEED certified winery and became a certified B Corp. They were among the first to be certified organic. Today, the second generation oversees the winery. Co-presidents Alison (CEO/Winegrower), and brother Alex (Winemaker/Winegrower) lead the team.

VINEYARDS - The 89 acres of estate vines provide 90% of the fruit for their wines. The rest comes from local growers. Their new 22 acre Kalita Vineyard in the Yamhill-Carlton AVA in in transition to organic certification. The estate vineyards have been certified organic since 2005. Manuel "Luis" Fernandez is the vineyard manager.

PEOPLE - Mark Vlossak established St. Innocent Winery in 1988 specializing in Pinot Noir becoming a renowned producer of single vineyard bottlings from great sites in the Willamette Valley. He has also branched out into Chardonnay and sparkling wine. Believing wine is food, he added a full kitchen in his new tasting room in 2019 for wine and food pairings. His wife, attorney Vickianne Vlossak, manages the business and events.

VINEYARDS - Though the winery has a 15 acres estate vineyard, it primarily source fruit from top tier Willamette Valley sites under long term block leases. Some are certified organic or biodynamic including 8 acres at Momtazi Vineyard (biodynamic) in McMinnville and 11 acres at Temperance Hill Vineyard (organic). The list also includes 17 acres Freedom Hill Vineyard (converting to organics in 2022) and 6 acres at Shea Vineyard.

WINES - The Sokol Blosser family celebrated their 50th anniversary with a celebratory wine to mark the milestone.

● **Dundee Hills Old Vineyard Block 50th Anniversary Pinot Noir 2018** SLOW WINE ● 496 cs; $ 60 - ⊞ - A mouthwatering floral aroma with a palate of black cherries, earthiness, forest berries, pie spice, oak nuances, and traces of herbs. Pure and complex with a velvety texture.
● **Willamette Valley Rosé of Pinot Noir 2020** ◉ EVERYDAY WINE 5,000 cs; $ 25 - 🍶 - Rose petals on the nose lead to refreshing flavors of Sweetheart cherries, strawberry rhubarb pie, orange zest, and fresh watermelon. Crisp acidity complements the juicy fruit, and the wine concludes with good lift.
Dundee Hills Twelve Row Block Estate Pinot Noir 2018 ● 397 cs; $ 60 - ⊞ - Scents of warm berry pie with intense layers of black raspberries, sassafras, mulberries, wild mushrooms, nutmeg, and a thread of earthiness unfold in the mouth. A silky texture and long finish.

WINES - The style of the winemaking is hands off including gravity flow racking, minimal use of new oak, and native yeast fermentations.

● **McMinnville Momtazi Vineyard Pinot Noir 2017** SLOW WINE ● 996 cs; $ 45 - ⊞ - Expressive and sophisticated. Black cherries, exotic spice, wild mushrooms, and toasty oak nuances unfold (aged 16 months in 27% new French oak barrels) unfold. Remarkable acidity and refined tannins.
● **Willamette Valley Freedom Hill Vineyard Cuvée la Liberté Chardonnay 2018** ○ 99 cs; $ 60 - ⊞ - Citrus blossom and sautéed pear armomas followed by a luxurious palate of peaches, Crunchy Gold apple pears, nutmeg, Valencia oranges, minerality, and subtle toasty barrel spice steering the wine to a prolonged finish.
Eola-Amity Hills Temperance Hill Vineyard Pinot Noir 2017 ● 1,021 cs; $ 45 - ⊞ - Bing cherries and dusty earth on the nose with wild berries and cherries, savory spice, dried cranberries, and oak barrel nuances on the midpalate.

acres 128 - cases 16,000
Fertilizers compost, organic-mineral
Plant protection organic, sulfur
Weed control mechanical
Yeasts commercial cultured yeasts spontaneous fermentation
Grapes purchase 10%
Certification organic

acres 15.5 - cases 6,000
Fertilizers compost, cover crops, organic
Plant protection biodynamic preparations, organic, sulfur
Weed control chemical, mechanical
Yeasts commercial cultured yeasts, spontaneous fermentation
Grapes purchase 73%
Certification converting to organics, some of the vineyards are certified biodynamic and/or organic

CARLTON

STATERA CELLARS

10501 NE Abbey Road - tel. (503) 522-2481
www.stateracellars.com – info@stateracellars.com

PEOPLE - Founded by Luke Wylde and Meredith Bell in 2014, the winery focuses on terroir driven Chardonnay. Wylde is the winemaker at Abbey Road Farm and owns his own small label, Lares. Bell is a former assistant winemaker at Craft Wine Company and works at EST. Wylde and Bell also engage their growers in conversations about wages with the goal of ensuring all workers are being paid a decent wage.

VINEYARDS - Given the emphasis on terroir, grapes come from sites with a range of elevations, soil types, AVAs and other distinguishing factors. Statera has typically sourced from a combination of sustainably and organically farmed vineyards. Beginning this year, they have partnered with farms that are organic or biodynamic certified (Johan Vineyard) or transitioning to organic.

WINES - Grapes are processed in the same manner to showcase place in the wine. Wylde and Bell are also now playing more with winemaking styles, exploring pet nats and skin-contact whites.

Willamette Valley Johan Vineyard Chardonnay 2018 ○ 24 cs; $ 35 - ⊞ - Beautiful in both flavor and texture, this wine is a winning combination of apple, lemon and salted caramel shortbread.
Columbia Gorge Cutis Chardonnay 2019 ○ 73 cs; $ 29 - ⊞ - Cutis means "skin" in Latin and is a nod to the whole berries that make it into this wine, which has an intriguing mix of nectarine skin, pineapple, apple blossom and earthy aromas.
Willamette Valley Imber Chardonnay 2019 ○ 95 cs; $ 21 - ⊞ - This is currently Statera's only cuvée of Chardonnay; watch for flavors of golden apple and lime.

acres 0 - cases 900
Fertilizers n/a
Plant protection n/a
Weed control n/a
Yeasts spontaneous fermentation
Grapes purchase 100%
Certification n/a

DAYTON

STOLLER FAMILY ESTATE

16161 NE McDougall Road - tel. (503) 864-3404
www.stollerfamilyestate.com
tastingroom@stollerfamilyestate.com

PEOPLE - Bill Stoller's family purchased a property in Oregon's Dundee Hills in 1943 and opened a turkey farm. Since 1995, the space has been reinvented as a vineyard and premium site for growing Pinot Noir and Chardonnay. Winemaking is done by Kate Payne-Brown, a graduate of the University of Adelaide, who has worked at Stoller full time since 2015. She is having fun making some experimental wines, including ones fermented and aged in concrete eggs.

VINEYARDS - Stoller's vineyard has only 225 planted acres on a 400-acre property, which leaves plenty of wild land to encourage diverse flora and fauna. Jason Tosch leads vineyard operations and has been farming some premium sections of the property organically. He is also looking at methods to conserve water by carefully measuring vine stress and adding moisture only when necessary. Communication between Tosch and the rest of the team is key, he notes, as "we're not growing grapes, we're growing wines."

WINES - Payne-Brown sees herself as a "storyteller for what's happening on the hill" and make wines that reflect place and season.

Club Exclusive Chardonnay 2019 ○ 760 cs; $ 40 - ⊞ - This wine was fermented in concrete using only native yeast and has a round texture with a nose and palate of apple, lime and lychee.
Dundee Hills LaRue's Brut Rosé 2017 ⁜ 322 cs; $ 65 - ⊞ - Made with 84% Pinot Noir and 16% Chardonnay, this wine shows flavors and aromas of yellow apple, white peach, brioche and apple blossom.
Club Exclusive Pinot Noir 2017 ● 282 cs; $ 35 - ⬗⊞ - Made with whole cluster grapes and carbonic maceration, bottlings of this Pinot Noir are a pleasing balance of fruity and savory, with a lighter weight and level of tannin.

acres 225 - cases 64,000
Fertilizers compost, humus, manure
Plant protection organic, sulfur, synthetic pesticides
Weed control mechanical
Yeasts commercial cultured yeasts, selected indigenous yeasts
Grapes purchase 23%
Certification none

DAYTON

SUZOR WINES

11400 Westland Lane - tel. (503) 593-4999
www.suzorwines.com – greg@suzorwines.com

PEOPLE - For 10 years, Greg McClellan and Mélissa Rondeau have slowly grown Suzor from a 100-case winery to one with a bigger-but-still-boutique presence. McClellan spent time in Burgundy and at notable Oregon wineries before launching his label. He calls himself "very much a traditionalist" and enjoys making wines from classic French grapes such as Pinot Noir, Chardonnay and Gamay (his family originally hails from the Loire Valley).

VINEYARDS - Suzor's wines are made primarily from organically-farmed Menefee Vineyard in the northwestern end of the Yamhill-Carlton AVA, which is owned by McClellan's mother. The 20-acre property contains Pinot Noir but has a few acres that were grafted to Chardonnay and Gamay that are just coming into production. Other partners include Left Coast Estate in the Van Duzer Corridor, Fennwood and Lazy River Vineyard in the Yamhill-Carlton AVA, and a new vineyard in the Eola-Amity Hills AVA.

WINES - McClellan's focus is making wines with high tension and acidity from high-elevation fruit. McClellan and Rondeau also aim to have fun and keep trying new things, including interesting blends and styles.

Willamette Valley The Sunflower Chardonnay 2019 ○ 92 cs; $ 30 - ⊞ - Flavors of bruléed lemon tart, lime popsicle and wet gravel.
Yamhill-Carlton Par Contre Gamay Noir 2020 ● 140 cs; $ 28 - ⊞ - Made with the first Gamay harvested from Menefee Vineyard, this wine shows pomegranate and earthy notes.
Willamette Valley The Tower Pinot Noir 2017 ● 225 cs; $ 32 - ⊞ - An earthy yet fresh Pinot with aromas and flavors of strawberry, red currant and forest floor.

ac 0 - cs 1,500
Fertilizers n/a
Plant protection n/a
Weed control n/a
Yeasts n/a
Grapes purchase 100%
Certification none

NEWBERG

TRISAETUM

18401 NE Ribbon Ridge Road - tel. (503) 538-9898
www.trisaetum.com – info@trisaetum.com

PEOPLE - California transplant James Frey and wife Andrea purchased land in Oregon's Coast Range in 2003, intent on planting a vineyard. Two years later, they bought another plot on Ribbon Ridge, established another vineyard, and built a winery. They named it Trisaetum, after their two children, Tristen and Tatum. The winery also displays Frey's work as a successful abstract artist. Entirely self-taught, Frey's winemaking mentors include Burgundian Jacques Lardiere and Oregonian Josh Bergström.

VINEYARDS - Trisaetum owns three vineyards, including 22 acres in the Coast Range, 17 acres on Ribbon Ridge, and 8 acres in Dundee. Concerned about future generations, Frey operates long-term, opting for dry-farming, no-tilling, no chemical herbicides or pesticides, hand-weeding and hand-harvesting, and composting post-harvest skins, seeds and stems for use in the vineyard.

WINES - A contemplative, holistic approach that avoids enzymes and additives, encourages native yeasts, and employs judicial use of whole cluster.

Ribbon Ridge Estate Pinot Noir 2018 ● 600 cs; $ 55 - ⊞ - A riot of red fruit, florals, spice, bright acids, silky tannins, and lingering finish.
Yamhill-Carlton Coast Range Estate Pinot Noir 2018 ● 400 cs; $ 55 - ⊞ - Beautiful notes of forest floor, black tea, dried marsh rose, pomegranate, cranberry and red berry, with a pleasing, subtle finish.
Dundee Hills Wichmann Dundee Riesling 2020 ○ 250 cs; $ 32 - ⌂ ⓖ - An off-dry, well-composed wine with lush golden apple, lychee, hazelnut, and stone fruit notes and energetic acidity.

acres 470 - cases 6,000
Fertilizers biodynamic compost, compost, cover crops
Plant protection sulfur
Weed control mechanical
Yeasts spontaneous fermentation
Grapes purchase 17%
Certification none

TROON VINEYARD

1475 Kubli Road - tel. (541) 846-9900
www.troonvineyard.com – tastingroom@troonvineyard.com

 Troon's vines and wines pulse with vitality.

PEOPLE - In 1972, Dick Troon planted some of the first vines in the Applegate Valley. Since the arrival of owners Texans Denise and Bryan White and general manager Craig Camp, Troon has transformed from the typical to the exceptional by achieving biodynamic certification then earning the first regenerative organic certificate for an Oregon winery. Converting to biodynamics reinvigorated soils and vines, offering to winemaker Nate Wall what's required for exceptional wines.

VINEYARDS - Located at 1400' above sea level where a gap in the coastal range allows cool Pacific air to seep, the Kubli Bench provides significant diurnal shift for ripeness and acidity, with soils on an ancient well draining river bed with layers of cobbles. Some of the vines from the previous era have been replanted and replaced with Grenache, Syrah, Mourvèdre, Malbec, Vermentino, Tannat, Marsanne, and Roussanne.

WINES - Troon offers natural, lively, elegant yet fun wines made in unusual styles from less typical varietals, grown using regenerative agricultural methods.

TOP **Applegate Valley Pét tanNat 2020** SLOW WINE ☀ 84 cs; $ 35 - ⬜ - Effervescent rose gold in the glass with aromas of fresh white nectarine with waxy white flowers while the palate is complex and textured with white stone fruit, pomelo and an earthy haunting finish.
Applegate Valley Kubli Bench Estate Syrah 2019 ● 400 cs; $ 35 - ⊞ - Troon makes several vivacious Syrah, each with its own personality; light in color, this one has both whole berry and whole cluster, presenting beautiful violet aromas, bright blue and bramble fruit, complexity, vitality, savory spices, and a long lifted finish.
Applegate Valley Kubli Bench Amber 2020 ◍ Riesling, Vermentino, Viognier; 250 cs; $ 35 - ⊞ - Herbs of provence with ample spicy citrus, tropical, and stone fruit wow the senses in this unusual passionate, vigorous, textural, and well-structured blend.

acres 45 - **cases** 5,500
Fertilizers biodynamic compost, cover crops
Plant protection biodynamic preparations, organic, sulfur
Weed control mechanical
Yeasts spontaneous fermentation
Grapes 100% estate-grown
Certification biodynamic, organic

TWILL CELLARS

21775 SW Ribera Lane - tel. (503) 638-7323
www.twillcellars.com – info@twillcellars.com

PEOPLE - The team at Twill includes winemaker Chris Dickson, vineyard manager Darrel Roby and sales and accounting manager Molly Roby. In addition to Pinot Noir and Chardonnay, Dickson makes a small amount of cool-climate Syrah and is exploring a sparkling program inspired by the Champagnes of Béreche et Fils. In years with perfect fruit, the juice will get stars; when vintage might be too ripe, the wine (a blend of Pinot Noir and Chardonnay) will be used for "orange" wine.

VINEYARDS - Since the 2.7-acre Molly's Vineyard, Twill's estate property, can only produce a fraction of the fruit needed each year, Twill also sources from four other vineyards around the Willamette Valley. The newest addition is the east-facing Vojtilla Vineyard near Wilsonville. Vojtilla, like Stormy Morning in the Tualatin Hills AVA and Bracken Vineyard in the Eola-Amity Hills AVA, is lovingly maintained by a single family and dry farmed with organic practices.

WINES - Twill's final fruit source is Johan Vineyards, which is certified organic and Demeter certified Biodynamic. Dickson's primary focus is to make wines with great structure and ageability while maintaining a sense of elegance and integrity.

Orange Wine 2020 ◉ 100 cs; $ 25 - ⊞ - A salty, complex with flavors and aromas of mandarin, lemon zest and white cherry blossom.
Willamette Valley Chardonnay 2019 ○ 200 cs; $ 25 - ⊞ - This fresh, mineral-driven Chardonnay is rich with lime zest, lime blossom and lemon yogurt.
Oregon Syrah 2019 ● 350 cs; $ 25 - ⊞ - Expect boysenberries and cream, cedar, black pepper and slate.

acres 2.7 - **cases** 1,500
Fertilizers none
Plant protection sulfur
Weed control mechanical
Yeasts spontaneous fermentation
Grapes purchase 82%
Certification none

TALENT

UPPER FIVE VINEYARD

1125 Morey Road - tel. (541) 285-8359
www.upperfivevineyard.com – terry@upperfivevineyard.com

 Terry and Molly represent the gold standard for the Slow Wine movement with their passion for organic and biodynamic farming and their diligence in winemaking.

PEOPLE - Proprietors, grapegrowers and winemakers Terry Sullivan and partner Molly Morison became serious about the wine world in the 90's which led to acquiring the property in Rogue Valley. In 2003 they converted the former pear orchard to vineyards, and Upper Five Vineyard was born. Each came from a scientific background. Terry has an MS in Ocean Engineering, and Molly an MS in Botany/Plant Biology.

VINEYARDS - The panoramic site of Upper Five Vineyards (elevation of 1920 feet) is planted to Sauvignon Blanc, Syrah, Tempranillo and Grenache. Their vineyard was the first to be certified organic in southern Oregon back in 2005, and today is also certified biodynamic. Their motto is "The best fertilizer is a farmer's footsteps, and wine is made in the vineyard."

WINES - Engaging in biodynamic practices while employing a minimal manipulation and natural winemaking philosophy yields an honest expression of their fruit and site in each vintage.

Rogue Valley Grenache 2019 SLOW WINE ● 50 cs; $ 26 - ⊞ - Rose petals and forest berries on the nose are inviting. It's true to variety on all fronts. Layers of raspberries, savory herbs, wild berries and red plums backed by lively acidity exhilarate the palate and it finishes elegantly.

Rogue Valley Sauvignon Blanc 2020 EVERYDAY WINE ○ 100 cs; $ 20 - ⬛⊞ - Expressive nose leads to passion fruit sorbet, lemon curd, jasmine green tea and herbs. Beautiful textural qualities and bright acids carry it to a vivid lime-scented finish.

Rogue Valley Tempranillo 2017 ● 130 cs; $ 28 - ⊞ - A warm berry pie aroma sets the stage for olallieberries, plums, a minerally edge, sun-dried tomatoes and savoriness. Elegant with refined tannins and a lingering finish.

acres 3.5 - **cases** 700
Fertilizers biodynamic compost, cover crops organic-mineral
Plant protection biodynamic preparations, organic, sulfur
Weed control mechanical, none
Yeasts spontaneous fermentation
Grapes 100% estate-grown
Certification biodynamic, organic

ASHLAND

WEISINGER FAMILY WINERY

3150 Siskiyou Boulevard - tel. (541) 488-5989
www.weisingers.com – wine@weisingers.com

PEOPLE - In 1978, John Weisinger enlisted his children to help him plant his first vineyard of gewurztraminer on land that had been farmed for 100 years. Ten years in, he started making wine; his son Eric followed in his footsteps, and in 1997, took over. Taking on the challenge to farm responsibly, Eric is moving toward organic and biodynamic practices which he also brings to the vineyards he manages and where he purchases his fruit. Winemaker Andy Meyers is helping research this task.

VINEYARDS - Located at 2,200', Weisinger's pioneering 4.5 acres are just up the hill from downtown Ashland. They produce wine from nearby sources which they manage in the Bear Creek Valley, and have a range of soil types and micro-climates. In addition to the Estate Gewurztraminer, Tempranillo, and Pinot Noir, they make Viognier, Mourvèdre, Malbec, and in 2020, released their first Roussanne.

WINES - With every growing year unique, an important goal for Eric Weisinger is to express the only true time capsule: that particular vintage. Lightly tempered by up to one third new oak, wines have acidity, spice, and fresh fruit.

Rogue Valley Avra Vineyard Grenache 2018 SLOW WINE ● 180 cs; $ 38 - ⊞ - A translucent cranberry with aromas of fresh grated nutmeg, carnation, and red fruit, this fun flirty grenache lovers' grenache has tart fresh raspberry on the palate.

Rogue Valley Estate Tempranillo 2018 ● 208 cs; $ 42 - ⊞ - Densely colored and richly spiced, the wine comes across dry with bold tannins, tart raspberry, tart cherry, and a crabapple finish.

Rogue Valley Estate Gewürztraminer 2020 ◎ 25 cs; $ 38 - ⊞ - Planted in 1978, this deep rose gold Gewürztraminer fermented 17 days on skins to produce exuberant aromas of stone fruit, spice, honeysuckle, and rose geranium with subtle fruit, depth, and texture on the palate.

acres 12 - **cases** 1,500
Fertilizers compost, cover crops
Plant protection n/a
Weed control mechanical
Yeasts commercial cultured yeasts, spontaneous fermentation
Grapes purchase 60%
Certification none

WILLAKENZIE ESTATE

19143 NE Laughlin Road - tel. (503) 662-3280
www.willakenzie.com – hospitality@willakenzie.com

PEOPLE - Burgundy native Bernie Lacroute and his wife Ronni Lacroute established the winery in 1991, naming it after the Willakenzie sedimentary soils found there. They purchased a former cattle ranch in what is now the Yamhill-Carlton AVA. In 2016 Jackson Family Wines acquired the property and brand and appointed Erik Kramer as winemaker. They have updated the winery dramatically over the past year, adding more Chardonnay acreage.

VINEYARDS - The Lacroutes first planted vines 30 years ago, releasing their first vintage in 1995. The estate grows Chardonnay, Pinot Blanc, Pinot Gris, Pinot Meunier, and Pinot Noir on 100 acres of the 420 acre site. Dozens of Longhorn cows graze the land, working the soil and increasing microflora. In 2008 they became the first LIVE certified winery. Solar panels (originally mounted in 2010) provide 40% to 50% of the estate's power.

WINES - The winery ferments each of their 43 blocks in separate tanks.

(TOP) Yamhill-Carlton Estate Cuvée Chardonnay 2019
SLOW WINE ○ 250 cs; $ 75 - ⊞ - Complex and refined, its mouthwatering aroma leads to well-balanced flavors of Honeycrisp apples, Meyer lemon, spicy accents, minerality, and nicely managed oak interlacing across the palate, through the long finish.

(TOP) Yamhill-Carlton Clairière Pinot Noir 2019 ●
375 cs; $ 80 - ⊞ - The fragrance of rose petals and black fruit on the nose is captivating. Shades of earthiness, black cherries, licorice drops, sandalwood, tayberries, spice box, and underlying oak entwine in harmony. Complex and precise with a zesty, memorable finish

Yamhill-Carlton Estate Pinot Noir 2018 ● 700 cs; $ 50 - ⊞ - Florals and earth-tinged aromatics meld with flavors of fresh Bing cherries, Lady Grey tea, black raspberries, and allspice. Silky in texture with lively balancing acidity and a satisfying savory finish.

---

acres 100 - **cases** 13,000
Fertilizers compost, humus, mineral fertilizer
Plant protection sulfur, synthetic pesticides
Weed control mechanical
Yeasts commercial cultured yeasts spontaneous fermentation
Grapes 100% estate-grown
Certification none

WINDERLEA VINEYARD & WINERY

8905 NE Worden Hill Road - tel. (503) 554-5900
www.winderlea.com – info@winderlea.com

PEOPLE - In 2006, after corporate careers in Boston, Bill Sweat and wife Donna Morris purchased an existing Dundee Hills vineyard, first planted in the 70s, and hired a LEED certified architect to built their sustainable, solar-powered tasting room. Viticulturalist Leigh Bartholomew oversees the vines. Robert Brittan is the winemaker. Demeter biodynamic and B Corporation certified since 2015, Winderlea donates part of their tasting fees to Oregon's ¡Salud! health care program for vineyard workers.

VINEYARDS - They source much fruit from local growers but have acquired two vineyards in recent years, growing their certified biodynamic estate to three sites. Winderlea Vineyard in Dundee Hills has Pinot Noir and Chardonnay on Jory soils. Meredith Mitchell Vineyard in McMinnville is 22 acres of Pinot Blanc, Pinot Noir, and Chardonnay on sedimentary and broken basalt. Worden Hill, a 25-acre site in Dundee Hills, is in transition to biodynamic certification.

WINES - Wines of gravitas, estate wines present three distinct styles: old-vine, own-rooted 'Legacy,' 100% whole cluster 'Imprint,' and panoramic 'Winderlea.'

Dundee Hills Winderlea Legacy Pinot Noir 2018 ●
243 cs; $ 85 - ⊞ - Brilliant ruby robe, subtle raspberry, floral and sous bois notes, ethereal structure, elegant finish.

Dundee Hills Winderlea Vineyard Estate Pinot Noir 2018 ● 477 cs; $ 65 - ⊞ - Heady clove, dried rose petal, potpourri, and red fruit aromas, supple morello cherry, raspberry, red plum notes, sublime struct

Dundee Hills Winderlea Imprint Pinot Noir 2018 ●
238 cs; $ 50 - ⊞ - Cherry, wild raspberry, red currant nose carries through on seamlessly on the palate. A wine of finesse, elegance and grace.

---

acres 65 - **cases** 6,000
Fertilizers biodynamic compost, cover crops, organic
Plant protection biodynamic preparations, organic, sulfur
Weed control mechanical, n/a
Yeasts spontaneous fermentation
Grapes purchase 55%
Certification some of the vineyards are certified biodynamic or organic

MCMINNVILLE

YOUNGBERG HILL

10660 SW Youngberg Hill Road - tel. (971) 901-2177
www.youngberghill.com – wine@youngberghill.com

PEOPLE - Wayne and Nicolette Bailey purchased
Youngberg Hill, a 50-acre hilltop farm, in 2003.
They revamped the entire estate. They are Salmon
Safe and LIVE certified and were formerly certified organic (until 2019). They specialize in events,
hosting guests in their nine room inn overlooking
the vineyards. Wayne is very active in promoting
wine tourism in the region. They raised their three
daughters here and name wines after each one of
them.

VINEYARDS - The original 12 acre site, formerly
known as Panther Creek vineyards, had own-rooted vines. The Baileys expanded to 23 total estate
acres. They grow Chardonnay, Pinot Gris and Pinot Noir at 600-800 feet of elevation. Cooling
breezes from the Pacific, 25 miles away, provide
optimal conditions for their cool climate varieties. The Baileys are passionate about their holistic
farming approach. Cattle and goats roam the property.

WINES - Nearly all of their wines are crafted from
estate fruit, including the three noted here. A small
percentage (5% - Grenache) is sourced from the
Rogue Valley.

TOP **McMinnville Bailey Family Pinot Noir 2017** ● 200 cs;
$ 115 - ⊞ - A nose of mixed berries and spice broaden
on the palate. Rich and mouthfilling with Bing cherries,
blueberry compote, raspberries, wild mushrooms, oak
nuances and savory spice linger far beyond the final sip.
Willamette Valley Cuvée Pinot Noir 2018 ● 365 cs;
$ 35 - ⊞ - Allspice and red fruits on the nose open to
cherries, black raspberries, pie spice, hints of plum, and
understated toasty oak enlivening the palate. Medium
bodied and elegant with bright acidity, it finishes with
verve; excellent value.
Willamette Valley Aspen Chardonnay 2019 ○ 175 cs;
$ 45 - ⊞ - Sleek and minerally with aromas of florals and
citrus up front. Layers of minerality, lemon gelato, hints
of salinity, a touch of oak and earthiness. Brisk acidity.

acres 23 - cases 2,500
Fertilizers compost, cover crops, manure
Plant protection organic, sulfur, synthetic pesticides
Weed control mechanical
Yeasts commercial cultured yeasts, selected
indigenous yeasts
Grapes purchase 5%
Certification some of the vineyards are certified organic

NEW YORK

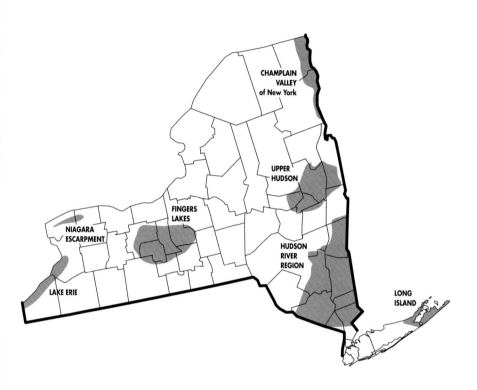

CHAMPLAIN
VALLEY
of New York

UPPER
HUDSON

FINGERS
LAKES

NIAGARA
ESCARPMENT

HUDSON
RIVER
REGION

LONG
ISLAND

LAKE ERIE

Bottle 🍾

Coin $

LODI

BOUNDARY BREAKS

1568 Porter Covert Road – tel. (607) 474-5030
www.boundarybreaks.com – info@boundarybreaks.com

PEOPLE - After a career in both publishing and tech, New York native Bruce Murray moved to the Finger Lakes, and purchased a 120-acre farm on the east side of Seneca Lake in 2007. Here he met wife and co-owner Diana Lyttle. Their goal: To make high-quality and terroir-driven wines from vinifera grape varieties, with a primary focus on Riesling. Vineyard manager Kees Stapel has been with Boundary Breaks since 2010. The estate works with a number of different contracted winemakers.

VINEYARDS - Boundary Breaks' estate vineyards slope toward Seneca Lake, where drainage tiles are used to prevent soils from becoming waterlogged. The team prefers to focus on manual work in the vineyard, rather than sprays and chemicals, to protect plants from disease and create optimally ripe fruit.

WINES - Today, Boundary Breaks crafts a wide variety of Rieslings, from dry versions to ice wines, alongside grapes like Cabernet Franc and Gewürztraminer.

🔝 **Finger Lakes #239 Dry Riesling 2019** ○ 2,730 cs; $ 23 - 🍷 - Has a round mouthfeel yet is well-balanced and shows a complex mix of lemon curd, lime zest, ginger and apple blossoms.
Finger Lakes Cabernet Franc 2019 ● 985 cs; $ 20 - ⊞ - This medium-bodied Cabernet Franc has notes of crunchy red fruit, graphite, violet and a touch of iron on the mid-palate.
Finger Lakes Chardonnay 2020 ○ 400 cs; $ n/a - 🍷 - This unoaked Chardonnay allows the lemon and floral aromatics of the variety to shine while still offering a velvety texture.

acres 38 - cases 10,000
Fertilizers organic-mineral
Plant protection sulfur, synthetic pesticides
Weed control mechanical
Yeasts commercial cultured yeasts
Grapes purchase 20%
Certification none

BURDETT

DAMIANI WINE CELLARS

4704 Route 414 – tel. (607) 546-5557
www.damianiwinecellars.com – info@damianiwinecellars.com

PEOPLE - Founders Lou Damiani and Phil David teamed up in 2004 to start Damiani Wine Cellars with a goal to prove that the Finger Lakes could make excellent red wines. Today, under head winemaker Phil Arras—who trained under Lou until taking over in 212—the winery does just that. In addition to working with red grapes like Cabernet Sauvignon, Merlot, Pinot Noir, Lemberger, and cabernet Franc, Damiani Wine Cellars makes an array of white, rosé, and sparkling wines as well, highlighting single-vineyard cuvees as much as possible.

VINEYARDS - Damiani Wine Cellars producers wines from several estate-owned and grower-partner vineyards along the eastern shores of Seneca Lake. Among them are the Damiani and Davis Vineyards, which are owned by the respective founders, and the vineyards of nearby wineries such as Standing Stone and Hazlitt. Sunrise Hill Vineyard is located on the west side of Cayuga Lake.

WINES - Exuberant and complex fruit in the reds is showcased by neutral oak while white wines find balance between fruit and acidity.

🔝 **Finger Lakes Barrel Fermented Chardonnay 2019** ⟨EVERYDAY WINE⟩ ○ 227 cs; $ 19 - 🍽 - Delivers varietal flavors like apple and lemon, accented by a hint of mineral and light oak.
Finger Lakes Meritage 2019 ● Cabernet Sauvignon, Cabernet Franc, Merlot; 665 cs; $ 45 - ⊞ - Damiani's flagship wine is a harmonious blend of dark berries, underbrush and spice with a good structure.
Finger Lakes Brut Méthode Champenoise 2013 ⟨⟩ Pinot Noir, Chardonnay, Pinot Meunier; 274 cs; $ 45 - 🍷 - Carries a vibrant acidity and fine perlage, alongside flavors of lemon, brioche and chamomile.

acres 41 - cases 6,000
Fertilizers mineral fertilizer
Plant protection organic, synthetic pesticides
Weed control mechanical
Yeasts commercial cultured yeasts
spontaneous fermentation
Grapes purchase 60%
Certification none

ARKPORT

ELEMENT WINERY

27 West Avenue – tel. (585) 943-7820
www.elementwinery.com – info@elementwinery.com

PEOPLE - Christopher Bates, MS., is committed to making fine wine in the Finger Lakes using carefully chosen grapes from the region. He started Element Winery as a boutique négociant that sources grapes from a broad array of terroirs that represent the Finger Lakes as a whole. Bates is working to establish a "big picture" Finger Lakes style more so than a particular site style.

VINEYARDS - Element Winery works with conscientious growers from various AVAs in the Finger Lakes to source fruit, but chooses to use only the Finger Lakes AVA on bottles to designate a Finger Lakes style. The winery focuses on grapes such as pinot noir, syrah, cabernet franc, chardonnay, and riesling. Although Element's wines are sourced from throughout the Finger Lakes, the winery purchased an estate vineyard in 2017 and will launch a separate label for estate vineyard wines.

WINES - Using low intervention and careful grape selection, Element Winery creates Finger Lake style wine that represent what the region can do as a whole.

Finger Lakes Until Next Time Riesling 2014 ○ 115 cs; $ 40 - 🍶 - Pale yellow colored wine with aromas of peach, petrol, pear and stone and a palate of tart granny smith apples and honey with savory salinity.
Finger Lakes Cabernet Franc 2015 ● 68 cs; $ 50 - 🛢 - Plum colored wine with satisfying aromas of mushroom, cherry, cranberry, plum, pepper and tomato leaves and a palate of cherry, crushed stone and tobacco.
Finger Lakes Pinot Noir 2016 ● 103 cs; $ 50 - 🛢 - Pale brick colored wine with aromas of cherry, violets and earth and a fresh, juicy palate saturated with cherries and minerality with smooth tannins.

acres 0 **cases** 600
Fertilizers compost, cover crops, manure
Plant protection organic, synthetic pesticides
Weed control mechanical
Yeasts spontaneous fermentation
Grapes purchase 100%
Certification none

PENN YAN

FOX RUN VINEYARDS 🍾

670 Route 14 – tel. (315) 536-4616
www.foxrunvineyards.com – bellpw@gmail.com

PEOPLE - Scott and Ruth Osborn purchased Fox Run in 1993 silent partners Albert and Kathleen Zafonte. Winemaker Peter Bell has a small ownership stake as well. Bell joined in 1995, after working across the New and Old World. He brought his love of cool climate viticulture and fortified wine, creating a diverse line of terroir-driven wines that pushes the boundaries of what is expected in the Finger Lakes. Lindsey VanKeuren is the assistant winemaker.

VINEYARDS - The estate and local growers face severe climactic and disease pressures in the Finger Lakes. Instead of using chemical herbicides to combat mildew and other diseases, they use mechanical weed whacking, compost and a vertical shoot canopy system to keep the grapes dry and give them plentiful access to the sun. Bell and Kaiser also use water diversion ditches to take capture rainfall. John Kaiser is the vineyard manager for the estate.

WINES - Riesling is what put the Finger Lakes on the map, but Bell make a broader selection of varietals, including Chardonnay, Merlot, Traminette, Cabernet Sauvignon, three fortified wines and sparkling wine.

🔝 Finger Lakes Cabernet Franc 2019 ● 420 cs; $ 22 - 🛢 - Cabernet Franc is a varietal on the rise in the Finger Lakes, and tasting this, it's easy to see why. Dense, dark, broody fruit. Black and red cherries. Blackberries, spice. Aging potential: sky's the limit.
Finger Lakes Reserve Riesling 2019 ○ 335 cs; $ 51 - 🍶 - Bell typically ferments about 12 Rieslings every year. This single tank wine is aromatically complex and juicy, with full-bodied orchard and floral notes, lemon curd, ripping acidity, heft and breadth.
Finger Lakes Fine Old Tawny ● 720 bt of 0,375 l; $ 50 - 🛢 - Made from estate grown Cabernet Franc and aged in old French and American barrels for seven years. All the brown things: coffee, toffee, figs, room temperature salted butter.

acres 35 - **cases** 18,000
Fertilizers mineral fertilizer
Plant protection copper, sulfur, synthetic pesticides
Weed control mechanical
Yeasts commercial cultured yeasts
Grapes purchase 65%
Certification none

HECTOR

RED NEWT CELLARS

3675 Tichenor Road – tel. (607) 546-4100
www.rednewt.com – info@rednewt.com

PEOPLE - David and Debra Whiting founded Red Newt in 1998, with the goal of creating a farm winery and a locally sourced farm-to-table destination. The in-house bistro, which overlooks Seneca Lake, became more casual in 2011 when Debra died, but still maintains the spirit of her mission and ethos. In 2013, Kelby Russell joined the winery as winemaker, and continued David's mission of sustainable farming, with the goal of crafting terroir-driven wines.

VINEYARDS - The team only leaves the best fruit on the vine, pulling out extraneous grapes to ensure that energy flows to the most promising grapes. The vineyard team uses a high-touch approach to ensure disease and pests stay under control in this tough climate, without chemical intervention. Turkeys, blue herons, bald eagles, coyotes and even bobcats that can occasionally be found there.

WINES - Russell and his assistant Meagz Goodwin work in collaboration with cellar master James Anderson. Most years, they make 12-15 Rieslings.

🔝 **Finger Lakes Tango Oaks Vineyard Riesling 2016** ○ 116 cs; $ 24 - 🍶 - Another great vintage, hot and dry, the hand-picked the grapes in late October. They cold-soak the fruit, allow a long spontaneous fermentation, leave it on the lees in stainless steel, then bottle it and let it rest. Smoky, savory, notes of white peaches and Thai basil.
Finger Lakes Pinot Gris 2017 ○ 308 cs; $ 17 - 🍶 - This was a cool and really late vintage, and the team picked through Thanksgiving. The fruit is cold-soaked for 24 hours to pick up mid-palate texture and weight. Fruit-forward, light and fresh, ripe pears, notes of almonds and flint.
Finger Lakes Cabernet Franc 2019 ● 625 cs; $ 20 A really cold vintage that produced intense and fruity, red and black fruit, black pepper, smoke, underlying minerality.

acres 40 - cases 12,500
Fertilizers compost
Plant protection sulfur, synthetic pesticides
Weed control mechanical
Yeasts spontaneous fermentation
Grapes 100% estate-grown
Certification none

LODI

SILVER THREAD VINEYARD $

1401 Caywood Road – tel. (607) 582-6116
www.silverthreadwine.com – info@silverthreadwine.com

PEOPLE - Richard Figiel founded Silver Thread in 1982, with the goal of embracing organic and sustainable growing practices on the eastern shores of Seneca Lake in the Finger Lakes. In 2011, Paul and Shannon Brock purchased the farm winery, with a vision of pushing it even further along the road to sustainability. They utilize cover crops, native vegetation and cultivate an array of biodiverse plants to deal with pests naturally. Working within the harsh realities of the Northeastern climate, they manage to deploy elements of both organic and biodynamic viticulture and eschew chemicals.

VINEYARDS - Silver Thread works with three grower-partners, and even during tough seasons—this past year they had 10 inches of rain in July, three times the normal rate of precipitation—their hands-on approach to vineyard management, with the help of chickens, geese and ducks, helps keep their vines and soils healthy.

WINES - The Brocks' desire to let their land speak through their wines can be tasted in every terroir-driven glass.

🔝 **Finger Lakes Estate Riesling 2020** SLOW WINE ○ 122 cs; $ 19 - 🍶🧊 - Juice from multiple pickings is separated into several fermentations, with malo, skin contact, whole-cluster press. This estate-grown Riesling gets three months in a combination of neutral oak and stainless steel. Quince, lemon pith, apricots, saline; medium body.
Finger Lakes Chardonnay 2018 ○ 124 cs; $ 19 - 🧊 - This estate-grown Chardonnay gets 10 months sur lie in neutral French oak. Crisp orchard apples, lemon, smoke, a complex minerality and hint of almonds.
Finger Lakes Blackbird Red Wine 2018 ● 133 cs; $ 32 - 🧊 - This blend of 62% Cabernet Franc, 30% Cabernet Sauvignon and 8% Merlot gets 22 months in neutral oak barriques. 2018 was a challenging year in terms of rainfall, but their determination shines through: red cherries, eucalyptus, wild flowers, tobacco, stones.

acres 10 - cases 3,000
Fertilizers compost, manure
Plant protection biodynamic preparations , organic, sulfur
Weed control n/a
Yeasts commercial cultured yeasts, spontaneous fermentation
Grapes purchase 15%
Certification converting to biodynamics
converting to organics

HECTOR

STANDING STONE VINEYARDS $

9934 Route 414 – tel. (607) 583-6051
www.standingstonewines.com – ssvny@standingstonewines.com

PEOPLE - The site that is now Standing Stone was first planted to vinifera grapes in the 1970s by the historic Gold Seal winery. In 2017, Fred Merwarth and Oskar Bynke of Hermann J. Wiemer purchased the property, moving away from conventional farming, eliminating herbicides, and transitioning winemaking to the Wiemer facility across Seneca Lake. Standing Stone is perhaps best known for specializing in Saperavi. All wines are made by head winemaker Fred Merwarth and winemaker Dillon Buckley.

VINEYARDS - Located on the east side of Seneca Lake, in front of the lake's deepest point, Standing Stone's amphitheater-style, hillside vineyards are well drained and have good ventilation. In addition to Saperavi, the vineyards consistently produce high-quality Gewürztraminer, as well as Riesling and Chardonnay, two varieties already planted back in 1972 and 1974 by Charles Fournier & Guy DeVeaux for Gold Seal.

WINES - It's all about balance at Standing Stone, managing weight and acidity.

● **Seneca Lake Timeline Dry Riesling 2019** ○ n/a; $ 25 - ⬚ - Coming from one of the oldest blocks of Riesling on Seneca Lake, this wine delivers great complexity and elegance; lemon rind and ginger abound with a fresh acidity and lingering minerality.
Seneca Lake Gewürztraminer 2019 ○ n/a; $ 25 - ⬚ - Made in an off-dry style, showing vibrant aromatics of rose, lychee, peach and orange blossom, with a good weight balanced by acidity.
Seneca Lake Teinturier Saperavi 2019 ● n/a; $ 27 - ⬚ - Medium-bodied, versatile and food-friendly, expressing flavors of mixed berries, mountain herbs, and spice.

acres 45 - cases 8,000
Fertilizers compost, manure
Plant protection organic
Weed control mechanical
Yeasts spontaneous fermentation
Grapes 100% estate-grown
Certification none

LODI

WAGNER VINEYARDS $

9322 State Route 414 – tel. (607) 582-6450
www.wagnervineyards.com

PEOPLE - For five generations, the Wagner family has grown grapes on the eastern slope of Seneca Lake. In 1979, Bill Wagner broke ground for the estate winery and the family has been making Wagner wines ever since. Bill's children, Laura and John Wagner run the winery since 2010. Ann Raffetto became the first female winemaker in the Finger Lakes when she started making wine for Wagner in 1983. Retiring in 2019, her shoes are now filled by Kevin Lee (part of the Wagner family) and Finger Lakes native Jess Johnson.

VINEYARDS - Wagner Vineyard is the biggest grower of Riesling in the Finger Lakes. In 1978, the family planted their first Riesling vines—which were their first vinifera vines. A second planting of 62 acres of Riesling were planted in 1995. The family grows 5 clones of Riesling as well as 19 other grape varieties (7 non-vinifera). All are dry-farmed, and harvested and vinified separately.

WINES - "Wine and food are a natural combination" is the philosophy behind Wagner's food-friendly wines.

Finger Lakes Riesling 2019 ○ 2,000 cs; $ 15 - ⬚ - Mineral-driven and with a lively acidity, this wine delivers bright citrus flavors and a light touch of pineapple.
Finger Lakes Cabernet Franc 2019 ● 902 cs; $ 17 - ● - A medium-bodied, well-structured wine bursting with red fruit, spice, rose, and black pepper.
Finger Lakes Dry Rosé of Cabernet Franc 2020 ● 700 cs; $ 15 - ⬚ - Has a zesty acidity, showing fresh watermelon, strawberry, and lime with the lightest touch of tannin on the finish.

acres 240 - cases 30,000
Fertilizers compost
Plant protection organic
Weed control n/a
Yeasts commercial cultured yeasts
Grapes 100% estate-grown
Certification none

SAGAPONACK

WÖLFFER ESTATE VINEYARD

139 Sagg Road Sagaponack – tel. (631) 537-5106
www.wolffer.com – eely@wolffer.com

PEOPLE - Founded in 1988 by Christian Wölffer, Wölffer's children, Marc and Joey, and winemaker Roman Roth now own and operate what has become an iconic producer of premium wines, ciders and spirits. Vineyard manager Richie Pisacano works with partner growers and the team at the estate to grow Merlot, Chardonnay, Cabernet Franc, Cabernet Sauvignon as sustainably as possible. In recent years, Wölffer has doubled down on its eco-initiatives.

VINEYARDS - The 170 acre property has estate stretches has 55 acres of planted vines which are farmed sustainably. An additional 52 acres is in the North Fork of Long Island with 160 more acres farmed with partner growers in the North Fork. estate is on loam soil. To combat pests and climactic challenges without chemicals, Wölffer's year-round crew pull leaves and adjust canopies as needed. Indigenous flora and fauna thrive on the unplanted estate areas.

WINES - Wölffer produces about 25 different wines a year. For oenophiles, the Cellar Series is the main event: it's a collection of small-quantity, limited release varietals and styles that speak of vintage and terroir.

Long Island Perle Chardonnay 2019 ◯ 1,328 cs; $ 30 - ▦ - From Dijon clone 76, planted in 1993, and Davis clone 4, planted in 1988. Hand-harvested, settled, racked and fermented in oak barriques and puncheons, 19% new. Fresh, focused, peaches and pears, with papayas. Rich but vibrant.

Long Island Antonov Sauvignon Blanc 2020 ◯ 717 cs; $ 32 - ▯ ▦ - A small portion was fermented in 3-year-old French Oak Puncheon. Ripe gooseberries, white flowers, ripe pears.

Long Island Grandioso Rosé 2020 ● 1,477 cs; $ 31 - ▦ - Made from 66% Merlot, 30% Chardonnay, 3% Cabernet Sauvignon, and 1% Sauvignon Blanc. Picked early to preserve freshness, then aged sur lie for five months. Lush ripe cranberries and cream, crushed stones, bright acidity.

acres 55 - **cases** 100,000
Fertilizers n/a
Plant protection organic, synthetic pesticides
Weed control mechanical
Yeasts commercial cultured yeasts, spontaneous fermentation
Grapes purchase 90%
Certification none

WASHINGTON

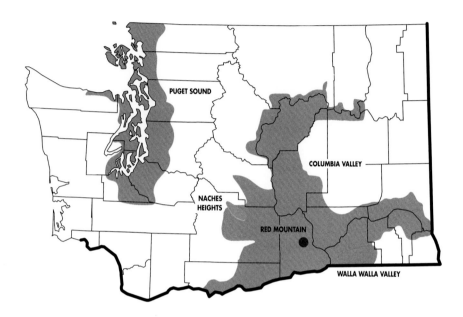

PUGET SOUND

COLUMBIA VALLEY

NACHES
HEIGHTS

RED MOUNTAIN

WALLA WALLA VALLEY

Snail 🌀

Bottle 🍾

BADGER MOUNTAIN VINEYARD

1106 N Jurupa Street – tel. (509) 627-4986
www.badgermtnvineyard.com info@badgermtnvineyard.com

PEOPLE - Founded by Bill Powers in 1982, Badger Mountain became the state's first winery certified as an organic food processor in 1986. Managing Partner Mickey Dunne gives considerable credit to Inez Duenas, Vineyard Manager, who has been with the winery 27 years. Following winemaker Jose Mendoza's departure after more than three decades with the winery, Steve Rothwell joined as head winemaker in 2021 bringing extensive experience with WSDA organic wine.

VINEYARDS - Badger Mountain became the state's first certified organic vineyard in 1990. Duenas worked closely with Powers and together the two developed the equipment used in the vineyards for pest control. Systems have been put into place to monitor water usage more closely and help conserve that resource. Additionally, certification as a regenerative agricultural site is being pursued which they hope will lead other agricultural operations down that road.

....

WINES - Between the popularity of the varieties and reasonable prices, these approachable wines crafted from estate fruit as well as other organic vineyards provide an option for any night of the week.

Columbia Valley Badger Mountain Organic Riesling 2020 ○ 3,750 cs; $ 15 - 🖰 - Sourced from two sites known for their higher acid, the resulting wine is zippy and mouthwatering with flavors of apple sauce, white peach, and a minerally finish.
Columbia Valley Badger Mountain Organic Cabernet Sauvignon 2020 ● 3,750 cs; $ 18 - 🖰 - Grapes from three vineyards were harvested mid-October to create this juicy outcome that delivers flavors of smoked meats, black cherry, English breakfast tea, and cocoa on the finish.
Columbia Valley Badger Mountain Organic Merlot 2020 ● 2,500 cs; $ 16 - 🖰 - Having only been in contact with stainless-steel tanks, the result is approachable fruit forward flavors with cherry in the leading role.

---

acres 73 - cases 50,000
Fertilizers compost, organic-mineral
Plant protection organic, sulfur
Weed control mechanical
Yeasts commercial cultured yeasts
Grapes purchase 50%
Certification organic

BAINBRIDGE VINEYARDS

8989 NE Day Road – tel. (206) 842-9463
www.bainbridgevineyards.com – info@bainbridgevineyards.com

 A Puget Sound pioneer who creates wines tended with horses and cultivates future farmers through an internship program.

PEOPLE - Gerard and Jo Ann Bentryn founded Bainbridge Vineyards in 1977. Working with Dr. Norton at Washington State University, they imported Sieggerebe and other verieties from Canada. After they retired, longtime employee Betsey Whittick, viticulturist and winemaker, reopened the winery under cooperative ownership. She certified it organic in 2014, and earned status as a Certified B Corporation in 2018.

VINEYARDS - Bentryn is credited for planting the first vitis vinifera grapes in the Puget Sound region and selected cool climate varieties that thrive here. Betsey began farming the land with one horse in the mid-90's and today works with two draft horses to spread compost, harrow, and seed cover crops.

....

WINES - The beautifully aromatic cool climate wines are inspired by the lower alcohol, delicate, fragrant wines of northern Europe.

🔵 **Puget Sound Madeleine Angevine 2018** SLOW WINE ○ 215 cs; $ 27 - 🖰 - Aromatic, crisp, and fresh with an intriguing flavor profile of grassiness, pear, and tangerine peel.
Puget Sound Müller Thurgau 2018 ○ 120 cs; $ 28 - 🖰 - Harvested from the estate's 40 year-old vines; crisp green apple and Asian pear are met with the verve of Mandarin orange mid-palate and contrasted by an opulent texture.
Puget Sound Siegerrebe 2019 ○ 105 cs; $ 28 - 🖰 - Bainbridge Vineyards was the first winery in the Puget Sound AVA to plant this variety for commercial use. Heady aromas of a pretty rose garden in full bloom lead to a vibrant combination of lychee fruit, rose water, and pink grapefruit.

---

acres 8 - cases 1,200
Fertilizers compost, humus, manure
Plant protection organic, sulfur
Weed control mechanical
Yeasts commercial cultured yeasts, spontaneous fermentation
Grapes 100% estate-grown
Certification organic

BIONIC WINES

53863 Highway 332 – tel. (509) 526-0686
www.bionicwines.com – hello@bionicwines.com

 A team of six Belgian draft horses are a "horse-powered" means used to cultivate the narrow rows among the rocks at Bionic Wines.

PEOPLE - Christophe Baron grew up among vines in Champagne, studied viticulture, then traveled and worked in different wine regions. On his way to acquire a vineyard in the Willamette Valley, a stop in Walla Walla changed everything. He laid eyes on a property covered in stones similar to those in Chateauneuf du Pâpe. Christophe purchased it and began planting vines in 1997. The first employee he hired in 1998 is still with him, and today 44 people are part of the venture.

VINEYARDS - Around 860' elevation, the 14 vineyards sit on an alluvial fan of compacted basalt stones that came out of the Blue Mountains. The estate is farmed according to biodynamic principles, the first in the Walla Walla Valley to do so. As part of that practice, animals inhabit the farm including chickens, cows, goats, and the team of 6 horses that tend the rows of the Horsepower Vineyards.

WINES - The unique character of the terroir is revealed through an exciting array of lively and distinct wines that offer savory, saline, and mineral qualities.

TOP Walla Walla Valley Cayuse Vineyards Cailloux Syrah 2018 SLOW WINE ● 866 cs; $ 92 - ▦ - Co-fermented with Viognier, graceful tannins accompany a compelling range of flavors from chocolate and deep fruits along with slight herbaceousness, ending with a lingering mocha finish.

TOP Walla Walla Valley No Girls La Paciencia Vineyard Grenache 2018 SLOW WINE ● 355 cs; $ 76 - ▦ - An exhilarating wine by Assistant Vigneronne, Elizabeth Boucier, that opens with the rocky terroir's signature smoky nose, a mouthful of bacon, and deftly delivers intensity without being heavy.

Walla Walla Valley Horsepower The Tribe Vineyard Syrah 2018 ● 735 cs; $ 121 - ▦ - A complex red with a smoky nose and layer upon layer of rich and savory umami notes redolent of soy sauce that linger in the lengthy finish.

acres 70.5 - cases 9,563
Fertilizers compost
Plant protection organic, sulfur
Weed control mechanical
Yeasts spontaneous fermentation
Grapes 100% estate-grown
Certification none

CASCADE CLIFFS VINEYARD AND WINERY

8866 Highway14 – tel. (509) 767-1100
www.cascadecliffs.com – cascadecliffshoodriver@gmail.com

PEOPLE - Formerly a banker, Bob Lorkowski was wise in the ways of how to finance a property purchase. In 1997, he acquired 5 acres of vineyards and a winery located 260 feet above the picturesque Columbia River. The winery enabled him to utilize knowledge acquired from previous work experience with forerunners in Washington wine including Kay Simon of Chinook Wines. Bob asserts that his vineyard and winery is one of the very first in Washington to grow and bottle Barbera.

VINEYARDS - Over two decades Bob has expanded the vineyard to 18 acres that are farmed sustainably utilizing a mix of biodynamic and organic techniques. For example, sheep manure has been combined with the previous year's pressings for fertilizer. As harvest nears, the windy and arid climate enables grapes to get longer hang time resulting in more sugars. Grapes are also sourced from five other vineyards, some of which are farmed conventionally.

WINES - Varieties beyond the mainstream can be found here, and while fifty new barrels a year are purchased for aging Cabernet Sauvignon and Barbera other varieties are matured in used oak.

TOP Columbia Valley Estate Barbera 2019 ● 625 cs; $ 65 - ▦ - Wonderfully old world scents of antique shops, libraries, and pencil lead precede lively yet lush flavors of pomegranate, milk chocolate, and a touch of herbs.

Columbia Gorge Grüner Veltliner 2020 ○ 310 cs; $ 30 - ▯ - From Flume Vineyard, this bottling reveals a happy marriage of lemongrass, herbal notes, and fresh citrus brightness, then finishes with chalky minerality.

Columbia Valley Syrah 2019 ● 520 cs; $ 40 - ▦ - A combination of Syrah from the estate and Chukar Ridge where clean farming practices are also employed results in a juicy and fresh example of the variety overflowing with raspberry, black cherry, and ripe red fruits.

acres 18 - cases 10,000
Fertilizers compost, green manure, manure
Plant protection biodynamic preparations, organic, sulfur
Weed control n/a
Yeasts commercial cultured yeasts
Grapes purchase 75%
Certification none

WALLA WALLA

FOUNDRY VINEYARDS

1111 Abadie Street – tel. (509) 529-0736
www.foundryvineyards.com – jay@foundryvineyards.com

PEOPLE - Walla Walla natives and siblings Jay and Lisa Anderson are second generation owners. Established in 1998 as an intersection between art and wine, the Walla Walla tasting room is a visual showcase designed to also function as an art gallery. In 2017 Jay took over production with the realization that he didn't want the winery to bottle a product made according to a formula that forces it to taste a certain way. Lisa is general manager.

VINEYARDS - In 2018 Jay began a transition toward organic grapes and indigenous yeasts. Roughly 10% of grapes come from the estate vineyard, which completed the three-year organic certification process in 2020. Established in 1998 at an elevation of 976 feet, it is planted to Cabernet Sauvignon, Merlot, Malbec, and Cabernet Franc on silt loam, and harvested by hand. The rest of the wine is thoughtfully sourced from four other organic sites.

WINES - All decisions from picking to fermentation are regularly examined. Jay explains, "We're trying to create a broad spectrum. We don't want seven wines that are all the same."

Columbia Valley GSM 2020 ● 50 cs; $ 36 - Whole cluster pressed, some of the juice underwent carbonic maceration, then the blend was co-fermented resulting in a fresh mix of Beaujolais juiciness meets Rhône spice character. A bit of violet in the background is followed by a cool swath of eucalyptus.
Columbia Valley White on White 2020 ○ Grenache Blanc, roussanne, Marsanne; 170 cs; $ 24 - Conveys a mix of beautiful stone fruits including nectarine and ripe peach then gives way to a richly textured mouth feel, contrasted by an invigorating light spritz that dances across the palate
Columbia Valley Carbonic Syrah 2018 ● 30 cs; $ 36 - From Conley Vineyard, this vibrant wine is inky purple with pleasing notes of mocha, hazelnut, and smoked meats.

acres 3.5 - **cases** 1,500
Fertilizers compost, green manure, manure
Plant protection biodynamic preparations, organic, sulfur
Weed control none
Yeasts spontaneous fermentation
Grapes purchase 90%
Certification organic

MANSON

HARD ROW TO HOE VINEYARDS

300 Ivan Morse Road – tel. (509) 687-3000
hardrow.com – judyphelps@gmail.com

PEOPLE - In 2004, after careers as a biologist and a civil engineer, Judy and Don Phelps bought 20 acres in Manson on the north shore of Lake Chelan and started Hard Row to Hoe Vineyards. At the time, it was the 9th winery in the region. Their first vintage yielded 500 cases of wine, and they opened the tasting room in 2006. Judy oversees winemaking with her son, Julian Shaver, assisting along with Clint Hepper while Don oversees the vineyards.

VINEYARDS - The estate vineyards, although not certified, have been farmed organically since the beginning. Judy and Don recognized that whatever goes on the ground is going to end up in the lake and didn't want to use anything toxic. Their efforts resulted in first certified LIVE and Salmon-Safe vineyard in north central Washington. The soil is very rocky, sandy, and not surprisingly hard to hoe.

WINES - Winemaking strives to let the varieties and region express themselves, so there is an emphasis on small lot, single vineyard bottlings. All wines undergo native fermentation.

Lake Chelan Whole Picture Au Naturel Pét Nat 2019 SLOW WINE 150 cs; $ 38 - A special project by assistant Winemaker Julian Shaver resulting in a clean, easy drinking sparkler awash in citrus and strawberry along with notes of brioche.
Lake Chelan SMS 2019 2019 ○ sauvignon blanc, muscadelle, Sémillon; 200 cs; $ 25 - The blend combined with sur lie aging in Acacia barrels results in a charming white both sleek yet voluptuous with Meyer lemon, a rounder mid-palate, and a lingering finish of orange marmalade, honey, and Semillon's tell-tale waxy notes.
Lake Chelan Whole Picture Estate Cabernet Franc 2018 ● 400 cs; $ 45 - Rich yet not overripe, savory tobacco and leather surround black cherry all served up with lively acidity.

acres 20 - **cases** 4,000
Fertilizers compost
Plant protection organic, sulfur
Weed control mechanical
Yeasts spontaneous fermentation
Grapes purchase 20%
Certification none

BENTON CITY

HEDGES FAMILY ESTATE

53511 N Sunset Road – tel. (509) 588-3155
www.hedgesfamilyestate.com – info@hedgesfamilyestate.com

PEOPLE - In 1990 Tom and Anne-Marie Hedges purchased their first 50 acres of land in the up and coming Red Mountain area and planted Bordeaux varieties. The region celebrated 20 years of AVA status in 2021. Daughter Sarah Goedhart started her wine career in California where she observed biodynamic approaches being practiced. She returned home and joined the family winery in 2005 and has been head winemaker since 2015.

VINEYARDS - Sarah believes that although many people think farming biodynamic and organic vineyards is harder, the climate on Red Mountain is well suited for these practices. For example, they avoid pest pressure because of the high winds and cold winters. Vineyard Manager, James Bukovinsky, says they try to limit mowing and cultivate less. They've also added a few more biodynamic practices such as spraying with cinnamon oil and horsetail tea to address some mildew pressure.

WINES - Native ferments are employed to lure out tertiary notes. The wines are complex and dynamic.

TOP Red Mountain Hedges Family Estate Biodynamic Syrah 2018 ● 284 cs; $ 40 - ⊞ - Dark and brooding, this fragrant wine entices with robust chocolate and smoky aromas, then delivers a flavorful mix of raspberry, blackberry, and blueberry along with dusty tannins.
Red Mountain La Haute Cuvée 2017 ● Cabernet Sauvignon, Petit Verdot; 274 cs; $ 60 - ⊞ - An appealing blend with cherry, pomegranate, raspberry, and chocolate flavors laced with holiday baking spices followed by a hint of eucalyptus on the lingering finish.
Red Mountain Descendants Liégeois Dupont Le Blanc 2019 ○ Marsanne, Viognier; 470 cs; $ 38 - ⏲⊞ - Sourced from the estate's highest elevation vineyard, this elegant white is well textured and redolent of ripe melons and peaches while offering both refreshment and heft.

acres 125 - **cases** 80,000
Fertilizers organic-mineral
Plant protection biodynamic preparations, organic
Weed control mechanical
Yeasts spontaneous fermentation
Grapes 100% estate-grown
Certification some of the vineyards are certified biodynamic, some of the vineyards are certified organic

ZILLAH

PARADISOS DEL SOL

3230 Highland Drive – tel. (509) 829-9000
www.paradisosdelsol.com – paul@paradisosdelsol.com

PEOPLE - A self-professed science geek and organic gardener since childhood, Paul Vandenberg took up winemaking as a hobby at 19. He started his own winery in 1999 after years of work at other wineries. In 2003, with a goal to grow grapes without pesticides, he and wife Barbara purchased property in Zillah. Planting began in 2005. Today the winery and farm is adorned with a community oven and inhabited by dogs and chickens that roam the grounds to their hearts' content.

VINEYARDS - The site has deep, silt-loam soils. Above ground there is good air movement. Paul works by hand among the vines mostly on his own. Although early plantings of Sangiovese weren't necessarily on his wish list, the vines were one of the few virus-free options at the time. Other varieties grown include Semillon, Chenin Blanc, Riesling, Orange Muscat, Tempranillo, Pinot Meunier, Teroldego, Cabernet Sauvignon, and Lemberger.

WINES - Paul's philosophy is to let the wine be what it is, not to adjust pH and acidity to some textbook standard.

Rattlesnake Hills Rosé Paradiso 2018 ● 1,092 cs; $ 22 - ⊞ - A combination of co-fermenting and blending, the depth of the wine hints at its sur lie aging while vibrancy is still present along with offerings of fresh strawberry and candied orange peel.
Rattlesnake Hills Sangiovese 2015 ● 252 cs; $ 14 - ⏲ - Lively although nicely aged before release, cherry leads on the palate followed by dried figs and a mouthwatering finish.
Rattlesnake Hills Angelica MRS ● 1104 bt of 0,375l; $ 25 - ⊞ - A fortified dessert wine crafted with estate Sémillon, Riesling, Muscat Blanc, and Orange Muscat that showcases Semillon's classic textural expression.

acres 6 - **cases** 1,000
Fertilizers compost, humus, manure
Plant protection organic
Weed control none
Yeasts commercial cultured yeasts selected indigenous yeasts
Grapes 100% estate-grown
Certification organic

PÉT PROJECT

SYNCLINE

1111 Abadie Street – tel. (509) 529-0736
www.petprojectwines.com – jay@petprojectwines.com

111 Balch Road – tel. (509) 365-4361
www.synclinewine.com – poppie@synclinewine.com

PEOPLE - At this sister winery to Foundry Vineyards, a desire to craft sparkling wine led owner/winemaker Jay Anderson to explore easier methods to make it. The outcome is this exciting project based on the ancestral method of winemaking. Jay holds a culinary degree from Seattle's Art Institute and cooked at some of Seattle's premier fine dining establishments. That training informs his minimalist techniques to preserve the integrity of the ingredient.

VINEYARDS - Starting in 2018 organic grapes were sourced for the project. Current vintage wines come from three vineyards. Pear Ridge, the source for Pinot Gris and Riesling, resides on Underwood Mountain at an elevation of 1,300 feet. Arete Vineyard provides Gewürztraminer and Chenin Blanc. Conley Vineyard supplies Syrah. In 2021, the estate vineyard was certified organic. 2022 will be the first vintage that Pét Project utilizes those grapes.

PEOPLE - Although Syncline's first vintage was 1999, it wasn't until 2003 that James and Poppie Mantone purchased an old farmhouse on fallow land in the Columbia River Gorge where they subsequently built a winery and planted vineyards. With the desire to let their kids play in an herbicide free zone, they chose to farm the land using biodynamic principles – practices that Poppie learned while working vineyards in Oregon. James tends the vines along with Miguel Flores.

VINEYARDS - At of 340 feet, the estate is among the lower elevation vineyards in Washington. Given that the vineyards aren't contiguous, some risks of virus spread are mitigated. Vines are planted to avoid direct sun on the grapes and get sprayed with clay to prevent sunburn. Rows follow the contours of the soil. The Mantones also purchase grapes from other growers, two of which they've convinced to go herbicide free.

WINES - Grapes for these pét nats are picked at 17-20 brix. The cellar is kept at cooler temperatures for these wines in order to achieve a low and slow fermentation and bring out aromatics.

Columbia Valley Chenin Blanc 2020 ☼ 120 cs; $ 29 - 🍶 - This tongue tingling sparkler is crafted with grapes from Arete Vineyard in the Columbia Valley AVA. With bright citrus on the palate, the finish offers contrasting richness.
Columbia Gorge Riesling 2020 ☼ 55 cs; $ 29 - 🍶 - Sourced from Pear Ridge (formerly Acadia Vineyard) in the cooler climate Columbia Gorge AVA, this bright wine opens with beautiful ripe pear on the nose leading to Asian pear on the palate and a dry finish.
Columbia Gorge Pinot Gris 2020 ☼ 120 cs; $ 29 - 🍶 - This lightly sparkling wine delivers Honeycrisp apple and a brioche finish.

WINES - In accordance with his philosophy that wines should mirror where they come from, James plants varieties that reflect the casual and wild environment in the Gorge and believe the wines should have some rugged edges.

🔴 **Columbia Gorge Estate Grown Gamay Noir 2019** SLOW WINE ● 400 cs; $ 40 - 🍶 - From one of the few vineyards in the state growing Gamay, this juicy example surges across the palate in a lively wave of bright fruit and watermelon rind, then finishes with complexities of black tea.
Columbia Gorge Estate Grown Grüner Veltliner 2019 ○ 100 cs; $ 25 - 🍶 🍷 - To avoid potential contaminants from smoke this vintage, the grapes got a quick press to get the juice off the lees then went into concrete and acacia barrels. It greets with lemongrass, leaves the lips tingling, and is a textural delight.

---

acres 3.5 - cases 600
Fertilizers compost, green manure, manure
Plant protection organic, sulfur
Weed control none
Yeasts spontaneous fermentation
Grapes purchase 100%
Certification organic

acres 11 - cases 4,500
Fertilizers compost, manure
Plant protection biodynamic preparations, organic, sulfur
Weed control mechanical
Yeasts spontaneous fermentation
Grapes purchase 50%
Certification none

RICHLAND

TAGARIS WINERY

844 Tulip Lane – tel. (509) 628-1619
www.tagariswines.com – info@tagariswines.com

PEOPLE - Owner Michael Taggares started out propagating apple trees. Eventually he planted wine grapes and the crops led to the creation of a winery. The current facility, finished in 2005, accommodates production as well as a restaurant that inspires food friendly winemaking. To oversee that, Winemaker Frank Roth joined Tagaris that same year. Remarkably, he started his first winery job while still a teenager and tackled winemaking roles in Canada at the age of 16. Eliseo Silva is Vineyard Manager.

VINEYARDS - Vines are planted at high elevation in the Wahluke Slope AVA, an appellation formed when the Missoula Floods raged through the area thousands of years ago. The region is considered one of the warmest and driest climates in Washington State. Of 750 cultivated acres among six vineyards, nearly half are certified organic. Locations are also Global GAP certified.

WINES - The goal is to make acid driven wines with as little oak as possible so that fruit flavors are dominant. Although the wines have been crafted with organic grapes for years, the winery produced its first certified organic wine in 2018.

● **Columbia Valley Organic Chenin Blanc 2020** EVERYDAY WINE ○ 400 cs; $ 16 - 🍷 - From high elevation vines planted in 1984. Lemon cream and ripe pear aromas carry through to an electric wine that finishes with mineral notes.
Columbia Valley Organic Gewürztraminer 2020 ○ 500 cs; $ 16 - 🍷 - Orange blossom perfume greets yet doesn't overpower, then leads to a lively yet delicate wine with ripe apricot, mango, honey, and lavender that leave behind a touch of beeswax.
Wahluke Slope Michael Vineyard | King Organics Cabernet Sauvignon 2018 ● 800 cs; $ 34 - 🍷 - An approachable and fruit forward example of the variety that showcases ripe red cherry, plum, black currant, creamy milk chocolate, and a hint of eucalyptus.

acres 750 - cases 10,000
Fertilizers compost, humus, manure
Plant protection organic, sulfur
Weed control mechanical
Yeasts commercial cultured yeasts, spontaneous fermentation
Grapes 100% estate-grown
Certification some of the vineyards are certified organic

YAKIMA

WILRIDGE VINEYARD, WINERY & DISTILLERY

250 Ehler Road – tel. (509) 966-0686
www.wilridgewinery.com – info@wilridgewinery.com

PEOPLE - Paul Beveridge founded Wilridge, Seattle's Original Winery™ in 1988. Two hours from that location lies the estate vineyard with a tasting room that operates on 100% self-generated power in spring and fall. The vineyard is tended by Abraham Gonzalez. Also a distiller, Paul transforms the grape must leftover from wine production into grappa and crafts fruit brandies from the bounty of orchard fruits grown on the property.

VINEYARDS - What was once an abandoned apple orchard is now an organic vineyard with sweeping vistas, where resident marmots help fertilize the vineyards. The original plantings of Sagrantino in Washington State reside here along with 22 other varieties at this Salmon Safe, organic, and Biodynamic® certified estate trademarked as Washington's Greenest™ Winery. Newer blocks of Zweigelt, Touriga Nacional, and Sagrantino are head trained.

WINES - Paul focuses on wines that reflect the "terroir" of their vineyard sites rather than current fashion or the latest winemaking trends. New labels depict the flora and fauna from the diverse ecosystem on the property.

● **Naches Heights Wilridge Vineyard Estate Organic & Biodynamic Sagrantino 2016** SLOW WINE ● 112 cs; $ 40 - 🍴 - Offers an inviting albeit faint floral nose with a mouthful of delightful crunchy red fruit and bramble berries that dance across the tongue.
Naches Heights Wilridge Vineyard Estate Organic & Biodynamic Nebbiolo 2016 ● 465 cs; $ 35 - 🍴 - Exudes flavors of plum fruit leather, fig, cola, and spicy undertones along with a lively energy and understated tannins for the variety.
Naches Heights Wilridge Vineyard Estate Biodynamic Rosé of Sangiovese 2019 🍷 117 cs; $ 28 - 🍷 - Begins with pepper and licorice on the nose then delivers a bright, refreshing mouthful of cherry with an old world minerally finish.

acres 14 - cases 6,000
Fertilizers compost
Plant protection biodynamic preparations, organic, sulfur
Weed control mechanical
Yeasts spontaneous fermentation
Grapes purchase 20%
Certification biodynamic, organic

INDEX OF WINERIES

INDEX OF PLACES

INDEX OF PLACES